WOMEN AND HAIR LOSS

A PHYSICIAN'S PERSPECTIVE
BY DR. MATT L. LEAVITT

♀

Women and Hair Loss: A Physician's Perspective

Neither the publishers nor the author are engaged in rendering professional advice or services to the individual reader. The ideas, procedures, and suggestions in this book are not intended as a substitute for consulting with a physician. All health matters require medical supervision.

While the author has made every effort to provide accurate information at the time of publication, neither the publisher nor the author assumes any responsibility for changes that occur after publication.

Most Beautiful Media books are available at special quantity discounts for bulk purchase for sales promotions, premiums, fund raising, and educational needs. Special books or book excerpts can also be created to fit specific needs. For details, write Beautiful Media, 5652 Kingsport Drive, Atlanta, Georgia U.S.A. 30342.

Library of Congress Cataloging Number: 2004109861

ISBN: 0-9755398-1-7

Printed in the Unites States of America

BEAUTIFUL MEDIA
5652 Kingsport Drive
Atlanta, GA 30342
404-847-0282

www.beautimedia.com

DONATION

With the help of our great physicians and employees at Advanced Dermatology & Cosmetic Surgery and Medical Hair Restoration, accompanied by contributing medical researchers and medical companies willing to fund hair research projects, I have been privileged to establish and maintain a national hair transplantation practice, multiple dermatology practices and to continue my incessant journey to seek answers for arresting and treating diseases of the hair.

A portion of the proceeds from this book will be donated to the National Alopecia Areata Foundation* in order to assist in its mission to continue research on finding a cure or advanced treatments, its support to those with the disease, and its endeavors to educate the public about alopecia areata. It is with great respect, affection and hope for this organization that these donations are given.

* The designation of the National Alopecia Areata Foundation as a recipient of a portion of the proceeds from the sale of this publication does not imply approval, endorsement or recommendation by the Foundation of the information contained in the publication.

ACKNOWLEDGEMENTS

The publishing of this book has been the fulfillment of my long-held mission to provide a reliable source of information for women who are suffering from all forms of hair loss. I am grateful to the following individuals for their invaluable assistance and unwavering support:

Thanks 110,000 times to my understanding wife Judye, who is a brunette and a total of 360,000 times to my children - Lauren (brunette), Adam (brunette) and Danielle (blonde).

Thanks countless times to my editor and researcher, Nancy Martin, who was bald for two years.

Thanks 140,000 times or 110,000 times to my Director of Physician Affairs, Valarie Montalbano, who is a blonde or a brunette, for her management of this book.

Thanks 108,000 times to Tim Harmon and Stacey Hayden, who have black hair, for their journalistic expertise and editing prowess.

Without their help, this book would not have been possible.

Special gratitude goes to my publisher, Katherine Phelps, for her professional expertise and belief in this project.

The figures refer to the numbers of follicles for each category of natural hair pigmentation: Brunettes have 110,000 follicles, Black-haired individuals have 108,000 follicles, people born with red hair have 90,000 follicles and Blondes have 140,000 follicles.

FOREWORD FROM RICHARD SIMMONS

"Our society is filled with myths and misinformation about hair loss in general, but even more so when it relates to women. That's why I'm so proud of my friend, Dr. Matt Leavitt, for taking the time to write a book about such an important topic.

It's clear to me that Dr. Leavitt cares about women and wants to help them make informed medical decisions. I believe 'Women and Hair Loss' is an important addition to the books currently available dealing with women's health and self-awareness related topics. I praise Matt for listening and responding to thousands of women who have not had such an in-depth source prior to this book. His attention to issues of the physical as well as the emotional aspects of female hair loss, as well as his commitment to improved doctor/patient communication is to be commended.

So read, become informed, and find your own solution on the pages of this wonderful book. You no longer have to suffer in silence. You can find answers!"

Richard Simmons
International diet, fitness and nutrition expert

WOMEN AND HAIR LOSS: A PHYSICIAN'S PERSPECTIVE

TABLE OF CONTENTS

ABOUT THE AUTHOR

Dr. Matt Leavitt is a Board Certified dermatologist and the Founder and Medical Director of Advanced Dermatology & Cosmetic Surgery, one of the largest dermatology practices in the country, and of Medical Hair Restoration, a national practice associated with surgical hair transplantation. He is a founding father of the American Board of Hair Restoration Surgery, where he served as its first vice president. This group administers board examinations and establishes standards for hair transplant surgeons. He was also one of the founders of the World Hair Society. Additionally, he has served as President of the American Osteopathic College of Dermatology (AOCD) and as Advisor and Trustee for the North American Academy of Cosmetic and Restorative Surgery.

As a clinical advisor for Merck Pharmaceutical, Dr. Leavitt was among the original physicians selected to study the effects of the hair-growth drug Propecia on hair transplantation. He sits on the advisory boards of Pfizer Consumer Health, manufacturers of Rogaine, as well as the Physicians Advisory Board for the National Congressional Republican Committee, which studies health care reform. Additionally, he is on the Board of Directors for ProCyte, a skin, hair, anti-aging and wound-care company. Dr. Leavitt has been asked to be on the Clinical Advisory Boards for Bradley Pharmaceuticals and Allergan, both pharmaceutical companies specializing in dermatology products. He also sat on Connetic's Clinical Advisory Board, a company specializing in skin, dermatology and scalp related medications.

Dr. Leavitt's hair restoration group was originally selected to research and evaluate the CO_2 laser and again chosen as a beta site to study the practicality and use of the Erbium laser on hair transplantation. He was the 2002 recipient of the prestigious "Golden Follicle," an award presented by nomination from an elite group of leaders and peers involved in hair transplantation surgery, known as the International Society of Hair Restoration Surgery (ISHRS), and selected for two consecutive years for the Milestone Award by the Italian Society of Hair Restoration. In 2002, he was also elected to the board of governors of the

ISHRS. He has lectured both nationally and internationally on hair loss in men and women for such groups as the AOCD, American Hair Loss Council, Premier Hair Show, European Cosmetic Surgeons, ISHRS, and for the Masters Teaching Workshop in Mexico.

Dr. Leavitt is a founder and 10 time chairman of the annual Live Surgery Workshop, which is acclaimed worldwide for its scope of training doctors in hair transplant surgery, its scientific presentations by the Who's Who in the field of hair research and for the showcasing of innovative surgical techniques, procedures and patented instruments. Dr. Leavitt is credited with originating "crosshatching," a technique used in hair transplantation and responsible for inventing several surgical instruments, of which one facilitates in the precision of hair transplantation. He has received three research grants from the ISHRS and was a recipient of an educational monograph where he collaborated with a group of other physicians to develop teaching and instructive programs for doctors.

Dr. Leavitt has penned numerous articles for dermatology, hair and cosmetic journals and has served three times as editor for special hair loss editions of the International Journal of Cosmetic Surgery. He published a chapter on corrective hair surgery in the first edition of Hair Restoration, a medical textbook. Recently, he authored chapters on scalp anatomy and the consultation process in the Fourth Edition of another textbook, Hair Transplantation, which was published this year. He has been interviewed by

Forbes, Parents Magazine, International Herald Tribune, MD News, Cosmetic Surgery Times, 20/20, WGN radio, MuscleMag and Men's Health. Dr. Leavitt has appeared on America's Health Network, CBS's "The Early Show," The Learning Channel, plus numerous local news programs nationwide. The Florida Medical Business Journal selected Dr. Leavitt as the recipient of the Physician Business Leadership award in 2003, and deemed his Advanced Dermatology & Cosmetic Surgery offices as the "Best Dermatology Practice" in 2004.

Dr. Leavitt is recognized internationally as an accomplished author, clinical researcher, surgeon and lecturer on the subject of hair loss. His speaking engagements include specific lectures on female hair loss.

A graduate of the University of Michigan and Michigan State University College of Osteopathic Medicine, Dr. Leavitt performed his residency at Ohio University Grandview Medical Center. He is a member of the American Academy of Cosmetic Surgeons, American Society of Dermatological Surgery, American Academy of Facial Plastic and Reconstructive Surgery, American Hair Loss Council, American Academy of Dermatology, American Osteopathic College of Dermatology, and International Society of Hair Restoration Surgery.

INTRODUCTION

"The hair is the richest
ornament of women."

Martin Luther, German Reformer 1483-1546

As a dermatologist, cosmetic surgeon, researcher and hair transplant specialist, I have seen and felt the frustration of thousands of female patients with hair loss. With this book, I sought to provide sound scientific answers and current medical information, as well as offer support for females seeking to learn more about their own hair loss. Viable avenues for treatment and valid options are also revealed. Most of all, the purpose of this book is to educate and to offer hope for women experiencing hair loss.

Since 1997, my dermatology practice has examined more than 19,000 patients seeking answers regarding hair loss. My nationally recognized hair restoration group, Medical Hair Restoration (MHR), has received in excess of 126,000 female-specific inquiries over the past twelve years, with nearly 2,000 females opting for hair transplantation surgery. In fact, 7% of MHR's practice is devoted specifically to performing transplantation surgery on women.

In the early '90s, information in women's magazines, on talk shows and on the Internet was limited, if it existed at all. In addressing the taboo subject of female hair loss, I was as perplexed as my patients. This led me to become more determined than ever to provide women with hair loss the answers they so desperately sought. I began my compelling journey seven years ago with a mission to research, seek out and examine any and all literature available on the topic of female hair loss. Several female medical doctors, including Vera Price, Elise Olsen, Maria Hordinsky, Marty Sawaya, Wilma Bergfeld and Janet Roberts had already begun their own vital research on women with hair loss. This valuable quest continues even today.

Due to society's views on baldness, women with hair loss often endure stares, humiliation, anguish and worst of all, depression. A man can comfortably walk into the boardroom, or the bedroom with a bald or balding head, but the same definitely does not hold true for his female counterpart. It is no wonder that women who suffer from hair loss can be devastated physically, psychologically and socially. "Why me?" is most often the prevailing thought. While it may be deemed okay and publicly acceptable for a man to lose his hair, that is certainly not the case for a woman.

A female patient generally presents herself differently from a male in that her approach to hair loss begins with a battery of carefully prepared, organized and well thought-out questions about her specific hair loss needs. Her approach to the dilemma is quite methodical, and she demands a logical explanation for what she perceives is an unreasonable phenomenon. Today's woman will no longer sit back passively and merely accept what she feels are the standard, prescribed, patterned and rehearsed answers. Women want and deserve options!

AN ANCIENT REMEDY FOR HAIR LOSS IN EGYPTIAN HIEROGLYPHICS

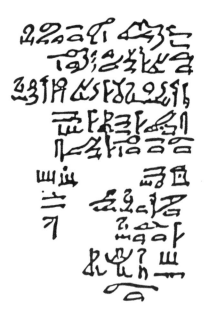

For the growth of the
hair on a head which
is becoming Bald

Fat-of-the-Lion
Fat-of-the-Hippopotamus
Fat-of-the-Crocodile
Fat-of-the-Cat
Fat-of-the-Serpent
Fat-of-the-Egypt Goat

Make into one and
rub the head of the
Bald one therewith

CHAPTER ONE

———

A LITTLE SNIP OF HAIR HISTORY

———

"Beware of her fair locks, for when she winds them around a young man's neck, she will not set him free again."

Johann Wolfgang von Goethe, Poet 1749-1832

Decorative significance aside, hair has a logical, functional and essential purpose as it was designed by nature to provide protection for the skull. It also plays a large role in regulating body temperature, both hot and cold. Hair serves as a protective covering for many areas of the body, but women experiencing hair loss do not consider these factors pertinent or relevant when seeking "the reason" for their loss. The truth be known, the major factor does not remain elusive, mysterious or unknown; as most physicians will agree that 65-75% of hair loss in women is due to hereditary or genetic reasons.

Perhaps the discovery of a comb made of boxwood from the Stone Age 10,000 years ago was a premonition to the modern era of things to come, and that attention to hair care and hairdressing was a viable practice even long, long ago. Thus, historically speaking our long-term obsession with hair has existed for millenniums. It seems that ensuing emphasis on hair loss can also be traced back to around 4000 BC and the Egyptians (even though pharaohs and nobility often wore wigs and shaved their heads) where a detailed and highly complex formula for hair loss was discovered. Deciphered from ancient hieroglyphics came the first known potion, an elixir, touted to be the ultimate cure-all remedy for baldness. The Egyptians advised mixing the fats of ibex (wild goat), crocodile, lion, serpents and geese with hedgehog bristles immersed in oil. This concoction was combined with fingernail scrapings, honey, alabaster and red ocher and then all were ceremoniously rubbed onto the head and scalp. Cleopatra is said to have lathered Julius Caesar's balding pate with a nostrum comprised of burnt domestic mice, horse teeth, bear grease, and deer marrow. The word "Caesar," hence Kaiser and Czar, are derivatives of the word hair, and even the first barber shop is believed to have been established in Rome in 296 BC. Hippocrates, the Father of Medicine, equated a bald dome as a sign of virility. He was bald, as you might well imagine, and recommended an ointment of opium, essence of rose and olive oil as a potion for balding. The poultice was enhanced for more severe cases by adding cumin, pigeon droppings, horseradish and beet root. All things considered, most of these mixtures were extremely difficult to put together, and in most cases had exceptionally unpleasant aromatic qualities!

Mythology, legends, folklore, religions and superstitions from various cultures all contributed to our historically overwhelming fascination with hair. The Egyptian nature goddess Isis cut off a lock of her hair to insure the preservation of the soul of her husband and brother, Osiris, god of the underworld. Widows often buried snippets of hair with their husbands to insure after-life protection. Maidens were forbidden to marry until their tresses were shorn and offered to the Greek god, Hippolytos and the goddess of wisdom, Athena.

In 247 BC, Berenices, the wife of Ptolemy III, a prominent astronomer during that time, adorned the altar of Aphrodite, goddess of love, with her hair as a means of protecting her husband in battle. The hair was stolen and according to mythology, appears today as the constellation Coma Berenices. It was believed that Berenices or "Berenice's Hair," and the Mother goddess's unbraided hair could control the weather. The ancient Romans even imagined haircuts to be a major cause of severe storms. During Medieval times, Christian Europe further suspected that witches, by unbinding their hair, could raise storms, summon demons and unleash an array of various forms of devastation.

Inquisitors in the Medieval church, as well as the ancients, shaved the heads of witches before torturing them, whereas, the Aztec Indians also removed hair from the condemned prior to execution in order to reduce their ability to work their supposedly magical spells. In contrast, Joan of Arc enraged the clergy when she took it upon herself to shave her own head. Only members of the clergy were supposed to do this. This act of utter defiance was ultimately added to her list of crimes. Conversely, Jewish wives and Christian nuns were compelled to have their heads shaved, thus portraying them as pure and harmless or powerless. Even today many Orthodox Jewish women cut off all their hair when they marry, and don a special wig called a "shatel" in public, only removing it in the privacy of their homes in the presence of immediate family. Women practicing the Muslim religion around the world cover their hair completely with the traditional hajeb. This is for religious reasons and also because the hair is deemed to be seductive.

Only spouses, immediate relatives, or other females may view their tresses. Puritans kept their short, uncurled strands under caps in the 17th century to be opposite of the curly and frilly English kings whom they opposed.

Throughout the Middle Ages, lovers toted lockets filled with their admirer's hair, while knights carried a tuft of their mistress' locks in their helmets during battle. Scottish girls were forbidden to comb their hair at night while their brothers were away at sea for fear a storm would be raised and sink the boats.

There are countless myths and superstitions attached to hair and its significance. In the practice of, and belief in magic throughout history, numerous cults and religions (including voodoo or black magic) believed that whoever got possession of someone's shorn hair could cast a magical spell upon that person. Many elaborate and ritualistic systems were created to cope with the hair shorn from infants, adults, and the deceased. The Santal tribes from India ceremoniously shaved an infant's head and carefully disposed of the hair, while some barbers meticulously gathered and hid the trimmed tufts before bad luck or spirits had a chance to enter the person's soul or before the hair was used in magical ceremonies to harm another.

Cultural differences abound when it comes to the subject of hair. Many French women who collaborated with the Nazis during World War II were publicly ostracized when their former allegiance was revealed by their presence in public with a sheared head. Yet, women from the Masai tribe in Africa shave their heads as a routine part of their culture, and South American Amazon Indian tribes pluck the hair off the heads of young girls when they reach puberty.

These actions, and considerably more, support our preoccupation with hair. In earlier times, girls were told not to cut their hair in March lest it becomes lifeless or after dark for fear of reducing sexuality. Europeans held that if birds built nests with discarded hair, the hair's owner would suffer severe headaches or even become insane. In Ireland, a love-smitten man could make his girlfriend mad with love by threading a strand of her hair through the leg of a corpse. Loss of hair could be viewed as an omen foretelling tragedies such as the loss of property, health and or a child. In many parts of the world, a widow's peak, a prominent pointed shock of hair on the forehead, forecasted impending misfortune; in America the same trait was purported to be a sign of good luck. Folklore further related that if a dressmaker accidentally sewed one of her own hairs into a garment intended for a trousseau, it foretold her own wedding.

Then of course there is the fairy-tale princess Rapunzel, portrayed in "Tales of the Brothers Grimm," who allowed her prince to climb into the tower where she was held captive, on a ladder created of her own beautiful flaxen locks. Perhaps this story helped to perpetuate the theory that blondes have more fun!

"To be or not to be...blonde?" was really the question in days of yore as light hair was sought even then. As early as 4000 BC, records show that Greek women dyed and bleached their hair, a regimen later adopted by Romans. In the 16th century Titian, the Italian artist, popularized a red-blonde hair color in his paintings. Venetian women who wished to achieve the color applied mixtures of alum, sulfur, soda, and rhubarb and sat in the sun. Also used for bleaching during the Middle Ages were henna, saffron, egg and calf kidneys. Conditioners were concoctions of lizard boiled in olive oil and egg whites.

In rural districts of Europe, parents kept locks of their children's hair put away for safekeeping to ensure the child's longevity. A more violent act of tearing ones' hair out was practiced in ancient times during mourning with the strands of the deceased's hair scattered over the corpse as a demonstration of sorrow.

There are approximately 80 references to hair in the Bible. Here too, hair is important. Mary Magdalene, often portrayed in illustrations with flowing red locks, wiped Jesus' feet with her provocative mane. St. Paul, in Corinthians II states plainly: "If a woman has long hair, it is a glory to her. If a man has long hair, it is a shame unto him." In the book of Mark, girls were told not to cut their hair lest it become lifeless. According to the Bible, Satan told worshipers no harm could come to them if they had hair. A hero in Apollo's day supposedly reduced the virility of an opponent by cutting off his locks on the hill site where Jesus was crucified known as Calvary, or "Bald Skull."

Beginning in the 14th Century, the concept of beauty, or what was perceived beautiful was beginning to expand. Many women from this era plucked their eyebrows and frontal scalp in order to enlarge and emphasize the forehead. For example, think of the most recognizable beauty with ample brow area that comes to mind: Queen Elizabeth I. Known for her fiery temper, she only had a few red locks remaining after a childhood bout with scarlet fever. There are numerous historical portraits of her, and written documentation testifying that she wore a variety of wigs.

In the 1800s, English noblemen's preparation of Indian teas and fresh lemon was applied to the scalp supposedly to rid one of baldness. Commoners were reduced to massaging their pates with chicken excrement. During this same period in history, hair was decorated with jewels, feathers and flowers, and then supported with wire frames two feet tall. The higher the hair, the more elite you were. Japanese women achieved this rigidity and elevation with lacquer, a precursor to modern-day hair spray! About this same time in America women accused of being witches or practicing witchcraft were being hung in Salem. Commonly, they were not executed until after their heads were shorn and shaved.

The roaring twenties saw women take on "masculine pursuits," of the times like smoking, drinking, voting and working. Along with this trend came more masculine hairstyles, with the "bob" being the most popular cut created to celebrate their newly found freedom. In 1925, it was said that an estimated 2,000 females per day were chopping off their hair in this outrageous blunt cut. Marshall Fields, the prominent Chicago department store, along with numerous other companies of merit, refused to employ "bobbed" women. Yet during World War II Veronica Lake, probably the most famous actress recognized solely by her long, blonde "peek-a-boo" hairstyle over one eye, was asked by the U.S. War Department (through Paramount Pictures) to change the seductive style. At this time in our history, females were operating machinery in factories for the war effort and there was fear that the long tresses were likely to become entangled in the equipment.

A mid-20th century poultice of dove urine, oil of worm toad, and spider webs was a hopeful remedy for hair loss to be followed later by acupuncture, the Japanese baldness brush, a 70s prevention of female sex hormones, sulfur, vitamins, antibiotics, nucleic acid, amino acids, urea, and wheat germ. In 1989, an extensive study of 300,000 over-the-counter lotions and potions were reviewed by the Federal Drug Association (FDA). They found that countless "hair-in-a-bottle" nostrums, which claimed to be effective for growing, replacing, restoring or saving the hair, were worthless. These preventative drugs and products were determined to be "not especially safe and/or effective, and further as being misbranded." **Period**. If hair loss precipitates in an individual, it is considered to be a genuine form of disease by the FDA. They are therefore able to regulate hair-growing restorative drugs and products.

Reflecting upon the history of hair, it is evident that it has proven to be an important historical, religious, political, cultural and socio-economic statement.

FOREIGN WORDS FOR HAIR

Albanian	*flok*
Bengali	*chool*
Chinese	*tou fa*
Czech	*vlas*
French	*cheveux*
German	*haar*
Hawaiian	*lauoho*
Hungarian	*haj*
Irish	*gruaige*
Italian	*capelli*
Latin	*capillus*
Latvian	*mati*
Lithuanian	*plaukas*
Portuguese	*cabelo*
Spanish	*pelo*
Swedish	*har*
Turkish	*sac*
Vietnamese	*toc*

CHAPTER TWO

HAIR 101:
THE BASICS

"Hair 'tis the robe which curious nature weaves to hang upon the head, and to adorn our bodies."

Thomas Decker, English Dramatist 1572-1632

It's official. Americans now spend in excess of $7 billion each year attempting to fight hair loss with drugs, surgery, cosmetics and non-surgical hair replacement (wigs, weaves and toupees) in order to restore their highly prized heads of hair. Cumulatively, hair transplantation accounts for the greatest dollar amount to date. Nearly $1 billion! Yes, it is true that the hair we fuss, muss, and brood over if lost; and which is purported in past and present literature, societal culture, and in religion to be our strength, our weakness, our glory, elixir of youth, and identifier of our sexuality; is oddly enough, not real. Or better said; it is dead! Hair may be chemically broken down as follows:

50% CARBON	What diamonds are made from
20% OXYGEN	The same as the air we breathe
17% NITROGEN	Used to make dynamite
6% HYDROGEN	The same element found in rocket fuel
5% SULFUR	Used to make gunpowder
2% RANDOM	Trace elements

Alopecia, the medical word for hair loss, is Greek in origin and literally translated means fox. It refers to the wild animal's mangy fur that often fell out in patches. The scientific term for the study of the anatomy, growth and diseases of the hair is **trichology**. **Trichophobia** means one who fears the sight of hair, and not the loss of it. **Thrix** is the Greek word for hair and **oulos** means curly or wavy. Thus, **ulotrichous** means having wiry or wooly hair. **Trichauxis** is excessive growth of hair in length and quantity, **trichoglossia** (glossia = tongue) is having a hairy tongue, **trichotrophy** (trophy = nourishment) refers to nutrition of the hair, and the list goes on and on.

Pelage is the furry coat of an animal and hair is its human counterpart. Humans possess about the least amount of cover found among the members of the animal species; yet, hair grows on virtually every part of our body except our lips, the palms of the hands and the bottoms of our feet. Microscopic cells even grow in the cochlea (our inner ear) where 15,000 tiny hairs are responsible for stimulating the nerves that transmit vibrations. It is interesting to note that without these hairs we could not hear, and with age they reduce in number. Even our respiratory tract comprises hair-like cilia that filter out unwanted pollutants. Internal tumors, since they are composed of skin tissue similar to hair, can also be covered with hair. Surprisingly, tiny tubes enclose miniscule hairs that protrude from our taste buds and aid in discerning tastes, flavors and temperatures.

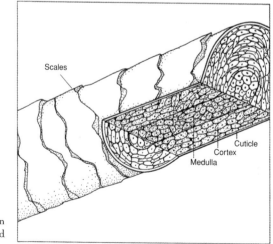

Scales

Cuticle
Cortex
Medulla

Human
Hair Strand

Here are a few facts about human hair:

- We have in excess of five million hairs on our body, most of these never growing more than one-half inch in length or exceeding .0035 inches in diameter.

- Hair on our head grows approximately one-half inch per month, or six inches per year reaching a maximum of forty plus inches in length over the course of its individual lifetime.

- Hair grows at the rate of .00000001 miles per hour, so if we placed end-to-end each fully grown hair we shed, it would extend over seven hundred miles!

- In any given 24 hour period, hair grows .039 mm at our temples and .044 mm at the vertex (top of our head).

- On our entire body, approximately 40 yards of new hair is grown every day.

- Hair cells divide every twelve hours.

- Women's hair grows faster in the summertime than in winter by about one-quarter of an inch.

- With increased humidity, hair absorbs moisture, stretches and elongates, thus allowing it to vary in length by up to 2½%.

- If our hair was twisted into a rope, it could pull a weight of 15 tons!

Although hair comes in various and versatile forms, basically it functions as **protection**. It performs as a signaling mechanism in animals: fur stands up to show aggression. Scalp hairs also aid in regulating and insulating against heat and cold. However, the 30 million or more females experiencing hair loss and/or thinning hair do not consider these factors relevant when seeking solutions for their own hair loss. Notice that in our society the word balding is rarely used with regard to women. We always manage to sanitize or soften the reference.

Delicate eyebrows are the first hairs to form on the fetus in the womb at approximately two months. At birth, this hair functions to shelter the eyes by decreasing the amount of sunlight invading the eye. Pollen and other debris are kept at bay by nasal hairs and eyelashes.

In reference to our external tresses, the scalp secures the shafts, or strands, that are so fervently desired. The underlying portion of the scalp, which is a mass of bulbs and follicles, shields the hair's internal structure, and it is here where growth occurs. Actually, scalp can be translated into an acronym for its five distinctive layers:

S kin: contains the epidermis or outer layer of skin and the dermis 3 to 8 mm thick

Sub **C** utaneous Layer: consists of fat and fibrous tissue

A poneurotica: located between frontal muscle and occipitus

L oose Connective Tissue: thin portion of scalp and mostly avascular

P ericranium: is attached to the skull and is the deepest layer of the scalp

Perhaps the most discussed, pampered and vilified hair component is the sac-like **follicle**. Contrary to popular belief, it does not get clogged, and DNA is not present for identification purposes as it is typically found only in cells that have a nucleus (hair does not). What the crime labs and detectives look for is mitochondrial DNA, which is a more primitive form of genetic coding. In 2001, a piece to the puzzle of one of the most infamous unsolved mysteries was found as a result of a hair identified by

DNA. A longtime friend of missing Teamster leader Jimmy Hoffa had testified nearly 30 years prior that Hoffa had never been inside his car. Yet a hair found in the vehicle conclusively matched that of Mr. Hoffa's.

Human Hair Follicle

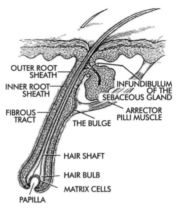

OUTER ROOT SHEATH
INNER ROOT SHEATH
FIBROUS TRACT
THE BULGE
INFUNDIBULUM OF THE SEBACEOUS GLAND
ARRECTOR PILLI MUSCLE
HAIR SHAFT
HAIR BULB
MATRIX CELLS
PAPILLA

Since the hair we see on top of our skin (simply as a result of being pushed out) is not a living organism, the active live hair actually rests beneath the surface or **epidermis**. The **root sheath**, which is the lowest section of the hair, enlarges at the end into a soft, light-colored structure called the **hair bulb**. A structure called the **papilla** projects into the hair bulb at the base of the follicle. It contains a vascular network that provides oxygen and nutrients like blood, blood vessels, nerves, arteries and connective tissue needed for growth and cell division. (Hair cells are one of the fastest dividing types of cells found in the body.) As the cells reproduce, the old ones are pushed upward toward the exterior, and they are denied nourishment and therefore harden (**keratinize**), die, and undergo **pigmentation** (colorization). This hard protein, or **keratin**, starts to form about one third of the way on its journey up to the surface. It is at this point it is referred to as the shaft or the visible part of the hair. Tensile strength is reduced in the hair strands of women with alopecia. If hair is cut, pain is avoided since the keratin and nerve fibers are lifeless, or dead. This goes for your nails also, as they too are comprised of keratin.

We are born with approximately 100,000 hair follicles and some of these follicles have more than one hair in each sac. Persons with certain hair colors have more or less hair, depending on the particular color. The breakdown is as follows:

All Hair Colors Are Not Created Equal	
Blonde:	About 140,000 hairs on the head
Brown:	About 110,000 hairs on the head
Black:	About 108,000 hairs on the head
Red:	About 90,000 hairs on the head

If a blonde wanted to count all of the hairs on her head, it would take 40 hours, or an entire workweek!

Follicles contain an oil gland called the **sebaceous gland** that lubricates the hair and keeps it soft. Here scents, smells and odors are trapped and often give away where you might have been the night before. The term "muscle head" is actually true of all of us, as each follicle has an **arrector pilli muscle**, though limited in its usefulness in humans because of the weight of our hair. But, when contracted this muscle causes our hair to literally "stand on end." When we are chilled or frightened, goose bumps abound. And no, the arrector pilli muscle **cannot** be exercised to make our hair bulk up!

There are three types of hair: **lanugo, vellus** and **terminal**. At around four months of age while in the womb, a fine, colorless hair starts spreading all over our body (except on our palms, lips and soles of our feet, and it is already on our eyebrows). The result is lanugo hair. Then it is about one or two months before birth that in the womb we have our first, albeit unbeknownst to us, bout with baldness as all of the hair sheds.

However, the original number of follicles remains with us for the rest of our lives, and they only **shrink in size and become less dense and less active**, thereby disallowing hairs to "push through" the scalp. Under ordinary circumstances, hair gradually thins as we age. Newborns possess the most follicles with approximately 1,135 per centimeter of scalp; by age one, the number of active follicles decreases to 795; then between the ages of twenty to thirty, the count is down to 615; age forty to sixty, 484; and finally at age eighty, the active follicles number only about 435. The end number represents only slightly more than one third of the original follicles with which we started.

Genetically programmed follicles endure an ongoing **miniaturization**, or shrinking process, until the hair shafts are too thin and too short to cover a full head of hair. With age these hairs appear as "peach fuzz," and possess a fine texture around our temples and on our pate.

At birth, hair coverage is minimal, soft, and wispy, usually limited in its location (head), and is barely pigmented. This baby fluff, which is also eventually shed for more permanent hair, is known as **vellus hair**, and it returns to haunt us as we age. Rarely does it exceed two centimeters in length.

Terminal hair is the third type of hair, and certainly the most desirable. It is what typically covers most of our scalp in our youth before thinning begins. Terminal hair is strong, larger in size and length than lanugo or vellus hair, and it is pigmented.

HAIR TYPES

Lanugo-occurs in utero on fetal skin and may be seen in prematurely born babies

Vellus-short, fine, very little pigmentation at birth

        — replaces terminal hair as we age

        — sometimes referred to as miniaturized hair

Terminal-thick and long hair-most desirous

        — in children occurs only as scalp hair, eyebrows/eyelashes

        — in adults, spreads to other body parts

Hair color is ascertained at birth and determined at the base of the follicle by the length and type of the **melanin granules** (pigment). Darker hair contains more of the substance and gray hair is absent of melanin as it (the melanin) diminishes with age. Eventually white, transparent, or yellowish hair takes over as melanin wanes. In dark hair, these melanin granules are large and rich in color pigment; in red hair they are a bit smaller and spherical in shape. The fewest granules are found in blonde, gray and white hair. Therefore, women who are born in warm, sunny climates have elongated granules, and there is a predisposition to black or very dark hair. Females in moderate climate zones have fewer elongated granules, resulting in more brown hair, and

---

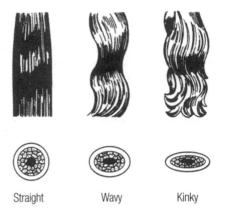

Straight   Wavy   Kinky

women in cooler or cold geographic regions like Scandinavia have far less melanin, thus giving them blondish hues.

A Caucasian woman's hair may begin turning gray in her early thirties, an Asian's slightly later, and an African American woman's often resists the graying process until sometime in her mid-forties. Gradual thinning of hair with age is a natural condition and is called **involutional alopecia** or **senescent balding**. Many elderly women seem to exhibit a bluish hue to their once white hair. This is due to a hair tinting process used in an attempt to try and camouflage the yellow tinge by applying a blue rinse that can eventually cause build up, with blue becoming the more predominant color over time.

Hair varies in shape according to ethnicity: Asians have the thickest and roundest hair shafts causing their hair to be straight or medically defined as **leiotrichous**. They also have a lesser incidence of baldness than Caucasians whose hair is slender, elliptical (kidney shaped), often curved and exhibits medium thickness. **Cynotrichous** medically defines Caucasian hair.

African Americans, on the other hand, have a ribbon like, slightly flattened, medium-thick hair shaft. This results in a hair strand that is wavy, curly or kinky and is called **heliotrichosis**.

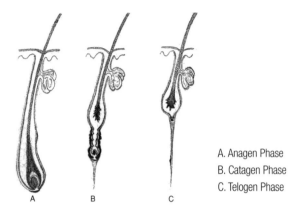

A. Anagen Phase
B. Catagen Phase
C. Telogen Phase

There are three primary phases of hair cycle activity: **anagen phase**, **catagen phase**, and **telogen phase**. **Anagen phase** is the growing cycle of the hair follicle with approximately 90% of the hair being in this mode at any given time. It is in this stage that the terminal hairs reside. Remember, these are the "good hairs" that have not been affected by age, disease, or dihydrotestosterone (DHT). The anagen cycle lasts between two and seven years.

The **catagen phase** begins when follicle growth ceases; the hair follicle shrinks; the melanin (pigment) is lost; and the follicle separates from the **capillary plexus**, which provides oxygen and nutrition to the area. In this transitional phase, which lasts about one to two weeks before going into the next phase, hair loss is not usually apparent. Only 1-2% of hair is in this state at any given time.

The third phase of hair growth activity is the **telogen phase**, which occupies around 8-10% of the hairs on our head. In this phase cell division ceases, hair growth stops and the attachment of the hair at the base of the follicle becomes progressively weaker. Panic sometimes reigns in this phase because, even in a thoroughly normal and healthy scalp, we see hair mound in our brushes, pile in the shower, and pepper the sink. These hairs have not been abused by hair products, coloring, poor diet, stress or improper hair care, but rather have simply lived their full life cycle of two to seven years. They have remained intact, for a three-month resting period, and then shed as part of the **normal hair loss process** consisting of 50 to 100 hairs per day. Finally, the old hair is shed as a result of ordinary daily traction from combing, washing, its own weight, or a push from a newly growing hair as it works its way up the follicle toward the scalp to replace the lost hair. Viewed under a microscope, the bulb of the hair shaft of a hair in the telogen phase is white and thicker and appears similar to an exclamation point. Now the cycle begins all over again: anagen, catagen, telogen.

The telogen phase can cause considerable concern for women. It is often associated with stress, pregnancy, weight loss, drug usage or illness. During pregnancy, all of a woman's hormones go toward development of a new baby. While the anagen phase normally comprises 90% of our hair, during gestation as little as 2% may be in this phase. After the baby is born, all of those growing hairs go into the resting phase (telogen) and can represent as much 30-50% of our hair at this time (usually telogen is only 8-10% of our total hair). Thus, there can be an accelerated amount of hair loss. Fortunately, this is only temporary, and the cycle will correct itself within three to six months and hair will reappear.

RULES OF 10 (Dr. Elise Olsen)	
100,000	Scalp Hairs
10,000	Telogen Hairs
1,000	Days of Anagen Phase
100	Hairs lost per day
1	Centimeter of hair growth per month

The Hair Loss Gene

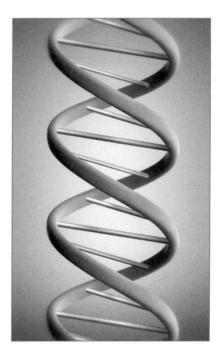

The Hair loss gene can be inherited by a child from either parent.

Female   **Male**

CHAPTER THREE

WHY WOMEN
LOSE THEIR HAIR:
FOUR MAIN REASONS

"Experience is the comb that nature
gives us when we are bald."

Ancient Proverb

For most women, the first approach to solving the problem and the disturbing dilemma of hair loss is simply denial. Next, most will try out a few different hairstyles designed to create the illusion of fuller, thicker hair in an attempt to camouflage the misfortune. Subsequently, a new shampoo "guaranteed to thicken or stimulate hair growth," frequently coupled with a vitamin regime is undertaken. Finally, realizing that all of their frantic, reactionary efforts have failed, and often several hundred dollars later, an appointment with the family physician and or a dermatologist is scheduled to obtain answers that will hopefully resolve the situation.

Hair loss can be gradual or quite sudden and can go virtually unnoticed for many months. It solely depends on the underlying cause or origin of the problem. There are four types of hair loss that account for most, or approximately 90 to 95% of the loss: androgenetic alopecia (hereditary hair loss), telogen effluvium, alopecia areata, and traction and chemical alopecia.

Androgenetic Alopecia

In 1962, Dr. Erich Ludwig combined the words andros and genetic to create a single term to describe the type of hair loss most common to both sexes, and the culprit responsible for approximately 85 to 95% of all alopecia: androgenetic alopecia. Andros refers to male hormones called androgens that contribute to this type of hair loss. Genetic refers to hereditary factors, and of course alopecia is the general word for hair loss. Women also have male hormones (androgens) that circulate throughout their body, and likewise, men have female hormones (estrogens), only at different levels. Men and

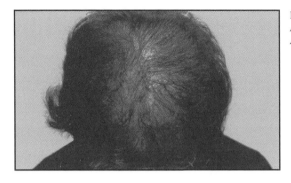

Example of Androgenetic Alopecia

women will be affected by some hair loss, the difference being degree and the onset of when androgenetic alopecia occurs. It is transmitted from both parents, not just from the mother's side, as is commonly thought. The condition is referred to not as only androgenetic alopecia, but common baldness, male pattern baldness, androgenetic hair loss, hereditary thinning, and diffuse androgen-dependent alopecia. When solely referring to women, the hair loss is called female pattern baldness, female pattern alopecia or most often female pattern hair loss. For simplicity, when discussing androgenetic-type hair loss in women, the condition shall be referenced as female pattern hair loss (FPHL).

Female pattern hair loss, which may begin as early as puberty or as late as the forties, is gradual and appears milder at first in women because they are so adept at concealing hair loss with creative styling. **Close to 25% of women ages thirty-five to forty, and nearly 50% of women beyond the age of forty, show signs of the condition**. Androgenetic alopecia happens almost as frequently in women as in men; it is just less severe. An average of 20% of females presenting with diffuse hair loss will have a family history. A study to determine the incidence of androgenetic alopecia (FPHL) in 1,006 Caucasian women found that it was quite common beginning in their late twenties and peaked after fifty years of age.

Age Group (Years)	No. of Patients Examined	No. with Female Androgenetic Alopecia	Percentage %
20-29	121	4	3
30-39	196	34	17
40-49	251	39	16
50-59	144	33	23
60-69	154	39	25
70-79	80	22	28
80-89	60	19	32
TOTAL	**1006**	**190**	**19**

Although physicians know that it exists, we are still not certain what change or action occurs in genetically susceptible individuals that makes hair fall out. That is to say that the role of androgens is not **completely** understood as they pertain to hair loss. The hair loss is caused by the attachment of an androgenetic hormone to specific receptor sites on the hair follicle cells. Just like there is good and bad cholesterol, there is good and bad testosterone. An enzyme called **5a-reductase**, which is produced in the adrenal glands and ovaries of women, attaches to and converts testosterone (good) to **dihydrotestosterone** (bad), which in turn attaches to a genetically susceptible follicle. There is now an overabundance of dihydrotestosterone (DHT), which does its damage by choking off the blood supply and denying nutrients to the follicle, triggering the hair loss process.

Additionally, androgens reduce the caliber and the diameter of the shaft, the rate of growth, and they curtail the duration of the anagen (growing) phase in the scalp. The anagen-telogen ratio falls from a usual average of nine to one, to about seven to one. Accompanying this abbreviated stage is the gradual shrinking or alteration of the follicle. It can take years to transform the terminal hairs to the shorter, peach fuzz, vellus hairs. This change to vellus hairs is called **miniaturization** or the beginning of androgenetic alopecia (FPHL). Unlike men, women do not necessarily have to have an excess of DHT in order for androgenetic alopecia (FPHL) to manifest. It is interesting to note that in a study of stump-tailed macaques, all of the monkeys (both male and female) developed frontal baldness after four years of age. The frontal hair follicles had produced elevated amounts of DHT. Again, the specific reason for the influence of DHT on androgenetic alopecia is unknown.

How do you know if you have androgenetic alopecia (FPHL)? Typically the male pattern begins with the familiar M-shape or receding frontal hairline. If women exhibit this type of hair loss, it may be accompanied by acne, **hirsuitism** (an over abundance of body and facial hair), reduced breast size, menstrual abnormalities or possibly **virilism** (the presence of male secondary sexual characteristics). This pattern usually indicates an incidence of a high level of testosterone, or of a higher level of circulating androgens. Men who lose their hair tend to have more vellus hairs remain on their head so their hair may seem thinner than that of a female's. Although women have fewer hair counts per cm2 than men, the hair that remains is similar in diameter and length to the hair fibers in non-balding women. Thus, they tend to have a much better cosmetic covering.

Female androgenetic alopecia, on the other hand, is considerably more dominant, and presents as a more diffuse pattern of loss over the crown or top of the head. With androgenetic alopecia (FPHL), 90% is of a diffuse pattern in women and 10% includes **temporal** (by the temples) thinning similar to the hair loss pattern of a man's. Retention of the frontal hairline is maintained 85% of the time for women. Here too, one of the first signals for this type of alopecia is that over time there is progressive shrinking of the genetically pre-programmed hair follicles, hairs are smaller in diameter, finer, unpigmented, and the now slower growing hair gradually ascends the follicle and replaces the terminal hair. A ratio of less than four terminal hairs to one of these miniaturized hairs usually indicates androgenetic alopecia.

The anagen, or growth phase, which includes the terminal hair, becomes shorter in its duration, thereby affecting the telogen phase (where we lose the 100 plus hairs per day). The telogen phase usually encompasses only 10% of the scalp hair, but can now represent about 30%. The result is more hair fall-out. Eventually the follicle simply ceases production of hair. Other signs of possible androgenetic alopecia (FPHL) are reduced hair volume and density, widening of the partings, and **skull-cap pattern baldness**. This condition is a diffuse loss of hair in the vertex area (highest point of the skull) and is seen mostly in postmenopausal women.

SIGNS AND SYMPTOMS OF HYPERANDROGENISM IN WOMEN
(An excess of male hormones)
Sperling and Heimer, Continuing Medical Education,
American Academy of Dermatology 1993

Loss of breast tissue	Hirsuitism
Acne	Alopecia
Deepening of voice	Primary or secondary memenorrhea
	(absence or abnormal cessation of the menses)
Increased libido	Increased muscle mass

The sebaceous gland, located in the follicle and responsible for the hair's oily sheen, continues to function after miniaturization, therefore often making the hair seem oilier and flatter. There has been preliminary research regarding the effect of the gland, and some believe the excess surface sebum may be responsible for higher levels of the 5-alpha reductase enzyme. The excess, in turn elevates the dihydrotestosterone. This supports the belief that perhaps uncleanliness can lead to a greater vulnerability of the hair follicles succumbing to DHT. Some doctors suggest daily washing of the hair to help reduce surface sebum.

Women usually experience a lesser level of hair loss than men. It is thought that this is due to their higher estrogen levels (believed to aid in hair retention) and lower androgen levels. In a 1988 study of pre- and post-menopausal women regarding patterns of hair loss, the doctors hypothesized that such a presence of increased estrogen vs. decreased androgens could alter hair loss. They labeled this phenomenon "anti-androgenetic influence." Also, it is theorized that women may have less

---

dramatic hair loss than men due to the fact that they have lower levels of circulating testosterone, lower levels of the 5-alpha reductase enzyme in scalp follicles, and an increased amount of **aromatase,** an enzyme that helps block the conversion of testosterone to DHT. It is believed that androgenetic hair loss may increase in females after menopause due to the decrease of the protective effects of estrogen on the hair follicles.

Misconceptions and Facts about Androgenetic Alopecia in Women

Vera Price, MD The New England Journal of Medicine, September 23, 1999
"Treatment of Hair Loss"

Factor	Misconception	Fact
Decade of onset	Age 50, 60, or 70s	Teens, 20, 30s, or 40s
Incidence	15 to 20%	50% of women less than 50 years of age
Mode of transmission	Maternal	Polygenic (both parents)
Menses and pregnancy	Abnormal	Normal
Androgen levels	High	Normal
Need for hormonal evaluation	Extensive evaluation	None needed unless any of the following are present: irregular menses, infertility, hirsuitism, severe cystic acne, virilization, or glactorrhea (excessive milk production)
Restrictions on hair care and grooming	Use of teasing, hair spray, hair color, permanents or frequent washing forbidden	Use of hair styling, teasing, hair spray, hair color, or permanents are fine; no restrictions on the frequency of washing

(Medical) Evaluation of Women with Androgenetic Alopecia
Vera Price, MD

Conditions To Be Ruled Out Or Assessed	Means of Evaluation
Androgen excess*	Measurement of serum total or free testosterone, Dehydroepiandrosterone sulfate (DHEAS), and prolactin
Hypothyroidism and Hyperthyroidism	Measurement of serum thyrotropin
Chronic inadequate intake of dietary protein	History taking
Chronic blood loss	Measurement of serum iron, iron-binding capacity, ferritin, and hemoglobin
Severe acute or chronic illness	Tests as indicated

*Androgen excess should be considered if any of the following are present: irregular menses, infertility, hirsuitism, severe cystic acne, virilization, or galactorrhea.

Telogen Effluvium

The second most common type of hair loss in females is called **telogen effluvium**. Because of its visibility and rapid progression, it can be frightening and of enormous concern to women. With this condition, too much hair prematurely and quickly goes from the growing stage (anagen) to the resting state of telogen that can now represent as much as 30 to 50% of

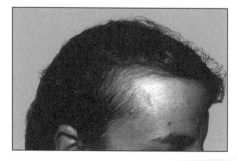

Example of
Telogen Effluvium

the hair on the scalp with daily loss now ranging from 150 to 700 hairs. The ends of the hair shaft, or roots, appear as bulbous or onion-shaped and fall out easily. A physician can diagnose the condition with a simple hair-pull test to view the club-shaped bulbs. Telogen effluvium almost always lags behind a stressful event by about two or three months. Depending on the medical history of a patient, tests such as thyroid function, iron studies, serum zinc, an antinuclear factor antibody titer, or a syphilis serology might be performed. With syphilis, there is often a patchy, moth-eaten appearance to the scalp area.

The good news about the shedding that occurs during telogen effluvium is that the old hair is making way for a new strand that is already forming and pushing its way up the hair shaft. Telogen effluvium generally corrects itself within six to eighteen months, once the contributing factor is removed. It is most commonly associated with postpartum, syphilis, major surgery, poor diet, birth control pills, anemia, certain medications, and thyroid irregularities.

The most frequently observed cases of telogen effluvium are the result of postpartum, with one-third to one-half of mothers reporting mild to moderate hair loss. This type of telogen effluvium is called **telogen gravidarum** (meaning birthing). During pregnancy, with all of the extra hormones present, the anagen phase is prolonged (sometimes as much as 95% of the hair remains in this phase during the later stages of pregnancy) instead of transitioning into the hair's usual telogen phase. Thus the scalp hair is usually very full with up to 6,500 extra hairs still remaining in this phase.

Upon birth, hormones are withdrawn suddenly, and the overdue amount of anagen hairs go into a short period of catagen (a few days to a few weeks duration), and then on to the longer telogen phase. Here the hair usually starts shedding profusely three to four months after delivery. During this time too, there may be changes in the nails. All types of telogen effluvium are corrected 90% of the time without medical intervention. If treatment is necessary, it often consists of a topical steroid regime, topical irritants such as salicylic acid and allergic sensitizers, squaric acid, dibutyl ester, estrogens or progesterones. Because of the normal cycle of hair, re-growth takes about three to six months after the initial fallout. **In 8% of telogen effluvium** cases, the condition recurs within the next twenty years.

Since birth has been the recent topic, this is an opportune time to address genetics. Baldness occurs when a single, dominant gene is inherited. That "singleness" is somewhat of a good thing and somewhat hurtful because it is "easier" to get one dominant gene passed on. If baldness would require two genes to be present, the instance of it would be less frequent. This gene is passed on to a child by either parent. The myth, "It's inherited from your mother," is **false**. If only one parent (remember it does not matter which) carries the dominant gene, a child has a 50% chance of inheriting the trait for baldness. The ante is raised to a 75% chance for being bald if both parents possess the gene. Although individuals may inherit the gene for hair loss, the condition may not manifest unless other genetic factors are present.

Oral contraceptives, which can be responsible for sudden hormonal changes, can cause telogen effluvium, either from discontinuing their use or from using them. The levels of progesterone, which are today less than in earlier doses, can affect hair loss. Stopping birth control pills can also cause this type of hair loss even up to three months after cessation. This is because higher levels of estrogen increase the percentage of anagen hairs while the patient is taking contraceptives. When stopped, more hairs go from the anagen phase into the telogen phase. Again, profuse shedding will subside in about three months.

If hair loss continues past three to six months, it is then called **chronic telogen effluvium**. The exact reason for this condition is not fully understood, but it is thought that stress might play a role.

Causes of Telogen Effluvium

Acute Stress (hemorrhage)	**Drugs**
Childbirth, postpartum	Allopurinol (Zyloprim)
Chronic Systemic Illness	Clofibrate (Atromid-S)
Cancer	Cocaine
Leukemia	Warafin (Coumadin)
Hodgkin's Disease	Heparin
Tuberculosis	Oral contraceptives
Cirrhosis	Propylthiouracil
Crash Dieting	**Febrile Illness**
	Influenza
Chronic Iron Deficiency*	Lobar pneumonia
	Pertussis
Psychogenic Stress	Scarlet Fever

* Added by Dr. Matt Leavitt

Poor nutrition, even with our rich Western diet, a proclivity for women to crash diet, and a change in the increased daily nutritional needs for women required after puberty, have all contributed to the presence of telogen effluvium in women. Low iron, fiber and calcium intake top the list for deficiencies in a study conducted by the British Ministry of Agriculture, Fisheries and Food.

The Dietary and Nutritional Survey of British Adults- Further Analysis

Item	Units	*RNI	% Below RNI
Fiber	grams	30	95%
Calcium	mg	800	48%
Iron	mg	14.8	89%
Magnesium	mg	300	72%
Potassium	mg	3,500	94%
Zinc	mg	7	31%
Copper	mg	1.2	59%
Folate	micro g	200	47%
Vitamin A	micro g	600	31%
Vitamin C	mg	40	34%
Vitamin B6	micro g	1.2	22%

*RNI (Reference Nutrient Intake) is equivalent to United States RDA (Recommended Daily Allowance)

Women should first eat a balanced diet, and if necessary consider taking a multivitamin or supplement in order to reverse this particular form of hair loss. Hair loss due to a severe protein deficiency is called **kwashiorkor** or **marasmus** if the deficiency includes both protein and caloric deprivation. In these conditions the remaining hair is brittle, dull, sometimes reddish in color, and the hair shaft diameter is smaller. Re-growth is probable if the diet is improved, and there has not been irreversible damage to the hair follicles. Malabsorption states or syndromes (gastrointestinal) can be associated with diffuse hair loss, also. Women intolerant to gluten can abate possible hair loss by going on a gluten-free diet.

Anagen effluvium, another type of sudden diffuse hair loss, presents during the anagen phase, rather than the telogen. Whereas telogen effluvium takes three months to manifest, anagen effluvium's onset is within a few days to a few weeks after the insult. It is extensive, with thousands of hairs lost daily, and may result in as much as 80 to 90% of the hair being lost. Anagen effluvium is the result of hair shafts that have been damaged from the effects of poisoning, drugs, or endocrine disorders, and is most often associated with chemotherapy, radiation, exposure to toxins (arsenic or thallium in insecticides), or a metabolic catastrophe. Except in cases of radiation to the scalp area, the hair will almost always re-grow when the offending cause is removed.

Causes of Anagen Effluvium
(Nonscarring Hair Loss Disorders)

Chemotherapy	Poisoning	Ionizing Radiation	Starvation
Antimetabolites	Arsenic		Acute prolonged
Azathioprine (Imuran)	Bismuth		protein deprivation
Colchicine	Borate		especially during
Cyclophosphamide (Cytoxan)	Lead		fad diets and fasting
Hydroxyurea (Hydrea)	Thallium		
Methotrexate			
Gentamicin (Garamycin)			

Alopecia Areata

Alopecia areata is considered by a vast number of physicians to be the third leading cause for hair loss in women. The condition most often affects the younger population, and its onset is usually sudden. The Egyptians first described such a condition in hieroglyphics, and in 1790 the term alopecia areata first appeared. It simply means hair loss in a specific area. Alopecia areata has an incidence of 1 to 4% in dermatology clinics, affects almost 2% of the population and is seen in the same families 10 to 20% of the time. It usually presents either as spotty, patchy or circular areas, or can be seen as breakage or clumps of lost hair. The hairs in the affected spot or spots can easily be removed or pulled with the fingers. Sometimes it is evident on the eyebrows. Wherever it manifests, the female views it as loathsome and as an affliction. In the most severe forms of alopecia areata, all scalp hair is lost. This is called **alopecia totalis**. When all scalp hair and all body hair is lost, including the eyebrows and eyelashes, the condition is referred to as **alopecia universalis**. Progression to alopecia totalis occurs more frequently in younger patients. The hair normally takes two years to fall out, with one-third of the patients having no significant re-growth. About one-third of those afflicted with these two conditions will have their hair grow back within one year.

The causes of alopecia areata are thought to be varied and frequently unknown, but most often the hair loss is associated with an immunological disorder (or autoimmune deficiency), which causes the body to produce antibodies that attack the

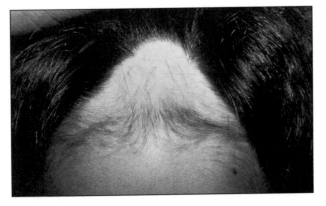

Example of
Alopecia Areata

hair follicles. Basically, the body's own defense system malfunctions, and the immune system acts as if the hair follicles are foreign and assaults them. The loss can follow a stressful event, such as divorce, death in the family, or even cataract surgery, and is primarily seen in twenty to thirty year olds. But 25% of the cases are seen after age forty and 60% of those cases have re-growth within one year and 40% have a relapse with 40% of those incidences occurring within the first year. Greater instances of alopecia areata are seen with those patients having thyroid disease, Down syndrome, vitiligo, diabetes and atopic dermatitis. Nail pitting is sometimes associated with the condition.

With alopecia areata, it ordinarily takes three to six months for the hair to fall out and then it ceases. This is followed by a three to six month period of no activity, and then re-growth occurs in approximately 90% of patients. Eight percent have a recurrence, and it can be even as late as twenty years past the initial attack. Sometimes the new growth can be a little lighter in color.

Alopecia areata usually resolves on its own. A doctor can tell if the hair shaft is in the state of alopecia areata as the hairs look like an exclamation point when plucked. That is, the ends are "fatter" and wider and have a blunt tip, whereas the bulb portion is thinner. Medical intervention is often limited as there is no real evidence that any form of treatment alters the ultimate course of the situation. If doctors do prescribe care, the first line of defense is usually a topical or intralesional steroid (glucocorticoid), topical irritant, such as salicylic acid and allergic sensitizers and squaric acid and dibutyl ester. Dithranol, a tar-like shampoo, topical Retin A with minoxidil added, and oral zinc are sometimes given. All are safe and may be effective. Why these agents allow re-growth and stimulation is not totally understood, but it is believed that they encourage stimulation of T-cells, thus creating an apparent autoimmune process, which restores the hair. Prednisone (oral steroid) is used in limited quantities with more severe cases, and may be combined with PUVA treatments. Here a physician prescribes a light-sensitive drug that is then followed by short exposures to ultraviolet light two to three times a week, lasting three to six weeks. Minoxidil 5% solution lends a 20 to 45% cosmetically acceptable re-growth and is even safe enough for children. Anthralin can be recommended and is safe for children with 25% having acceptable re-growth within approximately six months. Of course, a physician should prescribe a medical regime on a case-by-case basis.

Protocol for Treatment of Adult Alopecia Areata

Patients with less than 50% hair loss

1. Do nothing
2. Intralesional triamcinolone acetonide injections
3. Minoxidil 5% solution and superpotent topical corticosteroids
4. Combination of minoxidil 5% solution and anthralin
5. Topical immunotherapy if the above do not work

Patients with more than 50% hair loss

1. Topical immunotherapy with diphencyprone
2. Minoxidil 5% solution plus superpotent topical corticosteroids
3. Minoxidil 5% solution plus anthralin
4. PUVA (undergoing short exposure to UVA ultraviolet light)
5. Systemic corticosteroid therapy (rarely)

International Journal of Dermatology 1999
University of British Columbia
Hair Research and Treatment Center, 1998: Chart

More information on alopecia areata can be found at the National Alopecia Areata Foundation: www.naaf.org Telephone: (415) 456-4644

Traction and Chemical Alopecia

Traction alopecia accounts for the fourth most common cause of hair loss in females and is usually seen in conjunction with chemical alopecia. Traction alopecia involves hairstyles and hair care practices that contribute to, or put excess tension or pull on the hair. The condition is usually more common in African Americans, and presents in specific areas or in a pattern where the hair is being stressed over a period of time. When pulled too tightly the hair is traumatized, resulting in premature hair breakage and or patches of baldness, both of which can be reversed if the severe styling practice is ceased early enough, especially in children.

Two to four months is the time period for re-growth if it is to occur. Permanent scarring, fibrosis of the hair root, and loss of functioning hair follicles, can follow the continued repetition of harmful hair care and hair styling. Braiding, plaiting, cornrows, ponytails, elastic hair bands, excessive teasing and use of sponge rollers (they "grab" the hair tighter) can all contribute to traction alopecia.

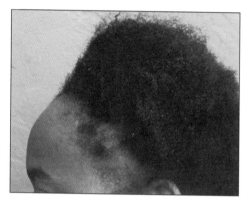

Example of
Traction Alopecia

Occasionally there is swelling, pustules or scaling. A related form of traction alopecia is called **friction alopecia** and can be seen when the choice is made to wear snug-fitting hats or wigs for a prolonged period. Advice from a physician would be to cease the abusive hairstyles and hair care, including hot combs. The use of cream rinses (conditioners) can help reduce friction and strengthen the individual hair strands.

Chemical alopecia occurs when tints, bleaches, straighteners, and permanents are used too frequently and improperly. These practices can weaken the hair so that it breaks off easily or falls out (temporarily or permanently). Injury to the scalp is also a possibility. Care should be given to always patronize a reputable and experienced hair-care professional when having any of these types of hair treatments. If the damage is not too severe and the abuse is corrected, hair will usually re-grow. A severe form of hair breakage that can sometimes be seen along with hair straightening procedures performed over an extended period of time is called **proximal trichorrhexis nodosa**. This particular hair damage resembles a "brush cut." If straightening is stopped, hair will usually recover after one or two years.

CHAPTER FOUR

MEDICAL TREATMENTS FOR ANDROGENETIC ALOPECIA

"Those curious locks, so aptly twined,
whose every hair a soul doth bind."

Thomas Carew, Poet 1594-1640

As recently as 20 years ago, there was virtually no medical path along which women with androgenetic alopecia (female pattern hair loss) could venture. The condition was rarely discussed, often avoided, ignored, covered up, and left undisclosed by women. It frequently remained untreated by physicians since they had few, if any, solutions for this specific type of hair loss.

There are thousands of non-medical "cures," lotions, potions, herbs, home remedies and concoctions for hair loss, some of which defy all believability. (Remember the Egyptian's formula?) If any of these were effective, there would be significant medical studies revealing such. And too, why has hair transplantation, which is mostly performed on patients with androgenetic alopecia, become a billion dollar industry, and one that is still growing? Vitamins, supplements, etc. may offer certain benefits, although most doctors do not profoundly recommend this route. Patients can be encouraged to try one or two various methods, if for no other reason than to eliminate their inherent curiosity and perhaps provide an element of comfort. The best advice from a physician's point of view is to beware of scams, unsubstantiated promises and unregulated products. Unfortunately, what often happens is that someone tries one of these unproven remedies as an answer to hair loss without seeking a physician's advice for what may be the symptom of an underlying disease. Hair loss patients may then miss out on a treatment that has been exclusively identified as medically providing beneficial results for hair loss.

The medical community must address several challenges in order to attempt to arrest the problem of androgenetic alopecia (FPHL). They are: improving and adding to the drugs currently available for hair loss, controlling or altering androgens (male hormones) that can affect hair follicles, surpressing of excessive DHT and reversing or stabilizing the miniturization of follicles.

Presently the only Food and Drug Administration (FDA) approved medication for androgenetic alopecia or thinning hair in women that can claim re-growth of hair is minoxidil, or as recognized by most as the product brand name, Rogaine for Women. (Rogaine claims 87% of the consumer market share even though their patent expired in 1996.) Other remedies touted to re-grow and retain hair slide through the FDA scrutiny by not stating that the product is a cure for hair loss, but rather is used to clean clogged pores on the scalp. Minoxidil, which is applied topically twice daily to the scalp, first surfaced in 1988 in the U.S. as a treatment for male hair loss, not as a cure, and could only be obtained with a prescription from a physician. Touted as real "hope in a bottle," minoxidil can provide a safe, effective, substantiated treatment option.

Initially sold in August 1991 as a hair loss treatment for women, minoxidil was still available by prescription only. The advertising promotion for Rogaine began in January of 1992. This campaign, with the familiar feminine pink boxes, succeeded in making 54% of females aware of minoxidil as a treatment for thinning hair. In April of 1996, it was approved as an over-the-counter drug (OTC) and currently is sold as a 2% solution for females and males, and a 5% solution for males (1997).

In a published study, 5% minoxidil, generally recommended solely for use by men, showed minimal benefits for women beyond what the 2% solution provided. In some instances the 5% can be beneficial, but the decision to use it should be discussed with a physician. Caution with use of the 5% solution is especially warranted for women as hirsuitism, or excessive hair growth, may result on the face or spread to the hands and/or arms (hypertrichosis). Hands should always be washed after application of minoxidil to prevent this possible side effect, and any contact with the eye area should be avoided. The most frequently reported side effect with its use is itching of the scalp and other minor skin irritations, which occur in approximately 6% of female consumers.

Use of minoxidil to abate hair loss or re-grow hair should be viewed as a lifetime commitment if the re-growth is to be maintained. More density to the hair is achieved with continuous use, which allows for easier styling, but bear in mind that it does not replace all of the missing hair and that the response to treatment is individual. Based on a photographic evaluation more than 4 out of 5 men will see an effect from treatment either as no continued hair loss, minimal growth, moderate growth, or dense growth (Olsen et al, 2002). If application should cease, the hair gained will be lost and will most likely return to the density prior to treatment. Patience must be exercised, as noticeable results are not usually seen for up to four months, with eight months being the best time to fully evaluate minoxidil's efficacy. If the product does not show any hair growth or cessation of hair loss after using twice daily for one year, it is probably not the appropriate choice. Discovered in the 1970s, minoxidil was first prescribed as an oral treatment for severe hypertension or high blood pressure. During human studies for use of minoxidil in this capacity, a significant number of patients grew a measurable amount of hair (70% got some hypertrichosis with the initial oral hypertension drug) on various parts of their bodies (eyebrows merged, cheeks and arms became hairy). Thus, the Upjohn Pharmaceutical Company began a scientific study for a topical 2% minoxidil solution for the treatment of male pattern baldness that involved nearly 6,000 men. The absorbed dose of the original topical minoxidil formula represents only about 1% of the minimal oral dose used for hypertension. To date, minoxidil has the highest dermatological usage of any hair loss product in the United States, and an estimated 10-15% of Rogaine sales are Rogaine for Women (now owned by Pfizer). In excess of one million women have tried the product.

No one is completely sure exactly how or why minoxidil works to make hair grow. However, one theory, based on scientific research, holds that the drug stimulates and enlarges the miniaturized follicles, advancing the resting hair (telogen phase) to enter the hair growth cycle (anagen phase), thereby prolonging that enviable phase. Consequently, the miniaturization process can be partially reversed, but only if miniaturization is not too advanced.

Since minoxidil is a vasodilator, it increases blood flow, hence another unproven theory that more nutrients are delivered to the follicles, providing for a healthier follicle that can possibly be coaxed out of its dormancy. Other popular presumptions include that minoxidil has an effect on the promotion of cell division at the hair follicle site, which increases hair growth. Minoxidil continuously fights the genetic programming of the hair follicles that want to cease production. With an extended growth phase, which may be lengthened with its use, the hair can grow longer and become thicker.

Minoxidil is not a miracle drug and cannot activate any follicles that are no longer capable of producing hair. For example, scarring alopecia or burned areas cannot re-grow hair. The initial studies for females revealed that 59% of the women using 2% Rogaine reported some hair re-growth (19% reported moderate re-growth, 40% reported minimal re-growth), and 40% reported no re-growth. Interestingly, in a user survey, four out of five women reported that they had gradual slowing or stopping of hair loss. Two percent minoxidil was shown to increase the hair weight by nearly 43% in women treated with the drug in a clinical trial that lasted for 32 weeks, compared to only 1.9% for those females treated with a placebo. In another study, 3% minoxidil solution increased the diameter of hair fibers in women, which made the hair appear thicker overall.

Most of the short, downy-like (vellus), colorless hair produced by minoxidil will eventually be replaced with longer, thicker, and pigmented hairs like others on the scalp. Hair re-growth usually appears first in balding or thinning areas (as vellus hair) or at the edges of a bald spot. Then gradually the hairless area is filled.

Women who wish to become pregnant should discontinue the use of minoxidil one month prior to stopping birth control. Nursing females should not use the drug as it may be absorbed into the blood stream and excreted in breast milk. One of the main complaints from women about the use of minoxidil is that since most have longer hair (than men), the product can be messy and interfere with their hairstyling routine. The good news is that manufacturers of minoxidil continue to develop optional delivery systems and improved application methods.

What to Expect from Minoxidil Use

Partial enlargement of follicles
Longer, coarser, darker hair
Hair 1 cm long becoming approximately 3-5 cm long
Increased coverage of the scalp

Vera Price, M.D.

A second group of drugs used to specifically help abate hereditary hair loss or androgenetic alopecia, are called antiandrogens, androgen blockers, or antagonizing androgens. All are words used to describe the deliberate interference with androgens (male hormones that are even present in females) in the body to help alter the course of hair loss. The goal is to reverse or stabilize hair loss. Since these male hormones are thought to be a prime suspect in this type of hair loss, these inhibitors (the drugs) seem to be the likely route to prevent the androgens from expressing their hair loss activity at target sites. Most medications are oral, as attempts at using topical antiandrogens, which were once believed to shrink the sebaceous gland, proved to be disappointing.

Spironolactone is approved in the U.S. as a medication for high blood pressure. As an off-label drug, it is commonly used to treat alopecia, acne, and hirsuitism in females. It is believed to work in arresting hair loss by interfering with testosterone synthesis or its production and by suppressing the 5-alpha reductase activity. Further, spironolactone increases peripheral conversion of testosterone to estrodial. (Remember female estrogens are believed to extend the anagen phase and provide protection against hair loss.) It also competes with DHT for the androgen receptor, and may decrease androgen production of male hormones. In a few small clinical trials, hair growth was not seen, but the trials did show spironolactone might slow down hair loss. If dosages over 100 mg per day are taken, uterine bleeding can be a side effect, and there may be a possible risk of developing breast cancer. Spironolactone may also cause abnormal fetal development (teratogenesis), so a form of birth control is also recommended when taking this drug. Although not approved by the FDA specifically for use as an antiandrogen, it is widely administered for this purpose and should be carefully supervised by a doctor.

Cyproterone acetate (CPA) is an androgen (male hormone) antagonist and a potent progestin (as in progesterone) commonly used in Europe and Canada to treat hirsuitism, but it is not available nor FDA approved in the U.S. Although no rigorous studies have been performed, some have shown that combining cyproterone acetate with ethinyestradiol (the most common estrogen found in birth control pills) may prevent, slow down, or reverse androgenetic alopecia (FPHL). Side effects can include weight gain, breast tenderness, loss of libido and nausea. Birth control pills that contain small amounts of cyproterone acetate are Diane and Dianette, but they are not available in the U.S.

Flutamide is a potent antiandrogen that blocks androgen receptors and is approved for use in the treatment of prostate cancer, but it is not approved for treatment of acne, hirsuitism or hair loss. Flutamide must also be used in conjunction with contraception, as feminization of the male fetus is a possible side effect if pregnancy occurs. Liver toxicity is another possible reaction. Because of these adverse side effects, scientists are presently researching the efficacy of a topical flutamide.

Cimetidine is a weak antiandrogen that may have some affect on slowing the hair loss process. It is often used effectively when treating children and adults with alopecia areata. Cimetidine can also be given in combination with minoxidil.

Finasteride is most commonly known in relation to hair as Propecia. It was developed by Merck Pharmaceuticals and has proven to be a great success for treating men with androgenetic hair loss, but the initial studies with postmenopausal women using it have proven to be disappointing. Finasteride was originally prescribed for benign prostate conditions under the brand name Proscar. It was then successfully marketed in 1998 as Propecia for use as a hair loss drug with the approval of the FDA. Dosage for Propecia 1mg was approximately one-fifth the original amount that was in Proscar.

Finasteride does not inhibit the actual male hormones (androgens), but the drug inhibits the 5-alpha reductase type 2 enzymes. It prevents testosterone from converting to dihydrotestosterone (DHT). Since these enzymes enable DHT, the "bad" testosterone, to be more prominent than the simple "good" testosterone, the hair loss cycle is broken. At birth DHT is necessary for the development of normal male genitalia but is not necessary for adults. Studies show that the concentration of finasteride in the sperm of men taking it is so minimal, that it is considered to be risk-free to pregnant women and their embryos. However, women of child bearing age cannot take Propecia, nor should they even handle any broken or crushed tablets. At present there are no plans for Merck to continue trials of finasteride for women, and testing has been abandoned. In some cases, doctors do prescribe the drug off-label for **post-menopausal** women in the treatment of androgenetic hair loss (FPHL).

Retinoic acid, known as Retin-A has no significant effect on circulating androgens, especially testosterone. It is believed to shrink the sebaceous glands where DHT harbors. There is less DHT available in the follicle area so hair loss theoretically, is decreased. Retin-A is not indicated for hair loss treatment, but it is used by many doctors for such. Pharmacists, with a doctor's prescription, frequently add Retin-A to minoxidil for a boost to hair growth because it may help increase absorption of the minoxidil.

CHAPTER FIVE

THE DOCTOR'S ROLE IN FEMALE HAIR LOSS

"Even a single hair casts its shadow."

Publilius Syrus, Roman Author, 1st Century BC

In a recent report, approximately half of all females seen for hair loss when surveyed stated that they were dissatisfied with the initial contact they had with their physicians. This was primarily due to the fact that they had been dismissed as too worrisome, depressed, having marital or sexual problems, or deemed "lucky" to have as much hair as they did. The women felt patronized as less than sympathetic interjections such as, "At least you're not bald," and "It's really nothing," were imparted upon them. Forty-three percent of the doctors advised their patients to wait for a while before taking any further action, and of the more aggressive ones, 10% suggested vitamins. Often the patients were merely dismissed altogether, since 90-95% of standard tests performed for their hair loss produced results considered to be within "normal" ranges. Frequently the women were prescribed the obligatory regimen of treatment with antidepressants.

Women's Degrees of Concern About Hair Loss, A Survey of 2,000+ Households

Extremely Concerned	19%
Somewhat Concerned	24%
Slightly Concerned	28%
Not at all Concerned	29%

Physicians have become increasingly aware of the need to listen. Sensing extreme patient frustration, most doctors ceased the patronizing manner in which female patients were treated in the past by eliminating any aloofness being projected, and by adopting a more compassionate and comforting approach toward solving the problem. The goal of the physician should be to educate the patient, let her know the medical plan in regards to her hair loss, and discuss a timeline for managing the hair loss. To date, approximately 20% of females with hair loss seek advice from their primary care physician, 47% see a dermatologist, 39% see a general or family practitioner and 1% see an obstetrician/gynecologist.

Since women are adept at camouflaging hair loss with creative styles, and since their loss is usually masked by retention of the frontal hairline 85% of the time, initially, the doctor may not recognize hair loss. In fact, a woman must lose more than 50% of her hair before it is readily visible, or others notice the loss. The physician may hesitate and wait for the female patient to initiate conversation regarding hair loss since the topic is such a sensitive one. Hence, there is the added importance of the patient posing in-depth questions, and the doctor attentively listening.

What Women Who Are Concerned About Hair Loss Do

Discuss it with their hair care professional	59%
Discuss it with a friend/family member	57%
Change shampoo/conditioner or frequency	53%
Change their hairstyles	50%
Start massaging their scalps regularly	36%
Consult a doctor	20%
Try an over-the-counter product	14%
Try minoxidil	3% (approx)

What Doctors Recommend for Women With Hair Loss

Nothing, just wait	43%
Vitamins	10%
Topical ointment/scalp cream	8%
Shampoo/dandruff shampoo	7%
Stress management/medication	5%
Referred to dermatologist	5%
Rogaine/minoxidil	3%
Scalp massage	3%
Change shampoo	3%
Nutrition/diet	3%

It is reasonable to say that an inordinate amount of the current research on hair and hair loss has come about just in the past 12 years and is being conducted by a group of highly talented, dedicated female researchers who are medical doctors, Ph.D.s and clinicians. In fact, Angela Christiano, Ph.D., discovered the first hair loss gene for alopecia areata, and Drs. Elise Olsen and Vera Price were involved in the initial discussions and journal articles on the use of minoxidil for women with hair loss.

Hair loss begins to bother its sufferers at various stages, but it can have a direct effect on personal comfort, impacting a variety of day-to-day scenarios. At home, at work, and in social situations, a woman with hair loss often feels that all eyes are upon her. Many women engage in laborious regimens and hairstyling routines as an initial quick fix, but eventually they become discouraged as the problem worsens and they tend to begin distancing themselves from social and professional settings. Women tend to think that their "problem" is only temporary and will be fine once stress abates. It takes them a great deal of time to develop the courage to discuss their hair loss with a physician.

When hair loss becomes a challenge, the first step in dealing with the situation should be to consult a qualified physician, preferably a dermatologist since his/her training is specific to treating hair, skin and nail disorders. The doctor should be made aware of the affects of hair loss on the patient's life, bearing in mind that his/her initial role is to listen. It is important that a trusting relationship is established from the onset and that there is free and open communication and dialogue. The staff should be sensitive toward the need for privacy, and the patient's possible reluctance to even being there. The chart below identifies how long a woman may have hair loss before she really notices it and sees it as a problem.

Duration of Hair Loss

First Observation	Percentage %
Less than 5 years	44%
5 to 9 years	19%
10 to 14 years	17%
Greater than 15 years ago	17%

Usually the first contact for consultation or assessment at a clinic or medical facility is covered by insurance, as is any lab work or tests. As a patient, demand a full physical, consultation, and diagnostic or lab tests, plus a hair biopsy if needed. All hair concerns should be diligently explored, not just to offer peace of mind, but also to examine and possibly detect any serious underlying health problems or disorders. The physician and the patient should discuss the diagnosis, prognosis and the plan of action thoroughly. Referral to a sub-specialist (such as an endocrinologist) might be advantageous at this point. Female patients experiencing hair loss should always be treated on a case-by-case basis in order to find the cause or origin of the problem. Many causes of hair loss, other than heredity, are reversible.

During the consultation and examination, the doctor is looking for a possible association between the hair loss and other diseases, such as lupus or a thyroid condition; reaction to certain drugs, such as birth control pills or beta-blockers; and a relationship between symptoms, for example, an infection. Also, unusual diets, family hair loss history, any episodes of high fever, diabetes, Hodgkin's disease, illnesses the past eight months, vitamin usage and kidney or liver problems are questioned. The tests can aid in the possible detection of structural hair defects, possible hair or scalp disorders, or assist in detecting any substantial trauma.

As mentioned, the physician is looking for any connection between symptoms, incidents or family history as well as ruling out any causes. During the examination, hair color, texture, diameter, and damage to the hair are studied as well as looking for signs of erythema, scale, pustules, and evaluating the degree and density of hair loss. After ascertaining any drug usage that may cause hair loss, a battery of tests may be ordered, followed by several others specific to hair loss. To accompany the history, physical examination, tests and reports, photographs may be taken for further documentation.

Still, regardless of extensive testing, the two main causes of hair loss remain androgenetic alopecia (genetic) and aging. Further, relatives of women severely affected with androgenetic alopecia have a greater risk of hair loss than the relatives of women with mild cases of the disease. Few women believe that they lose their hair because of genetic or hormonal influences (as men do). Instead most attribute the loss to external causes. A survey of 300 females experiencing hair loss revealed:

Belief of Cause of Hair Loss

Permanents, excessive coloring and bleaching, over processing	20%
Serious illness, medications	17%
Hereditary	14%
Age	14%
Stress, nerves	11%
Pregnancy, childbirth	10%

*Some women suggested more than one cause

The absence of intact hair follicles, which will not grow any hair (due to burns or certain diseases), is called **scarring alopecia**. Conversely, follicles are present in **non-scarring** hair loss disorders such as androgenetic alopecia and tinea capitis (scalp ringworm). Fungal infections like ringworm, psoriasis and seborrhea that may cause hair loss are common in younger patients, whereas bacterial scalp infections associated with hair loss are more common in adults. **Folliculitis** is a bacterial infection of the hair follicle, which causes small follicular pustules and diffuse hair loss. According to one study, the common causes of overall alopecia and their frequency are:

Androgenetic alopecia	68.8% of patients
Diffuse alopecia (may be Androgenetic)	11.3% of patients
Alopecia Areata	9.9% of patients
Cicatrical alopecia (many causes)	4.9% of patients
Trichotillomania	1.3% of patients
Trauma, traction	1.1% of patients
Other	2.7% of patients

Source: David Whiting, MD

Alopecia May Be Related to Any of Several Factors
Source: Dr. Maria Hordinsky

A well thought out, detailed questionnaire is crucial in order to obtain an essential patient history regarding her hair loss. Questions should cover a broad range of topics including family history of hair loss, illnesses, hair-care habits, medications, emotional stresses, and recent surgeries.

Patient Information and History Form for Hair Loss
(Developed by Dr. Paul Cotteril with additions by Dr. Matt Leavitt)

Hair:

What area or areas of hair loss are you experiencing?

What is the main problem? (itching, scaling, thinning areas, etc.)

Have you previously been affected by any type of hair loss? If so explain.

When did this particular hair loss begin?

Does anyone in your family have hair loss? What is the amount, age of onset and relationship to you? Be specific.

Has the hair loss increased, decreased or stayed the same?

How many hairs are you losing daily?

Do you feel that you have been shedding excessive numbers of hair?

Do you feel that your scalp hair is slowly thinning out over the top without losing excessive numbers of hairs daily?

Are you losing hair from the entire scalp, or is it more noticeable on the top?

Are any of the hairs short and without color (pigment)?

Where do you mainly lose them? (tub, sink, brush or comb, etc.)

Do your hairs come out at the root or break off?

Do you pull and or twist your hair?

Has your hairline or temporal area receded?

Have you noticed the middle part in your hair widening?

Does the hair seem dull, brittle, or uncombable?

Has the appearance changed; is it straight vs. curly?

Has anyone other than you noticed or mentioned your hair loss?

Have there been any changes in your nails, skin, teeth or mouth?

Do you sweat normally?

Does hair loss affect your daily routine? (more time spent styling, less social contact)

Does hair loss affect you emotionally? (feel less attractive, lower self-esteem)

Hair Care:

How often do you shampoo? List all products used on your hair.

Did you shampoo today?

Have you changed your hairstyle recently or within the last 6 months?

Do you wear a fall or use hair extensions?

Do you braid, plait, tease or wear a bun or ponytail? How often?

Do you use relaxers, pomades, or straighteners?

Do you perm, color, dye or bleach your hair? How often and with what products?

Do you use hot or sponge rollers, hot combs? How often?

Do you use rubber bands, hairpins or other hair ornaments?

Do you blow-dry your hair?

Medical:

List any health problems that you have or have had. Be specific.

Do you have any history of diabetes, anemia, iron deficiency, thyroid or glandular disease?

Have you donated blood in the last 3 years? How many times?

List any high fevers or drug allergies.

List any medication that you take along with duration and dosage.

List all vitamins and supplements you take and the duration and amounts.

List any surgeries, anesthesia, or hospital admissions.

Is there anything unusual about your period? Describe your period. Have you gone through menopause?

Are you tired excessively?

Have you ever had, or do you currently have any ovarian cysts?

Have you ever been pregnant?

Do you have any children? How many?

Were there any complications with pre and postpartum?

When were you last pregnant, and when did you last deliver?

Did you lose any hair after childbirth?

Do you take birth control pills? For how long and what brand? Be specific.

Have you changed jobs, moved, married, had a death in the family or had any life changes in the year prior to hair loss?

Have you had surgery or general anesthesia in the last year?

Have you had a prolonged high fever within the last 6 months?

Are you bothered by being too hot or too cold?

Have you dieted within the last 8 to 12 months? Has your weight changed?

Are you a vegetarian? Do you eat red meat?

Have you ever had chemotherapy or radiation treatments? When?

Have you ever been exposed to any animals or persons with hair loss diseases?

Physician's Hair Loss Examination Form

PHYSICAL EXAM

Hair Density:

_____ normal

_____ mild thinning-crown

_____ mild thinning-diffuse

_____ sparse-crown

_____ sparse-diffuse

Scalp:

_____ normal

_____ erythema

_____ papules/pustules

_____ excoriations

_____ scaling

_____ facial hair loss

_____ scarring

_____ follicular plugging

Hair Pull Test:

_____ negative

_____ positive

Broken Hairs:

_____ absent

_____ present

Laboratory:

KOH exam (for fungal) _____

Trichogram _____

Hair shaft exam _____

Diagnosis:

Plan:

Three day hair count requested: _____

5 mm punch biopsy performed: _____

Blood tests ordered

_____ CBC

_____ ferritin

_____ TSH

_____ total testosterone

_____ DHEAS

_____ RPR (syphilis)

Return to clinic _____ weeks _____ months _____ prn (as needed)

The hair that is lost from oral medications and chemotherapy drugs is certainly tolerated, as the life-saving potential is great. **Alopecia medicamentosa** is the term used to describe diffuse hair loss, usually of the scalp area, caused by the administration or use of various types of drugs. There are close to three hundred medications that can cause hair loss as a side effect, and many are quite familiar. Most physicians and or pharmacists, mostly because of the plethora of drugs, impart little acknowledgement of this fact. The list of medications is just too vast. But be sure to ask at the time the prescription is offered if hair loss is a possibility. When these drugs are no longer taken, hair loss almost always ceases and re-growth occurs within three to six months.

Common Drugs That [May] Cause Hair Loss

Cholesterol lowering drugs- clofibrate (Atromis-S) and gemfibrozil (Lopid)

Parkinson medications- levodopa (Dopar, Larodopa)

Ulcer drugs- cimetidine (Tagamet), ranitidine (Zantac) and famotidine (Pepcid)

Anti-coagulants- Coumadin and Heparin

Agents for gout- Allopurinol (Loporin, Zyloprim)

Anti-arthritics- penicillimine, auranofin (Ridaura), Indomethacin (Indocin), naproxen (Naprosyn), sulindac (Clinoril), and methotrexate (Folex)

Drugs devised from vitamin-A- isotretinoin (Accutane), and etretinate (Tegison)

Anti-convulsants for epilepsy- trimethadione (Tridione)

Anti-depressants- tricyclics, amphetamines

Beta blockers for high blood pressure- atenolol (Tenormin) metoprolol (Lopressor), nadolol (Corgard), propranolol (Inderal), and timolol (Blocadren)

Anti-thyroid agents- carbinazole, iodine, thiocyanate, thiouracil

Others- blood thinners, male hormones (anabolic steroids)

Source: USA Library Publishing, Inc. Copyright(c) 1996

Your doctor may not realize this side effect, and if made aware of it he/she may be able to prescribe an alternative medication that will be just as effective for treating your condition. To ascertain possible side effects, you can ask your doctor to look up your medication in the **Physician's Desk Reference**, which lists the side effects of all medications. When you get a prescription filled, ask your pharmacist this question as well.

Additional Drugs that Can Cause Hair Loss

Anti-cancer drugs (chemotherapy): Actinomycin Amsacrine, Carboplatin, Cisplatinum, Cytosine Arabinoside, Cyclophosphamide (Cytoxan), Bleomycin, Cyclophosphamide, Cytarabine, Dactinomycin, Daunorubicin, Fluorouracil, Methotrexate, Procarbazine, Doxorubicin (Adriamycin), Epirubicin, Etoposide (Taxol), Floxuridine, Ifosfamide, Thioguanine, Vinblastine, Vincristine (Oncovin)

Anti-coagulant drugs (blood thinners): Dicumarol, Warfarin

Anti-convulsant drugs: Carbimazole, Methimazole, Methylthiouracil, Propylthiouracil

Beta Blockers (heart): Acebutolol, Labetalol, Pinolol

Calcium Channel Blockers: Calan 240mg

Non steroidal anti-inflammatory drugs: Fenoprofen, Ibuprofen, Indomethacin, Ketoprofen, Meclomen, Naproxen, Piroxicam

---

Retinoids and Retinol: Acitretin, Etretinate (Tegison), Vitamin A overdose

Tricyclic anti-depressants: Amitriptyline, Amoxapine, Desipramine, Doxepin, Imipramine, Nortriptoline, Protriptyline, Trimpramine, Lithium

Birth Control

Misc.: Valproic acid, Octreocide, Fluoxetine, Fluroxamine, Fluconazole (in large doses), Lamivudine

Source: Health Review Magazine, January 1996

When examining a patient, two hair loss charts, designed specifically for females, can be used. The two physicians who were among the first to take an interest in women's hair loss developed both charts: Doctors Erich Ludwig and Ronald C. Savin. The use of these charts was intended to establish the presence of a pattern of female androgenetic alopecia.

The Ludwig Classification, developed in 1977, defined three stages of hair loss: I, II, and III; with III indicating the most advanced hair loss.

Stage I reveals hair beginning to thin on the crown while the frontal hairline remains preserved. In **Stage II**, the crown continues to thin; the hair loss has advanced and is quite noticeable to others. There may be various shorter and thinner hairs with some being vellus-like and un-pigmented. Again the frontal hairline is relatively intact. **Stage III** is full baldness in the crown area with an increased number of shorter and thinner hairs. The frontal hairline is not preserved and hairstyling cannot hide the loss, as it is too great. Dr. Ludwig is credited with coining the term androgenetic alopecia which means that male hormones, or "andros" combined with a hereditary predisposition, or "genetics," can produce common baldness.

Dr. Ronald C. Savin developed **The Savin Female Density Scale** in the early 1980s. It is based on a scale of 1 through 7, with 7 representing the lowest density. This scale shows hair that is lost

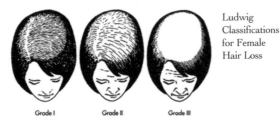

Grade I   Grade II   Grade III

Ludwig
Classifications
for Female
Hair Loss

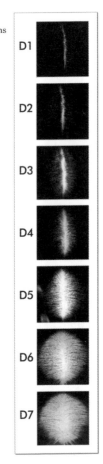

D1

D2

D3

D4

D5

D6

D7

Savin Female
Density Scale

diffusely over the entire scalp. This is the most typical hair loss pattern for females.

Also of note is **The Norwood Classification System**. First developed by Dr. James Hamilton as the Hamilton Hair Loss Chart, and then modified by Dr. O'Tar Norwood, this system is used mostly for describing male pattern baldness—the most common pattern of hair loss found in men. Doctors use this chart to determine the pattern and degree of female hair loss when loss is in the typical horseshoe pattern prevalent in men.

Exams, work-ups, and testing for the individual patient should always be custom tailored. However, the following labs and tests are somewhat standard for patients with alopecia. Even though approximately 90% of the labs and tests will not provide a definitive answer, the information gathered for evaluation, review and interpretation may lead to the underlying cause of hair loss. "Normal" ranges do not negate the fact that hair loss exists; it simply means that finding the reason will be more challenging.

LABS

The lab work-up should consist of a blood count, routine chemistry studies, a urinalysis, a **seriological** test for syphilis, and tests for thyroid function. Additional useful and helpful tests are: testosterone levels, sex hormone binding globulin (SHBG), dehydroepiandrosterone sulfate (DHEAS), androstenedione, lutenizing hormone, follicle-stimulating hormone (FSH), and prolactin counts. Useful too, is serum iron, total iron-binding capacity and ferritin levels. An abnormal endocrinopathy reading can suggest that the hair loss is the male pattern type.

Norwood Classifications System for Male Pattern Baldness

TESTS

Daily Hair Loss Test

This test is performed by the patient daily for one week. Hairs that fall out during the day are counted. These include those lost in the bathroom area, on pillows and in brushes and combs. Hairs should be saved for further examination by the physician, who can then determine the anagen-telogen ratio.

Hair Density Test

It is necessary to determine the width difference of hair loss from various parts of the scalp. This test can be performed on the first visit to the doctor with a hand-held instrument, and simply entails parting hair from different areas and measuring the various widths. Since there are supposed to be approximately 800 to 1,000 hairs per square inch, a relatively close visual estimate can be assumed.

Hair Pull Test

This test is performed in order to determine degree and stage of loss. A section of eight to ten hairs from various parts of the base of the scalp are gently grasped by the doctor and pulled outward to the ends of the hair. One to two hairs are an acceptable number for being detached or lost. Be sure to avoid a recent shampooing as it may alter the number of lost hairs. If four to six hairs are removed by this method, the test indicates active shedding. The hairs can then be examined under a light microscope checking for broken hair (chemical or heat damage), dystrophic hair (seen with congenital hair abnormalities), or for intact telogen hair. This test has significance in patients with alopecia areata as a positive hair pull test suggests that hair loss may possibly be progressing to encompass the entire scalp.

Hair Mount

This is a microscopic examination of the hair shaft to observe hair shaft abnormalities. The type of hair, texture, color, length and condition (dry, oily or brittle) is observed in addition to noting if hairs are broken. If broken hairs are visible, it can be due to **hair shaft fragility** from chemicals such as shampoos, dyes, heat, activators or strong sunlight, which can weaken the shaft's disulfide bonds. Many fungal scalp infections can be identified using this method. This test is useful in identifying various congenital hair disorders, hair breakage, hair shaft fragility and fungal or bacterial infections.

Microscopic Trichogram

This is a microscopic examination of the hair bulb. Several hairs (fifteen to twenty) from the affected area are pulled and examined to compare the anagen-telogen relationship, as well as hair shaft diameters. If hair bulbs are excessively clubbed, have a smaller than normal hair shaft diameter, and pigment is limited, then the hair is dystrophic or abnormal. Anticancer drugs (chemotherapy) can cause this condition.

Scalp Biopsy

A scalp biopsy is warranted in most cases using very small (4-5mm) sites on the scalp. The doctor can do this in the office and the procedure is quick and virtually painless. Ask for a vertical and horizontal biopsy. It will reveal a decreased number of terminal hairs with a proportional increase in vellus hairs if hair loss is present. The test can also ascertain the presence of seborrhea, psoriasis, alopecia areata and lupus.

Source: Stephanie Gardner, M.D.

Assembling, studying, and evaluating the total medical information package should result in a defining diagnosis for the patient. Remember, photo documentation is an important part of fact gathering and compilation on hair loss.

CHAPTER SIX

PSYCHOLOGY
OF HAIR LOSS

"It is foolish to tear one's hair in grief,
as though sorrow would be made
less with baldness."

Marcus Tullius Cicero, Roman Philosopher 106 BC - 43 BC

The importance of hair loss to women is ultimately revealed in their answers to the psychological questions typically posed to hair loss patients by their doctors. Devastating words and phrases such as inadequacy, low self-esteem, anxiety, lack of confidence, maladjustment and depression are used to describe the effects of hair loss on women. Feelings of embarrassment, emotional wounding and lost femininity are referenced repeatedly throughout literature available on this topic. While it is deemed acceptable for a man to lose his hair (not that he necessarily likes it), for a woman it is perceived as a decline in sexuality, or even worse, as the result of poor health, illness or disease. The female with hair loss is often slighted socially and professionally and is frequently the recipient of impolite and embarrassing stares. One of the most memorable episodes from the popular television show, "The Simpson's" portrayed the usually overweight and bald Homer Simpson with hair. He quickly rose to the top of the corporate ladder after a hair growth product gave him a full, luxurious head of hair. As soon as the miracle tonic waned, and baldness prevailed once again, he was unceremoniously hurled back to the bottom rung.

Females with hair loss are not marred or scarred, but many women feel that hair loss and its onset is a disability, unfair, unjust and their undoing, both socially and psychologically. The shedding seems unnecessary, excessive and abnormal to them, and our societal preoccupation with physical perfection adds to the tremendous pressure associated with women losing their hair. While women carefully camouflage thinning hair with scarves, hats, creative hairstyles and wigs, the stigma associated with women experiencing hair loss still remains. Women, in general, are much more private and secretive about their hair loss than men.

While the perception of what defines abnormal hair loss runs the gamut, for most it begins with visible strands in brushes and sinks. For others it may be noticing considerably less scalp hair when braiding or in attempting to "volumize" or style hair with various products. Hair loss typically affects approximately 50% of total overall coverage before it becomes visibly apparent to others. Of course individuals affected by loss are conscious of it much sooner.

Cultural influences and social norms dictate, influence and emphasize the importance of hair. It provides instant information about us. It further divulges our gender, approximate age, possible socio-economic level and even certain expressions of one's personality...defiant or rebellious sporting red, blue or green hair, one's political or cultural associations, such as the long-haired hippies of the 60s era, or it can define one's religious persuasion (Hasidic Jew or Amish).

Psychological studies have demonstrated that individuals who are rated as being physically attractive (with beautiful hair being one of the most outward signs of physical beauty), are perceived to be more successful, to enjoy more respect, to have more friends, to be more happily married and perceived to be better adjusted socially than their less physically attractive counterparts.

Having combed medical literature on the psychological effects of hair loss in females, numerous well-researched and well-documented papers were found to exist. The psychological importance of hair, the stigma attached to losing it and coping with excessive loss is presented in literature with several encompassing studies that reveal the truly alarming effects and the devastating repercussions that hair loss has on women.

When faced with hair loss patients, physicians should reiterate the advantages of positive thinking and explain that although hair loss is a stressful incident, the stress can sometimes compound the problem and cause more hair loss. Doctors should avoid such platitudes as, "Don't worry," "Relax," "Be patient," and "It's not so bad." These may seem like words of comfort, but they can possibly be interpreted as irritating or patronizing to a patient.

The results and conclusions from selected studies covering the psychological effects of hair loss on women have been complied. Various studies are confined to the impact of androgenetic alopecia (FPHL) and not alopecia areata, trichotillomania (pulling one's hair out), telogen effluvium, or other hair loss conditions.

References:
Psychological Characteristics of Women With Androgenetic Alopecia; A Controlled Study, by J. van der Donk, J. Passchier, C. Knegt-Junk, M.H. van der Wegen-Keijser, C. Nieboer, E. Stolz and F. Verhage. British Journal of Dermatology, 1991, 125, 248-252.

This group of doctors included specialists in gynecology, dermatology and psychology.

A group of 58 women, a group of men with androgenetic alopecia and a group of 40 women with no hair loss concerns (non-apparent dermatological disease) as a control group were selected to compare various psychological characteristics regarding the effect of hair loss. Results showed that women with androgenetic alopecia had higher scores for social inadequacy than the other women in the control group. They also had significantly lower scores for self-evaluation and self-esteem when compared to men, and they scored higher on general psychological maladjustment. Additionally, the females with hair loss showed a trend toward greater inadequacy and rigidity, and more than one-third felt ashamed and less attractive than the men. Nearly five times more women were worried about their hair loss than the men, and these women were more uncomfortable in public than males with androgenetic alopecia. They were also less active socially. However, the men were reminded by others about their hair loss more and commonly said that their hair loss made them feel older.

Hair problem/dermatological complaint statements	Women with androgenetic alopecia %	Dermatological control group %	Men with androgenetic alopecia %
Tried medical therapy	76 (43)	54 (25)	26 (43)
Compares own hair with that of others	68 (39)	—	51 (85)
Tried Remedies	58 (33)	35 (16)	42 (70)
Worries about hair loss / complaint	54 (31)	17 (8)	11 (19)
Annoyed by jokes about hair loss / complaint	47 (27)	11 (5)	28 (47)
Feels ashamed	42 (24)	15 (7)	8 (13)
Becomes reminded of hair loss / complaint	37 (21)	7 (3)	54 (90)
Others underestimate hair problems / complaint	37 (21)	11 (5)	39 (65)
Feels less attractive	37 (21)	9 (4)	28 (48)
Discomfort in presence of men	37 (21)	7 (3)	4 (6)
Discomfort in presence of women	35 (20)	2 (1)	12 (20)
Considered a wig	33 (19)	—	11 (18)
Talks frequently about hair loss / complaint	30 (17)	15 (7)	8 (13)
Considered hair transplant	26 (15)	—	20 (34)
Goes out less	23 (13)	4 (2)	5 (8)
Little understanding from others	19 (11)	9 (4)	20 (34)
Others make hair loss / complaint a problem	18 (10)	2 (1)	20 (34)
Feels much older	12 (7)	7 (3)	25 (41)
Less able to make contact	7 (4)	2 (1)	2 (4)
Feels excluded	7 (4)	2 (1)	1 (2)

Further, on the basis of in-depth interviews with women with androgenetic alopecia (unpublished data), it was concluded that almost 30% of the women had a difficult time coping with the problems of hair loss and were preoccupied by the negative consequences.

Quality of Life and Maladjustment Associated With Hair Loss In Women With Alopecia Androgenetica by J. van der Donk, J.A.M. Hunfeld, J. Passchier, K.J. Knegt-Junk and C. Nieber 1994 Soc. Sci. Med. Vol. 38, pp. 159-163, 1994.

This group of doctors included specialists in dermatology, gynecology and psychology.

This examination was a continuation with the original 58 women from the previously mentioned 1991 study. This time there were no men and no control group of women without hair loss (non-visible dermatological complaints). The researchers' questions were:

1. What problems exist in various life areas in the women with androgenetic alopecia (FPHL) who applied for treatment?

2. How many females with androgenetic alopecia show general psychological maladjustment, which is attributable to androgenetic alopecia?

The predominant attitude of women to hair and hair loss held that 62% felt it was an important aspect of physical appearance and an important means of self-expression. Comments by women included, "If you are employed as some sort of representative, you can't go around with wispy, thin hair or bald spots," "A wife without hair is no real wife for a man," "If I had beautiful hair, I'd have more self-esteem, confidence, and then I wouldn't need to be so uncivil to everyone."

Characteristics of women with alopecia androgenetica

Characteristics	Mean	(SD)	No.	%
Age (in years)	36	(6.6)		
History of hair loss (in years)	12	(7.5)		
History of visible hair loss (in years)	9	(7.0)		
Marital status*				
With a partner			36	63
Single			12	21
Divorced			8	14
Widowed			1	2
Educational level				
Low (secondary education or less)			15	26
High (more than secondary education)			43	74

*Characteristics of one subject are missing

For 15% of the women, hair loss was a physical handicap, and they wished to be relieved of the encumbrance of the wig or prosthesis, which they regarded as an artificial part of their body.

Most women (72%) felt that hair loss affected their self-esteem in terms of decreased self-confidence, uncertainty, shame, feelings of inferiority, and age. More than half (57%) felt less attractive.

Approximately 88% of these women altered their behavior in their daily routine. They felt restricted, and adopted numerous precautionary measures to cope. Many stated they felt tense in public. Women went so far as to avoid check writing to keep from bending their heads, which would reveal hair loss. Others stayed away from places with strong illumination. Most stayed home when it was raining or windy. They also avoided swimming and walking in the sun.

Psychosocial problems associated with hair loss: number of responses and percentage for each life area and response category

Life area and response category*	Absolute number of responses	(%)
Attitude to hair and hair loss	54	93
Hair forms an expression of oneself	36	62
Major factor in female appearance	22	41
Hair loss is a handicap	9	15
Negative effects on self-esteem	42	72
Less attractive	33	57
Reduced confidence	31	54
Uncertainty	19	33
Shame	15	26
Inferiority complex	12	21
Feeling old	7	12
Negative activities in daily life	51	88
Conceals hair loss	40	69
Takes more care	35	60
Pays more attention to the hair of others	17	29
Takes care where to sit	13	22
Goes out less or stays at home	10	17
Negative feelings during social contact	28	48
Is worried	15	26
Is afraid of remarks about hair loss	9	16
Inhibited	7	13
Inferiority complex	4	7
Is jealous of others	4	7

*Subjects could give more than one answer
Responses given by fewer than 5% of the subjects are not mentioned in this table

The majority (69%) attempted to hide hair loss with frequent washing, drying, and cutting, while nearly one-third stated they frequently looked at other women's hair. For 48% of the women interviewed, hair loss created a problem socially. More than one-fourth of these women felt worried others would see the thinning patches, and one in seven was afraid that others would make remarks about her hair loss. Three women in the study went so far as to say hair loss was comparable to a physical impairment, such as the loss of a limb, while others considered it to be an affliction.

Stressful Life Events and Loss of Hair Among Adult Women, A Case-Control Study by: Janine York, Thomas Nicholson and Patricia Minors. Psychological Reports, 1998, 82, 1044-1046.

Psychological stress has been identified as a cause of human hair loss; however, this is most often only temporary and usually the hair grows back as stress is alleviated. In this study, 25 women who had recent, unexplained hair loss were compared with 25 women with no complaint of hair loss. High stress was reported by 22 of the 25 women with hair loss and in 10 not experiencing hair loss. In this analysis, results suggest that women who experience high stress are more likely to have hair loss.

Diffuse Hair Loss in Women: The Psychopathology of Those Who Complain by: J. Eckert. ACCA PSYCHIAT. Scand, 1976, 53, 321-327.

A psychiatrist examined 32 women complaining of diffuse alopecia. Seven were found to have severe marital and sexual problems, and two of the females studied were overtly depressed. In a previous investigation, the results of tests to assess the degree of hair loss of these seven women showed no significant difference from the values obtained on a control series of women.

Eckert suggested this focus on women whose anxiety seemed to be disproportionate to their hair loss should be carefully questioned regarding possible depression and marital difficulties. These factors may cause them to be unusually sensitive to hair loss, which normally might not be significant enough of a worry to seek further advice. However, women may then choose to use their hair loss as a means or as an excuse to obtain help with their other underlying problems.

Psychological Problems with Hair Loss in General Practice and the Treatment Policies of General Practitioners by: E.B.G. de Koning, J. Passchier, F.W. Dekker. Psychological Reports, 1990, 67, 775-778.

In this study of men and women, 28% of the men complained about diffuse hair loss and 48% about baldness. This tendency was reversed in women: 68% complained about diffuse hair loss and 8% about baldness. Even though both sexes had the same problem, men received information on baldness 58% of the time, while women only received such 39% of the time. Women were more often given vitamins and shampoos, and twice the amount of psychological advice was bestowed upon them as opposed to the men. Seldom were either referred to a psychologist or a psychiatrist, although 50% were diagnosed with psychological problems. Thirty-nine percent of the men and 20% of the women were referred to a dermatologist.

Psychological Effects of Androgenetic Alopecia on Women: Comparisons with balding men and with female control subjects by Thomas Cash, PhD, Vera Price, MD and Ronald Savin, MD Journal of the American Academy of Dermatology, 1993, VOLUME 29, Number 4.

Ninety-six women, 60 men and 56 female control patients completed questionnaires to assess the psychological reactions to their respective conditions and to measure body language, personality and overall adjustment. Perceptions, feelings and reactions concerning hair loss were also assessed. Results clearly revealed that androgenetic alopecia was a stressful

Female and Male Androgenetic Alopecia Patients' Reports of Specific Effects Attributed to Hair Loss

% Women	% Men	EFFECTS ATTRIBUTED TO HAIR LOSS
		Adverse Effects
98%	90%	Wish that I had more hair.
97%	93%	Think about my hair loss.
95%	87%	Try to figure out if I am losing more hair (by inspecting my head, brush, sink, etc.).
93%	88%	Feel frustrated/helpless about my hair loss.
92%	92%	Spend time looking at my head/hair in the mirror.
92%	85%	Worry about my looks.
92%	78%	Feel self-conscious about my looks.
91%	85%	Have negative thoughts about my hair/head.
90%	82%	Worry about whether others will notice my hair loss.
89%	93%	Worry about how much hair I am going to lose.
83%	90%	Notice people who are balding.
78%	77%	Think about how I used to look.
78%	73%	Notice what other people look like.
75%	68%	Have the thought, "Why Me?"
72%	73%	Think that I am not as attractive as I used to be.
71%	65%	Wonder what other people think about my looks.
68%	53%	Have thoughts that I am unattractive.
67%	80%	Try to imagine what I would look like with more hair loss.
63%	38%	Feel depressed or despondent.
62%	62%	Worry about getting older.
60%	52%	Worry that my spouse or partner will find me less attractive.
55%	53%	Feel embarrassment.
53%	47%	Feel envious of good-looking people of my sex.
50%	53%	Feel sensitive to personal criticism.
43%	50%	Am conscious of how others react to me.
42%	70%	Feel I look older than I am.
36%	65%	People comment about my hair loss.
20%	60%	Get friendly teasing or kidding from others.
		Behavioral Coping:
98%	90%	Try to figure out what to do about my hair loss.
94%	63%	Try to hide my hair loss.
82%	58%	Talk to my hairstylist/barber about my hair loss.
79%	63%	Try to improve my hairstyle.
75%	55%	Do things to improve my looks.
71%	52%	Talk to friends of my own sex about my hair loss.
70%	55%	Spend time on my appearance.
64%	57%	Talk to my partner about my hair loss.
62%	57%	Seek reassurance about my looks.
44%	52%	Try to improve my figure or physique.

Note: Positive percentages refer to the percentage of each group who reported an increase in the event. Negative percentages reflect reported decreases in events. Of the 69-item HLEQ (Hair Loss Effects Questionnaire), only those items endorsed by a majority of female and/or male patients are listed. Source: Cash, Price, and Savin (J Am Acad Dermatol, 1993) experience for both sexes but substantially more distressing for women. Relative to control subjects, women with androgenetic alopecia possessed a more negative body image and a pattern of less adaptive functioning.

In addition, patients were asked questions to measure their social self-esteem, their public self-image, their belief in self-determined control over life events, public self-consciousness, social anxiety, life satisfaction and psychosocial well-being.

Women were almost twice as likely as men to feel "very to extremely" upset with negative effects of hair loss and with the emotional distress of hair loss. Females reported greater social anxiety, lower self-esteem and less life satisfaction. They also felt more depressed, and wondered more how others would think about their appearance and additionally were more embarrassed than men were about their hair loss.

Feelings of helplessness and diminished attractiveness were reported. The women with hair loss worried that others would observe their hair loss and that the condition would progress and become even more noticeable. To cope, they sought information, selective social support, struggled to control negative thoughts and feelings about the condition, and tried to conceal hair loss with altered styling.

The results confirmed that the psychological impact of androgenetic alopecia (FPHL) is more severe for women than for men. In fact, the only effect that may be more difficult for men than women regarding hair loss is that men tend to receive more teasing and social comments about their loss. The study also revealed men's belief that hair loss aged their appearance more.

Personality Disorders and Psychological Symptoms In Patients With Androgenetic Alopecia by: Cesare Maffei, M.D., Andrea Fossati, M.D. Fabio Rinaldi, M.D. Elisabetta Riva, M.D. Arch. Dermatology; 1994, Vol. 730: 868-872.

In this study of men and women, patients with hair loss proved to have a significantly higher (10.3%) diagnosis for personality disorders than seen in the general population. Of these, 76.3% were diagnosed with at least one personality disorder.

Patient-Perceived Importance of Negative Effects of Androgenetic Alopecia in Women by: Cynthia J. Girman, PhD, Susan Hartmaier, PhD, Janet Roberts, MD, Wilma Bergfeld, MD, and Joanne Waldstreicher, MD. Journal of Women's Health & Gender-Based Medicine, 1999, vol. 8; number 8: pp. 1091-1095.

A questionnaire was given to 120 women with at least mild (Ludwig I) androgenetic alopecia regarding the effect of hair loss and its importance on their lives. The inability to style their hair, dissatisfaction with their appearance, concern about hair loss continuing and uneasiness about others noticing their loss were most important to females. Emotional aspects also ranked high, including self-consciousness, jealousy, embarrassment, and feeling powerless to stop the hair loss.

In addition, the thought prevailed that the psychological impact of androgenetic alopecia might be more pronounced and amplified in females than in males, particularly because of society's increased pressure for physical attractiveness in women, and because of the female's own psychological investment in her

Descriptive Characteristics of Participating Women With Hair Loss

	No.	(%)
Ethnicity		
Caucasian	104	86.7
African American	9	7.5
Other	7	5.8
Marital status		
Single	30	25.0
Married / cohabitating	63	52.5
Separated / divorced / widowed	27	22.6
Education level		
Some high school	3	2.5
High school graduate	11	9.2
Some college	51	42.5
College graduate	25	20.8
Some graduate school	16	13.3
Graduate degree	14	11.7
Severity of hair loss (Savin scale)		
Savin 3, mild	37	30.8
Savin 4	34	28.3
Savin 5, moderate	29	24.2
Savin 6	10	8.3
Savin 7, severe	9	7.5
Savin 8	1	0.8
Severity of hair loss (Ludwig scale)		
Ludwig 1, mild	54	45.0
Ludwig 2, moderate	51	42.5
Ludwig 3, severe	15	12.5

appearance. This study was the first to ask women directly how important potential negative effects of androgenetic alopecia were to them. The results showed that approximately 45% experienced mild hair loss (Ludwig I), 42.5% experienced moderate, and 12.5% experienced severe loss. The item perceived as most important to women was, "My hair loss negatively affects the way I like to style my hair." Negative effects on self-satisfaction with the appearance of the hair were the second most important factor, third was its effect on personal appearance and fourth, dissatisfaction with one's overall appearance.

The psychological aspects of hair loss or thinning in women have been described in terms of maladjustment, difficulty in coping with hair loss, and as displaying poor psychological well-being by researchers. Personality disorders, depression and greater dissatisfaction with hair, life, and negative feelings about body image have been suggested as being associated with androgenetic alopecia in women. Negative effects on daily living and changes, or restrictions in lifestyle in order to hide hair loss have been noted previously in psychological studies and are consistent with and support this examination. Some similarities include combing the hair differently to hide the hair loss and avoidance of certain activities such as swimming or going out in inclement weather.

Emotions reported earlier in other studies as associated with hair loss in females included frustration, shame, envy and feeling less feminine. Lower self-esteem, reduced self-confidence, and insecurity are commonly accepted complaints and considered to be the norm for women with hair loss.

Several items in this questionnaire had not been emphasized in prior reports but were uncovered during the open-ended focus group discussion. One of these items included the negative effects of androgenetic alopecia (FPHL) on hair styling, which again ranked highest. In addition, annoyance about the time spent

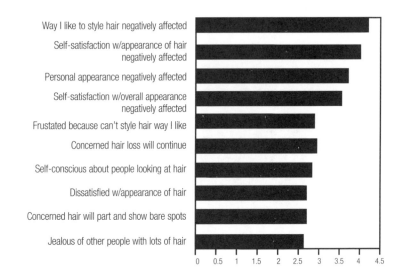

Way I like to style hair negatively affected	
Self-satisfaction w/appearance of hair negatively affected	
Personal appearance negatively affected	
Self-satisfaction w/overall appearance negatively affected	
Frustated because can't style hair way I like	
Concerned hair loss will continue	
Self-conscious about people looking at hair	
Dissatisfied w/appearance of hair	
Concerned hair will part and show bare spots	
Jealous of other people with lots of hair	

0   0.5   1   1.5   2   2.5   3   3.5   4   4.5

The 10 most important items as ranked by women with androgenetic alopecia. For each item, the bar reflects the mean importance ranking given by patients on a scale of 1 (not very important) to 5 (extremely important).

trying to make their hair look fuller, checking their hair in the morning and trying to cover bare spots were quite important to the participants. Conversely, some previously highly ranked negative effects of hair loss were lower. These included preoccupation with hair loss, feeling older because of hair loss and avoidance of swimming or going out in inclement weather.

Understanding the Link Between Hair Disorders and Self-Image by: Richard Fried, M.D., Ph.D. Skin & Aging, March 2001, pp 55-59.

For men, alopecia is an embarrassment and has many unfortunate connotations, but the fact that it is so prevalent and socially acceptable softens the blow to some extent. By contrast, in women it can trigger a full-blown emotional crisis. In addition to the stigma of age and decline, female alopecia patients must fend off misconceptions of poor health that others may associate with their change in appearance.

Losing Hair, Losing Points?: The Effects of Male Pattern Baldness on Social Impression Formation by: Thomas F. Cash, Ph.D., Journal of Applied Social Psychology, 1990, 20, 2, pp. 154-167.

This experiment examined the influence of male pattern baldness on the initial social perception of men by both men and women by using photographic slides of balding and non-balding men. It was intended to demonstrate that even women show a prejudice toward hair loss. Women were responsible for rating the men with male pattern baldness as less favorable on things such as physical attractiveness, personal characteristics, and they invariably misjudged age.

All the women regarded the older balding men as less successful and less physically attractive than the non-balding controls. As the younger female controls viewed the slides, they perceived the younger balding men as less intelligent, less successful and less likeable. In contrast, the older female control group perceived younger balding men as somewhat more intelligent, successful and likeable. Hair loss also added five years to the perceived age of the younger men.

Suffice to say that the psychological impact of hair loss on women truly causes extensive trauma and elicits a formidable emotional upheaval. Numerous support groups and Internet access to chat rooms and medical information regarding hair loss are readily available. Be proactive and start delving into the plethora of information available on alopecia, but adhere to caution when seeking answers on the web as the range of data can be inconsistent and questionable. The old adage reigns, "If it seems too good to be true, then it probably isn't so." However, a self-quest does not negate the fact that all medical questions should be professionally addressed by a member of the medical community and or by a psychologist. The quicker such help is sought, the sooner the underlying cause or causes of hair loss, whether medical, physical, psychological or hereditary, can be addressed.

CHAPTER SEVEN

CANCER AND HAIR LOSS

"Hair brings one's self-image into focus; it is vanity's proving ground. Hair is terribly personal, a tangle of mysterious prejudices."

Shana Alexander, American Author 1925-

Approximately 400,000 people undergo chemotherapy treatments for cancer in the United States annually. In a recent study, nausea, vomiting and hair loss were revealed to be the three most distressing side effects of chemotherapy, with hair loss being far more distressing to women than to men. Hair loss that follows chemotherapy is reported to be the most anticipated traumatic side effect in up to **58% of female patients**. In fact, **8% of women** with a diagnosis of cancer are at risk of refusing chemotherapy treatment simply because the idea of potential baldness would prove to be too overwhelming.

Reaction Experienced by Females to Chemotherapy-Induced Hair Loss:
Not prepared; shock
Personal embarrassment
Losing sense of self
Distraught over the reaction of others

One study of a group of women with breast cancer reported that for some women the loss of their hair was harder to cope with than the loss of a breast. Others said that hair loss robbed them of their privacy about having cancer and increased feelings of personal shame. Another study showed that 73% of patients had a decrease in self-esteem after alopecia, regardless of the degree of hair loss. Additionally, alopecia during chemotherapy treatment may be associated with specific sexual problems that are not related to the effects of medication, resulting in difficulty with maintaining successful personal relationships.

Differing from androgenetic alopecia, which is gradual, hair loss as a side effect of chemotherapy is usually sudden—all of the hair is shed, and it is accompanied by a life threatening disease. The reason for hair loss during chemotherapy is that drugs destroy the rapidly reproducing cells in the body, and hair cells are of this type. These hair cells, along with white blood cells and **epithelial cells** (which line the mouth, esophagus and stomach, thus one of the causes of nausea) are usually the first cells affected. Chemotherapy treatment is also injurious to the cells of the hair root responsible for hair shaft formation. No hair-growth stimulants, shampoos, conditioners or other cosmetic treatments can prevent or retard this form of hair loss. Although limited use of ice packs applied to the head by oncologists (cancer specialists) during chemotherapy treatments were originally thought to help abate the initial fall out of hair, this exercise has proven to be futile, as the end result is that the hair usually disappears completely. During the 1980s, considerable research was performed in an effort to find methods of preventing alopecia in cancer patients by use of tourniquets or cooling devices. Results were questionable and because of the risk of scalp metastasis (possible transmission of the cancer from one site to another), the FDA stopped the commercial sale of these devices.

The good news is that once chemotherapy is completed, hair generally grows back. Since hair grows at a rate of approximately one-half inch per month, and usually does not even start re-growing until two months after therapy has ended, substantial hair growth may take from four months to a year. The new hair may vary in volume, texture, thickness and color from that of the original. Any color difference from previous coverage is due to the absence or alteration of pigment in the hair shaft. It is not unusual for hair to become gray or white due to these changes. Also, previously curly hair may become straight and formerly straight hair may become curly. Remember that the body has suffered a serious assault due to this disease; therefore the follicles may take some time to recover.

Hair that has returned to the scalp should be treated gently, as it may be prone to breakage. Shampooing two to three times per week with a mild shampoo, and then applying a conditioner and gently massaging the scalp to remove any remaining scales, is recommended. Using the hair dryer sparingly and avoiding harsh brushes, combs, hairpins and tight curlers are also suggested. The American Hair Loss Council (AHLC) recommends that cancer patients wait until the hair is at least three inches long before performing permanent waving, chemical curling, or coloring. A mild body wave left on the hair for a short time is suggested to achieve volume. The AHLC further stresses the importance of being cognizant of the chemical smells associated with various processing procedures since chemotherapy patients are especially sensitive to odors that can cause nausea or vomiting.

There are an estimated 17,000 brain tumors diagnosed in the United States each year. Of those cases, approximately 80%

receive radiation treatments. Unlike chemotherapy, which targets the entire body, radiation penetrates a specific area or areas. If the intended section to be treated is in the proximity of the head, this results in permanent hair loss on the particular section being radiated. Those who are treated for other types of cancer with radiation on other parts of the body will not lose their hair. Hair loss due to radiation treatment usually occurs within two or three weeks after the initial treatment and the affected area feels similar to sunburn. Although creams can be prescribed for relief, elasticity usually diminishes due to reduced amounts of collagen in the region. According to the AHLC, direct sunlight, tanning beds and hot showers should all be avoided (the same as for those receiving chemotherapy treatments).

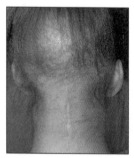

While the tumor doctors removed from Allison's head was benign, the radiation treatments she received left a permanent bald area. Allison recently underwent hair transplantation surgery to restore the area.

Having personally spoken with hundreds of females who knew specifically that cancer was their diagnosis, resilience and a determination to beat the disease prevailed. However, a common link between the women was an overwhelming fear of hair loss. Fear of the disease itself was not an all-consuming factor, yet the fear of hair loss was. Women tend to be optimistic and believe that medicine will triumph and ultimately banish their illness. But the dismay over the loss of hair, even in the face of a life and death situation, often surpassed the frightfulness of the disease.

One of the researchers for this book was diagnosed with Hodgkin's disease, a form of lymphatic cancer, six months into the project. The very first question she asked her oncologist after being told that she might lose her life from this dreaded disease was, "Will I lose my hair?" Even she was shocked, retrospectively, at the words that came from her mouth! She went on to finish her chemotherapy and radiation regimens, and continue a year later with bone marrow transplantation moving on to finally complete the assignment. And yes, she lost her hair twice, only to have it re-grow entirely after the cessation of treatments.

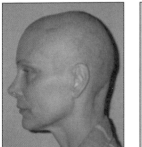 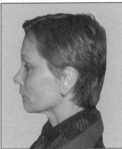

Nancy experienced temporary hair loss from chemotherapy treatments, but today enjoys a full head of hair.

Women with cancer who have children need to be especially careful in their explanation of "mommy's hair loss." Children are extremely sensitive to change. The hair loss may trigger withdrawal, depression or other unusual social behavior. A child may think that part of the mother's body is no longer there to love them.

(This can also occur with women who lose a great deal of weight.) Cancer patients need to remain positive, so the mood and tone of those surrounding them should be upbeat, energetic and caring.

So what should a patient do when her hair loss becomes noticeable? The answer is…whatever she wants to in order to feel more comfortable and confident. There is no right or wrong here. It is an extremely personal, as well as an emotional decision. Some cancer patients choose to shave their heads or cut their hair very short before all of the hair falls out. Psychologically, these transitions can sometimes soften the shock of total loss. Shaving the remains of the uncontrolled hair fall-out can also help eliminate what can potentially be embarrassing shedding. Some women feel that total baldness is more attractive than patchy hair loss. An AHLC survey revealed that after hair loss of 50%, males or females look healthier with no hair at all.

The choices for dealing with the hair loss are basic: wearing a wig or prosthetic; covering the head with turbans, hats or scarves; or leaving it as is…in other words facing the world bald. There are thousands of stores, web sites, hospitals and cancer centers that cater specifically to the needs of those who wish to take the head-covering route of hats, scarves, wigs, etc. These coverings can be used not only for emotional support, but also to offer protection from the elements. For shaving one's head, the use of a good disposable razor is advised, and it should be only used once, and then discarded in order to reduce the possibility of infection. If a cancer patient opts for purchasing a wig, it is recommended that this is done before the hair falls out and that a simple style, in a color slightly lighter than her own natural hair, is selected. In order to achieve a look that is as natural as possible, ample time should be given for the hand-making or individual styling of any type of hair system. Here again, shaving one's head allows for the use of a prosthetic (wig or hair piece) providing security and comfort. Glue-ons, adhesives, tapes and vacuum-base prosthetics will fit better on a completely bald scalp. Radiation patients need to be more cautious when selecting and attaching any hair system. They should never use two-way medical tape, medical adhesives, or glues on the treated area for about two weeks and then only with physician approval.

One measure that doctors and cancer centers are introducing to ease and aid in decision making about hair loss is computer imaging. This is interactive and allows the patient to participate. It is a software program that modifies hairstyles and was originally developed for the hair salon industry. Patients can view themselves with new hairstyles, hair color, scarves, and hats before they plunge into making any decision about their impending hair loss or before making any purchases. As part of this pilot program, a one-hour session with a psychologist was incorporated. The American Cancer Society has extensive resources on support groups, drug research, clinical trials and the "Look Good, Feel

Better" program provides information and answers questions on what to do about the physical changes and appearance of women experiencing cancer.

Remember, many insurance companies will pay for a wig or prosthetic, but inquire early as to the terms that apply to your particular policy, as it can be an extremely slow process. In order to increase the odds of being reimbursed, have your primary physician write a prescription for a "**cranial prosthesis**" and submit this with your claim. Hand-made or special order custom wigs can take up to six months or more to process. Avoid the initial expense of partial hair additions such as integration systems or hair weaves, as more than likely most of the hair will fall out quickly, and there will be nothing to attach an addition to.

A 1991 survey revealed that 82% of all cancer patients preferred a nurse rather than a beautician to assist them in coping with their hair loss. These same 40 cancer patients were also surveyed about their hair loss needs. Nearly 47% indicated a need for a hospital or home visit for hair loss care and all stated that they had not been given prior information about hair and scalp care. Additionally, 58% responded that their physician was the first to inform them of anticipated hair loss. Patients commented that they valued a nurse's knowledge regarding their disease and perceived that a nurse would better meet their needs. They were also more comfortable exposing the visible consequences of treatment to a nurse. However, 42% had initially attempted to obtain assistance from their beauticians and had walked away with very little help or knowledge. In the past decade however, the beauty industry has made a successful effort to better communicate and serve cancer patients. This improvement has exposed a more empathetic stylist as well as a concerted conviction on the part of stylists to further educate themselves in recognizing and addressing the special needs of the client with cancer.

At an Oncology Nursing Society chapter meeting, 66% of the nurses reported that the patients they came in contact with preferred the concept of a nurse-cosmetologist team approach and 92% requested instructional sessions to increase their knowledge of wigs, alternatives, and hair and scalp care.

Twelve years ago, one of my patients, Kristine was diagnosed with a cancerous brain tumor. After beating cancer with a combination of surgery, seven weeks of radiation treatment and a year of chemotherapy, Kristine survived but found herself balding on the top of her head. Her hair follicles had been severely damaged by the radiation, and scar tissue was a concern with regard to her candidacy for surgical hair restoration when she initially approached me.

After my preliminary consultation with her, it was determined that Kristine had sufficient donor hair for a successful transplant. My associate, Dr. Mel Mayer performed her procedure in 1997, at the Third Annual Live Surgery Workshop, a physician's symposium sponsored by the International Society of Hair Restoration Surgery. Her bravery and kindness allowed the medical team to share her transplant with more than 100 other doctors for educational purposes. "It took a few months before any hair grew in, so I was becoming a little disappointed," said Kristine. "But when I got bangs…oh, you just don't know. I got so excited and that made everything worthwhile. It's just amazing that this could happen to me…that they could actually take my own hair and transplant it. I never thought I would be given the chance to have completely restored hair." Seven years after her procedure, Kristine is cancer free, works as an orthodontic assistant, is married and has one child.

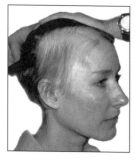 

Kristine experienced permanent hair loss from radiation treatments, but had her hair restored through surgical transplantation.

Nann Chafin as a child prior to losing her hair.

Nann as a young adult, proudly displaying the beauty of her baldness.

CHAPTER EIGHT

CHILDREN AND HAIR LOSS

"And forget not that the earth delights
to feel your bare feet and the winds
long to play with your hair."

Kahlil Gibran, Lebanese Author 1883-1931

A 12-year old girl and a 40-year old woman might well share the fact that both of them are losing or have lost their hair, but each brings to the table a different set of coping skills and ways of integrating the problem into their lives. Each must find her own unique methodology for adjusting to different emotional experiences and social environments. We should always remember that adults have far more refined abilities for dealing with the emotional and psychological traumas often associated with hair loss than children do.

Unfortunately, while alopecia occurs in males and females of all ages, it is young people, particularly girls, who are affected most often. Teasing, poking fun, taunting and bullying may be deemed child's play but when these actions are directed toward children with hair loss, it becomes cruel and can be both emotionally and psychologically damaging. The basic tenet of teasing is, if it doesn't push your buttons, it won't be fun or effective for the teaser. Children should be advised that no matter how much it hurts or how embarrassed they are, learn to ignore it. Do not respond. Read a book. Look up at the sky. Hum. Walk away. This is the proper mindset for dealing with teasing.

We are all driven to be different in our looks, yet we feel the need to conform to what is mandated as acceptable by magazines, Hollywood, the music scene, and of course the "in group," or our peers. Whoever or whatever that group is, often defies all logic. A child with hair loss, whether it is from chemotherapy, alopecia areata, chemical hair loss or any one of another numerous childhood diseases manifested by hair loss, should be encouraged to be positive. These children should be taught to hold their heads up high and try doing something different, imaginary or whimsical. Some of the fashion-making statements that might be suggested are placing temporary tattoos (stressing the word temporary) on the head just for fun, or perhaps donning a fashionable scarf, hat or a wig that is "just the style" she always wanted her hair to be.

The most difficult time of all for a female with hair loss is adolescence. This is a time when girls are blossoming into young womanhood, and what is more symbolic as a testament to femininity than a beautiful head of long, flowing hair. Nann Chafin began losing her hair at age 13 and thought she would never be whole again. Now in her twenties, Nann reflects, "At first I thought that I would never fit in. I didn't want to go to school or even go out at all. I tried every treatment, saw every doctor, and took every test that was. Once I accepted the fact that my hair was never coming back, I decided to jump on the bandwagon for young people who shared my same problem and take on as many speaking engagements as possible. And FYI, today I always go out without my hair. I am me and happy to be alive! They say that clothes don't make the man, well, hair doesn't make the woman either!"

Most of all, it is important that being different is played up as being a plus. Encourage children to educate others so they too will feel differently about hair loss. Take the time to stop and explain to those who stare. Remember, they are staring for two reasons. First, they are curious, and secondly, at the same time they are afraid because they do not understand what is wrong.

Children should be given the opportunity to explain to classmates and friends that hair loss is not contagious or painful (in most cases), and that hair loss does not necessarily mean that you have cancer or some other dreaded disease. In fact, show-and-tell is a terrific way to get that message out. Let the other children touch the affected area; talk about the loss; ask the other children what they think about it, and if they respond negatively, let them know that being different can be a positive. One high school basketball team in Nicholasville, Kentucky shaved their heads in support of a player who went through chemotherapy and lost all of his hair. It is also extremely important to educate school administration and teachers as well.

Of course, none of this would be possible without the full support of the parents. Parenting a child with alopecia can be described as difficult at best. However, according to the National Alopecia Areata Foundation (NAAF), parents need to keep two important things in mind. One, children can be much more resilient than we imagine. They are generally optimistic and do not have the expectation for rejection that adults have because they have not experienced it or observed it as much as adults. Two, children take their cues from the adults in their world. If a child perceives her hair loss as being a source of anxiety or sadness from a parent, she will internalize those feelings. This does not mean that a parent should ignore or repress feelings of loss, sorrow, or anger when trying to cope. Rather, parents should realize feelings of guilt or responsibility for their child's hair loss as perfectly natural and to be expected. Families are encouraged not to hide the hair loss but to try and make the situation as acceptable and as much a part of the norm as possible.

The choice to wear any type of wig or prosthesis should strictly be left up to the child. By giving the child a choice, as a parent you are validating her decision by saying that she is okay just the way she is. Even if you feel that your child's life may be enhanced by wearing a head covering, you should never insist. A suggestion from the American Hair Loss Council is to purchase an inexpensive wig, preferably a shade slightly lighter than your child's own hair color and add it to her toy collection. Make it a possession she will see almost daily, allowing the wig to become an item that no one is saying to "play with" or "not play with." It may be months, years, or never when your child decides to wear some type of hair system. But, by presenting a wig as an alternative in this manner, the fear of such an item is eliminated by making it seem normal and commonly available.

Also extremely important to remember is the sensitivity factor as it relates to age. Parents must keep in mind that the 10-year old who seems totally accepting of her condition will turn into a 13-year old who is totally intolerant and unable to cope with her alopecia and wearing a hairpiece. Comments can range from, "I am ashamed every time someone mistakenly calls me 'son' or 'young man' when I wear my hat." Another child stated, "The worst is when someone takes off my hat or pulls my wig off at school. I never want to go back again but know that I have to."

Children with hair loss are not plagued with androgenetic alopecia, the more common form of hair loss typically seen in adults, but their loss is more often associated with a genetic disorder. Many of the diseases and syndromes to which hair loss can be attributed are rare. The onset of any severe physical (febrile illness, surgery) or mental stress (depression) may induce hair loss and cause telogen effluvium. Certain prescription drugs, such as synthetic retinoids, anti-thyroids, anti-coagulants and sodium valproate can also be the culprits. The causes of hair loss are sometimes hard to identify, even by members of the medical community. Typically, diffuse hair loss occurs three to four months after the initial stress or injurious aggravation. It is the result of the premature conversion of growing (anagen) hairs to the resting phase (telogen). Loss continues for a few months but re-growth follows when the irritations are eliminated.

Most common causes of hair loss in children
Alopecia areata
Trichotillomania
Ringworm of the scalp (Tinea capitis)
Telogen effluvium
Endocrine disorders
Nevus sebaceous
Chemical
Nutritional
Trauma: Traction, loose anagen shaft defects, pulled hair
Aplasia cutis/other scarring alopecias

Alopecia areata, recognized since the days when ancient Egyptians wrote about it on papyrus, affects more than four million Americans (both male and female). It is hair loss that has no specific cause, but may be due in part to a relationship with or a connection to certain autoimmune diseases. Some of the autoimmune disorders associated with alopecia areata are Addison's disease, pernicious anemia, juvenile diabetes mellitus, Hashimoto's thyroiditis and Graves' disease.

With alopecia areata, the anagen follicles prematurely enter into the telogen phase. Bald patches that are usually oval or round with well-defined borders are the end result. Initially, the new hair tends to be finer than normal and can be un-pigmented. Alopecia areata is the most common form of hair loss in children with 60% of the new cases reported being patients younger than age 20. An onset before the age of two is unusual and generally the children appear healthy and asymptomatic. This is the disease that most often progresses into **alopecia totalis** (total loss of hair from the scalp) or **alopecia universalis** (total loss of hair from the entire body) in children. Re-growth within one year is seen in 95% of children, but the earlier the onset of alopecia areata, the poorer the prognosis. A 40-50% relapse in all cases may be seen and upwards of 25% may be permanent. Nearly one-third of patients have a family history and emotional stress can also play a possible role in some cases. Alopecia areata is frequently associated with nail changes, like pitting or nail bed distortion. In patients with Down syndrome, an increased incidence of alopecia areata is noted, as well as with those children who have asthma and atopic dermatitis. (See also Chapter 3 "*Why Women Lose Their Hair*")

The psychological trauma that alopecia areata might inflict upon a child was examined over a one year period in a study comparing children who had the disease and those free from it used as a control group. The children with alopecia areata had more psychological problems, were more anxious, withdrawn, aggressive and delinquent.

No specific treatment is known to alter the disease's ultimate natural course. Shampoo, mild sulfur cream, Tagamet, Retin-A, dithranol, as well as topical intralesional or systemic steroids that produce prompt re-growth, may be used.

Trichotillomania, thought to affect eight million people in the United States, is a term that describes a particular condition where one pulls out one's own hair. Medically speaking, the psychiatric definition of trichotillomania is an irresistible urge to pull out the hair, thus obtaining a sense of relief after the hair has been plucked. It is the second most common cause for hair loss in children and seven times more likely to affect children than adults. Many times the children themselves (and often even their parents) are unaware of this behavior, and it can be comparable to nail biting or finger sucking. However, trichotillomania is not considered to be a form of self-mutilation. Although girls are mostly affected, when trichotillomania occurs in children under the age of six, the percentage of occurrence is higher in boys. The frontal area of the head is usually affected first. Parents can observe the condition as it progresses, as the affected hairs are broken and are varied in lengths. Nail biting, nail pulling and bulimia nervosa (self-induced vomiting) may accompany or follow this condition. An association is sometimes seen with vitiligo, and some hairs are actually swallowed, which may cause intestinal obstructions or "hairballs." Onset of the habit may manifest unexpectedly. It is most often a sign of chronic social depravation partly thought to be provoked by difficulty at home, troubles at school or by an illness, particularly emotional depravation in the maternal relationship. Mothers will frequently even deny that their child is pulling out her own hair. Children with the condition are rarely depressed, and it is interesting to note the younger child will more readily admit to hair pulling, whereas the older child often unequivocally denies the act.

Educating both the child and the parents, coupled with empathetic discussions between the patient and her doctor, should be the first steps in treatment. On a case-by-case basis, a decision should be made as to whether the use of a topical cream or injected cortisone is appropriate. If these measures prove unsuccessful, the child and the parent should be referred for family counseling with a psychologist or psychiatrist.

Example of Trichotillomania

Scalp ringworm, or tinea capitis, is the third most common hair disease in children. Fungal organisms acquired from other humans or animals invade the hair shaft at the epidermis. The hairs are sometimes broken in the affected areas. Swollen areas known as **kerion**, which contain fungus or boggy tumors, are soft and spongy and plague the affected area. The skin in the area is dry, scaly and sometimes totally devoid of the hair. This particular disease mainly affects African Americans and can easily be diagnosed by observing tissue from the affected area under a microscope. Contagious children must stay home from school a few days, due to the fact that ringworm is highly infectious. Administered orally for four to six weeks, griseofulvin is the usual treatment medication of choice. When combined with a topical antifungal and medicated shampoo, the condition will almost always clear.

Endocrine disorders - Hair loss may be seen in hypopituitarism, hypothyroidism and hyperthyroidism, hypoparathyroidism and poorly controlled diabetes mellitus.

Chemical Hair Loss - When discussing chemical hair loss, the cause can be relaxers, straighteners or faulty permanents that can damage the hair and possibly the hair follicle. It can be from chemicals used in chemotherapy, radiation or certain drugs such as arsenic, beta blockers, bismuth or thallium. Upon discontinuance of the event or agent, hair loss is almost always reversed. Toxic hair loss is seen with anti-metabolites, alkylating agents and mitotic (cell division) inhibitors all of which hamper the synthesis of hair in growing follicles (anagen) and as a result, the hair is lost. **Anagen**

effluvium (sudden diffuse hair loss) follows, but usually re-growth occurs when the caustic drug is discontinued.

Nutritional deficiencies can cause hair loss. A lack of iron, protein, biotin, zinc and essential fatty acids and of course **marasmus** (malnutrition) can all be considered culprits. Diffuse alopecia is one of the visible features of anorexia nervosa (eating disorder).

Traction alopecia is another form of traumatic hair loss and may be unintentionally caused by repeated hair styles like braiding, tight pony tails, hot combing, excessive blow drying, tight rollers, hair pins or exaggerated rubbing. Hair extensions or weaves can also contribute to this condition. Traction alopecia is most often seen in African American women and children. (See Chapter 9 *"Ethnic Hair Loss"*)

Loose anagen syndrome, first reported in 1986, is a more recently discovered cause of diffuse hair loss. With this disease, which is most commonly associated with girls under the age of eight, the hair can easily and painlessly be plucked away while in the anagen or growth phase. It is seen more in girls who are fair-haired. The hair is uniform in length but is short and may have never been cut. Also, the shaft is typically frizzy, kinky, without luster, and often difficult to comb. There is no treatment for loose anagen syndrome, but it usually improves with time, and the hair then becomes denser. Although children with loose anagen syndrome are healthy, it is frequently associated with a family history of the disease.

Congenital Causes of Hair Loss in Infancy, Childhood and Young Adults

Aplasia Cutis Congenital (ACC): Absence of skin in a specific, wide area commonly affecting 70% of the scalp

Hydrotic Ectodermal Dysplasia (Clouston Syndrome): Presents as malformed or absent nails, sparse hair, and pigmentation changes in the skin

Conraedi's Syndrome: Degenerative bone disease

Incontinentia Pigmenti: Neurological gene-linked disease; skin discolors, usually within two weeks of birth

Menkes' Syndrome: Inherited copper deficiency

Netherton's Syndrome: Skin disorder with reddish scaling in a circular pattern, seen mostly in females in the first ten days of birth

Progeria: Premature old age; hair can be gray or thin; stature may be small and skin wrinkled

Darier's Disease: Skin is lumpy, itchy, with stubborn scales and or blisters, mostly in young adults

Ichthyosis: Skin builds up and scales, is extremely dry, is usually diagnosed at birth and is lifelong

For the child whose hair loss has stabilized, **hair transplantation surgery** definitely has its place. A section of the scalp exhibiting a burn, scar or other disfigurement can easily be remedied. Trauma associated with hair loss during birth is sometimes observed. Forceps used in delivery can damage follicles near the ears or around the side of the face. Or, fetal scalp electrodes that are placed in the womb on the infant's head for heart monitoring before and during delivery, can also injure or destroy an area of hair follicles. However, be sure that you discuss hair transplantation as an option with a reputable surgeon. She/he should always be cautious about performing a hair transplant procedure at too early an age. In most practices, it is recommended that the child has reached 12 years of age, and the area of hair loss should have been stabilized for at least two full years. Complete parental support is always essential.

When a child is diagnosed with medically related hair loss, in some instances one parent must stop working to stay home and care for the child or to be available to accompany the child on medical trips for treatment. Discretionary income may decline drastically (virtually being cut in half or less), as unexpected costs mount up quickly, and wigs can be difficult to work into the family budget with such dramatically reduced earnings. Additionally, there are expenses for transportation and lodging when traveling to a medical facility. When a child begins taking certain medications her weight often fluctuates, necessitating the purchase of new clothing. Buying clothing in various sizes over a short period of time puts yet another strain on an already overly taxed family budget. Insurance may not always cover all of the costs for treatment and medication. Depending upon the policy, it may not cover a wig or **cranial prosthesis**. Some insurers cover only a portion of these costs and the reimbursement period is usually long and complicated. When a child loses her hair due to a medical condition, there is often no time to wait six months for an insurance company to process a claim or approve a prescription. For a family to spend $800 to $3,500 for a hair replacement system is not possible in many cases.

There are several organizations that offer gifts of hair to economically challenged children. If your child has a need for hair, you may qualify for a free prosthesis through **www.locksoflove.org**, **www.angellocks.org**, or **www.wigsforkids.org**.

The National Alopecia Areata Foundation (NAAF) publishes letters and articles by and about parents and children with hair loss in their newsletters, and provides informational brochures, pen pal lists and support group information. NAAF also holds an annual national convention that offers children with alopecia a chance to come together along with their parents for three days of education, networking, support and fun.

Suggested reading for children:

The Princess Who Lost Her Hair
Tololwa M. Mollel
Troll Associates, 1993
ISBN: 081672816X

The Paper Princess
Elisa Kleven
EP Dutton, 1994
ISBN: 0525452311

CHAPTER NINE

ETHNIC HAIR LOSS

"Her head was bare but for her native
ornament of hair, which in a simple knot was
tied; sweet negligence…unheeded bait of love."

John Dryden, English Poet 1631-1700

There are unique properties associated with ethnic hair. A physician should address ethnic hair loss noting these characteristics and manage any hair loss or hair care accordingly. Focus should particularly be directed toward texture, diameter, caliber, density, and any skin abnormalities that might surround the hair shaft.

Special attention and care must be given to the hair and skin when working with the African American patient in order to avoid possible **keloid** formation, a type of disfiguring often accompanied by **hypopigmentation** (loss of color on the skin, or lightening of the skin). Both must be seriously regarded, especially when a patient is considering **hair grooming and hair or eyebrow transplantation**.

Women of color tend to experience hair loss more often than women of other ethnic backgrounds, yet they are no more likely to expect it to happen, as noted in the chart below.

Thinning Hair and/or Hair Loss Experience and Expectation by Ethnicity (Forbes Consulting Group, Inc.)				
	Caucasian	**African American**	**Asian/Pacific or Islander**	**Other**
Actually Experience Hair Loss	22%	37%	23%	29%
Expect to Lose Hair	7%	8%	6%	5%

Keloiding, which is most frequently associated with dark-skinned individuals, may result after an injury, laceration or incision to the skin or scalp area, therefore injuring or destroying hair follicles. The affected area becomes raised and spreads beyond the parameters of the original wound. This scarred area, often irregular in shape and lacking in pigmented color, may take on a pinkish hue. The tissue itself can sometimes be tender and painful for an extended period. Injections of Kenelog (a steroid), use of a topical preparation, Mederma (a healing cream for treating scars) or laser treatments, especially if used in the early stages, may minimize keloids. Keloids can be genetic; they can occur at any age and may recur in some patients. In other words, there is very little predictability with this particular condition. Caucasians can also develop keloids, but this occurs far less frequently than amongst women of color.

Hypopigmentation is a discolorization of the skin where melanin is destroyed in an area for several different reasons. It can be caused by treatments for keloiding, inflammation which further injures the pigment cells, or when skin bleaching creams have been applied incorrectly. This results in tissue being lighter in tone than that of the surrounding area. At the same time the skin may appear bleached or unhealthy, although there is nothing infectious or contagious about the phenomena. Hypopigmentation is more prevalent in darker skinned individuals and in those patients with olive–toned skin. Conversely, **hyperpigmentation** is seen more in Caucasians and fairer–skinned people whereby the skin becomes darker and takes on a splotchy appearance.

When treating any condition involving a hair-bearing surface, always be sure to consult with a physician. This decision can help in the treatment plan for any affected areas of skin that may be potential sites for hyperpigmentation or hypopigmentation.

Due to the nature of curly hair, meticulous consideration must be paid to avoid a condition called **pseudofolliculitis barbae** in African Americans. This condition is commonly known as ingrown hair or "razor bumps." These ingrown hairs should only be opened by a physician utilizing a sterile needle and treated with either an oral or topical antibiotic. They can appear on the face, scalp or the body and should never be plucked or tweezed. Abscesses can form and ultimately cause the death of the affected hair follicles. Since women do not usually shave their faces or heads, this is not as much a problem for them as it is for men. However, shaving arms, legs and eyebrows may bring on the same condition.

If permanent makeup is applied to the eyelid or eyebrow area where hair is missing, the possible danger of developing keloids, hypopigmentation, or hyperpigmentation must be carefully weighed. A test area should be performed and checked within 6-8 months to evaluate just how well the skin will tolerate the introduction of permanent makeup dyes. Most physicians advise against permanent makeup procedures for women of color, as the inherent risk for keloiding or hypopigmentation is high.

African American hair is normally less dense than Caucasian hair. It grows at a slower rate and the telogen (shedding phase) hair counts are usually higher, thus one might see more hair fall out during the course of the day. Additionally, the combination of dark scalp and dark hair provides very little contrast, thus giving the illusion of increased hair density.

Hair transplantation in African Americans can yield excellent results due to the quality of the caliber of the hair and the lack of contrast between scalp and hair, but there are definite challenges for the surgeon. There are certain techniques that can be used to improve the outcome. The surgeon must utilize special methods perfected from years of expertise in order to improve and enhance the outcome of an ethnic hair transplant. A potential patient should be certain to select a hair transplant surgeon with proven results.

Ethnic hair restoration patients are more prone to a condition known as **cobblestoning**, an irregularly textured skin surface that is raised, hardened and bumpy. This can occur when harvested follicles (grafts) are transplanted or placed too high or too low into the scalp, thus presenting a displeasing appearance. The follicle is not destroyed; the hair will still grow, but the end result will be cosmetically less attractive. (This is more common with older hair transplant procedures.)

One successful technique is to inject a saline solution around the soon-to-be harvested donor site. The mixture swells the scalp section adding plumpness and firmness to the area, thus the predominantly curved hair follicles can be straightened. By doing this, it then becomes easier to divide the donor strip of hair into smaller grafts, thus avoiding damage to the follicle. At the same time, the curl pattern is lessened. To solve the issue of less density in some African American hair, donor hair can be taken from the fringe area located above the ears, where the follicles are more densely packed. Special attention is given to the recipient site or the area on the scalp where the follicular unit grafts will be placed. The method used here, whether a slit or a puncture, must be made at a 75- to 90-degree angle so that the curl-prone hair does not grow and "curl back" upon itself.

The use of larger, but fewer grafts for African American hair transplantation candidates may be preferable in some cases because fewer incisions in the recipient area (usually the top of the head and the crown) are necessary. Fewer incisions decrease the chance of possible formation of keloids. However, grafts that are too large can increase the chances of hypopigmentation, cobblestoning and of creating a "halo" effect. This is a round, white (depigmented), area of tissue surrounding the placed graft that forms on the outer edge of the graft.

The chances of **hypertrophic** scarring, a lesser form of scars than keloids, is also a concern for African American patients. A session of test grafts may be advisable before launching into a full hair transplant. This consists of 15 to 20 grafts that should be placed inconspicuously in the scalp, and then carefully analyzed in six to eight months before the decision to proceed is made. If a surgeon adheres to this practice, the transplant should yield no unwelcome surprises, and the result should be satisfactory for the patient. In areas where the overuse of hair straighteners and relaxers is visible, resulting in hypopigmentation on the scalp, grafts can be placed in this location in order to camouflage the loss of color in an effected area.

Approximately 80% of all African American women use chemical straightening agents. Besides making a fashion statement for a woman, straightening the hair allows for easier grooming. Specialty products for straightening, chemical relaxing, "straight perming," or "hot-pressing" curly hair can be harmful to the normal growth process as they can cause breakage or damage to hair follicles. The downside of these products can be the cause of a condition known as **chemically induced alopecia** or **relaxer-induced alopecia**. Often ingredients such as **sodium hydroxide** (lye), used mainly in salons, or **guanidine hydroxide** (non-lye), used mainly at home, are used to chemically straighten the hair shaft. Both agents weaken the hair, but the guanidine is the less harsh of the two. Chemically treated hair is more susceptible to breakage when wet, with the nape of the neck being the most common area to be affected. Burns from the caustic straightening agents can be profound and caution must be exercised not to get any of the chemicals on the hands or face. Hair can possibly be further damaged by relaxer creams: **by causing** a 40-50% decrease in the strength of the hair fiber; **by causing** cuticular (cuticle) damage secondary to the swelling of the hair fiber by 40-80%; **by causing** the loss of the protective cuticle; **by causing** increased porosity (the hair's ability to absorb a specific amount of water); and **by causing** a decrease in the hair's moisture content.

Genetically, in African Americans, the follicle is curly because the hair shaft in the scalp has an acute curve. Adding relaxers and straighteners, thus causing the exposed hair shaft to lose its original texture and curl, can temporarily fool Mother Nature. However, if over used or abused, these chemicals can cause permanent destruction to the hair follicle as well as hypopigmented scarring. Although straightening is permanent for the existing hair on the scalp, it must be repeated on new growth every four to eight weeks to smooth the new hair. This repetitive procedure, particularly in inexperienced hands, can have catastrophic results and presents a genuine danger of continually over-processing the hair. Additionally, the hair of African Americans has a lower water content than that of Caucasians or Asians and all hair types weaken by a mere five-minute heat treatment above 239 degrees Fahrenheit, with African American's being the most vulnerable. Following the recommendations of a professional stylist who has successfully used a particular product or having hair straightened professionally is the best advice.

Hair straightening over an extended period of time can cause a severe condition known as **proximal trichorrhexis nodosa** (Vera Price, M.D.). The hair is similar to a "brush cut," and the hair will recover after two years if the straightening practice is abolished. If a return to a more natural hairstyle is desired during this recovery time period, a mild permanent is recommended.

In 1994 and 1995, the Food and Drug Administration received a staggering 3,244 complaints regarding adverse effects of a specific hair relaxer known by the product name "Rio." This was the largest number ever recorded for a cosmetic product. (Unlike drugs, cosmetics are not subject to stringent pre-market review and approval by the FDA.) Ninety-eight percent of the complaints were registered by African American women. The FDA discovered that the product, Rio Hair Naturalizer System, was adulterated, misbranded and falsely labeled. This product, eventually responsible for subsequent hair breakage and fall-out, was found to have extremely high acidic levels.

Of those responding to a survey regarding usage of this product, 95% of respondents experienced loss at the temples and the crown of the head. The quantity of hair lost was substantial, and according to three-quarters of those surveyed, at least one spot was completely bald. Most Rio users had re-grown some hair in eight months, but 9% had no re-growth at all.

Adverse Effects Associated with Use of Rio Hair Naturalizer System Products

Reported by 464 Respondents to the FDA Survey, 1994

Problem	No.	(%)
Hair breakage and/or hair loss	440	(95)
Dry or coarse hair	325	(70)
Unusually dry scalp (flaking or scaling)	246	(53)
Severe anxiety or depression	231	(50)
Hair discoloration	128	(28)
Burning sensation during application	117	(25)
Discoloration of fingernails	105	(23)

Madame C.J. Walker, purported to be the first female African American millionaire, was an innovator and entrepreneur from the pages of hair care history. She started her business with only $1.50. In 1900, distressed over her own hair loss due to the use of harsh chemical straighteners, she invented and obtained a patent for hot pressing, or as it is more commonly called today, a "hot-comb." The hot-comb works by reaching temperatures between 300 and 500 degrees Fahrenheit, and is used along with a hot oil or pomade product to straighten the hair, reduce static electricity, and make styling easier. (Remember, damage to hair can occur at 239 degrees Fahrenheit, and hair dryers typically reach 150 degrees Fahrenheit.) Madame Walker later formulated and sold entire product lines for African American hair-care and styling.

A condition known as **hot-comb alopecia** can be the result of this grooming practice. It is also referred to as **follicular degeneration syndrome**. Clinically speaking, it is an area characterized by a well-defined region of partial hair loss. Inflammation and scarring may occur because of the hot oil running down the hair shaft and into the follicle. It is usually worse on the top of the head because the hair shafts on the crown run perpendicular to the scalp. The follicles around the sides and back are horizontal; therefore not as much oil seeps into the hair shaft. If scarring occurs, the hair loss will be slowly progressive and be permanent.

Besides chemical agents for straightening hair, numerous oils are used. Certain oils such as lecithin, peanut, castor, olive, jojoba and mineral oil respond differently to African American hair than to other hair types. In some cases, the oil tends to cause the hair to become even curlier, and can aggravate seborrheic dermatitis (excess secretion of sebum), or even induce folliculitis (small pustules and redness) from areas of infection. It must be noted that lanolin, a key ingredient in many products, is the most likely ingredient to intensify seborrheic dermatitis. Mineral oil and jojoba oil are considered less likely to cause such problems. Hot-comb straightening, unlike its chemical counterpart, is not permanent and requires only moisture to allow the hair to re-curl.

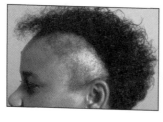 

Maxine experienced traction alopecia, but had her hair restored through surgical hair transplantation.

When observed in African Americans, **traction alopecia** is almost entirely confined to females. The condition is caused mostly from trauma related to hairstyles that put too much tension or pressure on the hair follicle over an extended period of time, usually three to five years. Tight cornrows stress the hair follicles along the temporal region and ponytails have a tendency to cause hair loss along the frontal hairline. If the hair loss is confined to the hairline, a condition most commonly seen in African Americans called **alopecia marginalis**, results. Hair extensions or weaving can also add significantly to the problem. Sponge rollers add insult to injury because they have "no give" once the hair is wound around the roller. The hair loss experienced as a result of traction alopecia is in excess of the acceptable 50 to 100 hairs normally lost each day during the telogen phase. If the condition is caught early on, the effected hair follicles can potentially be saved. It is critical to discontinue the practice of these hairstyles if hair breakage or hair loss prevails. Damage can be irreversible if the follicles are repeatedly strained.

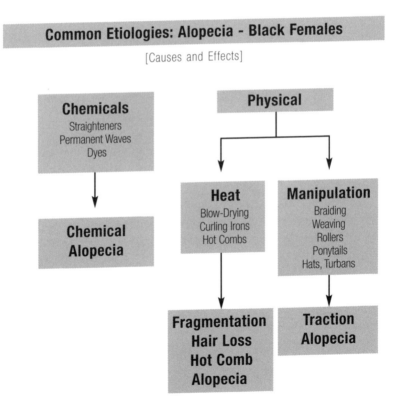

Common Etiologies: Alopecia - Black Females
[Causes and Effects]

Chemicals
Straighteners
Permanent Waves
Dyes

↓

Chemical Alopecia

Physical

Heat
Blow-Drying
Curling Irons
Hot Combs

↓

Fragmentation Hair Loss Hot Comb Alopecia

Manipulation
Braiding
Weaving
Rollers
Ponytails
Hats, Turbans

↓

Traction Alopecia

Management of Hair and Scalp Disorders in African Americans

Condition or Disease Entity	Causative Agent(s) or Factors	Therapy and Management
Traction Alopecia	Tight ponytails and braids, sponge or other tight rollers	Avoid tension on hair. Topical minoxidil in severe cases. *Possible hair transplant surgery.
Hair breakage in nape and suboccipital regions, generally from relaxers; breakage in crown area usually associated with scratching	Hydroxide relaxers Scratching	Protein and cationic conditioners, Leave in conditioners/emollients Use milder relaxer. Treat cause of itching.
Hair shaft very weak distally; crumbles with minimal trauma; severe breakage in parietal area (top/sides of skull)	Thioglycolates	Lipid moisturizers. Avoid protein conditioners. Use milder formulation or booster alone to curl or wave hair.
Severe breakage that cannot be masked by own hair	All causes	Hair weave or wig. *Possible hair transplant surgery.
Seborrheic dermatitis	Lanolin, squalene, wheat germ oil, castor oil, stress, genetics*	Topical corticosteroids with: a) propylene glycol or ointment base for curls, waves and natural hairstyles; b) an ointment base for hotpressed hair; and c) any vehicle for chemically relaxed hair.
Hot-comb alopecia (follicular degeneration syndrome)	Use of hot-combs, curling irons, and hood dryers	Avoid heat where possible. Use spacer between hot-comb and curling iron. Decrease time spent under hood dryers.
Pseudofolliculitis barbae	Plucking or electrolysis in females, some shaving	Avoid shaving if possible or shave in direction of hair growth. Use clipper with 3 (0) blade or depilatory if tolerated. Topical retinoic acid, corticosteroid, topical or oral antibiotic, and benzoyl peroxide. Laser hair removal*.
Folliculitis keloidalis	Genetic predisposition; shaving or close-cutting of hair in nape and posterior scalp	Avoid close-cutting of hair in affected areas. Topical or systemic antibiotics. Liquid nitrogen cryotherapy, intralesional corticosteroids. Surgical or CO_2 laser excision.

*Added by Dr. Matt Leavitt

The popularity of the Disney stage play "Lion King," which unfolds in the grasslands of Africa, features cast members laden with towering headdresses to accompany this kingdom of giraffes, lions, and elephants. During the show's nine-month tour in Canada, four actors were seen at the University of Toronto Hair Clinic who had experienced hair loss from the tiered wigs. Members' hair had to be worn short so that the headdresses could be securely attached. Dry Toronto air and increased relaxer usage (to obtain straight hair for a tighter wig fit) both led to brittle hair and traction alopecia in all four patients. One actor left the production, and the other three vastly improved as Dr. Charlene Linzon from the Clinic worked with management to make several adaptations.

Because of extensive pride, cultural endeavors, and societal beliefs, enormous attention and care is given to hair in all parts of the world. This is especially true in the African American population, and at one clinic, medical problems associated with **caring** for hair crept up instead of from **neglecting** the hair.

At the Martin Luther King Jr./Charles R. Drew Medical Center in Los Angeles, 23 of 62 African American women who visited the dermatology clinic for reasons other than hair problems, were additionally diagnosed with hair and scalp disorders. It is interesting to note that clearly three-fourths of the cases would not have been discovered since the women wore decorative braids, weaves, wigs and hair attachments to disguise some of the conditions. Hair loss is frequently hidden

Ethnic Hair Loss ♀

for years from family and friends, owing to possible cultural and psychological reasons. This group ranged from having the condition(s) from one month to 10 years, and with most believing that the hair and scalp issues were genetic or possibly a "family trait." Nearly half had never mentioned their problem because they did not realize that dermatologists treated these disorders. Education, by doctors and hairstylists, early diagnosis, and early treatment could have prevented almost all these women's plight.

Hispanic Hair

Hispanic patients generally have dark hair that is medium to coarse in texture, average in density, and the follicle is not as deep as found in other ethnic backgrounds. Many have a light curl or wave to their hair. Hispanic women have a high level of contrast between their skin and hair color. The diameter of the hair shaft is usually less than that of the Asian female and some Caucasians. Also, Hispanic women tend to have hair loss due to androgenetic alopecia (FPHL) more often than African American women who have loss most frequently because of traction alopecia. Hair transplantations have proven to be successful for both ethnic groups.

Asian Hair

Asian hair presents its own considerations. In general, Asian women's hair is dark in color and is usually coarse and straight. Asian women normally have a lower hair density than women from other ethnic backgrounds, in some cases less than half the density found in Caucasian women's hair. However, the hair is stronger than African American's and Caucasian's, and their hair loss is usually less.

Similar to African American and Hispanic women, Asian women have a tendency to form keloids or hypertrophic scars. Because of these factors, old conventional punch or mini-grafts are not suitable for hair transplants on Asian patients. The use of small slit grafts, follicular units and micro-grafts is recommended. Also, they will usually need fewer grafts than most Caucasians due to the existence of their larger hair shaft diameter, thus providing more coverage. The dermis layer of the Asian woman's scalp is thicker, and the length of the follicle is longer with fewer hairs per follicle on average when compared to the hair of Caucasian women.

Ethnic Differences in Skin and Hair

Characteristic	White American	African American
Collagen Fiber Bundles	Bigger	Smaller, closely stacked
Corneocyte size	No significant difference	No significant difference
Cutaneous blood vessel reactivity	Greater	Less
Dermis	Thinner; less compact	Thicker; more compact
Elastic Fiber Staining	In photodamage, stain pink in papillary, recticular dermis	All stain pink; elastosis uncommon
Elastic Fibers	More	Fewer
Fiber Fragments	Sparse	Prominent; numerous
Fibroblasts	Not numerous; some binucleated/ multinucleated cells	Numerous; large; many binucleated/ multinucleated cells
Glycoprotein molecules	Variable	Numerous in dermis
Hair diameter	Larger	Smaller
Hair follicles	Ovoid; anchored by more elastic fibers	Elliptical; anchored by fewer elastic fibers
Melanin	Greater protective capability in stratum corneum	Less protective capability in stratum corneum
Melanophages	Numerous	Numerous; larger
Melanosomes	Smaller; in groups of keratinocytes; more numerous in stratu corneum	Larger; individually dispersed in keratinocytes; more numerous in basal layer
Minimal erythema dose	Low (~2 J/m)	High (~11 - 13 l/m)
Photodamage response	Significant epidermal change	Marginal epidermal change
Recovery from pertubation	Slower	Faster
Resistance to skin stripping	Lower	Higher
Response to irritation	Mainly erythema	Mainly hyperpigmentation
Response to irritation: using transepidermal water loss	Lower	Higher
Severe acne incidence	Greater	Less
Skin thickness	No significant difference	No significant difference
Stratum corneum layers	17	22
Stratum corneum lipids: ceramide	High	Low
Stratum corneum lipids: total	Lower	Higher
Stratum corneum thickness	7.2 mm	6.5 mm
Stratum lucidum	1 - 2 layers; swells with sun exposure	1 - 2 layers; unaltered by sun exposure
Superficial blood vessels	Sparse to moderate	Numerous; mostly dilated
Susceptibility to stinging, burning and itching	May be greater	May be less
Sweat glands	Few apocrine-eccrine mixed glands	More apocrine-eccrine mixed glands
Vitamin D production	Higher	Lower
Water barrier	May be greater	May be less

Note: This information presented at an international symposium in Chicago, sponsored by L'Oreal Institute for Ethnic Hair and Skin Research and by Howard University.

Source: Dr. Christian Oresajo of the Ethnic Skin Research Institute, Howard University, Washington, D.C.

COMPARISON BETWEEN FEMALES AND MALES WHO HAVE HAD HAIR TRANSPLANTATION

Non-Scientific Observation of Medical Hair Restoration Patients

♀ typically start out with a diffuse hair loss pattern

♀ are not as bald

♀ donor area can be poorer…soft and spongy

♂ donor area is rarely bad…it is poor to great

♂ tissue is tougher

♀ have a higher pain tolerance

♀ due to less available donor area, harder to initially provide density; typically need multiple hair transplant sessions

♀ are happy and extremely grateful for almost any improvement

♂ frontal hairline reconstruction is more important

♀ want better overall coverage to allow for more length and styling options

CHAPTER TEN

HAIR
TRANSPLANTATION

"A hair divides what is false and true."

Omar Khayyam, Persian Poet 1048 - 1131

There are three main means of surgical hair restoration procedures. The most common is **hair transplantation** where hair-bearing follicles or grafts are moved or redistributed from an area of stable growth and density on the scalp to an area that is thinning or balding. The grafts are typically moved from the back of the head from an area known as the **occipital** area. Most of these hairs are genetically programmed to grow for a lifetime, unaffected by DHT. Next is a procedure called a **flap surgery**, where hair is moved from the hair-bearing sides of the scalp and rotated or transposed across the bald area. The third procedure, a **scalp reduction**, consists of removing a section of bald tissue, generally from the crown region. All are performed today, but the use of flaps and scalp reductions has dramatically decreased as vastly modified and improved hair transplantation techniques have been developed.

The idea that scalp tissue could be surgically moved or transposed from one area of the head to another was the initial premise for hair transplantation surgery. It first appeared in 1897 when flap surgery was performed to cover a denuded area of the scalp (a wound), only to be followed in 1926 by the first scalp reduction. Hair replacement surgery, the procedure for moving one's own hair from an area of stable growth and density to an area of little or no growth probably had its true beginnings in 1931 when for the first time, the French surgeon Passot moved hair from a viable hair-bearing section of the scalp to a bald area...or basically, a more involved version of a comb-over!

Following flap surgery and scalp reduction was the introduction of **hair grafts** or **follicular unit transplantation**, as we know it today. A Japanese dermatologist, Dr. Shojui Okuda, published his results from this procedure in 1939 only to have his endeavor go unnoticed at the time, probably because his works occurred during World War II. Dr. James B. Hamilton opened research into male pattern baldness in the 1940s. His work supported the androgenetic (male hormone) theory of common baldness, and he further developed the system of hair loss classification and identification still in use today. As mentioned previously, androgenetic alopecia is the number one cause of hair loss in both men and women.

Present day credit for the foundation and popularizing of hair transplantation is given to Dr. Norman Orentreich, a New York dermatologist, for his work in the early 1950s and later, his published material in 1959. As a pioneer, he developed the theory of "donor dominance," whereby scalp grafts were moved or transplanted from the hair-bearing occipital area to the frontal bald or thinning areas of the head, and at the same time the grafts maintained their integrity and behaved as they did at their original site. They were expected to grow and last for a lifetime. His theory was proven four years later when his patient still had the transplanted hair. The procedure was endorsed by celebrities who openly discussed their own hair transplantation. This act helped to increase the popularity and make hair transplants the second most performed cosmetic surgery in the United States.

Doll hair, hedgerow, toothbrush, cornrows, spikes, telephone poles, and plugs are all monikers for the older, all too visible, results of hair transplantation. Things have definitely changed, with these former methods emerging as the basis for an improved generation of instruments and advanced techniques. Now hair transplantation serves as a way to not only reduce balding or thinning, but also as a means to replace eyebrows, eyelashes, camouflage scars from burns, and to cover disfigurement from radiation, accident trauma and traction alopecia.

At times the ensuing scars from a face-lift or a brow-lift, cause hair loss along the suture line or the scar can widen over time. In these instances, hair transplantation can be valuable, as small follicles can actually be inserted in and around the hairless and scarred area. The transplanted follicular units can follow the path of the frontal hairline and or be hidden in the hair at the temporal region, successfully masking or covering any obvious face or brow-lift scars. This modern procedure is also recognized as a means to treat various autoimmune diseases that cause balding.

Hair transplant surgery appears to be a relatively simple concept; however, there are many nuances that contribute to good vs. bad results. Remember, the procedure does not replace every hair lost with a new hair. The result creates an illusion of fullness, an artistic sort of *trompe l'oeil*. Technical aspects, physician expertise, patient expectations, the quality, quantity, density of hair, the pattern of loss, the emotional needs, family history, budget, the ability of the medical technicians, donor availability, health, age, race, the rate of loss over time, as well as present hair loss, must all be measured and considered when evaluating whether or not to proceed with hair transplantation.

A potential patient must do her own screening of the physician. How long has she/he been performing hair transplants, is she/he using the most current methods, is she/he **board certified** in hair transplant surgery? Does she/he display an interest in helping women, seem meticulous, present a neat personal appearance as well as maintain a tidy office environment? Does she/he intently listen and take time to answer all questions, have photos of previous patients and agree for you to meet or talk with several patients? Furthermore, does she/he encourage that laboratory, endocrine, and hormonal tests be done, does she/he keep the conversation positive and provide reasonable answers, and does she/he not dismiss you as an obsessive female? Lastly, an interest only in the bottom line by a doctor should not be tolerated. That particular physician should be eliminated as a potential surgeon if that is her/his primary motivation.

After a physician ascertains who is a qualified patient, and after a candidate selects a doctor as her hair transplant surgeon, a planning session follows. Again, this depends on many of the previously mentioned variables. Until approximately 20 years ago, the majority of women were not perceived as good hair transplant patients by most physicians because of their unique pattern of hair loss, which is typically more diffuse or exhibits an overall thinning of the entire scalp area, including the donor area. Thus that crucial area, necessary for a successful surgery, was considered compromised.

To put all of the transformation of hair replacement into proper perspective and sequence, a brief time line or explanation of transitional periods is necessary. Since few scalp reductions and flap surgeries are performed on women, the discussion deals almost solely with graft and follicular transplantation.

In the early to mid 80s, physicians began to take note of the female patient for hair transplantation due to the presence of new and improved techniques in instrumentation in the hair replacement arena, as noted earlier. The upside was that unlike men, women rarely lost all of their hair and did not have large areas that were totally bald. Their loss was less severe, coupled with the fact that women's hair loss developed at a slower rate. Another plus, female patients usually did not need to have the frontal hair line recreated (the most difficult region to mimic naturally) which could result in a hair line that was too abrupt or too thick if done improperly.

The evolution from the original 15-18 hairs per graft (and only 30-50 were transplanted per session) or **plugs**, to the current one to three hair grafts benefited females tremendously. The newer process additionally introduced the improved technique of harvesting the grafts. Gone was the old punch method where grafts were removed from the shaved donor area in four to five mm round circles with an instrument resembling a hollow bullet that was used to extract the donor graft like a cookie cutter. This left unused hair-bearing tissue, similar to what remained after cutting dough. This donor area in the occipital (back of head) region was left to heal with little round wounds on its own. This method wasted precious grafts and was more uncomfortable for the patient. (This waste was called "islands" because it fell in small parallel strips within the donor area. Later an updated surgical method was used to salvage this region, and this once discarded tissue was then used as transplantable small grafts.) By the early 1990s, a power-driven punch was utilized to harvest grafts from the donor area, with the biggest advantage being speed and accuracy, and the disadvantage being heat damage or possible trauma to the hair bulbs. The number of grafts now transplanted had risen from an average of 60-100 by the late 1980s and increased from 200-500 up to the mid 1990s.

Improvements in harvesting the donor site came with newer techniques. Linear strips of scalp tissue were now being taken from the occipital area, thus eliminating the island waste and the old style punch grafts that both tended to damage surrounding tissue and destroy follicles. Conservation of donor hair follicles was a result, scarring was minimized since there was only one horizontal suture in the area now, and patient comfort heightened as healing time decreased.

These advancements created an environment of excitement, a platform for research, a basis for education, and launched an influx of hair transplant surgeons. The plugs, which were no longer acceptable, were making way for a cosmetically superior leap in grafting that was appearing on the horizon: **micro- and mini-grafts**, which consisted of 1-3 hairs per micro-graft and 4-6 hairs per mini-graft. In addition to these virtually microscopic grafts, **slit grafts**, which placed 1-3 hairs per graft in between the existing areas of hairs in women with diffuse hair loss, were introduced. The micro- and mini-grafts were placed or inserted into an area where a tiny amount of bald tissue had previously been removed. Slit grafts, on the other hand, were inserted into a small cut in the recipient area without disturbing surrounding hair. This technique eliminated any scarring because tissue was not removed. Thus greater density was achieved for the woman with diffuse hair loss. Slit grafts were also used for large thinning areas of hair loss to camouflage scars and to repair previously unappealing hair transplants. Slit grafts, which resulted in a very natural aesthetically pleasing hair transplant, combined with the micro- and mini-grafts were a major advancement for females with this diffuse pattern of hair loss. About this time, an escalating awareness of women's hair loss emerged, thanks to increased public consciousness and the media. Other contributing factors were an accelerated interest among an aging baby boomer population (thinning hair and its possible association with menopause), and the prolific amount of information disseminated via the Internet. Hair transplantation was now a viable option for women experiencing hair loss.

The late 1990s introduced the current revolution in hair transplantation, again benefiting women. The new method that is currently utilized is now called follicular unit transplantation. This technique provided the impetus for mega sessions in hair transplantation where 1,000 to 3,000 grafts can be placed at one time. Instead of randomly cutting one, two, three, etc. sections of hairs from a donor strip and inordinately splitting follicles, as was formerly done, today the strip is examined with high-power magnification and cut into naturally occurring groups of follicles or follicular units. Note that each follicular unit may hold one, two, or even three hairs, so none of the follicles are split or cut, but the hairs remain in their original follicular units without being damaged. A dense donor area is one that yields an average of 25 hairs per four millimeters. The end result of this improved hair transplantation method took the procedure one step closer toward refinement and solidified the inability for detection of it as surgically relocated hair.

An innovative technique developed by my practice, Medical Hair Restoration, for the placement of these follicular units is called "cross-hatching." Here the follicles are placed in the recipient area in a seemingly random pattern (because nature does not adhere to straight lines and is asymmetric), and they are positioned in various directions so that an appearance similar to a textured painting is achieved. The brush strokes are made in overlapping directions, thus creating an illusion of increased volume and density. Also, it is critical to use precise angulation in the placement of the follicular unit as much as possible. Cross-hatching and acute angles are state-of-the-art techniques and provide a more natural, feathered-like hairline. Creating the right spacing, angle and direction for each graft is essential to achieve the best result.

The use of lasers in hair transplant surgery has been limited and mostly confined to making incisions in the recipient area. The benefit of lasers in most surgical procedures is that they minimize bleeding, thus healing time may be decreased. However, their use in hair transplantation has not been as successful because the intense heat generated by the laser can compromise blood supply to the newly transplanted graft.

Most often, more than one session of hair replacement surgery is recommended. Ideally, 6-8 months are necessary for the transplanted hair to grow. Since women are usually thin and not bald, this lets the newly transplanted hair grow virtually undetected and causes less shock to existing hairs in surrounding areas. Additionally, it gives the physician a chance to evaluate the session. Usually 9-12 months separate the time between any subsequent surgeries. However, if a patient desires, another session of hair transplantation can be done as soon as 4-6 weeks later, just as long as it is not in the same region as the previous one. If the areas to be transplanted are far enough apart, for example the crown and the frontal part of the head, transplants can be performed within a period of a few weeks. However it is more practical to have the desired area of treatment transplanted in the one session. If further density is required, subsequent surgery is usually performed 9-12 months later. Follicular grafts are the most often used graft for creating the hairline and the frontal area. Hair located a little higher in the donor area usually best matches the hair lost on the vertex (top of the head) and is used in that area first.

Making the decision to proceed with hair transplantation takes more time than the actual procedure itself. Prior to surgery, labs may be drawn and patients are encouraged to use **minoxidil at least two weeks before surgery to enhance circulation, to minimize**

telogen effluvium of existing hairs, and to further aid in the rapid growth of the transplanted hair. The procedure lasts approximately 3-4 hours for the patient, depending upon the number of grafts to be placed. However, it actually entails a total of about 4-8 hours of intensive work for the highly skilled medical team that prepares everything for the physician. A light sedative is administered with most patients reporting little or no discomfort. Because of the smaller incisions, the post-operative turban-like bandage is used less frequently. Patients may return the next day to be shampooed, and sutures in the donor area are removed in 10-14 days. Small crusting appears over the grafts and fall off in 7-10 days, thus leaving tiny, pinkish areas that blend in with the scalp and hair. These disappear in approximately 10 days to three weeks. A wig may be worn almost immediately post operatively if preferred. Actually, the most difficult part of hair transplantation comes next—the waiting.

Hair that was transplanted may initially fall out...this is expected and referred to as "shock loss." Then it takes 3-4 months to see the new growth and approximately 6-8 months for the hair to reach a length of about 2-3 inches. Complications are rare, and if they occur, are most often limited to swelling, tenderness, slight bleeding or itching that is usually confined to the donor area. All of these conditions are temporary and have no long-term harmful effects. If the surgeon's technique is flawed, a cosmetically unappealing transplant can result, once again stressing the importance of selecting the right physician. The longevity of a hair transplant does not wane. You can bleach it, perm it, dye it, style it, cut it, mousse it, spike it, or even shave it — the point being that it lasts forever.

It should be noted that not every woman is a candidate for this procedure. An evaluation of the cause and degree of loss must determine if the patient can be helped by hair transplantation. While hair restoration surgery is time consuming, labor intensive and tedious, it is extremely gratifying when a physician knows and is able to witness what a difference it makes in a person's life.

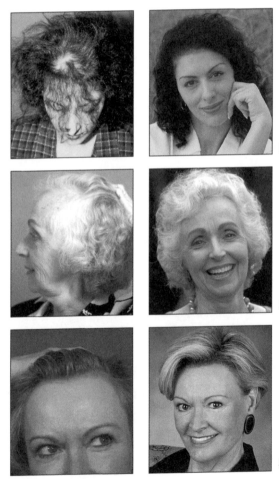

Examples of female patients who solved their individual hair loss needs with hair transplants through Medical Hair Restoration.

Mary G.

Dottie A.

Sheryl L.

BIBLIOGRAPHY

Alexander, Suzanne, MB 1985. "Common Baldness In Women." Seminars In Dermatology. March 4:l:l-3.

American Academy of Dermatology. 1993. "Hair Loss." Internet site: www.aad.org/pamphlets/hairloss.html.

American Academy of Dermatology. 1999. "Hair Diseases In African Americans Require Specialized Knowledge." Internet site: www.aad.org/PressReleases/hairdisease.html.

American Hair Loss Council (Editor). 1989. "Maintaining A Positive Body Image With Hair Loss Related To Cancer Treatment." Hair Loss Journal. 5:2:1-11.

American Hair Loss Council (Editor). 1990. "Understanding Hair Loss In Females." Hair Loss Journal. 6:2:103.

American Hair Loss Council (Editor). 1992. "Hair Transplantation In Females." Hair Loss Journal. 7:3:1-7.

American Hair Loss Council (Editor). 2000. "Female Pattern Hair Loss." Internet site: www.ahlc.org/female.htm.

American Hair Loss Council (Editor). 2000. "Alopecia Areata." Internet site: www.ahlc.org/alopec.htm.

American Hair Loss Council (Editor). 2000. "What Is A Non-Surgical Hair Addition?" Internet site: www.ahlc.org/nsurg.htm.

American Hair Loss Council (Editor). 1993. "American Hair Loss Council Hair Loss Estimates." 1-10.

Aram, Homayoum, MD. 1987. "Treatment Of Female Androgenetic Alopecia With Cimetidine." International Journal of Dermatology. March 26:2:128-130.

Astley, Amy. 1994. "The Politics Of Hair." Vogue. December 229-234.

Avram, Marc R., MD. 1999. "Hair Transplantation In Women." Seminars in Cutaneous Medicine and Surgery. June 18:2:172-176.

Baden, Howard P., MD. 1987. Diseases Of The Hair And Nails. Chicago: Year Book Medical Publishers, Inc. 105-143, 166-184.

Bates, Betsy. 2003. "Hidden Hair Disorders Common In Black Women." Skin and Allergy News. November 34:11: 40.

Bates, Betsy. 2003. "Lab Studies Untangle Ethnic Differences In Hair." Skin and Allergy News. November 34:11: 41.

Bates, Betsy. 2003. "'Lion King Alopecia' Tamed By Dermatologist." Skin and Allergy News. November 34:11:28.

Bergfeld, Wilma F., MD and Redmond, Geoffrey P., MD. 1987. "Androgenic Alopecia." Dermatologic Clinics. July 5:3:491-498.

Bergfeld, Wilma F., MD. 1978. "Diffuse Hair Loss In Women." CUTIS. August 22:190-195.

Berland, Theodore. 1993. "Baldness 'Cures:' Does Anything Really Work?" Consumers Digest. July/August 68-70.

Brodland, David G., MD, and Muller, Sigfrid A., MD. 1991. "Androgenetic Alopecia (Common Baldness)." CUTIS. March 47:173-176.

Bulengo-Ransby, S.M., MD, and Bergfeld, W. F., MD. 1992. "Chemical And Traumatic Alopecia From Thioglycolate In A Black Woman: A Case Report With Unusual Clinical and Histologic Findings." CUTIS. February 49:99-103.

Bundles, A'Lelia. 2001. On Her Own Ground: The Life and Times of Madam C. J. Walker. New York: Scribner.

Burke, Karen E. MD, PhD. 1989. "Hair Loss." Postgraduate Medicine. May 52-74.

Cash, Thomas F., PhD, Price, Vera H., MD, and Savin, Ronald C., MD. 1993. "Psychological Effects Of Androgenetic Alopecia On Women: Comparisons With Balding Men And With Female Control Subjects." Journal of the American Academy of Dermatology. 29:4.

Cash, Thomas, F., PhD and Pruzinsky, Thomas, PhD. 1994. "The Psychological Effects Of Androgenetic Alopecia And Their Implications For Patient Care."

Cotterill, Paul C., MD and Unger, Walter P., MD, FRCP(C), FACP. 1992. "Hair Transplantation In Females." Journal of Dermatologic Surgery and Oncology. 18:477-481.

Cotterill, Paul, MD. 2000. "A Review Of Scalp Hair Loss In Women-Part I." Hair Transplant Forum International. May/June 10:3.

Dawber, Rodney P.R., MA, MB, FRCP. 1981. "Common Baldness In Women." International Journal of Dermatology. December 20:10:647-650.

Desai, Sukumar P., MD, and Roaf, Edward R., MD. 1984. "Telogen Effluvium After Anesthesia And Surgery." Anesthesia Analg. 63:83-84.

DeKoning, E.B., Passchier, J., and Dekker, F.W. 1990. "Psychological Problems With Hair Loss In General Practice And The Treatment Policies Of General Practioners." Psychological Reports. 67:775-778.

DeVillez, Richard L., MD, and Dunn, James, MD. 1986. "Female Androgenic Alopecia." Arch Dermatol. Sept 122:1011-1014.

DeVillez, Richard L., MD, et al. 1994. "Androgenetic Alopecia In The Female." Arch Dermatology. March 130:303-307.

DeVillez, Richard L., MD. 2000. "Growth and Loss of Hair." Internet site: www.regrowth.com/story.cfm?id=10147.

Dolte, K.S., Girman, C. J., Hartmaier, S., Roberts, J., Bergfeld, W., and Waldstreicher, J. 2000. (Chart) "Development Of A Health Related Quality Of Life Questionnaire For Women With Androgenetic Alopecia." Clinical and Experimental Dermatology. July 25: 637-642.

Dorius, David A., MD. 2000. "Recognizing And Treating Androgenic Alopecia In Women." Internet site: www.minoxidil.com/female.htm/female.htm.

Dover, Robin, PhD. 1995. "Hair Loss In Women." Internet site: www.docnet.org.uk/hair/femaleloss.html.

Draelos, Zoe Diana, MD. 1990. "Augmentation Of Hair Through Artificial And Natural Hair Additions." Cosmetic Dermatology. January 12-18.

Draelos, Zoe Diana, MD. 1990. "Evaluating The Patient With Diffuse, Nonscarring Hair Loss - Part 1 - Part 2." Cosmetic Dermatology. March 10-14.

Earles, R. Martin, MD. 1986. "Surgical Correction Of Traumatic Alopecia Marginalis Or Traction Alopecia In Black Women." Journal of Dermatologic Surgery and Oncology. January 12:1:78-82.

Eckert, J., MD. 1976. "Diffuse Hair Loss In Women: The Psychopathology Of Those Who Complain." Acta Psych (Scand). 53:321-327.

Editor. 1994. "Secret Signals For Women." Prevention. November 27-29.

Editor. 1997. "Genes." Internet site: www.newhairinstitute.com.

Editor. 1997. "Producers of Baldness Remedies Turn To Women For Fresh Growth." Internet site: www.chicago.tribune.com/pris/9703/31/business/9703310118.html.

Editor. 2000. "Glossary Of Terms." Internet site: www.follicle.con/section4/1.htm/.

Editor. 2000. "The Social Dimension Of Hair Loss." Internet site: www.health-library.com/library/health/part1/htm.

Editor. 2000. "Hair Transplant Terminology." Internet site: www.regrowth.com/documentscfm?id=10626.

Editor. 2001. "Gender And Ethnicity May Deter Choice Of Techniques For Hair Restoration." Internet site: www.docguide.com/news/content.nsf/News/85256790004EDE3285256530004F6A55?

Editor. 2000. "What Do FDA And FTC Say About Hair Loss Scams?" Internet site: www.hairlossscams.com/FDAandFTC.htm.

Editor. 1983. Man Myth & Magic: The Illustrated Encyclopedia Of Mythology, Religion And The Unknown. New York: Marshall Cavendish. v:5:1201-1204.

Editor. 1997. The New Book Of Knowledge. Danbury, CT: Grolier, Inc. v:8:5-8.

Editor. 1998. The New Encyclopedia Britannica. Chicago: Encyclopedia Britannica: v:5:622.

Editor. 2002. The World Book Encyclopedia. Chicago: World Book, Inc. v9: 9-10.

Editors. 2000. 2000 Compton's Encyclopedia & Fact-Index. Chicago: Success Publishing Group. v:10: 7-8.

Editor. 2001. Physicians' Desk Reference. Montvale, NJ: Medical Economics Co., Inc.

Editors. 1990. Orfanos, C.E., MD and Happle, R., MD. Hair and Hair Diseases. Forslind, B. "The Growing Anagen Hair." Berlin: Springer-Verlag. Chapter 4. 73-97.

Editor. 1995. Dermatology In General Medicine. Bertolino, Arthur P., and Freedberg, Irwin. (Hair) "Disorders Of Epidermal Appendages And Related Disorders." Dermatology In General Medicine. New York: McGraw-Hill Book Company. 627-651.

Editors. 1996. The Hairy Book: The (Uncut) Truth About The Weirdness of Hair. Canada: Planet Dexter.

Editors. 1998. "Mites Indicated In All Baldness Cases." Internet site: www.regrowth.com/documents.cfm?id=10083.

Editors. 2000. "The Facts About Fine, Thin And Thinning Hair." Internet site: www.womenshairinstitute.com/facts.htm.

Eisner, Robin. February 14, 2001. "American Men Spend More Than $1 Billion Each Year to Treat Baldness." Internet site: www.abcnews.com-health.

Epstein, Franklin, MD, (Editor). Paus, Ralf, MD, and Cotsarelis, George, MD. 1999. "The Biology Of Hair Follicles." The New England Journal of Medicine. August 341:7:491-497.

Ertel, John. 1998. "New Hair Loss Drug May Be Approved In 2000." Internet site: www.regrowth.com/documents.cfm?id=10094.

Falcon, Mike. 2001. "Female Baldness Still Under Cover." Internet site: www.usatoday.com/life/health/doctor/1hdoc314.htm.

Fred, Herbert L., MD, and Accad, Michel F., MD. 1997. "Abdominal Pain, Leg Weakness, And Alopecia In A Teenage Boy." Hospital Practice. April 15:69-70.

Fried, Richard, MD, PhD. 2001. "Understanding The Link Between Hair Disorders And Self-Image." Skin and Aging. March 55-59.

Garcia-Hernandez, Maria-Jose, MD. 1999. "Chronic Telogen Effluvium: Incidence, Clinical And Biochemical Features, And Treatment." Arch Dermatol. 135:1123-1124.

Gardner, Stephanie S., MD, Conte, Melissa A., MD and McKay, Marilynne, MD. 1991. "Hair Loss In Women. Part I: An Approach To Evaluation." The Female Patient. May 16:39-48.

Girman, C.J., et al. 2000. "Development Of A Health-Related Quality Of Life Questionnaire For Women With Androgenetic Alopecia." Clinical and Experimental Dermatology. 25:637-642.

Girman, C.J., Hartmaier, S., Roberts, J., Bergfeld, Waldstreicher, J. 1999. "Patient-Perceived Importance Of Negative Effects Of Androgenetic Alopecia In Women." Journal of Women's Health & Gender-Based Medicine. 8:8:1091-1095.

Greenwood-Robinson, Maggie, PhD. 2000. Hair Savers For Women. New York: Three Rivers Press.

Grimalt, R., Ferrando, J. 1999. "Partial Response Of Severe Alopecia Areata To Cyclosporine A." Dermatology: Letters to Dermatology. 67-69.

Guendert, Denise V., MD, and Calhoun, Karen H., MD, FACS. 1995. "Management Of Alopecia." Internet site: www.npntserver.mcg.edu/htm1/alopecia/documents/baldness-95.html.

Guttman, Cheryl, (Editor). "Iron Deficiencies Most Common Hair Problem In Healthy Women." Dermatology Times. April 1993.

Hanlon, Phyllis. 2001. "Hair Loss In Women: No Longer A Guy Thing." Healthy Skin & Hair. Fall 6-7.

Hanover, Larry. 2000. "Hair Replacement: What Works, What Doesn't." Internet site: www.verity.fda.gov/search97c.

Herten, R. Jeffrey, MD. 1982. "Nonscarring Hair Loss Disorders." Postgraduate Medicine. October 72:4:231-245.

Hitzig, Gary S., MD. 1997. Help & Hope For Hair Loss. New York: Avon Books.

Hoffman, Rolf, MD, Happle, Rudolf, MD. 2000. "Current Understanding Of Androgenetic Alopecia. Part II: Clinical Aspects And Treatment." European Journal of Dermatology. July/August 10:410-417.

Hordinsky, Maria K., MD. 1987. "General Evaluation Of The Patient With Alopecia." Dermatologic Clinics. 5:3:483-488.

Hutchinson, P.E, MB, MRCP. 1980. "Diagnosis Of Hair Disease." The Practitioner. November 224:1159-1167.

Hwang, Sang Min, MD, et al. 1999. "Nurse's Cap Alopecia." International Journal of Dermatology. 38:187-191.

INK Electronic Media Limited. 1998. "Androgenetic Alopecia Male Pattern Baldness/Female Pattern Baldness." Internet site: www.follicle.com/typesandrogenetic.html.

INK Electronic Media Limited. 2000. "Anagen Effluvium: Cancer Treatment Hair Loss." Internet site: www.follicle.com/section2/3.html.

INK Electronic Media. 2000. "Hair Structure And Life Cycle." Internet site: www.follicle.com/2.html.

Jackson, Edward A., MD. 2000. "Hair Disorders." Primary Care. June 27:2:319-324.

Kasick, James M., MD, Bergfeld, Wilma F., MD, Steck, Willard D., MD, Gupta, Manjula K., PhD. 1983. "Adrenal Androgenic Female-Pattern Alopecia: Sex Hormones and the Balding Woman." Cleveland Clinic Quarterly. Summer 50:2:111-122.

Kim, Jung-Chul. 2001. "Oriental Hair." International Society of Hair Restoration Surgery/The World Hair Society. Abstract.

Kluger, Jeffrey. 2002. "How Science Solves Crimes." Time Magazine. October 21, 39.

Knowles, W. Roy, MD. 1987. "Hair Transplantation: A Review." Dermatologic Clinics. July 5:3:515-530.

Kobren, Spencer D. 2000. The Truth About Women's Hair Loss. Chicago: Contemporary Books.

Levy, Moise L. MD. 1991. "Disorders Of The Hair And Scalp In Children." Archives of Disease In Childhood. 63:702-706.

Li, Vincent W., MD; Baden, Howard P., MD; and Kvedar, Joseph C., MD. 1996. "Loose Anagen Syndrome And Loose Anagen Hair." Dermatologic Clinics. October 745-751.

Lucky, A.W., MD, et al. 2004. "A Randomized, Placebo-Controlled Trial Of 5% and 2% Topical Minoxidil Solutions In The Treatment Of Female Pattern Hair Loss. Journal of the American Academy of Dermatology. 50: 541-553.

Ludwig, Erich. 1977. "Classification Of The Types Of Androgenetic Alopecia (Common Baldness) Occurring In The Female Sex." British Journal of Dermatology. 97:247-254.

Macquire, Henry C., MD and Kligman, Albert M., MD, PhD. 1963. "Common Baldness In Women." Geriatrics. April 329-334.

Maffei, Cesare, MD, Fossati, Andrea, MD, Rinaldi, Fabio, MD, Riva, Elisabetta, MD. "Personality Disorders And Psychopathologic Symptoms In Patients With Androgenetic Alopecia." Arch Derm. July 130:868-872.

Marin, Rick. 1992. "Kiss It Goodbye." GQ. August 172-177.

Mayer, Toby G., MD and Fleming, Richard W., MD. 1992. Aesthetic and Reconstructive Surgery of the Scalp. St. Louis: Mosby Yearbook. 38-45.

McGarvey, Elizabeth L., (Editor). 2001. Baum, Lora D., PhD, Rogers, Laura, M., BS. "Psychological Sequelae And Alopecia Among Women With Cancer." Cancer Practice. November/December 9:6:283-289.

Meisler, Jodi, MS, RD. 1998. "Conversation With The Experts-Toward Optimal Health: The Experts Respond To Hair Loss In Women." Journal of Women's Health. 7:3:307-310.

Mercke, Yekaterina, Sheng, Huaibao, Khan, Tehmina, and Lippmann, Steven. 2000. "Hair Loss In Psychopharmacology." American Academy of Clinical Psychiatry. 12:1:35-42.

Messenger A.G. MD and Rundegren J., MD. 2004. "Minoxidil: Mechanisms Of Action On Hair Growth." Brit J Dermatol. 150: 186-194.

Milgraum, Sandy S., MD. 1987. "Alopecia Areata, Endocrine Function, And Autoantibodies In Patients 16 Years Of Age Or Younger." Journal of the American Academy of Dermatology. July 17:1:57-61.

Miller, Jeffrey J, MD. 2001. "Relaxer-Induced Alopecia." Division of Dermatology. Penn State College of Medicine, Hershey, PA. 238-239

Morris, Desmond. 1985. Body Watching. New York: Crown Publishers, Inc.

Muller, Sigfrid A. MD. 1987. "Trichotillomania" Dermatologic Clinics. July 5:3:595-601.

Nelson, Bruce R.,MD, Stough, Dowling B., MD, Stough, D. Bluford, MD, and Johnson, Timothy, MD. 1991. "Hair Transplantation In Advanced Male Pattern Alopecia." Journal of Dermatologic Surgery and Oncology. 17:567-773.

Norwood, O'Tar T., MD. 2001. "Incidence Of Female Androgenetic Alopecia (Female Pattern Alopecia)." Dermatologic Surgery. January 27:53-54.

Olsen, Elise A., MD. 1999. "The Midline Part: An Important Physical Clue To The Clinical Diagnosis Of Androgenetic Alopecia In Women." Journal of the American Academy of Dermatology. January 40:1:106-109.

Olsen, Elise A., MD. 1989. "Alopecia: Evaluation And Management." Primary Care. September 16:3:765-787.

Olsen, Elise, MD. 1991. "Topical Minoxidil In The Treatment Of Androgenetic Alopecia In Women." CUTIS. September 48:243-248.

Olsen, Elise, MD (Editor). 1994. Disorders Of Hair Growth: Diagnosis And Treatment. Olsen, Elise A., MD. "Hair Loss In Childhood." New York: McGraw-Hill. Chapter 7. 139-194.

Olsen, Elise, MD (Editor). 1994. Disorders Of Hair Growth: Diagnosis And Treatment. Olsen, Elise A., MD. "Androgenetic Alopecia." New York: McGraw-Hill. Chapter 11. 257-283.

Olsen E.A.MD, et al. 2002. "A Randomized Clinical Trial Of 5% Topical Minoxidil Versus 2% Topical Minoxidil And Placebo In The Treatment Of Androgenetic Alopecia In Men." Journal of the American Academy of Dermatology. 47: 377-385.

Orentreich, Norman, MD. 1978. "Medical Treatment Of Baldness." Annals of Plastic Surgery. January 1:1:116-118.

Parkinson, Richard, W., MD. 1992. "Hair Loss In Women: What To Say And Do To Ease These Patients' Distress." Postgraduate Medicine. March 91:4:417-431.

Pathomvanich, Damkemg, MD, FACS. 2001. "What Do You Want to Know When Doing Asian Hair Transplantation?" International Society of Hair Restoration Surgery/ World Hair Society. February 21-24.

Paus, Ralf, MD and Cotsarelis, George, MD. 1999. "The Biology of Hair Follicles." New England Journal of Medicine. August 341:7:491-497.

Perez-Meza, David, MD. 2001. "Hispanic Patient." International Society of Hair Restoration Surgery/World Hair Society. February 21-24.

Phillips III, J. Hunter, MD, et al. 1986. "Hair Loss: Common Congenital And Acquired Causes." Postgraduate Medicine. April 79:5:207-215.

Piacquadio, Daniel J., MD, Rad, Farhad S., MD, PharmD, Spellman, Mary C., MD and Hollenbach, Kathryn A., PhD. 1994. "Obesity And Female Androgenic Alopecia: A Cause And An Effect?" Journal of the American Academy of Dermatology. June 30:6:1028-1030.

Pine, Devera. 1991. "Hair! From Personal Statement To Personal Problem." U.S. Food and Drug Administration/FDA Consumer. December.

Price, Vera H., MD (Task Force Chairman). Baden, Howard, MD, DeVillez, Richard L., MD, Drake, Lynn A., MD, Hordinsky, Maria K., MD, Olsen, Elise, MD, and Shupack, Jerome L., MD. 1996. Drake, Lynn A., MD (Guidelines/Outcomes Committee). "Guidelines Of Care For Androgenetic Alopecia." Journal of the American Academy of Dermatology. September 35:3 (Part 1): 465-469.

Price, Vera H., MD, FRCP(C). 1988. "Androgenetic Alopecia And Hair Growth Promotion State-Of-The-Art: Present And Future." Clinics in Dermatology. October-December 6:4:218-227.

Price, Vera, MD, FRCP(C), et al. 2000. "Lack Of Efficacy Of Finasteride In Postmenopausal Women With Androgenetic Alopecia." Journal of American Academy of Dermatology. November 43:5:768-776.

Pride, Howard B. MD, and Tunnessen, Jr., Walter W., MD. 1995. "Picture Of The Month." Arch Pediatric Adolescent Medicine. July 149:819-820.

Redmond, Geoffrey P., MD, and Bergfeld, Wilma F., MD. 1990. "Treatment Of Androgenic Disorders In Women: Acne, Hirsutism, And Alopecia." Cleveland Clinic Journal of Medicine. July/August 57:5:428-432.

Redmond, Geoffrey P., MD. 1998. "Androgens And Women's Health." International Journal of Fertility. 43:2:91-97.

Reid, Robert L., MD and Van Vugt, Dean A., MD. 1988. "Hair Loss In The Female." Obstetrical and Gynecological Survey. 43:3:135-141.

Roenigk, Randall K., and Roenigk, Jr., Henry H., (Eds). 1989. Pinski, James B. "Hair Transplantation." New York: Marcel Dekker, Inc. 1047-1064.

Rosenfield, Robert L., MD, and Lucky, A.W., MD. 1993. "Acne, Hirsuitism, And Alopecia In Adolescent Girls." Endocrinology and Metabolism Clinics of North America. September 22:3:507-525.

Rushton, D. H., PhD, Ramsay, I. D., James, K. C., Norris, M. J., and Gilkes, J. J. H. 1990. "Biochemical And Trichological Characterization Of Diffuse Alopecia In Women." British Journal of Dermatology. 123:187-197

Rushton, D. Hugh, PhD. 1993. "Management Of Hair Loss In Women." Dermatologic Clinics. January 11:1:47-53.

Rushton, D.H., PhD. 2002. "Nutritional Factors And Hair Loss." Clinical and Experimental Dermatology. 27:396-404.

S & G Research/Hair Loss Research Laboratories. 1999. "Hair Growth Cycle, The Genetic Link, Why You Lose Your Hair, Solutions To Thinning Hair." Internet site: www.info@hairloss-sq.com.

Sawaya, Marty E., MD, PhD, and Shapiro, Jerry, MD, FRCPC. 2000. "Androgenetic Alopecia: New Approved And Unapproved Treatments." Dermatologic Clinics. January 18:1:43-63.

Sawaya, Marty, MD. 2000. "WHS 1999-Hormones & Hair." Internet site: www.regrowth.com/documents.cfm?id=10033.

Sawaya, Marty, MD, PhD. 1998. "Novel Agents For The Treatment Of Alopecia." Seminars In Cutaneous Medicine and Surgery. December 17:4:276-283.

Schmidt, Jolanta B. 1994. "Hormonal Basis Of Male And Female Androgenic Alopecia: Clinical Relevance." Skin Pharmacol. 7:61-66.

Segell, Michael. 1994. "The Bald Truth About Hair." Esquire. May 111-117.

Shapiro, Jerry, MD, FRCPC and Madani, Shabnam, MD. 1999. "Alopecia Areata: Diagnosis And Management." International Journal of Dermatology. 38 (Supp6Dermatology Nursing. April 4:2:93-99.

Stroud, James D., MD. 1987. "Diagnosis And Management Of The Hair Loss Patient." CUTIS. September 40:272-276.

Sullivan, John R., MB, and Kossard, Steven, FACD. 1998. "Acquired Scalp Alopecia. Part I: A Review." Australian Journal of Dermatology. 39:207-221.

Swee, Warren, MPH, et al. 2000. "A Nationwide Outbreak Of Alopecia Associated With The Use Of A Hair-Relaxing Formulation." Arch Dermatology. September 136:1104-1108.

Swinehart, James M., MD, and Griffin, Edmond I., MD. 1991. "Slit Grafting: The Use Of Serrated Island Grafts In Male And Female-Pattern Alopecia." Journal of Dermatologic Surgery and Oncology. 17:243-253.

Tosti, A., MD, Camacho-Martinez, F., MD, and Dawber, R., MD. 1999. "Management Of Androgenetic Alopecia." Journal of the European Academy of Dermatology and Venereology. December 12:205-214.

Tosti, Antonella, MD and Piraccini, Bianca M., MD. 1999. "Androgenetic Alopecia." International Journal of Dermatology. 38 (Suppl. 1): 1-7.

Tran, Diana. MBBS, Sinclair, Rodney, D., MD. 1999. "Understanding And Managing Common Baldness." Australian Family Physician. March 28:3:248-253.

Unger, Walter, MD and Shapiro, Ron, MD (Editors). 2004. Hair Transplantation: Fourth Edition. Rose, Paul, MD, Leavitt, Matt L., DO, and Cartwright, Mont J., MD. "Anatomy Of The Scalp." New York: Marcel Dekker. 33-37.

Unger, Walter, MD and Shapiro, Ron, MD (Editors). 2004. Hair Transplantation: Fourth Edition. Mayer, Melvin L., MD. "Hair Restoration In Black Patients." New York: Marcel Dekker. 595-602.

Uno, Hideo, MD. 1997. "The Histopathology Of Hair Loss." Internet site: www.regrowth.com/documents.cfm?id=10153.

Upjohn. 1993. The Patient. "Hair-Loss Patient." Seminar for Doctors. Chapter IX:3-10

Upjohn. 1990 "Medical Management Of Female Androgenetic Alopecia." Proceedings from the Roundtable Discussion. Chicago, IL. November 15-17

Van Der Donk, J., Hunfeld, J. A. M., Passchier, J., Knegt-Junk, K. J., Nieboer, C. 1994. "Quality Of Life And Maladjustment Associated With Hair Loss In Women With Alopecia Androgenetica." Soc. Sci. Med. 38:1:159-163.

Van Der Donk, J., Passchier, J., Knegt-Junk, C., Van Der Wegen-Keijser, M.H., Nieboer, C., Stolz, E., and Verhage, F. 1991. "Psychological Characteristics Of Women With Androgenetic Alopecia: A Controlled Study." British Journal of Dermatology. 125:248-252.

Venning, V.A., MRCP, and Dawber, RPR, MA, FRCP. 1988. "Patterned Androgenic Alopecia In Women." Journal of The American Academy of Dermatology. May 18:5 (Part 1): 1073-1077.

Walker, Barbara G. 1996. The Woman's Encyclopedia of Myths and Secrets. Edison, NJ: Castle Books. 366-371.

Whiting, David A., MD. 1998. "Male Pattern Hair Loss: Current Understanding." International Journal of Dermatology. 37:561-566.

Whiting, David A, MD. 2000. "The Diagnosis Of Alopecia." Internet site: www.diagnosisaa.htmlatnpntserver.meg.edu.

Wilborn, Wesley S., MD. "Disorders Of Hair Growth In African Americans." New York: McGraw-Hill. Chapter 17. 389-407.

Wood, Alastair J. J., MD (Editor). 1999. Price, Vera, H., MD. "Treatment Of Hair Loss." New England Journal of Medicine. September 23: 13:964-973.

York, Janine, Nicholson, Thomas, and Minors, Patricia. 1998. "Stressful Life Events And Loss Of Hair Among Adult Women, A Case-Control Study." Psychological Reports. 82:1044-1046.

RESOURCES AND SUPPORT GROUPS FOR WOMEN WITH HAIR LOSS

Today more than ever before, we realize the impact that hair loss is making on millions of women's lives and the importance of the topic. Below is a list of medical associations and support groups that can provide reliable, up-to-date information for females.

American Academy of Cosmetic Surgery (AACS)
737 N. Michigan Ave.
Suite 820
Chicago, IL 60611
312-981-6760
www.cosmeticsurgery.org

American Academy of Dermatology
P.O. Box 4014
Schaumburg, IL 60168-4014
847-330-0230 or 1-888-462-3376
www.aad.org

American Cancer Society

1599 Cliff Valley Way
Atlanta, GA 30329
1-800-ACS-2345
www.cancer.org

American Hair Loss Council

Susan Kettering- Executive Director
125 Seventh Street, Suite 625
Pittsburgh, PA 15222
412-765-3666
www.ahlc.org

American Society for Dermatologic Surgery

5550 Meadowbrook Dr. • Suite 120
Rolling Meadows, IL 60008
847-956-0900
1-800-441-2737
www.asds-net.org

International Society of Hair Restoration Surgery (ISHRS)

13 South 2nd Street
Geneva, IL 60134 USA
1-800-444-2737 or 630-262-5399
www.ishrs.org

Locks of Love

2925 10th Avenue North
Suite 102
Lake Worth, FL 33461
561-963-1677
1-888-896-1588
www.locksoflove.org

NAAF- National Alopecia Areata Foundation

P.O. Box 150760
San Rafael, CA 94915
415-472-3780
www.alopeciaareata.com

The Phoenix Society for Burn Survivors
2153 Wealthy St., SE, Suite 215
E. Grand Rapids, MI 49506
1-800-888-2876
www.phoenix-society.org

Rogaine for Women
1-800-ROGAINE (1-800-764-2463)
www.womensrogaine.com

Trichotillomania Learning Center
303 Potrero #51
Santa Cruz, CA 95060
831-457-1004
www.trich.org

Wigs for Kids
21330 Center Ridge Road
Rocky Ridge, OH 44116
440-333-4433
www.wigsforkids.org

Dr. Matt Leavitt's Organizations:

Medical Hair Restoration
More than 40 locations nationwide
1-800-444-0055
www.medicalhairrestoration.com

Advanced Dermatology & Cosmetic Surgery
More than 19 locations throughout Florida
1-888-540-9660
www.advancedderm.com

Women and Hair Loss: A Physician's Perspective
www.womenandhairloss.com

NAMES FOR HAIR STYLES

Beehive…Wedge…Dreadlocks…BoxTop…FrenchTwist…Braided…Plaited…Ponytail…

Buzz…Mohawk…Afro…Pigtail…Caesar…Pixie…Flip…Pompadour…French

Bob…Pudding Head…Crew Cut…Burr…Sidewinder…The Mullet…East- to-

West…Ringlets…Rat Tail…Surfer Cut…Bangs…Locks…Page Boy…Spiked…Brush

Top…High and Tight…Shafts…Butch…Coiffure…Punk…Jordan

Look…Shag…Kojak Look…Big Hair…Pixie Cut…Step Cut…Brush Cut…Dolly

Parton Look…Blow Out…Tape Up…Fades…Farrah Fawcett Style…Feather

Cut…French Cut…French Braid…Bun…Duck Tail…Dorothy Hamill Cut…Flat

Top…Bowl Cut…Up-Do…Boy Cut…Crimp…Helmet Head…Swinging Bob…Spiral

Curls…Popcorn Curls…Pineapple Waves…Fishbone Braid…Mall Hair…Marilyn

Monroe…Wave Nouveaux…Cornrows…Zig Zag…Fingerwaves…Crochet Braids…Bi-

Level…Gibson Girl…Bo Derek…Stacked Bob…Italian Boy-Cut…Shingle…Asymmetrical

Cut…Bubble Flip…Geometric Cut…Zulu Knots…Spiked…Weaves…Basketball

Net…Water Fall…Jennifer Aniston…Sassy Bob…Mushroom…Afro

Puffs…Fade…Princess Di Cut…Gypsy Shag…Faith Hill Cut…Love Knots…The

Box…Bed Head Look…Rat's Nest…Basket Weave…Princess Knots…Comb Over…That-

Girl Flip…Meg Ryan Look…Cleopatra Cut…Skater Style…The Soccer Mom…Spider

Web…Bouffant…Pom Poms…Shirley Temple…Chignon…Bologna Curls…Marcel

Weave…Sheep Dog…Veronica Lake…Venus' Hair…Page Boy…Piece Cut …

Chopped…Kinky…Wind Blown…Rope Braid…Ami-ties…Sugar Ray Cut…Twisties…

♀   ♂

The Book of
Latin American Cooking

The Book
of
Latin
American
Cooking

Elisabeth Lambert Ortiz

Vintage Books
A Division of Random House • New York

Some of the recipes in this book first appeared in *House & Garden* magazine, copyright
© 1969 by The Condé Nast Publications, Inc., and in *Gourmet* magazine in July, September, and October 1969, September 1971, December 1973, January and December
1974, October 1975, and December 1977.

Library of Congress Cataloging in Publication Data

Ortiz, Elisabeth Lambert.
  The book of Latin American cooking.

  Includes index.
  1. Cookery, Latin American.   I. Title.
[TX716.A1077 1980]   641.598   80-11250
ISBN 0-394-74514-0

Manufactured in the United States of America
6789

For my husband and colleague, César Ortiz-Tinoco,
whose knowledge and enthusiasm were of
inestimable help in writing this book,
and for Judith Jones, most perceptive and helpful of editors

Contents

Acknowledgments

It is hard to know where to begin with thanks. Surely no one has had friends more generous with their time, their knowledge, and their kitchens than I have had. I would like to thank Mr. and Mrs. José Fernández de Córdoba, Mr. and Mrs. Belisario Fernández de Córdoba, Mr. and Mrs. Arturo Montesinos, Mr. and Mrs. Galo Plaza, Col. and Mrs. Edmundo García Vivanco, Mr. and Mrs. Vincente Umaña Méndez, Margarita Pacini, Cecilia Blanco de Mendoza, Mr. and Mrs. Guillermo Power, Jorge Manchego, Mr. and Mrs. Genaro Carnero Checa, Noreen Maxwell, Dr. and Mrs. Alberto Gormaz, Alejandro Flores Zorilla, Mr. and Mrs. Salvador Ferret, Dr. Raúl Nass, Mr. and Mrs. Carlos August León, Simón Reyes Marcano, Raymond Joseph Fowkes, Lolita de Lleras Codazzi, Phyllis Bird, Emma Vásquez, Mirtha Stengel, Mr. and Mrs. Gilberto Rizzo, Mr. and Mrs. Raúl Trejos, María J. Troconis, Jeanne Lesem, José Wilson, Copeland Marks, Lua de Burt, Josefina Velilla de Aquino, María Teresa Casanueva, Mr. and Mrs. Abél Quezada, Mr. and Mrs. Humberto Ortiz Reyes, Humberto Ortiz Azoños, Mr. and Mrs. Héctor Fernández, Mr. and Mrs. Efraín Huerta, Dr. and Mrs. Antonio Delgado, Raquel Braune, Victor Simón Bovier, Alwyne Wheeler, James A. Beard, Mr. and Mrs. Victorino A. Althaparro, Dr. Raúl

Noriega, Dr. and Mrs. Andrés Iduarte, Elizabeth Borton de Treviño, Mr. and Mrs. Julio César Anzueto, Lucy de Arenales, Mr. and Mrs. Jason Vourvoulias, Mr. and Mrs. Mario Montero, Ruth Kariv, Mr. and Mrs. Antonio Carbajal, Mr. and Mrs. Eugenio Soler Alonso, Ambassador and Mrs. Mario Alvírez.

I am deeply indebted to Dr. David R. Harris of London University and Dr. Wolfgang Haberland of Munich for their scientific findings on the origins of agriculture in Latin America and for their advice and encouragement, and to Walter Sullivan, who first brought this new work to my attention. My thanks to my friend and colleague the late Dr. Alex D. Hawkes for helping me with botanical problems relating to tropical plants and herbs. I am immensely grateful to Alan Eaton Davidson CMG, that great authority on fish and shellfish and writer of cookbooks on the subject, and to Alwynne Wheeler of the British Museum of Natural History, who both helped me on the identification of the chilean fish *congrio*.

I would have been lost without the work done by Dr. Jorge Hardoy, of Argentina, and Dr. Leopoldo Castedo, of Brazil, who make brilliantly clear the urban nature of the great civilizations of pre-Columbian Latin America. I owe them a great debt.

I would also like to thank Charles B. Heiser, Jr., Distinguished Professor of Botany, Indiana University, Bloomington, Indiana, for telling me about new work being done on plant origins, and for letting me know that it was the Mexican green tomato (Physalis ixocarpa) that is known from 700 A.D. since, archaeologically, the ordinary red tomato has not yet been found.

My thanks also to Sally Berkeley at Knopf for the marvelous job she did in helping to find illustrative material for this book and to Karolina Harris, the designer, for her imaginative selection and placement of the illustrations.

Elisabeth Lambert Ortiz,
New York

Introduction

    I first became interested in Latin American food when I was at school for some time in Jamaica. It was the flavor of hot peppers that beguiled me, especially one that Jamaicans call a Scotch bonnet — small, lantern-shaped, fiery, and flavorful. I also had Cuban and Brazilian friends who gave me a tantalizing glimpse into this enormous cuisine that stretches from the Rio Bravo (Rio Grande) to the Antarctic. It wasn't until shortly after I was married, twenty odd years ago, and my husband was transferred from headquarters in New York to another United Nations assignment in Mexico, that I was able to pursue my research into flavors I have never been able to forget. So it was chance that I started with Mexico, perhaps the most complex and unique cooking of the whole region. Even now, when I have traveled to all the world's continents, Mexican food is still the most exotic of all.

    Mexican cooking still rests firmly on its Aztec, and to a lesser extent Mayan, origins, interwoven with the cooking of Spain. But Spain itself was for almost eight hundred years dominated by the Arab empire, so its food has a strong Middle Eastern influence. All through my investigation of Mexican cooking I kept stumbling into the Middle East. Later on I went to the Middle East, Spain, and Portugal to sort out the influences. So many strands are woven into this complicated tapestry that I still find it hard to unravel them completely.

But no matter the sources, the reward is in the eating. From the start I was enchanted by the dishes of the corn kitchen, the most purely Mexican aspect of the food. My palate was utterly bewitched by simple snacks like *quesadillas de flor de calabaza* where an unbaked tortilla is stuffed with a savory mixture of cooked squash blossoms, folded over, and fried, or more rarely, baked. I had mouth-watering deep-green peppers stuffed with mashed beans, batter-coated, and fried; or even more exotic, stuffed with meat and masked with a fresh cheese and walnut sauce and garnished with pomegranate seeds. I had *huachinango a la Veracruzana*, beautiful red snapper with mildly hot *jalapeño* peppers in a tomato sauce very lightly perfumed with cloves and cinnamon. And *Mole Poblano de Guajolote*, that extraordinary mixture of different types of dried peppers, nuts, herbs, spices, and a little bitter chocolate made into a sauce for turkey and origi- nally a favorite dish at Moctezuma's court. It was wholly unfamiliar, wholly delicious.

I found wonderful descriptions of the markets of pre-Conquest Mexico in the monumental work of a Spanish priest, Fray Bernardino de Sahagún, who was there before the Conquest was consolidated. A lively writer, he brought the markets to life, even describing how the local prostitutes lounged about, clicking their chewing gum. I hadn't realized that *chicle* (chewing gum) from the *zapote* tree was also a Mexican gift to the world, and that this same tree bears the pleasant *chico zapote* (sapodilla) fruit. Father Sahagún characterized and identified all the various kinds of tortil- las on sale, and clearly he was not averse to sampling some of the cooked foods since he described a shrimp stew and other dishes with such relish one can almost taste them. I needed no more urging — I went off to the markets, realizing they were still the best places in which to learn.

Because peppers, along with corn and beans, play such a vital role in the Mexican cuisine, and because my palate was still haunted by the flavor of the hot Jamaican peppers of my school days, I began to research this fascinating fruit. Botanically it is *Capsicum annuum* or *Capsicum frutes- cens* of the *Solanaceae* family, to which potatoes, tomatoes, and eggplant also belong. There has never been an accurate count of peppers, which were first cultivated as far back as 7000 B.C. Because they are self or insect pollinated and cross-fertilize easily, and since they have been doing this for thousands of years, there are now a great many different kinds. Some bota- nists put the number as low as sixty, while others can name over a hundred. Long before Columbus they had spread all over the Caribbean, as well as Central and South America. And since Columbus they have sprung up all over the world and have become so thoroughly naturalized that their national origin has been forgotten. They are sweet, pungent, or hot. They are first green, then change to yellow or red as they ripen — and some of them have all three colors in their cycle. They range from ¼ to 7 inches in length. They are used fresh or dried. Some are wrinkled; some are smooth; and quite apart from sweetness, pungency, or heat, they have flavor.

My first visit was to the large San Juan market. It was a blaze of color. There were enormous piles of ripe crimson tomatoes; and heaps of yellow squash blossoms, soft green zucchini, ripe red bell peppers and pimientos, bright green bell peppers and darker green *poblanos*; stalls selling the dried, wrinkled red peppers — *ancho, mulato,* and *pasilla* — brick red *chipotle* and *morita,* smooth red *guajillos,* and the little peppers, *cascabel* and *pequin.* There were more kinds than I could possibly take in at a single visit.

The sellers were mostly women with their dark hair in plaits, dressed in full cotton skirts and snowy white blouses with the traditional *rebozo* (stole) around their shoulders. Some, sitting on the ground, had before them only tiny piles of herbs or spices, or a pyramid of purple-skinned avocados. Others, often with husbands and children, had proper stalls laden with oranges; grapefruit; the paddles of the *nopal* (prickly pear) cactus, *nopalitos;* or its fruit, *tuna* — globes of green or purplish red. They called to me as I passed: *"Qué va a llevar, marchanta?"* ("What are you going to buy, customer?") and when I explained that I wanted to learn about Mexican food, they were generous with their help. I found the pepper I had remembered from my school days. It came from Yucatán and was called, paradoxically, *habanero* (pepper from Havana), a migrant returned. Later I found it all over the Caribbean, in Bahia in Brazil, and in Guatemala where it is called *caballero,* gentleman pepper — one clearly to be reckoned with.

I bought peppers of all kinds, took them home, photographed them, learned their names, and cooked them. I have listed them in the ingredients section — not all, of course, only the ones I think are useful to North American cooks.

That first day I asked one of the market women how to make *quesadillas de flor de calabaza* (squash blossom turnovers), and she was delighted. She shouted to a tortilla seller to come over, and gradually gathered all the ingredients needed, then showed me how to put them together, folding the squash-blossom mixture in a tortilla and then frying it. She was careful to explain that she was using an already baked tortilla for convenience. Whereupon she sent me off to a stall to buy a fresh lump of tortilla dough, which is made from the special cooked and ground corn that is sold dried as *masa harina* (literally "dough flour," in markets such as this one, it is already mixed with water). That was a lovely day and I became a regular visitor to markets whether in La Merced, San Juan; or Medellín in Mexico City; in Guadalajara, Querétaro; in Mérida, Yucatán; or in Cuernavaca. Wherever I went I found wonderfully knowledgeable teachers, good friends who introduced me with great generosity and enthusiasm to all manner of new foods.

Tortillas are an essential accompaniment to Mexican food. I learned easily to make them from packaged *masa harina,* using a tortilla press, which is a very splendid colonial invention. Mexican cooks can pat a tortilla with their hands into a thin pancake, then slap it on to a *comal* (griddle) to bake. But I found I could make only rather thick, clumsy ones this way, so I tried using a cast-iron tortilla press (the original presses were made of wood). It works very well and can be bought, as can *masa harina,* from specialty stores selling Mexican foods.

Beans are also an integral part of Mexican food, whether served in bowls as a separate course — not dry, rather soupy — or mashed and fried in lard to make *Frijoles Refritos,* a rich-tasting bean paste, used in all sorts of delectable ways.

A key ingredient is the tomato, and I can't imagine Mexican cooking without it, whether it is the familiar red or yellow tomato of everyday use, or the little Mexican green tomato (*Physalis ixocarpa*) — a small pale-green or yellow tomato covered with a papery husk, whose flavor develops only as it is cooked, and which is usually available to us only canned, except in parts of the Southwest. Both types of tomato are used in cooked and fresh sauces, and in *Guacamole,* the avocado salad cum sauce that is another essential on the Mexican table.

Mexico, and indeed all of Latin America, adopted rice enthusiastically and it goes excellently with the *mollis* (Mexican stews) and most other dishes. Cooks all over the continent pride themselves on their rice. No matter what method they use to cook it, each grain is tender and separate.

During the years I lived in Mexico I traveled all over the country, from the northern cattle ranges where my husband's family comes from to Mayan Yucatán, from the Caribbean to the Pacific, in enthusiastic pursuit of recipes from family, friends, strangers, markets, and restaurants, captivated as I was by the exuberance of this wonderfully varied food. I worked happily in my kitchen to faithfully reproduce the dishes I found so seductive, and back in New York I put my discoveries into a cookbook. Then chance again, or should I say good fortune, took me to Central America, beginning with Guatemala — once the heart of the Mayan empire — and I realized there was a whole continent of intriguing new cookery, linked with Mexican food, still to discover.

My interest was stimulated by recent discoveries of food origins that showed that agriculture had been born simultaneously in the Middle East and in the Valley of Mexico about 7000 B.C. In the Middle East animals such as sheep, goats, pigs, and cattle were domesticated, and barley, wheat, peas, and lentils cultivated. Gradually this produce spread all over Europe and Asia. Rice was introduced from Asia about 3500 B.C. Peanuts, Guinea yams, and millet came from Africa some centuries later. At the same time in Mexico, that other cradle of agriculture, peppers, squash, and avocados were the first cultivated food plants. A couple of thousand years later corn and the common bean followed, then lima beans, and later still, in 700 A.D., the tomato. These foods gradually spread all over the Americas. Potatoes and sweet potatoes, cultivated in the Andean highlands by the predecessors of the Incas about 2500 B.C., spread through the continent, and so did manioc (cassava) and peanuts from Brazil. Peanuts, as a matter of fact, have a dual origin, as they were independently cultivated both in Brazil and West Africa by 1500 B.C. and though of different genera behave the same in the cookpot. All this cultivation was, of course, an ongoing process, with more and more fruits, vegetables, and crops being developed, so that by the time Columbus arrived, he found not only a whole new world, but a whole new world of food. These discoveries gave me an insight into the nature of the cuisine, for very soon after the Conquest there was a blending of cooking strains that evolved into the rich and varied cookery of Latin America today.

I knew it would take me a long time to travel the huge continent, to visit markets, to talk to cooks, to collect recipes, to learn about the food, and to cook it back home in my own kitchen. I also knew I would have a magnificent time doing so and I set off with enthusiasm, this book beginning to take tentative shape in my mind.

I found visiting the archaeological sites of the old Mayan empire a good way to trace the boundaries of the ancient cuisine. The Mayan empire began in Guatemala, spread to nearby Honduras, and into the states of Yucatán, Chiapas, and Campeche and the territory of Quintana Roo in Mexico. In this area today the cooking is Mayan, not Aztec Mexican. Since the civilization was already in decline at the time of the Conquest, not a great deal has survived. I wish more had, as it is subtle and delicate, except when it comes to fresh hot pepper sauce, which is really fiery. I love to cook with ground annatto seeds, which have a flowery fragrance when used whole, quite unlike the flavor of the colored oil or lard made from just the reddish-orange pulp surrounding the seeds. The cooking of the rest of Central America — Belize, El Salvador, Nicaragua, Costa Rica, and Panama, which together with Guatemala and Honduras make a land bridge between North and South America — is a mixture of Mayan, Aztec Mexican, Colombian, and Spanish cuisines, with cosmopolitan influences from recent times. There is also a Caribbean influence, mostly from island people coming to work in the banana plantations.

The Caribbean seemed my next logical step, and I went off island-hopping and again found generous-hearted cooks who welcomed me with my notebook into their kitchens and shared their cooking secrets with me. Of that great arc of islands that stretches from Florida in the north to the coast of Venezuela in the south, and which Columbus discovered in 1492, only Cuba, the Dominican Republic, and Puerto Rico are part of Latin America. When Columbus arrived, first at Hispaniola (now the Dominican Republic and Haiti), the islands were inhabited by warlike Caribs and gentle Arawaks, both from South America. The Arawaks were good farmers and soon cultivated corn and peppers from Mexico, and sweet potatoes, yams, and manioc (cassava) which they must have brought with them. Their influence on the food of the islands persists in the wide use of root vegetables, hot peppers, allspice, and corn. African settlers brought okra and their own yams, but fundamentally the cooking of the Spanish-speaking islands is that of Spain — using a mixture of indigenous and introduced foods. It is a surprisingly rich and varied kitchen, particularly in the Dominican Republic where a *cocido* (stew) of chicken, beef, ham, and sausages, cooked with an assemblage of vegetables, is a veritable feast.

I could now see the pattern that the common heritage of Spain and Portugal and an early shared agriculture wove into the tapestry that makes Latin American food into a richly diverse unity. And so I set off on a series of journeys to South America, lucky to have friends all over the continent to help me. I began with the Andean countries — Venezuela, Colombia, Ecuador, Peru, Bolivia, and Chile — visiting them one by one.

The 4,000-mile mountain chain of the Andes, which runs along the Pacific coast of South America from Venezuela to the tip of Chile, dominates the continent. The foothills begin at the coast, which is lushly subtropical in the north and desert from Peru on south. The mountains rise range upon range interspersed with high plateaus and cut by wild mountain rivers, until they descend into the valley of the Amazon. It is awe-inspiring country, and traveling in it I felt as if I were in a sea of mountains. Before air travel became commonplace, journeys were difficult so that cuisines developed independently of each other. It was just as hard for people and goods to get from the coast to the highlands as from country to country, so there is a tropical and a temperate cuisine as well. Modern roads and transportation have changed this, blurring the distinctions.

Venezuela's cuisine is small, as there was no great indigenous Indian civilization. The country was discovered in 1498 by Columbus when he found the mouths of the Orinoco River. Spanish settlement began in 1520.

The basis of the cookery is colonial more than anything else with borrowings and adaptations from other Latin American countries. Black beans are a great favorite and Venezuelans call their mashed black beans *caviar criollo*, native caviar, surely the ultimate culinary compliment. The national dish is as eclectic as the rest of the cooking. It is based on a sixteenth-century Spanish recipe, *Ropa Vieja* (Old Clothes), made from shredded flank steak in a rich tomato sauce — very good, despite its name — and is served with fried eggs, black beans, rice, and fried plantains. There is also a good avocado sauce, *Guasacaca*, derived from Mexico's *Guacamole*, and a fine fish dish, *Corbullón Mantuano* (Striped Bass in Sweet Pepper Sauce), that echoes Mexico's famous *Pescado a la Veracruzana* (Fish, Veracruz Style). The local corn bread is the *arepa*, made in a similar way to Mexico's tortillas but with a different type of corn. *Arepas* are much thicker, more like buns than pancakes, and the corn flavor is much less pronounced than in tortillas. German settlers of the last century are responsible for the very good cheeses of Venzuela and the excellent beer, for that matter. There is a delicious runny fresh cream cheese that turns an *arepa* into a feast when the corn bread is served hot, then pulled apart and stuffed with the cheese.

Colombia has a very grand geography with two seacoasts — one on the Pacific, one on the Caribbean — which gives the country a large choice of fish and shellfish. Three great mountain ranges, from six thousand to nineteen thousand feet, rise from the coast like the steps of a giant staircase, forming a series of plateaus at different heights so that the country has every type of climate and produces every kind of food. Wandering around the markets in the capital, Bogotá, I found piles of coconuts, bananas, plantains, pineapples, cherimoyas, papayas, sugarcane, avocados, guavas, and tropical root vegetables like yams, taros, sweet potatoes, cassava roots, and *arracacha* sharing space with peaches, pears, apricots, apples, grapes, and plums.

The conquering Spanish intermarried with the dominant Indians, the Chibchas, great gold workers who had a highly advanced civilization. The modern cuisine is very varied, sophisticated, and original. The coastal kitchen makes imaginative use of coconut milk — with rice, fish, meats, and poultry. I particularly like *Arroz con Coco y Pasas* (Rice with Coconut and Raisins) and its twin dish *Arroz con Coco Frito y Pasas* (Rice with Fried Coconut and Raisins): the rice is dry and quite firm, *bien graneado*, which is the equivalent of *al dente* in pasta. I also like the subtle flavor of *Sábalo Guisado con Coco* (Shad Fillets in Coconut Milk), easy to make at home in the spring when shad is plentiful. The highlands produce wonderful stews, perhaps the most famous of which is *Ajiaco de Pollo Bogotano* (Bogotá Chicken Stew). There is the even grander *Sancocho Especial* (Special Boiled Dinner) with a great selection of meats and vegetables, some from the tropics. It is a splendid dish for a family gathering or a party. As in all of Latin America, fresh coriander is used a great deal and there is always a fresh hot pepper sauce on the table to be taken at one's discretion.

My next trip was to Ecuador. The highland region was part of the Incan empire. The tropical lowlands were not conquered until the arrival of the Spanish. Quito, the capital, at nearly ten thousand feet lies within an extinct volcano, Pichincha, which rises to fifteen thousand feet. Eight volcanoes — among them the fabled Chimborazo, over twenty thousand feet, and Cotopaxi, over nineteen thousand feet — can be seen on clear days from Quito. The equator is only fifteen miles away, giving the highlands a gentle climate. There is a great contrast between tropical sea level cuisine and highland cookery, especially as one was Incan, the other not.

On the wall of the cathedral in the main plaza of Quito is a plaque that says that the glory of Ecuador is that it discovered the Amazon River down which Francisco de Orellana floated in a homemade boat, arriving at the source in 1541. I think it could also be claimed that the glory of the Ecuadorian kitchen is its *seviches* (fish "cooked" in lime or lemon juice). They are quite different from other countries' *seviches* mostly because of the use of Seville (bitter) orange juice in a sauce of onion, garlic, and oil. I tasted *seviches* made from bass, shrimp, lobster, and an interesting black conch. They are best accompanied by chilled beer. In Latin America there is never any problem finding beer of excellent quality with a nice bite to it, sharp on the tongue, refreshingly dry.

Potatoes play a large role in Ecuadorian highland cooking. A favorite dish is *Locro*, a thick potato and cheese soup that is sometimes served with avocado slices. I find it makes a splendid light lunch or supper if followed by a dessert or fruit. With Ecuadorian friends at midday dinner, still the main meal in most of Latin America, I had it as a course that followed a corn soufflé and preceded the meat. It was made with a little sweet paprika, but the coastal version uses annatto (achiote), which has a more pronounced flavor. Another favorite potato dish is *Llapingachos*, fried potato and cheese patties that are served with various accompaniments either as a first or as a main course according to what goes with them. They make an admirable addition to broiled or grilled meat, fish, or poultry. On the coast they are usually fried in annatto lard or oil. Coastal rice is also usually cooked with annatto, which yellows it.

Vegetables are highly esteemed in Ecuador and are served in that gentle climate at room temperature, several at a time. Since water at ten thousand feet boils at a much lower temperature than at sea level, vegetables are always crisply tender without the cook making a great effort. I think of this as a cuisine that builds bridges between the exotic and the known, using mustard in imaginative ways and contrasting texture and flavor. I was once served hot roast pork, cut into cubes and arranged in a circle on a serving dish, the center filled with slightly chilled, chopped ripe tomatoes. Delicious. There is, as everywhere, a hot sauce, *Salsa de Aji*, to be taken or not as one pleases, this one made from fresh hot red or green peppers simply ground with salt and mixed with a little chopped onion.

Of all the Andean countries the cuisine of Peru is the most exciting, though in creating it the brilliant agriculturists of the region had a most formidable geography to contend with. The narrow coastal plain is desert except where rivers create a brief oasis. The mountains rise abruptly, completely barren, but they create fertile valleys with great rivers running through them, and wide plateaus with temperate farm- and pastureland, though already as high as eleven thousand feet. Higher still, at fourteen thousand feet, are only barren, windswept uplands.

It was in the temperate highlands, the steep mountainsides terraced to provide more land for crops, that the ancient people of the region developed the sweet potato and over a hundred varieties of the potato some time around 2500 B.C. They freeze-dried potatoes, using the cold of the Andean highlands to freeze the vegetables overnight, thawing them in the morning sun and squeezing out the moisture. The resulting rock-hard potatoes were called *chuño* and kept indefinitely. The only large domestic animals were the cameloids — the llama and the alpaca — used by the Incas for their wool, as pack animals, and for meat, and though I can't prove it, their cooking suggests they made a fresh cheese from their milk.

The Incan empire had an extensive highway system to which only the Roman is comparable, linking its more than thirty towns and cities. Farmers in this highly organized, highly urban society sent their produce to market in the town or city nearest them. A sophisticated cuisine developed with a characteristic use of hot peppers, *aji*. Peruvians like their food *picante* and are lavish in their use of peppers, of which they have a considerable variety, just about all of them hot. They are a wonderful sight in the markets, enormous piles of *rocotos* and *mirasols*, great heaps of sun yellow, flaming orange, or red as well as green peppers in various sizes, but it is the yellow ones that catch the eye. I like to speculate about this use of yellow in the food of countries that were sun worshipers before the Conquest brought Christianity. I don't think it can be an accident that Peru uses the herb *palillo*, ground to a sunshine-yellow powder, to color and flavor food. And there are the yellow potatoes — true potatoes, not sweet potatoes — which have yellow flesh, as well as yellow sweet potatoes, and plantains, yellow when ripe. The yellows continue in the squash family from the pale yellow of the huge *zapallo* to the deep yellow of other types, and in fresh corn. There are potato dishes that are a symphony of yellow and white, perhaps honoring the sun god and the moon goddess. In any case, they are lovely food in a cuisine full of marvelous dishes.

Little is known of the cooking of the Bolivian highlands, though this region was once the site of impressive civilizations. From the cook's point of view the altitude is rather daunting, for Bolivia tends to be high, higher, and highest. Lake Titicaca, which Bolivia shares with Peru, lies at 12,500 feet. Legend has it that an island in the lake is the legendary home of the Incas. Quite nearby are the ruins of Tiahuanaco, a pre-Incan city. After the Conquest Bolivia became part of Peru and was known as *El Alto Peru*, highland Peru. With independence the name was changed to Bolivia to honor the liberator, Simón Bolívar. Like the Peruvians, the Bolivians like their food hot and are lavish in their use of hot peppers. Their most popular dishes are stews and hearty soups. However, my favorite is a very good chicken pie with a corn topping, *Pastel de Choclo con Relleno de Pollo*, which I recommend with enthusiasm.

The geography of Chile poses very different problems. The northern third of this stringbean of a country, twenty-six hundred miles long and sandwiched between the Pacific Ocean and the Andes, is unrelieved desert, the most total desert on earth. Flying over it, the shadows are so intensely dark they look like pools of water, a tantalizing illusion. It is strangely, movingly beautiful. The southern third is mountainous and storm-swept, with more rain than it needs, but the middle third is lovely, temperate, and fertile, with green valleys full of vineyards that produce very fine wines, splendid vegetables and fruits, among them notable strawberries. The southern part of this felicitous third is heavily forested with a series of lakes, a landscape of rare loveliness. And, of course, the snowcapped Andes make a permanently dramatic backdrop.

The cold Humboldt Current gives Chile the most unusual seafood in the world. I can only think of the giant sea urchins, *erizos*; giant abalone, *locos*, tender as chicken when properly beaten; of *picoroccos*, strange, beaked shellfish that taste like crabs; giant crabs; mussels; clams; shrimp; langostines; oysters; and *congrio*, a splendid fish unique to these waters. Only in Chile can one enjoy these gifts of the cold current. All the same I found many interesting dishes that are not dependent on special ingredients — dishes like *Congrio en Fuente de Barro* (Fish with Tomatoes and Onions), *Pollo Escabechado* (Pickled Chicken), and *Porotos Granados* (Cranberry Beans with Corn and Squash).

There was no great Indian civilization in what is now Argentina and Uruguay. Though they are today separate countries, before independence from Spain they were both part of the viceroyalty of the River Plate. Spanish cooking methods using indigenous and introduced ingredients produced the local cuisine, which has been somewhat modified by newer arrivals — Italian influence being predominant. Like Chile, Argentina produces good wine, and its beef ranks with the best in the world. *Matambre*, which translates literally into kill hunger, and into kitchen parlance as stuffed rolled flank steak, is an example of what Argentine cooks can do with a comparatively humble cut of beef. And the *Empanadas*, the pastry turnovers, variously stuffed, are the best I've ever had. There are some unusual and good meat stews with fruit, such as *Carbonada Criolla* (Beef Stew, Argentine Style) with peaches and *Carbonada en Zapallo* (Veal Stew in Baked Pumpkin), which includes pears and peaches and finishes cooking in a large, hollowed-out squash. It is a delicious combination.

Paraguay is a small landlocked country where Guaraní, the language of the Indians of the region, is co-equal with Spanish as an official language. The cooking is Spanish and Guaraní, with some international food, mostly French and Italian. My favorite Paraguayan dish is the magnificently named *So'O-Yosopy* (the last syllable is pronounced with an explosive PEH), that translates into Spanish as *sopa de carne* (beef soup). I know of nothing more restorative when one is worn-out. I'm almost as fond of *Sopa Paraguaya,* which is not a soup at all but a rich cheese and cornmeal bread that is traditionally served with steak; but as far as I am concerned, it is good by itself and goes with almost everything. Paraguay is also the home of *Mate* tea, a very ancient Indian drink that is pleasantly stimulating, since it has a good deal of caffeine.

Of all the cuisines in South America, the Brazilian is the most exuberant and varied. The country, taking up nearly half the continent of South America, is enormous, stretching from the tropics in the north to the temperate south, with great highlands and a long coastline. It bulges generously out into the South Atlantic toward Africa with which it is once believed to have been joined — perhaps accounting for the dual origin of the peanut. The ethnic mix is as varied as the climate, which ranges from torrid to temperate. There are the original Indians, the Portuguese, Africans, Italians, Germans, and so on. And there are all the foods of the world plus many cooking techniques, making a rich amalgam. The sheer size of the country has made for authentic regional cooking.

There was no great Indian civilization in Brazil. Today's cuisine has developed since the arrival of the Portuguese who in 1539 founded Salvador in the state of Bahia on the northeast coast, planted sugarcane, and brought in African slaves to work in the cane fields. From a combination of the foods and cooking methods of local Indians, Africans, and Portuguese,

Brazil's most exciting cooking, the *cozinha baiana*, Bahian cookery, developed. The primary ingredients are *dendê* (palm) oil from Africa, which has a nutty flavor and colors food an attractive orangey-yellow, coconut, fresh coriander, fresh and dried shrimp, and nuts — almonds, cashews, peanuts — and of course, hot peppers. A hot sauce made with tiny *malaqueta* peppers steeped in *dendê* oil and *farofa* made from manioc (cassava) meal, often colored yellow with *dendê* oil, is always on the table. Brazilians in all parts of the country sprinkle meat, poultry, and other dishes with *farofa*, as others might use grated Parmesan cheese.

The cooking of Rio de Janeiro which supplanted Salvador as the capital in 1763 seems almost subdued by comparison. It is closer to Portuguese, using local ingredients, except for *Feijoada Completa*, a regional recipe from Rio which is now recognized as the national dish. It is a very splendid, colorful meal of meats and black beans cooked together so that the many flavors are blended, and it is served, lavishly garnished, with sliced oranges, rice, cooked kale or collard greens, *farofa*, and a hot pepper and lime juice sauce. I cannot think of a better dish for a party.

São Paulo and Minas Gerais to the south share a regional cuisine. It was the Paulistas who, in the seventeenth century, set out looking for gold and found it, together with diamonds and other mineral wealth in the mountainous country to the northeast. This is now the state of Minas Gerais, which means general mines, a succinct description of what the Paulistas found. It is hearty food, well suited to the cooler climate. One of its best dishes is *Cozido à Brasileira* (Stew, Brazilian Style), a splendidly robust pot-au-feu. The most famous dish is *Cuscuz Paulista*, an adaptation of the couscous that originated in Arabia and spread to North Africa. It is made with cornmeal instead of wheat, looks marvelously decorative, and is surprisingly easy to make.

Desserts all over Brazil are rich and very much in the Portuguese egg-yolk-and-sugar tradition with its strong Moorish overtones.

Throughout Latin America there are examples of the oldest form of cooking, the neolithic earth oven, now superseded for centuries by stoves of one kind or another from charcoal to electric or gas. It has persisted as holiday cooking. Country people in Mexico cook a whole lamb in an earth oven for a *barbacoa*, and less rural people have *barbacoa* parties on Sundays and holidays at special restaurants devoted to this form of cooking. In Yucatán the earth oven is called a *pib*; in the Andes it is called *pachamanca* from the Quechua words for earth and pot. In southern Chile they have a *curanto*, best described as a clambake like those in New England. It is often lavish and includes a suckling pig as well as Chile's magnificent shellfish.

Argentina, Uruguay, and Brazil all have barbecues like the kind popular in the United States. In Argentina there are splendid restaurants where meats are cooked on wall-size grills, and in Brazil there are *Churrascarias* where all manner of grilled meats are served. I think the best proof I ever had of the popularity of this form of cooking was on a main street in Montevideo, Uruguay, when I watched some road repairmen settle down to lunch. They made a fire, put a piece of wire netting on top of it, grilled a steak, opened a bottle of red wine, and with the addition of some good bread had an excellent meal.

Looking back to the day when I determined to collect Latin American recipes — true gems of cookery — into a book gives me a feeling of great pleasure. I have done what I so deeply wanted to do, to bring these delectable dishes into American kitchens. I have spent a long time on my research; I have made many exciting journeys and eaten a great deal of very good food. It has been infinitely worthwhile. I sought out the historical hows and whys of this intriguing cuisine and found academic answers which I recorded in my endless notebooks in a special kind of cook's shorthand. A fascinating analysis to be sure, of ancient peoples and cities, of the birth of agriculture, of the coming together, in the kitchen, of very different cultures. That was only part of what I sought. I found the rest quite simply in wonderful food, the focal point of family and social life. So the best part of my quest has been coming back to my own kitchen and bringing to life those scribbled words, turning them into dishes with the authentic flavors of Latin American cooking.

It isn't food that is difficult to cook or bristles with complicated techniques. For the most part it is straightforward and easy, though there are some cooking methods that may seem odd at first, like frying a paste of peppers and other ingredients in lard or oil as a preliminary to making a Mexican *mole*. And I did have to learn about unfamiliar fruits and vegetables and seek them out in my own markets back home, where I found them without much trouble. I remembered flavors, and altered recipes until the taste was right, and had loving friends and family in to share splendid meals with me. It was a joyous experience and I have never been happier than when I received the accolade bestowed on good cooks in Latin America, *"tiene buena mano,"* "She has a good hand." It is my hope that readers will want to share my experience, and will cook, enjoy, and adopt these recipes as family favorites.

The Book of
Latin American Cooking

Ingredients

Aceite o Manteca de Achiote (Annatto Oil or Lard) is made by briefly steeping annatto seeds in hot oil or lard, then straining and cooling the fat, colored a deep orange-gold by the seeds, see page 324. It is used for both color and flavor in Latin America as well as in some non-Spanish-speaking parts of the Caribbean.

Aliño Criollo (Creole Style Seasoning Powder), a Venezuelan seasoning mixture made of herbs and spices, used with meat and poultry, in stews, and so on. Available in shaker-top glass jars from the spice section of supermarkets. Easy to make at home, see recipe, page 325.

Allspice or **pimiento** (*Pimenta officinalis*), the *pimiento de Jamaica* or *pimienta gorda* of the Spanish-speaking countries is the small, dark brown berry of an evergreen tree of the myrtle family found by the Spaniards growing wild in Jamaica. Most exports still come from the island. The dried berries, which closely resemble peppercorns, combine the flavor of cinnamon, nutmeg, and cloves. Available whole or ground wherever spices are sold.

Annatto is the English name given to the seeds of a small flowering tree of tropical America. Known as *achiote* in Spanish from the Nahuatl (Aztec) *achiotl*, the seeds are sometimes called *bija* or *bijol* in the Spanish-speaking islands of the Caribbean. The Caribs and Arawaks called the seeds *roucou*, a name by which they are still known in parts of the region. The hard orange-red pulp surrounding the seeds is used to make *Aceite o Manteca de Achiote* (Annatto Oil or Lard) and serves as a coloring and flavoring for meat, poultry, and fish dishes in the Caribbean, Colombia, Ecuador, and Venezuela. In Yucatán the whole seed is ground with various spices (such as cumin and oregano) into a paste, giving a more pronounced flavor. The taste is hard to define, fragrant, light, and flowery. Available in stores specializing in foods from Latin America or India.

Antojitos, literally little whims or fancies, the name given by the Spanish to the finger foods made with a base of tortillas that they found in Aztec Mexico. These foods fit perfectly into today's meal patterns as hors d'oeuvres or first courses. A large version, the *antojos*, whims or fancies, are ideal for light lunches or suppers.

Apio — see **Arracacha.**

Arepas, the corn bread of Venezuela, made from special flour of pre-cooked Venezuelan corn, available, packaged, from Latin American groceries. See **Tortillas** for additional information.

Arracacha (*Arracacia xanthorrhiza*) is a leggy root vegetable found in markets in Colombia. It is a member of the celery family indigenous to the northern part of South America and a favorite pre-Columbian vegetable. Venezuela has a cylindrically shaped root vegetable called *apio*, also said to be *Arracacia xanthorrhiza*. They do taste the same, faintly reminiscent of celery with a hint of sweetness, a potatolike texture, and very pale yellow flesh. The only difference I've found is that *apio* is easier to peel. As *apio* is often available in tropical markets and *arracacha* only occasionally, they can be used interchangeably. Confusion arises from the fact that *apio* is the Spanish for celery. Venezuelans solve the problem by calling celery *apio de España* or *apio de Castilla* (Spanish celery). It can be a delicious substitute for potatoes, and makes a lovely dessert when cooked with pineapple.

Arrowroot, the edible starchy powder made from the underground rhizomes of *Maranta arundinacea*, is a delicate thickening agent for soups, stews, and sauces. It is widely available.

Avocado (*Persea americana*), of the laurel family, was cultivated in Mexico as far back as 7000 B.C. and was known as *ahuacatl* in Nahuatl, the language of the ancient Mexicans. Today it is called *aguacate*. It spread to South America before Columbus arrived and was cultivated in the Inca empire, where it was called *palta*. Today it is known in Quechua by that name though in many parts of South America it keeps its Mexican name. In Brazil it is called *abacate*. The fruit may be rough or smooth-skinned, green or black. It is hard when unripe but ripens in a few days if put into a brown paper bag and left at room temperature. An avocado is ripe when it yields to a gentle pressure at the stem end. Once an avocado is cut, it discolors quickly. Sprinkling lime or lemon juice on it helps, and if you are going to try to keep an unused portion of an avocado, leave the skin on, let the pit rest in the cavity, rub the cut sides with lemon or lime, wrap tightly in plastic wrap, and refrigerate.

An easy way to mash avocados is to cut them in half, remove the pits, and mash them in their shells with a fork, holding the shell in the palm of the left hand. Scoop out the flesh with a spoon and mash any bits that may have escaped the fork. This method is much easier than having them slither round a bowl and gives a texture with character. Avocado leaves are sometimes used in Mexican cooking in the same way as bay leaves and there is also the charming bonus of being able to grow the pits into very beautiful house plants. To toast avocado leaves, place them on an un-greased *comal* (griddle) or a heavy iron skillet and cook on both sides over moderate heat for about 1 minute.

Bacalao, Spanish for dried salted codfish, called *bacalhau* in Brazil, is extremely popular in all of Latin America. It is available in Latin American markets and in many supermarkets and fish stores, especially in the Northeast.

Bananas and banana leaves. Both green and ripe bananas are used in Latin American cooking, the green bananas as a vegetable. When a recipe calls for plantains (page 15), bananas make a good substitute. Banana leaves, sometimes available in specialty food stores, are used as a wrapping in which to cook foods. Kitchen parchment or aluminum foil make good substitutes.

Beans, black (turtle), red kidney, pink, mottled pinto, white Navy, or pea beans, all belong to the large grouping called *Phaseolus vulgaris* of the legume family, which originated in Mexico about 5000 B.C. They are an essential part of the Latin American kitchen and turn up in many guises. I follow the Mexican rules for cooking beans — namely, that they should not be soaked but should be put on to cook in cold water with their seasonings and that hot water is added as necessary during the cooking time. Salt should not be added until the beans are tender. It is impossible to give an exact time for cooking beans as it can vary from 1½ to 2½ hours according to the age of the beans. It is wise to buy beans from shops with a quick turnover, as stale beans may take a very long time to cook and even when cooked may have a dry texture. If there is reason to suspect that beans are stale, a desperate remedy may be in order. Soak them overnight in cold water with a little bicarbonate of soda (baking soda), ¼ teaspoon to 2 cups of beans, then rinse the beans very thoroughly before putting them on to cook in fresh water. It works wonders.

The Spanish and Portuguese brought chickpeas, sometimes called garbanzos or ceci (*Cicer arietinum*), also of the legume family, to the New World with them. These hard, round, yellow peas, native to the Middle East, do need soaking overnight in cold water before cooking. Another popular bean from the Middle East is the broad bean, also called fava or habas (*Vicia faba*). Other popular local beans are limas from Peru and cranberry or shell beans and, to a lesser extent, black-eyed peas, which originated in Africa. Whenever beans need soaking before cooking, instructions are given in individual recipes.

Calabaza, also called *ahuyama*, *zapallo*, *abóbora*, and, in English, West Indian or green pumpkin, is a winter squash available in Latin American and Caribbean markets. Not to be confused with American pumpkin, it comes in a variety of shapes and sizes but is usually large and either round or oval. Hubbard, or other winter squash, is a good substitute.

Carne sêca is the sun-dried salt beef, known in the United States as jerked beef, that is used in the Brazilian national dish *Feijoada Completa* (Black Beans with Mixed Meats). It is available in Latin American markets and in some specialty butcher shops. The salt beef used in *Sancocho Especial* (Special Boiled Dinner, see page 163) from Colombia could be used instead, as the technique of salting and drying is similar.

Cassava (*Manihot utilissima*), also called manioc, mandioca, aipím, or yucca, is a handsome tropical plant whose tuberous roots, at least 2 inches in diameter and about 8 to 10 inches long, are best known as the commercial source of tapioca. Cassava originated in 1500 B.C. in Brazil and is widely used in the kitchens of Latin America. The roots are covered with a brown, barklike, rather hairy skin. Cassava should be peeled under running water and immediately dropped into water, as its white flesh tends to discolor on contact with the air. It may be boiled and used as a potato substitute in stews, or to accompany meat and poultry dishes, or it may be fried and served like potato chips.

In Brazil manioc meal is used to make *farofa*: the meal is toasted and mixed with butter and other ingredients such as onion, eggs, or prunes and served with *Feijoada* or with poultry, steaks, or roasted meats. *Farofa*, which looks like coarsely grated Parmesan cheese, is as common on Brazilian tables as salt and pepper.

Cassava is also used for making bread or cakes, mostly sold commercially in South America. To make them, you need cassava that is finely ground like cornstarch, not easily obtainable in the United States — and, anyway, the results are not particularly delicious.

Chayote (*Sechium edule*), of the squash family, is also known a christophene, cho-cho, and chuchu. The vegetable originated in Mexico, and the name comes from the Mexican *chayotl*. It is now widely grown in semitropical regions throughout the world. About 6 to 8 inches long, and roughly pear-shaped, chayote is usually a light, pretty green (though there are white varieties), with a slightly prickly skin and a single edible seed. The texture is crisp with a delicate flavor a little like zucchini but more subtle. It is best when young and firm. Avoid soft or wrinkled ones.

Chicha, a beerlike drink made from dried corn. Usually only slightly alcoholic. Popular throughout South America.

Chicharrones are fried pork rinds available packaged in Latin American markets and in supermarkets.

Coconuts and **coconut milk.** Choose coconuts that are full of liquid. Shake them to check. Nuts with little liquid are stale. Avoid those with moldy or wet "eyes." With an ice pick, screwdriver, or similar sharp implement, pierce two out of the three eyes of the nut using a hammer to bang it through if necessary. Drain out and reserve the liquid. Strain it before use as there may be bits of coconut fiber in it. A medium-sized coconut yields about ½ cup liquid. Bake the coconut in a preheated hot (400° F.) oven for 15 minutes. Then put the coconut on a hard surface and hit it all over with a hammer. The hard shell will fall away. Lever out any bits that are left with a knife or screwdriver. If making coconut milk it is not necessary to peel off the brown inner skin, but if grated coconut is to be used in a recipe, peel this off with a small, sharp knife. Chop the coconut pieces coarsely, then put into a blender or food processor fitted with a steel blade and grate as fine as possible. The grated coconut is now ready for use. If the coconut water is not to be used separately in a recipe, add it to the blender or food processor with the coconut pieces as this helps in the grating. This makes about 4 cups per coconut.

To make thick (rich) coconut milk squeeze the grated coconut through a damp cloth, squeezing and twisting the cloth to remove as much liquid as possible. Set this aside. To make ordinary coconut milk put the squeezed-out coconut into a bowl and pour 1 cup boiling water over it. Let it stand 30 minutes. Squeeze out the liquid through a damp cloth, add the coconut water, and set aside. Repeat the entire process. Discard the coconut.

Unless a recipe calls for thick coconut milk to be used separately, mix the thick and ordinary coconut milk together and use. When thick coconut milk is left to stand, the cream rises to the top. This is delicious instead of cream with desserts. If the coconut water drained out of the nut at the beginning is not needed for any culinary purpose, it makes a wonderful mix with gin or vodka.

If coconuts are not available, canned moist coconut is a good substitute for grated fresh coconut. Creamed coconut available from tropical markets and specialty stores is a good substitute for coconut milk. Simply dilute to the desired consistency with warm water or milk.

Freshly grated coconut keeps well frozen.

Coriander (*Coriandrum sativum*), of the carrot family, indigenous to the Mediterranean and the Caucasus, is a very old herb, mentioned in Sanskrit and ancient Egyptian writings. Its antiquity is proved by the fact that the Romans introduced it to Britain before the end of the first century A.D. It has spread throughout the world and is very important in Indian and Thai cooking, indeed in most of Asia including China. It is often sold as Chinese parsley and though the leaves are a lighter green, it does resemble flat-leafed parsley, also of the carrot family and a close relative.

Many Mexicans think of coriander as indigenous. Certainly it is hard to imagine the Mexican green tomato dishes or *Guacamole* (Avocado Sauce) without it. If there could be said to be a favorite herb in the Mexican kitchen it would be coriander, though oregano, cumin, and to a lesser extent the indigenous herb *epazote* are all popular. I have never been able to find out when coriander first arrived in Mexico, but I think it was introduced after the Conquest and was adopted with enthusiasm. Certainly it is popular in all of Latin America. But there is a puzzle here. Coriander is not used in Spanish cooking today, although it is a favorite Middle Eastern herb and Spain was occupied for nearly eight centuries by the Arabs. In fact, Columbus had discovered America before Spain had reconquered all its occupied provinces, so the Spanish of that time, eating Arab foods, may have brought coriander with them to the New World. Or it may have arrived via the Philippines, where it is popular; there was a great deal of trade between Mexico and the Philippines, then a Spanish possession, in early colonial times. Some kitchen mysteries may never be solved, though it is great fun trying. There is no mystery, however, about its arrival in Brazil, as it is a favorite Portuguese herb.

The fresh herb is increasingly available. Latin American, Chinese, and

Korean markets, as well as some specialty stores, carry it. In Latin American markets it is called cilantro, less usually *culantro* or *culantrillo*. In Chinese and Korean markets it is called Chinese parsley, or, in Chinese, *yuen-sai.* It is sold with its roots on and it does not keep well. The roots should not be removed for storage and the coriander should not be washed but simply wrapped in paper towels, roots and all, and stored in a plastic bag in the refrigerator. This is the simplest method and the one I use. Some recommend washing the coriander with its roots on, drying thoroughly, and refrigerating in a jar with just enough water to cover the roots. Others simply refrigerate roots and all in a glass jar with a screw top.

To have coriander available for flavoring soups and stews, I remove the roots, wash the coriander well, and purée it, including the stems, without the addition of any water in a food processor, then freeze the purée in an ice cube tray. When frozen, I store the cubes in a plastic bag. One cube is the equivalent of about 1 tablespoon of the freshly chopped leaves. This works well where flavor — not appearance — is what matters. Sometimes the coriander roots are quite sizeable. In Thailand, the country, incidentally, in which I became a coriander addict, they are scraped and used in curries. They add a very intense flavor. I always keep an eye out for these fat roots, a happy bonus.

The tiny brown seedlike fruits of coriander are also used in cooking, especially in curries, and to flavor gin. They are available in jars in the spice section of supermarkets and I have grown coriander from them.

Crème fraîche. Venezuela has a lovely runny fresh cream cheese that is wonderful with hot *arepas* (corn bread). It is very like French *crème fraîche.* A good imitation of *crème fraîche* can be made by mixing 1 tablespoon of buttermilk with 1 cup heavy cream and heating the mixture to lukewarm in a small saucepan. Pour it into a jar and let it stand until it has thickened, about 8 hours in a warm room. It will then keep for several days refrigerated.

Dendê oil (palm oil), originally from Africa and very much used in Bahian cooking in Brazil. It is a deep, beautiful orange-gold and has a pleasant nutty flavor. Available in Latin American stores and specialty markets. It lends color and some flavor to dishes but one can manage without it.

Epazote (*Chenopodium ambrosioides*), one of the Anserinas, from the Nahuatl *epazotl,* known under a variety of names in English — Mexican tea, wormseed, lamb's quarters, goosefoot, and Jerusalem oak. It is ubiquitous, growing wild all over the Americas and in many parts of Europe. It dries excellently and is often available dried in Latin American markets.

To dry it yourself, pick the epazote or lamb's quarters on a dry morning (early if possible, as the sun draws out the volatile oil) and spread on paper towels in a dark, warm cupboard until dry, turning occasionally. This may take a week. Or put on a tray in the oven with the pilot light on. Turn from time to time. This will take only a matter of hours. Strip the leaves from the stalks when dry, put into a screw-top glass jar, and store away from light. It is used quite a lot in Mexican cooking, especially in the center and south, in black bean and tortilla dishes. There is no substitute. Fortunately the herb is not vital to the success of the dishes.

Garlic. Peruvian garlic, purple-skinned, and Mexican garlic, sometimes purple-skinned, sometimes white, are both often available in specialty food stores and supermarkets. They have quite enormous cloves, which comes in handy when one has to peel a number of them. The size of garlic cloves varies so widely, as does a taste for garlic, that I have adopted in most instances the system of simply giving the number of cloves needed so that those who are particularly fond of garlic may seek out the big ones with a clear conscience.

Guascas or **huascas** (*Galinsoga parviflora Lineo*) is a Colombian herb that grows in the Andes. It is sold in jars, dried and ground into a green powder, in Colombian food shops. Though it has no relationship whatsoever to Jerusalem artichokes, its smell is reminiscent of that vegetable. It adds a delicious flavor to soups and stews, particularly those made with chicken. Since specialty food stores constantly increase the range of their imports, I have included it here in case it should become available, but it is not essential to the success of any of the recipes in this book.

Hearts of palm, in Spanish and Portuguese *palmito*, are the tender heart buds of any one of several species of palm trees. Their delicate flavor is exquisite in salads and soups. Though they are eaten fresh in the countries of origin, they are always canned for export and are available in supermarkets.

Huacatay, an herb of the marigold family, is used in Peru in sauces and dishes such as *Picante de Yuca* (Cassava Root with Cheese Sauce). It is not available here and there is no substitute. The flavor is unusual and is certainly an acquired taste, rather rank at first try. I find I don't miss it.

Jerusalem artichokes, despite their name, are the edible tubers of a plant native to Canada and the northern United States. Their botanical name is *Helianthus tuberosus*, and they are a species of sunflower belonging to the daisy family. Jerusalem is apparently a corruption of *girasole*, the Italian word for sunflower. They are called *topinambur* in South America and are sometimes called sunchokes in U.S. markets. They have a lovely crisp texture reminiscent of water chestnuts. They make a delightful soup, an excellent salad, and are a lovely change of pace from the more usual potatoes as a starchy root vegetable. They are a little tricky to peel since the small tubers are knobby in shape. I always pick out the largest and least knobby ones available, but I have also found recently that newer varieties are easier to peel. When I scrape them I'm not all that fussy about a bit of skin left on, as it is not at all unpleasant, and I just shave off the little knobs. It is very important not to overcook them since they lose their crisp texture and turn mushy.

Jícama, pronounced HEE-kama (*Exogonium bracteatum*), of the morning glory family, is a tuberous turnip-shaped root vegetable with a light brown skin, originally from Mexico, where it is usually eaten raw, sliced, with a little salt and a sprinkling of hot chili powder (cayenne), or in salads. It has crispy, juicy white flesh. Water chestnuts or tart green cooking apples are the best substitutes. It is available in markets in the Southwest and in markets specializing in tropical fruits and vegetables.

Malanga — see **Taro.**

Mate, a tea made from the dried leaves of the South American evergreen *Ilex paraguayensis.* Especially popular in Paraguay, Uruguay, Argentina, and Brazil. Available in specialty and health food stores. Make according to package directions, or see page 337.

Mole, pronounced MO-lay, from the Nahuatl (Mexican) word *molli,* meaning a sauce made from any of the peppers, sweet, pungent, or hot, usually a combination, together with other ingredients. The most famous of the *moles* is the *Mole Poblano de Guajolote,* the turkey dish from Puebla using bitter chocolate, but there are a host of others playing variations on a theme.

Nopal is the prickly pear cactus. It is available canned in stores selling Mexican foods and fresh in some markets in the Southwest. Used mainly in salads, it has an attractive fruit, *tuna,* which may be green or pinkish red.

Oranges, bitter, sour, Seville, or Bigarade, to give this fruit all the names by which it is commonly known, are not raised commercially in the U.S., but can sometimes be found in specialty food stores or markets. The large, rough-skinned, reddish-orange fruit has a delicate and quite distinctive flavor, but the pulp is too sour to be eaten raw. The juice, which is used a great deal in Latin American cooking, freezes successfully, and the peel need not be wasted but can be used to make marmalade. A mixture of one-third lime or lemon juice to two-thirds sweet orange juice can be used as a substitute.

Palillo is a Peruvian herb used dried and ground to give a yellow color to food. Since so many Peruvian foods are yellow or white, I'm sure it is a reflection of pre-Conquest Inca sun (and moon) worship. *Palillo* is not available here but I have found that using half the amount of turmeric gives much the same result.

Pepitas, Mexican pumpkin seeds, available in jars in supermarkets and health food stores.

PEPPERS

Peppers, sweet, pungent, and hot, all belong to the genus *Capsicum annuum* or *Capsicum frutescens* of the *Solanaceae* family, to which potato, tomato, and eggplant also belong. They were first cultivated in the Valley of Mexico about 9,000 years ago and their original name in Nahuatl was *chilli*. Varieties are legion and have not yet been fully classified botanically. They have spread all over the world and become naturalized so quickly that their national origin has been forgotten. Peppers are widely used in Latin American cooking, especially in Mexico and Peru. The number of varieties used is, fortunately, limited. They are widely available in markets specializing in Latin American and tropical foods and often in supermarkets and neighborhood stores. They fall into two main categories, the dried and the fresh.

The Dried Peppers

Ancho. This is the most widely used of all the peppers in the Mexican kitchen. It is quite large, with a wrinkled skin, about 4 inches long by about 3 inches wide. It has a deep, lovely color and a rich, full, mild flavor. It is the base of many cooked sauces.

Chipotle and **morita.** These are dried wrinkled peppers, brick red in color. Both are smaller than *ancho* peppers, with the *morita* smaller than the *chipotle*. Though they are available dried and sometimes ground, they are more usually canned. They have the most distinctive flavor of all the

Mexican peppers and are very, very hot. If used sparingly, the exciting flavor comes through without excessive heat.

Guajillo. This is a long (4-inch), slender, tapering, smooth-skinned bright red pepper, which, like its fresh counterpart, the pale green *chile largo*, is mostly used whole to flavor pot-au-feu dishes.

Mulato. Much the same size and shape as the *ancho* but darker in color, closer to brown than red, and longer and more tapering. Its flavor is more pungent than the mild *ancho*. It is wrinkled.

Pasilla. This is a long, slender pepper, 6 to 7 inches in length and about an inch or so wide, and very much darker in color than the *ancho*. Like ancho and mulato peppers, it is wrinkled and some varieties are so dark they are called *chile negro* (black peppers). It is very hot but at the same time richly flavored. In Mexico these three peppers are often used in combination.

SMALL HOT DRIED PEPPERS

There are a number of small hot dried red peppers under various names, *cascabel, pequín, tepín*, which can be used interchangeably whenever dried hot red peppers are called for. One variety, a Japanese migrant, is called *hontaka* and should be treated with respect as it is very hot indeed. Hot paprika or cayenne pepper can be used instead: ⅛ teaspoon is about the equivalent of a whole *pequín*.

Mirasol. This is a medium-sized tapering, wrinkled, dried hot pepper from Peru, which may be either red or yellow. It is not available here, but dried hot red peppers are an excellent substitute. The larger ones like the Japanese *hontaka* are the most suitable.

How to Use Dried Red Peppers

The method used in Mexican cooking is the same for *ancho, pasilla, mulato, chipotle,* and *morita* chilies. Rinse in cold water, tear off the stem end, and shake out the seeds. Tear the chilies roughly into pieces and soak in warm water, about 6 to 1 cup, for half an hour. If they are very dry, soak them a little longer. Purée them with the water in which they have soaked in a blender or food processor fitted with a steel blade. The resulting almost pastelike purée is then ready to be cooked in hot lard or oil with the other ingredients specified in the recipe to make the sauce.

Canned *chipotle* and *morita* chilies are puréed right out of the can without soaking, or used as the recipe specifies. The small hot dried red chilies are usually just crumbled with the fingers.

Always wash the hands in warm soapy water after handling chilies. Hot chili accidentally rubbed in the eyes can be temporarily very painful.

Dried chilies are best stored in plastic bags in the refrigerator or another cool place. They dry out if exposed to the air.

The Fresh Peppers

HOT FRESH PEPPERS

A number of small and medium-sized hot green peppers are sold fresh in supermarkets and greengrocers all year round. They are not usually identified beyond being called hot peppers. In Mexico the most commonly used small fresh peppers are the *serrano*, about 1½ inches long, tapering, smooth-skinned, medium green, and the *jalapeño*, which is slightly darker in color and larger, about 2½ inches long. Both are quite hot. *Jalapeño is* sold interchangeably with *cuaresmeño*, a pepper so like it that some botanists classify them as the same. The shape is slightly different and I think the *cuaresmeño* is hotter. As most of the heat in these peppers is in the seeds and veins, remove them, unless fiery heat is wanted. These peppers are also sold canned in Mexican food stores and are very useful since they can be used when fresh peppers are not available.

There is a tiny hot pepper that in Brazil is called *malagueta*. It is fiery. A larger one, sometimes called cayenne chili, is widely available year round in greengrocers and can also be found in Chinese and Japanese markets. These two are sometimes sold ripe, when they have turned red. They are then slightly less hot, and have a somewhat richer flavor.

In the West Indies there is a lantern-shaped pepper that the Jamaicans call Scotch Bonnet, usually quite small, about 1½ inches long, with a most exquisite flavor. It is the *habanero* of Yucatán and is also popular in tropical Brazil. This pepper is sold green, yellow, and red in its three stages of ripening. It is fiery hot but has a flavor that makes it worth seeking. I have found it fresh in Caribbean markets and also bottled, usually imported from Trinidad. The bottled version keeps indefinitely in the refrigerator.

Any of these peppers can be used when fresh hot red or green peppers are called for.

Peppers vary a great deal in strength. There is only one way to find out how hot they are and that is by tasting. Nibble a tiny bit of hot pepper, and if it seems very fiery, use it sparingly. But tastes vary as much as peppers do, so the only true guide is to please yourself. As with dried peppers, always wash your hands in warm, soapy water after handling.

Visiting markets in Peru, I came upon great heaps of yellow peppers, *ají amarillo* (fresh hot yellow peppers), an astonishment to the eye. Surely nothing short of gold is as yellow as these peppers. Yellow peppers are almost never available here. Fresh hot red or green peppers are just as good from the point of view of flavor.

SWEET FRESH PEPPERS

Perhaps the most widely used of all peppers is the green bell pepper, available year round everywhere. There is a splendid Mexican pepper, the *poblano*, dark green and tapering and about the same size as the bell pepper, which is not available in Eastern markets. It is used especially for stuffed peppers and the bell pepper makes a good substitute. There is another sweet green pepper, pale green and tapering, called California or Italian pepper. It is similar to the Mexican *chile güero* and can be used whenever chopped bell peppers are called for. These tapering peppers are not usually large enough to be stuffed.

The green bell pepper turns red when ripe. A similar pepper, though a different variety, is the pimiento, tapering in shape where the bell pepper is squat. It is always sold canned or in jars, often labeled *pimientos morrones*. It is tomato red whereas the ripe bell pepper is a true crimson. When red bell peppers are unavailable, use the canned pimientos. Already peeled and cooked, they can be used straight from the jar and make a very attractive garnish.

How to Peel Red or Green Bell Peppers

Stick a cooking fork into the stem end of the peppers and toast them over a gas flame or electric burner, turning frequently, until the skin blisters and blackens. Wrap the peppers in a cloth wrung out in hot water and leave for 30 minutes. The burned part of the thin papery skin will rinse off easily under cold running water and most of the rest can be pulled away. If a few bits of skin remain, it does not matter. Toasting the peppers in this way also brings out their flavor.

Piloncillo, Mexican brown sugar packaged in pyramid-shaped pieces. Similar molded brown sugar is called by a variety of names. Use dark brown sugar instead.

Plantains, *plátanos* in Spanish, are members of the same family as bananas — bird-of-paradise (*Strelitzia*). They are much larger and are not edible until cooked even when they are quite ripe and their skins are black. They are fried or boiled green, half-ripe, and ripe, and are usually served as a starchy vegetable to accompany meat, poultry, or fish. They also make a good cocktail nibble when green (*verde*), thinly sliced, and deep fried.

How to Peel a Plantain or Green Banana

Neither plantains, except very ripe ones, nor green bananas peel readily by hand. The simplest method is to make shallow lengthwise cuts along the natural ridges of the fruit and pull the skin off in sections.

Potatoes. The people we call the Incas for convenience, though it was quite likely a much earlier civilization, now lost in time, first cultivated potatoes in the high Andes. They developed a bewildering variety, some of which survive today. Among the survivors are large, yellow-fleshed potatoes that look beautiful used in the Peruvian potato dishes. However, this is more a matter of aesthetics than flavor as any good-quality potato that takes to boiling can be used instead. Colombia has a small version of the Peruvian potato. They are also yellow-fleshed, are called *papas criollas*, and are the size of new potatoes. As they stay firm when cooked, Colombians use them in stews with other, softer potatoes, which disintegrate to thicken the gravy, leaving the *papas criollas* intact. Any good small new potato, especially a waxy one, does very well as a substitute.

Sausages. There are no problems in finding the right sausages for Latin American cooking. Chorizos, Spanish-style hot, spicy pork sausages, are widely available in the United States. Blood sausages are very little different from *morcilla*, and Polish *kielbasa,* available in supermarkets, is a splendid substitute for Spanish *longaniza* or Brazilian *linguiça*.

Shrimp (dried) are used a great deal in Bahian cooking in Brazil. They are tiny and are ground before being used in dishes like *vatapá*. A food processor fitted with a steel blade takes the hard work out of this chore. A blender can also be used. If the shrimp are very dry, a brief soaking in warm water helps. Available in Chinese and Japanese markets and in Latin American markets.

Sierra (Spanish mackerel) is a large fish that can reach 10 to 15 pounds. It is very attractive, with yellow the predominating color on its back scales instead of the steely blue of Atlantic mackerel. Found off Florida and the Gulf coast, it is a popular fish in South America and is used in *Sopa de Almejas* (Clam Soup) from Colombia. Red snapper, or similar fish, is a better substitute than Atlantic mackerel, which is too strongly flavored.

Smoked ham. When South American recipes call for smoked ham, the one most usually used is Spanish *jamón serrano*, which has been aged in spices. Italian prosciutto, German Westphalian, French Ardennes, or Bayonne hams are perfect substitutes.

Squash blossoms or **pumpkin flowers**, whatever they are called, are the pretty golden yellow blooms of one or other of the cucurbits of the squash family. They are not the female blossoms, which would turn into little squash, but are the male flowers, which if not gathered and cooked would die upon the vine. Female blossoms have recognizably squashlike swellings behind them; male blossoms do not. The latter make a marvelous soup among other things.

Sweet potato (*Ipomoea batatas*) is an edible tuber originally from tropical America, though its precise birthplace is not known. Only slightly sweet, it is in no way related to the potato family. The most popular variety grown in the United States is the Louisiana yam, with moist, orange-colored flesh and brown skin. Its name is also confusing as it is not related to the yams, which are an entirely different botanical group, the Dioscoreas. The white sweet potato with drier white flesh and pink or white skin is known as *boniato* (pronounced bon-ee-AH-toe) and is the variety most popular in Latin America. It is widely available in tropical markets and increasingly in ordinary greengrocers. It makes a delicious substitute for potatoes.

Taro and **malanga** are tropical plants that bear edible tubers and are members of the very large *Arum* family. There are a great many of them and they have been cultivated for more than 2,000 years. I think of all the root vegetables they are, apart from potatoes, the most subtly flavored, the most delicious. The type of taro most widely cultivated in the United States is called *dasheen* and can be found in tropical markets, though in some markets specializing in Caribbean foods it may be called *coco* or *eddo*. They can also be found in Japanese markets as *sato-imo*, or Japanese potatoes. A closely related group, the malangas, which belong to the genus *Xanthosoma*, are known by a wide variety of names, malanga, tannia, and *yautía* being the ones most likely to be encountered in tropical markets in the U.S. The skins are usually brown, the flesh white to yellow, and they can be cooked like potatoes. When I first went looking for them in markets, I wrote down all the names and asked for them in a sort of litany. I found people very understanding and helpful, and they sorted things out for me in a charmingly good-humored way.

Tomatoes, green or husk (*Physalis ixocarpa*), which have a loose, brown papery outer covering, should not be confused with ordinary green (unripe) tomatoes. Though members of the same family, they are a different species. The Aztecs called the fruit *miltomatl*, but today in Mexico it is usually called *tomatillo* (little tomato), as it is never very large, usually only about an inch across. It has other names, *tomate verde*, *tomatitto*, and *fresadilla*. In English it is sometimes called Spanish tomato. When the tomatoes, which cannot be skinned as nothing would be left of them, are marketed as peeled, it means that the papery brown husk has been removed. The green tomato is very important in Mexican, and to a lesser extent Guatemalan, cooking, giving a distinctive flavor to the "green" dishes and sauces. The flavor is delicate and slightly acid, and the fruit must be cooked for 2 or 3 minutes for its special flavor to develop. It is available fresh in markets in the Southwest and canned from stores specializing in Mexican foods. The canned version needs no further cooking and is ready to use. The flesh is rather delicate and the can may be full of broken fruit. When this happens, use the liquid from the can in a sauce, reducing the amount of stock or other liquid, and save the whole fruit for sauces where no liquid is required. Green tomatoes are grown easily from seed.

Tortillas and **arepas.** The tortilla of Mexico, and the *arepa* of Venezuela, and to a lesser extent Colombia, are unique in the world of bread since they are made from cooked flour. Dried corn kernels are boiled with lime (to loosen the skin), then the kernels are drained and ground, and, if not for immediate use, are dried and packaged as flour. Though the method of cooking the corn is the same for both tortillas and *arepas*, the end result is very different because of the difference in the type of corn used. The corn for *arepas* has very large kernels, giving a rather starchy flour. The packaged flours identify themselves very clearly as *masa harina* (literally dough flour) for tortillas, or flour for *arepas*. It is not possible to confuse them. Shops specializing in Latin American foods carry them.

Yams are members of a vast assemblage of edible tubers of the Dioscorea family, which has about 250 different species, most of them originating in the tropical regions of the world. They can be as small as a new potato or weigh up to 100 pounds, though most of them weigh about a pound and are the size of a large potato. The skins are usually brown and may be rough, smooth, or hairy, and the shape is usually cylindrical. The flesh is white or yellow, the texture mealy, and the flavor pleasantly nutlike. They are available in tropical markets and increasingly in supermarkets and greengrocers. They may be encountered in markets as *ñame* (pronounced ny-AH-may), yampi, cush-cush, mapuey, or a number of other names. A good plan on seeing an unfamiliar tuber in a market is to ask if it is a kind of yam, always remembering that these yams should not be confused with the Louisiana yam, which is a sweet potato. They may be cooked in the same way as potatoes. The smaller varieties are usually the best ones to buy for texture and flavor, and they are well worth getting to know.

Hors d'Oeuvres and Appetizers

Entremeses

Hors d'oeuvres and appetizers in our modern sense were not a large part of the traditional cooking of Latin America. But there are innumerable small foods that were once used as accompaniments to main dishes or were served only to gentlemen in bars or eaten from stalls in the market, which have been adapted for comparatively new styles of eating: finger foods to go with drinks, or light first courses at lunch or dinner, often taking the place of soup.

From country to country they rejoice in a variety of names, which are as different and varied as the hors d'oeuvres themselves. They are known as *botanas*, meaning literally the stoppers on leather wine bottles; *bacaditos*, little mouthfuls; *antojitos*, little whims or fancies; *boquillas*, things to stop the mouth; *fritangas*, fried things and fritters; *tapados*, nibbles; *picadas*, things on a toothpick; *entremeses*, side dishes; *entradas*, dishes to be served at table; *salgadinhos frios*, small, cold, salty things; and *salgadinhos quentes*, small, hot, salty things.

These are the hors d'oeuvres I find exciting, not the almost universal modern canapes, which are mostly borrowed or adapted from our own cocktail foods and have become popular throughout Latin America in recent years as industrialization has changed social patterns from feudal to modern. One comes upon canapes of caviar, ham, shrimp, anchovies; even *crudités* turn up. There are clam or onion-soup dips, cheese cubes alternating with pineapple on toothpicks, tiny frankfurters, salmon caviar with sour cream, and grilled bacon-wrapped prunes. They appear in recipe books under the heading *Cocina Internacional*, International Cookery, and have a certain glamour in Latin America because they are foreign and unfamiliar, which is very understandable.

But fortunately they have not elbowed out the traditional appetizers with exciting flavors that are new to us. These traditional foods range from the simplest of nibbles — toasted corn, fried chickpeas, tiny fried potatoes, French fried plantain slices, yucca and banana chips — to the heartier *Empanadas* (Turnovers) and the *seviches* (fish cooked in lime or lemon juice), which make particularly splendid first courses for summer dining. And the *antojitos* (little whims or fancies) and *tacos*, *chalupas*, *sopes*, *quesadillas*, which all derive from some form of tortillas imaginatively stuffed and seasoned, can compose a whole cocktail buffet or informal luncheon.

All of these appetizers are easy to make and most of them are served at room temperature. They can be prepared ahead of time, and some, like the *empanadas*, can be made well in advance and frozen. They make ideal hors d'oeuvres for a cocktail party. I have enjoyed them in restaurants and in the homes of friends throughout Latin America. They fit perfectly into the pattern of today's living, where meals tend to have fewer courses and be less elaborate than in the past, and where the habit of having drinks before lunch or dinner is increasingly accepted.

It is surprising that the hors d'oeuvres of the region owe so little to their Spanish heritage. Though one might have expected the *tapas* of Spain to appear on New World tables changed, but recognizable, this has not happened. It always surprises me in the world of culinary borrowings, what gets taken, what gets left — and this is especially true of appetizers. After nearly eight centuries of Moorish domination, Spain gained its independence and united its provinces into a nation, turning its back at the same time on the *mezze*, the hors d'oeuvres of the Middle East, which are one of the most attractive features of the food of that region. Latin America, with a few exceptions such as *empanadas*, has behaved in much the same way, so that it is the ancient dishes of the pre-Columbian kitchens and the dishes of the creole cuisine that have been adapted as today's appetizers.

The old tradition of foods eaten in the market has survived in Latin America in a very charming way. Snack foods, cakes, and drinks of all kinds are served in *confeitarías* in Brazil, in *sandwicherías* in Uruguay, and *whiskerías* in Argentina, while each station on the subway in Buenos

Aires has a stall selling coffee, a variety of drinks, and snack foods. In Chile *empanadas*, cakes, and snack foods of all kinds are sold in *salas de onces*. *Onces* (*once* is the number eleven), named for the English custom of having tea or coffee and cookies at eleven in the morning, have become, by some extraordinary transmutation, afternoon tea, so that a *sala de onces* is a tea shop. Ecuador has restaurants devoted to its famous *seviches* while Mexico has its *taquerías*, with an astonishing variety of fillings for the simple *tortilla*.

Anticuchos   PERU
Skewered Beef Heart

These are without doubt the most famous of all the Peruvian *entradas*, or appetizers — dishes traditionally served sometimes before, sometimes after the soup, but before the roast in the days when appetites were more robust than they are now. Many of the *entradas* make excellent lunches or suppers; some, like these spiced pieces of beef heart that are skewered and grilled, make a good first course but are also fine as a snack or an accompaniment to drinks. When served as lunch or supper they may be accompanied by corn on the cob, boiled sweet potatoes, and boiled yucca (cassava), bland foods that go very well with the spicy beef hearts. Peruvians like their *picante* foods to be really hot and *anticuchos* are no exception. The dried chili used is *mirasol*, not available here. I have found the *hontaka*, dried hot red chili peppers sold packaged in Japanese markets, to be an admirable substitute.

The amount of peppers given in the recipe, 1 cup, will make a very fiery sauce just the way Peruvians like it but too hot for most of us. A good idea is to begin with ⅛ cup peppers. If the sauce seems too bland, add more peppers. Peppers themselves vary a great deal in hotness, and I have found when dealing with them it is wise to experiment.

Anticuchos are a very old, pre-Columbian dish; I suspect they used to be made with llama hearts since there were no cattle until after the Conquest. The name translates from the Quechua into "a dish from the Andes cooked on sticks."

My favorite place to buy *anticuchos* is from stalls outside Lima's *plaza de toros*, built in 1768 and said to be the second oldest bullring in the world. Eaten right there, accompanied by beer and rounded out with a dessert of *picarones*, deep-fried sweet potato and pumpkin fritters, they make a wonderful impromptu meal.

Serves 8 to 10 as an hors d'oeuvre, or 6 as a main course

1 beef heart, weighing about 4
    pounds
1 head garlic (about 16 cloves),
    peeled and crushed
1 tablespoon fresh hot red or green
    peppers, seeded, coarsely
    chopped, and puréed in a
    blender or food processor

1 tablespoon ground cumin
Salt, freshly ground pepper
1 cup red wine vinegar

FOR THE SAUCE

1 cup dried hot red peppers
1 tablespoon ground annatto
    (achiote) seeds

1 tablespoon vegetable oil
Salt

Remove the nerves and fat from the beef heart, and cut it into 1-inch cubes. Place in a large bowl. Combine the garlic, fresh hot peppers, cumin, salt, pepper, and vinegar, stir to mix, and pour over the beef heart, adding more vinegar, if necessary, to cover. Refrigerate, covered, for 24 hours. Remove the beef heart from the marinade and set them both aside.

Shake the seeds out of the dried peppers and soak in hot water to cover for 30 minutes. Drain the peppers and put them into a blender or food processor with the annatto, oil, and about ¾ cup of the reserved marinade. Season to taste with a little more salt if necessary and blend until smooth. The sauce should be quite thick. Thread the beef-heart cubes on skewers. Brush them with the sauce, and broil, turning to cook all sides, either over charcoal or under a gas or electric broiler, about 3 inches from the heat, for about 4 minutes. Serve with the remaining sauce on the side. Accompany with boiled corn, sweet potato, and yucca (cassava root).

Acarajé
BRAZIL
Black-Eyed Pea Fritters

Black-eyed peas are originally African, brought to the New World by slaves. The fritters turn up all over the Caribbean as well as in South America. The most elegant version, *acarajé*, comes from Bahia in Brazil and makes an unusual cocktail nibble. I have occasionally come across packaged black-eyed pea flour, *harina para bollitos*, which I have found very good indeed and useful when one is in a hurry. It is worth looking out for in Latin markets. As the flour is a ready mix and needs only the addition of water, it saves one all the bother of soaking the peas, rubbing off the skins, and grinding them. To make the fritters from the pea flour, simply follow package instructions. The *dendê* (palm) oil, used a great deal in Bahian cooking, is also an African contribution. A rich reddish-orange in color, it turns the fritters a beautiful deep gold. They have a crispy texture and a nutty flavor with an attractive hint of shrimp from the sauce.

Makes 24

1 pound (2 cups) black-eyed peas
½ cup dried shrimp
1 medium onion, chopped

Salt
Dendê (palm) oil

Soak the black-eyed peas overnight in cold water to cover. Drain. Rub off and discard the skins. Soak the shrimp in cold water to cover for 30 minutes. Put the peas, shrimp, and onion through the fine blade of a food grinder, or purée them in a blender or food processor. Season to taste with salt if necessary. The shrimp may be quite salty. Pour enough *dendê* oil into a deep fryer or saucepan to fill it to a depth of 2 to 3 inches. When the oil is hot (365° F. on a frying thermometer), fry the mixture by the tablespoon, turning the fritters once, until they are golden. Drain on paper towels and serve at room temperature with *Môlho de Acarajé*.

Môlho de Acarajé
Black-Eyed Pea Fritter Sauce

BRAZIL

Makes about 1¼ cups

½ cup dried shrimp
1 medium onion, chopped
1 tablespoon crushed dried hot red peppers

½ teaspoon chopped fresh ginger root
3 tablespoons dendê (palm) oil

Soak the shrimp in cold water to cover for 30 minutes. Drain the shrimp and pulverize them in a blender or food processor with the onion, peppers, and ginger root. Heat the oil in a skillet and sauté the shrimp mixture for about 3 minutes. Transfer to a bowl and serve with the *acarajé*.

Variation: For *Abará* (Steamed Black-Eyed Peas), make 1 recipe *Acarajé* (Black-Eyed Pea Fritters), but do not fry them. Beat the mixture thoroughly until it is fluffy with 3 tablespoons *dendê* oil and fresh hot red peppers, seeded, coarsely chopped, and puréed in a blender or food processor, to taste. Place tablespoons of the mixture in the center of 6-inch squares of kitchen parchment or aluminum foil, push a whole dried shrimp into the center of the pea mixture, then fold up into a neat package. If using parchment, tie securely with kitchen string. Steam the packages for 1 hour and serve directly from the packages at room temperature. Traditionally, banana leaves, which are sometimes available from specialty shops, are used for *Abará*. Makes about 24.

Variation: There is a simpler, but very attractive, version, *Buñuelitos de Frijol* (Bean Fritters) from coastal Colombia. The black-eyed peas are soaked overnight in cold water and the skins rubbed off and discarded. The peas are ground fine and seasoned with salt, then beaten with a wooden spoon until they are light and fluffy. They are deep fried by the tablespoon in vegetable oil or lard until golden brown.

Garbanzos Compuestos   MEXICO
Toasted Chickpeas

Chickpeas were brought to the New World by the Spanish and even though the common bean (red kidney, etc.) was first cultivated in the Valley of Mexico as early as 5000 B.C. and had long spread to other parts of the continent by the time of the Conquest, chickpeas were given a warm welcome and have been widely used in the kitchen ever since. I think, however, that toasted chickpeas as a cocktail nibble are a piece of culinary borrowing from South America, where a special type of large-kernel white corn was developed by the Incas, presumably sometime after corn reached them from Mexico, its birthplace. Called *cancha* in Peru, the corn is soaked, fried in lard, seasoned with salt, and served alone, or with *seviche*, *anticuchos*, and so on. In Ecuador the same dish is called *Maíz Tostado* and is always served with the *seviches*.

Makes about 4 cups

Two 1-pound cans of chickpeas, or
   1 pound dried chickpeas,
   soaked overnight
1 teaspoon salt

½ cup olive oil
1 clove garlic
Ground hot red pepper

Drain the chickpeas, cover with fresh water, and simmer for 30 minutes. Add the salt and continue cooking until the chickpeas are tender. Drain and cool. Heat the olive oil in a skillet and sauté the chickpeas with the garlic until they are golden brown. Drain on paper towels and sprinkle with the hot pepper.

    If using cooked canned chickpeas, rinse, drain, and then fry them.

Patacones

COLOMBIA

Green Plantain Chips

Fried plantain slices are popular in many parts of Latin America under different names and cooked by slightly different methods. Sprinkled lightly with salt, they are served with drinks, or as an accompaniment to meat, fish, or poultry. My favorite is this one from the northern coast of Colombia.

Vegetable oil for deep frying
1 large green plantain, peeled and
    cut into 1½-inch slices
Salt

Pour enough oil into a deep fryer or saucepan to fill it to a depth of 2 to 3 inches. Heat to moderate, 325° F. on a frying thermometer. Drop in the plantain slices and fry until tender, about 5 minutes. Lift out and drain on paper towels. Cover with wax paper and press until each is about ¾ inch thick. I find a clenched fist does as well as anything. In fact in Costa Rica, where the usual name is *tostones*, they are sometimes called *plátanos a puñetazos*, "plantains hit with the fist."

Raise the temperature of the oil to hot, 375° F. on a frying thermometer, and fry the slices until they are brown and crispy on the outside, tender inside, a minute or two. Traditional cooks dip the slices in cold, salted water before this second frying to make them crustier. I don't find this extra fussiness makes much difference. Sprinkle lightly with salt before serving.

Variation: In Venezuela the chips are called *tostones de plátano*, and cut into 1-inch slices. Some cooks put them in overlapping pairs after the first frying and before flattening them. This gives a very thick, soft center with crispy edges. In lieu of the clenched fist, the heel of the hand, or a rolling pin, I've seen cooks on this coast use large stones from the beach to do the flattening for them.

Variation: *Tostones* in Puerto Rico, cut diagonally into ½-inch slices, are soaked for 30 minutes in cold, salted water before they are either sautéed, or deep fried in oil or lard. They are dipped again in salted water before the second frying.

Variation: Also in Puerto Rico green plantains are very thinly sliced, soaked in ice water for 30 minutes, drained, patted dry, deep fried until crisp in hot oil or lard, and sprinkled with salt before serving. Called *platanutri*, they are *tostoncitos* in the Dominican Republic and *chicharritas de plátano verde* in Costa Rica. Green bananas are often used in the same way. They make a pleasant change from potato chips.

Yuca Frita   COLOMBIA
Cassava Chips

In Colombia hors d'oeuvres are called *picadas* and any fried *picada* is called a *fritanga*. Cassava chips, deliciously light and crisp and no trouble at all to make, are among the *fritangas* I enjoy most. This root vegetable is such an astonishment. First cultivated in northern Brazil in 1500 B.C. it has now spread all over the world. I once saw it growing outside a country pub in Wiltshire, England, where its tall spike of white flowers towered flamboyantly over roses and wallflowers. We know it best as tapioca, but Latin America uses it much more widely, added to stews, boiled and mashed. Its squeezed-out juice is the basis of *cassareep*, used in the Guyanese national meat and poultry stew. And of course there is always a bowl of *farofa* (cassava meal) on the table in Brazilian restaurants and homes (see page 6). I like cassava in all its forms whether it is called yucca, manioc, mandioca, aipím, cassava, or botanically, *Manihot utilissima*.

1 pound cassava (yucca) root, about	Salt Vegetable oil or lard

Peel the vegetable under cold running water as it discolors quickly. Cut into 1-inch slices and boil in salted water to cover until tender, about 30 minutes. The pieces often break up during cooking but this does not matter. Drain, pat dry with paper towels. In a skillet heat about ½ inch oil or lard and fry the pieces until they are crisp and golden all over. Serve at room temperature with drinks. The chips are also a pleasant accompaniment to meats or poultry.

For crisper chips, freeze the boiled vegetable for an hour or so before frying it and fry it frozen. The chips can be deep fried if preferred.

Variation: In the Colombian highlands *Papas Criollas Fritas* (Fried Creole Potatoes) are a popular appetizer. These are small local potatoes with yellow flesh; the smallest bite-sized ones are chosen and deep fried, skin and all, sprinkled with salt and eaten while still hot as an accompaniment to drinks. They are sometimes available in tropical markets; if not, use very small new potatoes.

Variation: Puerto Ricans use breadfruit to make *Hojuelas de Panapén* (Breadfruit Chips). Peel and core a breadfruit and quarter it. Cut it into thin crosswise slices and drop into boiling salted water. Boil for 2 to 3 minutes, drain, and pat dry. Fry in deep oil or lard until the chips are golden and crisp. Sprinkle with salt and serve at room temperature. Canned breadfruit can be used, in which case simply pat it dry, slice, and fry it.

SEVICHE

Seviche or *ceviche* — the spelling varies — is raw fish marinated in lime or lemon juice. The fish loses its translucent look as the juice "cooks" it and needs no further cooking. It doesn't taste raw. The idea almost certainly originated in Polynesia and like all migrant dishes has evolved in its new home; I have found versions of it all over Latin America. The best *seviches* in Mexico are from the state of Guerrero, especially from Acapulco on the Pacific coast. The fish principally used are sierra, or Spanish, mackerel, pompano, and porgy. I am always rather surprised at how well the mackerel *seviche* comes out, with the full-flavored and oily fish tempered by the lime or lemon juice. *Seviche* in Peru, served with sweet potatoes, lettuce, ears of corn, and toasted corn (*cancha*), is almost a meal in itself. The most popular fish there is bass, which makes a very delicate *seviche*, though octopus, conch, and scallops are also used. I've enjoyed *seviche* in restaurants overlooking Acapulco Bay, with its indestructible charm, and at a beach club in the strangely beautiful desert landscape of the Peruvian coast, but I think the best *seviches* I've ever had were in Ecuador. They are quite different from the Mexican variety though not wholly unlike those from Peru since bitter (Seville) oranges are used in both countries. Made from shrimp, lobster, bass, and an interesting local black conch, they have a reputation for being a splendid pick-me-up, and one is encouraged to try them at noon with a glass of cold beer. Marinated fish or shellfish should be eaten 5 to 6 hours after the marinating was begun.

Aguacate Relleno con Seviche de Camarones   MEXICO
Avocado Stuffed with Marinated Shrimp

This unusual variation on the standard *seviche* is from Acapulco and makes a rather grand and rich beginning to a special lunch or dinner. It would make an admirable light lunch served with soup as a first course and a dessert to finish.

Serves 2

½ pound small shrimp, shelled and deveined
½ cup or more fresh lime or lemon juice
1 medium tomato, peeled and chopped
1 canned jalapeño chili, rinsed, seeded, and cut in strips
1 pimiento, chopped
1 tablespoon fresh coriander (cilantro), chopped, or use parsley

½ small white onion, finely chopped
6 small pitted green olives, halved
4 tablespoons vegetable oil
Salt, freshly ground pepper
1 large avocado, halved and pitted
Lettuce leaves

If small shrimp are not available, cut larger ones into ½-inch pieces. Put into a bowl with enough lime or lemon juice to cover, about ½ cup. Refrigerate for about 3 hours, or until the shrimp are opaque. Add the tomato, chili, pimiento, coriander, onion, olives, oil, and salt and pepper to taste. Toss lightly to mix.

Spoon the shrimp mixture into the avocado halves and serve on plates garnished with lettuce leaves.

Seviche de Sierra   MEXICO
Mackerel Marinated in Lime Juice

Serves 6

1 pound skinned fillets of mackerel, or use pompano or porgy, cut into ½-inch squares

1½ cups lime or lemon juice, about
2 medium tomatoes, peeled and chopped

4 canned serrano chilies, rinsed
    and chopped
¼ cup vegetable oil
1 teaspoon oregano

Salt, freshly ground pepper
1 medium onion, finely sliced
1 large avocado, peeled, pitted,
    and sliced

Put the fish into a glass or china bowl and pour the lime or lemon juice over it. There should be enough to cover the fish. Add a little more, if necessary. Refrigerate the fish for 3 hours, turning it from time to time. Add the tomatoes, chilies, oil, oregano, and salt and pepper to taste. Toss lightly to mix and divide among 6 bowls. Garnish with the onion slices and the avocado.

Seviche de Corvina
PERU
Bass Marinated in Lime Juice

Serves 8

1½ pounds fillets of striped bass,
    or similar fish, cut into 1-inch
    pieces
Salt, freshly ground pepper
2 fresh hot red peppers, seeded and
    thinly sliced
1 teaspoon paprika

1 large onion, thinly sliced
1 cup lemon or lime juice
1 cup bitter (Seville) orange juice*
1 pound sweet potato, preferably
    the white type
2 ears corn, each cut into 4 slices
Lettuce leaves

Put the fish into a large glass or china bowl and season to taste with salt and pepper. Add 1 of the peppers, the paprika, and the onion, reserving a few rings for the garnish. Add the lemon or lime and bitter orange juice, mix lightly, cover, and refrigerate for about 3 hours, or until the fish is opaque, "cooked" by the juices.

Peel the sweet potatoes, cut into 8 slices, drop into salted water, bring to a boil, and cook until tender, about 20 minutes. Drop the slices of corn into boiling salted water and boil for 5 minutes. Drain and reserve the vegetables.

Line a serving platter with lettuce leaves. Arrange the fish on the platter, garnish with the reserved onion rings and the hot pepper strips. Arrange the corn and sweet potato slices around the edge of the dish. Serve with *cancha* (toasted corn).

*If bitter (Seville) orange juice is not available, use 1½ cups lemon juice and ½ cup orange juice.

Seviche de Corvina   ECUADOR
Bass Marinated in Lime Juice

Serves 6 to 8

1½ pounds fillets of striped bass,
    or similar fish, cut into
    ½-inch pieces
1 cup lime or lemon juice
1 cup bitter (Seville) orange juice*
1 fresh hot red or green pepper,
    seeded and finely chopped

1 medium onion, thinly sliced
1 clove garlic, chopped
Salt, freshly ground pepper
1 cup vegetable oil

Put the fish into a large glass or china bowl and add the lime or lemon juice
to cover, adding a little more if necessary. Refrigerate for about 3 hours, or
until the fish is opaque, "cooked" by the lime or lemon juice. Drain.
Transfer to a serving bowl and mix with the bitter orange juice, pepper,
onion, garlic, salt and pepper to taste, and the oil. Serve with *Maíz Tostada*
(Toasted Corn) on the side.

Seviche de Camarones   ECUADOR
Marinated Shrimp

Serves 6

2 pounds medium shrimp, shelled
    and deveined
Salt
2 cups bitter (Seville) orange
    juice†
1 medium onion, finely chopped

1 fresh hot red or green pepper,
    seeded and finely chopped
1 large tomato, peeled, seeded,
    and chopped
Freshly ground pepper

Drop the shrimp into a large saucepan of boiling salted water and boil for 2
or 3 minutes, or until the shrimp are cooked. Drain and mix with the
orange juice, onion, hot pepper, tomato, and salt and pepper to taste. Let
stand an hour before serving. Serve with *Maíz Tostada* (Toasted Corn) on
the side.

*If bitter (Seville) orange juice is not available, use ½ cup lime or lemon juice and ½ cup orange juice.

†If bitter (Seville) orange juice is not available, use 1½ cups orange juice and ½ cup lemon juice.

Seviche de Ostras GUATEMALA
Oysters Marinated in Lime Juice

I came across this unusual *seviche* in Guatemala, where there are still echoes of the Mayan cuisine which must have been an exciting one.

Serves 8

4 dozen oysters, shucked
1 cup lime or lemon juice
3 large tomatoes, peeled and
    chopped
1 large onion, finely chopped
1 fresh hot red pepper, seeded and
    chopped

2 tablespoons mint leaves,
    chopped
Salt, freshly ground pepper
Lettuce leaves

Put the oysters into a large glass or china bowl with the lime or lemon juice, cover, and refrigerate overnight. Strain the oysters, reserving the juice. In the bowl combine the oysters with the tomatoes, onion, hot pepper, mint leaves, and ¼ cup of the reserved juice. Season to taste with salt and pepper. Line a serving bowl with lettuce leaves and pour in the oyster mixture.

Siri Recheado BRAZIL
Stuffed Crabs

A similar dish, *crabes farcies*, is popular in the French Caribbean islands. I think it is very probable that the original inspiration came from West Africa. Whether in the West Indies or in Brazil, I have never had exactly the same version of stuffed crabs, which makes eating them a perpetual adventure. Cooks let imagination, not rule books, guide them.

If live crabs are not available, use ¾ pound (12 ounces) fresh, frozen, or canned crab meat, picked over to remove any shell or cartilage, and stuff scallop shells.

Serves 3 to 6

6 small, live hard-shelled crabs
Olive oil
2 tablespoons lime or lemon juice
2 cloves garlic, crushed
Salt, freshly ground pepper
1 medium onion, grated
2 scallions, chopped, using white
   and green parts
2 medium tomatoes, peeled,
   seeded, and chopped

2 tablespoons fresh coriander
   (cilantro), chopped
1 or 2 fresh hot red peppers, seeded
   and chopped
1 cup fresh breadcrumbs
1 egg, beaten
Fine bulgar wheat
Lettuce leaves
Small black and green olives

Plunge the crabs into boiling water and boil for 10 minutes. Lift out and cool. Carefully remove the meat from the shells and claws, and chop. Discard the spongy fiber. Scrub the empty shells, dry them, and brush the insides with a little olive oil. Season the crab meat with the lime or lemon juice, garlic, salt and pepper to taste, and set aside.

Heat 2 tablespoons olive oil in a skillet and sauté the onion, scallions, and tomatoes until the mixture is soft and well blended. Cool to room temperature and combine it with the crab mixture. Add the coriander leaves, the hot peppers, and the breadcrumbs, and mix well. Stuff the crab shells with the mixture, brush with beaten egg, and sprinkle with a little bulgar wheat. Bake in a preheated moderate (350° F.) oven for 30 minutes, or until lightly browned. Garnish serving plates with the lettuce leaves and olives. Serve as a first course.

Variation: Parsley is sometimes used instead of coriander leaves and mandioca (cassava, or manioc, meal) is used instead of bulgar wheat. In Bahia *dendê* (palm) oil often replaces olive oil.

EMPANADAS
Turnovers

One could write a small book on *empanadas, empanaditas, pasteles, pastelitos, empadhinas,* and *pastèizinhos* — those delicious turnovers, patties, and pies, stuffed with meat, poultry, fish, shellfish, and other mixtures, and baked or fried, which are so popular throughout Latin America. Each country has its own favorite pastries, its own favorite filling, and the *empanadas* of Argentina and Chile are as different as one turnover can be from another. They come in small sizes for cocktails, larger ones for first courses, snacks, light luncheons, or picnics. They are very versatile, and I often use a pastry from one country, a filling from another, according to my fancy. I am not attempting to give a representative selection of these delights, only those I have especially enjoyed making and eating.

I remember at Viña del Mar, on the Chilean coast, sitting on the terrace of a friend's house overlooking the sea in the cold winter sunshine and eating *empanadas de locos* bought from a small shop in nearby Quintero and washing them down with the local, very acceptable champagne. *Locos* are the enormous abalone of this coast, where the cold Humboldt Current makes for a fabulous harvest of fish and shellfish. There were also turnovers with other fillings, but it is the juicy onion-enriched abalone ones I remember best, and for which I have worked out an approximation. Use the recipe for the 6-inch Argentine *Empanadas* (Turnovers) pastry, page 38, with 2 tablespoons filling. Have ready equal amounts of coarsely chopped, canned abalone and finely chopped onion. Sauté the onion in *Color Chilena* (Paprika Oil), page 324. Add the abalone, salt, pepper, and a little chopped parsley. Place the filling across the center of the pastry, top with 2 small black olives, pitted, and a slice of hardboiled egg.

As for the *empanadas* of Argentina, some of which I ate decorously in a *whiskería* (a felicitously evolved tea shop) in Buenos Aires, the crust was so light and flaky I felt the *empanada* might fly from the plate. The filling combined beef with pears and peaches — utterly delicious. I remember too taking some with me for an al fresco lunch on the banks of the River Plate, the Rio de la Plata, which looked like a vast sea of silver, not like a river at all. And on the other side of the river, later in Montevideo, in Uruguay, eating *empanadas* in a *sandwicheria*, which again belied its name by selling all manner of marvelous small foods as well as drinks.

Empanadas of course have strong echoes of Spain, Portugal, and the Middle East. They probably originated in the Middle East, which would be natural enough considering that wheat was cultivated there as early as 7000 B.C. But they are of mixed ancestry. The *pasteles* of the Middle East, for example, are believed to have been taken to Turkey from Spain or Portugal by Sephardic Jews a long while ago. They are very like the *empadhinas* of Brazil, which are cousins of the *empanadas*. However, many of the turnovers incorporate foods of the New World — potatoes, tomatoes, peppers, even using corn for the pastry, thus linking them with the indigenous Indian kitchens.

EMPADHINAS and PASTÈIZINHOS
Little Pies and Turnovers

One of my pleasantest memories of Brazil is of eating *empadhinas* and *pastèizinhos*, little savory pies and turnovers in a *confeitaria*, a pastry shop in downtown Rio which seemed to me to be full at all hours with people eating pies and cakes and drinking tiny cups of exquisitely strong coffee. The generic term for these pies and turnovers is *salgadinhos*, little salt things, and they form an enchanting part of the Brazilian cuisine, allowing the inventive cook endless freedom to experiment. If you make them in larger sizes, they are called *empadas* and *pastéis*, and they are fine for lunches.

Massa Para Empadhinas   BRAZIL
Pastry for Little Pies

Makes about 30

2½ cups all-purpose flour	2 egg yolks
½ teaspoon salt	Water
4 tablespoons (¼ cup) lard	1 egg
4 tablespoons (¼ cup) butter	

Sift the flour with the salt into a large bowl. Cut the lard and butter into little bits and rub into the flour with the fingertips to make a coarse meal. Make a well in the center of the flour and stir in the egg yolks with enough cold water (4 to 5 tablespoons) to make a soft but not sticky dough or mix quickly in a food processor. Cover with wax paper and refrigerate for 1 hour. Roll out on a lightly floured surface to ¹/₁₆th-inch thickness and cut into circles 1½ inches larger than the circumference of the cupcake, muffin, or tart tin you are using. Cut an equal number of circles the same size as the tins. Press the larger circles into the tins. Add enough filling to come about three-quarters of the way up the tin, and if the recipe calls for it a small piece of sliced hardboiled egg and a slice of pitted olive. Moisten the edges of the pastry with a little egg beaten with ½ teaspoon water, cover with the smaller circle of pastry, and seal firmly with the fingers. Brush the tops with egg and bake in a preheated moderate (350° F.) oven for 30 minutes or until golden brown. Makes about 30 in muffin tins measuring 2½ inches across.

The pastry may be used to make 1 large double-crust pie, in which case use a 9-inch pie tin and bake the pastry for about 10 minutes longer.

Picadinho de Carne
Meat Filling

Chopped beef fillings are popular all over Latin America. In this one the meat is steamed, making it moist and giving it a softer texture and more delicate flavor than its namesake, Mexican *picadillo*.

Makes about 2 cups

1 tablespoon olive oil
¾ pound lean ground beef
Salt, freshly ground pepper
2 cloves garlic, crushed
1 medium onion, grated

2 tomatoes, peeled and chopped
1 fresh hot red pepper, chopped
  (optional)
2 hardboiled eggs, sliced
Sliced pitted black or green olives

In a skillet heat the oil and add the beef, salt, pepper, and garlic, mixing well. Sauté for a minute or two, then add the onion, tomatoes, and the hot pepper, if liked. Stir to mix, cover, and cook over low heat until the meat is tender, about 20 minutes. Allow to cool. Then fill the pies three-quarters full and put a piece of sliced egg and a slice of olive on top of each before covering with the top crust.

Recheio de Sardinhas
Sardine Filling

Makes about 2 cups

1 tablespoon olive oil
1 medium onion, finely chopped
2 medium tomatoes, peeled,
  seeded, and chopped
½ fresh hot red pepper, seeded and
  chopped
Salt, freshly ground pepper

2 cans (4-ounce) sardines, drained
2 teaspoons lime or lemon juice
2 tablespoons chopped fresh green
  coriander (cilantro)
2 hardboiled eggs, chopped
4 pitted black or green olives,
  sliced

In a skillet heat the oil and sauté the onion until it is softened. Add the tomatoes and the pepper, season to taste with salt and pepper, and simmer, stirring from time to time, until the mixture is thick and well blended, about 10 minutes. Cool. Mash the sardines with the lime or lemon juice and coriander, and fold into the tomato mixture with the eggs and olives.

Recheio de Queijo
Cheese Filling

Makes about 2 cups

¾ pound (1 ½ cups) ricotta cheese
Salt, freshly ground white pepper
½ teaspoon sweet paprika

4 scallions, trimmed and chopped,
   using white and green parts
3 egg yolks, lightly beaten

Mix all the ingredients together. Chill slightly before using.

Recheio de Camarão Baiano
Shrimp Stuffing, Bahian Style

Makes about 2 cups

¼ cup dendê (palm) oil
1 medium onion, finely chopped
1 medium green bell pepper,
   seeded and chopped
1 fresh hot red or green pepper,
   seeded and chopped
1 pound fresh shrimp, peeled and
   chopped

Salt
½ cup palm hearts, chopped
2 egg yolks
½ cup thick coconut milk (page 7)
1 tablespoon fresh green coriander
   (cilantro), chopped

In a skillet heat the palm oil and sauté the onion and the peppers until they
are softened. Add the shrimp, salt to taste, and palm hearts, and cook for a
minute or two. Beat the egg yolks with the coconut milk and stir into the
shrimp mixture. Add the coriander and cook, stirring over low heat until
the mixture has thickened. It should have the consistency of a medium
white sauce. If necessary thicken with ½ teaspoon arrowroot or cornstarch
dissolved in 1 teaspoon water and cook for a minute or two longer. Cool.

Recheio de Galinha
Chicken Filling

Makes about 2 cups

2 tablespoons butter
½ cup mushrooms, finely chopped
4 scallions, trimmed and chopped, using white and green parts
1 cup finely diced cooked chicken breast

1 cup thick Béchamel sauce (page 325)
1 tablespoon grated Parmesan cheese (optional)

In a skillet melt the butter and sauté the mushrooms over fairly brisk heat until they have given up all their liquid and are very lightly browned, about 4 minutes. Stir the mushrooms, scallions, and chicken meat into the Béchamel sauce, which should be highly seasoned. Add the grated cheese, if liked. Cool before using.

I sometimes like to follow the example of Brazilian cooks who vary the sauce by using equal amounts of chicken stock and milk, making the sauce lighter with a beautiful chickeny flavor.

Massa Para Pastéis Fritos   BRAZIL
Pastry for Fried Turnovers

Makes 50 to 60 turnovers

2 cups all-purpose flour
½ teaspoon salt
2 tablespoons butter

2 eggs, lightly beaten
Vegetable oil for deep frying

Sift the flour with the salt into a large bowl. Cut the butter into little bits and rub into the flour with the fingertips to make a coarse meal. Make a well in the center of the flour and pour in the eggs. Stir with a fork to mix and add enough water (about 1 tablespoon) to make a soft but not sticky dough. Knead until the pastry is elastic. A food processor may be used to mix and knead the dough; spin until the dough forms a ball. Cover and allow to stand for 1 hour. Roll out on a floured surface to a thickness of ¹/₁₆ inch, cut into 3-inch rounds with a cookie cutter, or a glass, and stuff with 2 teaspoons of any of the fillings on pages 2–3. Moisten the edges with water or milk, fold over, and press together. Seal with the tines of a fork. I sometimes put a small piece of sliced hardboiled egg and a slice of black or green olive on top of the filling, a very popular touch in Brazil.

To fry: Pour enough oil into a fryer or saucepan to reach a depth of 2 to 3 inches. Heat to moderate, 350° to 360° F. on a frying thermometer. An easy way to check the temperature is to stir the oil with wooden chopsticks, then wait to see if tiny bubbles form on the sticks. If they do, the temperature is right. Fry the turnovers, a few at a time, until golden brown, turning once, cooking a total of 4 to 5 minutes. Drain on paper towels and keep warm.

Empanadas
Turnovers

ARGENTINA

Makes 16 first-course or luncheon-size turnovers

FOR THE PASTRY

4 cups all-purpose flour
2 teaspoons baking powder
1 teaspoon salt

1½ cups lard, or ¾ cup each lard
    and butter

Sift the flour, baking powder, and salt into a large bowl. Cut the fat into small pieces and rub into the flour with the fingertips to form a coarse meal. Mix to a fairly stiff dough with cold water, gather into a ball or mix in a food processor, and refrigerate, covered with wax paper, for 1 hour. Roll out on a floured surface to about ⅛ inch thick. Cut into 6-inch circles using a small plate or bowl as a guide.

FOR THE FILLING

2 medium onions, finely chopped
2 cups finely diced raw potatoes
1 pound finely chopped lean round
    steak

Salt, freshly ground black pepper
3 tablespoons beef stock
1 egg, beaten with ½ teaspoon
    water

Mix all the ingredients, except the egg, together. Spoon 2 tablespoons of the mixture across the center of each circle of pastry, leaving ¼ inch at the edges. Moisten the edges of the pastry with the egg and fold the pastry over to make a turnover, pressing the edges firmly together. Curve the turnover slightly to form a crescent shape, then turn about ¼ inch of the pastry back over itself, pinching it between the thumb and forefinger to form a rope-like pattern round the edge. Prick the tops of the turnovers 2 or 3 times with the tines of a fork and brush with the egg mixture. The *empanadas* are now ready to bake and may be frozen until ready to use. Let them thaw for 3 hours at room temperature before cooking.

To bake: Bake the turnovers on an ungreased cookie sheet for 10 minutes in a preheated hot (400° F.) oven. Reduce the heat to 350° F. and bake for 30 minutes longer, or until golden brown.

ANOTHER FILLING

2 tablespoons butter
1 medium onion, finely chopped
1 green bell pepper, seeded and
*   chopped*
1 pound lean ground beef
1 large tomato, peeled and
*   chopped*

1 large pear, peeled, cored, and
*   chopped*
2 large peaches, peeled, pitted,
*   and chopped*
Salt, freshly ground pepper
¼ cup dry white wine

Heat the butter in a skillet and sauté the onion and pepper over moderate heat until softened. Add the meat, breaking it up with a fork, and sauté for a few minutes longer. Add all the remaining ingredients and cook for 5 minutes over low heat. Cool and stuff the turnovers with the mixture in the same way as for the other filling. If using both fillings, double the amount of pastry.

Variation: In Cuba a similar pastry is enlivened by the addition of ½ cup dry sherry, 2 eggs and 2 egg yolks, and a tablespoon of sugar. The lard and butter are reduced to 2 tablespoons each. This is a very old recipe from colonial times and an attractive one. The fillings used are any cooked meat or poultry, chopped and mixed with chopped onion, sautéed in butter, peeled and chopped tomatoes, raisins, olives, capers, and chopped hardboiled eggs, combined and seasoned with salt and pepper. Wonderful for using leftovers.

Empanaditas
Little Turnovers

VENEZUELA

Makes 75 cocktail turnovers

FOR THE PASTRY

3 cups all-purpose flour
½ teaspoon salt

6 ounces (¾ cup) butter
1 egg and 1 yolk, lightly beaten

Sift the flour with the salt into a large bowl. Cut the butter into small pieces and rub into the flour with the fingertips to form a coarse meal. Or use a food processor. Make a well in the center of the flour and add the egg and yolk, stir to mix, and add water (about ⅓ cup), tablespoon by tablespoon, mixing with a fork, to make a soft but not sticky dough. Form the dough into a ball and refrigerate it, covered, for 1 hour. Roll out the dough on a floured surface to ¹/₁₆th inch thick and cut into 2½-inch squares. Put a teaspoon of filling into the center of each square, fold over, and seal the edges. The turnovers may be frozen at this point until ready to use. Let them thaw for 3 hours at room temperature before cooking. If preferred, they may be completely covered and simply reheated in the oven just before serving.

To fry: Fry as for the Colombian *Pastelitos Rellenos de Cerdo* (Pork-Filled Turnovers), page 41.

FOR THE FILLING

1 pound lean boneless pork, chopped
2 tablespoons vegetable oil
1 medium onion, finely chopped
1 green bell pepper, seeded and finely chopped
2 medium tomatoes, peeled and chopped

1 tablespoon small pimiento-stuffed green olives, chopped
1 tablespoon capers, chopped
1 tablespoon seedless raisins
Salt, freshly ground pepper
Aliños criollos en polvo, to taste*
½ cup dry sherry
1 hardboiled egg, chopped

Put the pork into a saucepan with water barely to cover and simmer, covered, until tender, about 30 minutes. Drain, reserving the pork stock. In a skillet heat the oil and sauté the onion and pepper until they are softened.

Aliños criollos en polvo is a Venezuelan seasoning sold ready made. It is a mixture of sweet paprika, cumin, black pepper, ground annatto, garlic powder, oregano, and salt. Add a little of all or any of the ingredients to the filling according to taste. *Aliño*, sold as *Aliño Preparado* by McCormick in a glass shaker bottle, may sometimes be available in Latin markets. It makes a characteristic and remarkably pleasant addition to soups, stews, etc., and also adds a little color. It is easy to make at home (see page 325).

Add the pork and sauté for a minute or two longer. Add the tomatoes, olives, capers, raisins, salt, pepper, *aliño criollo* to taste, and the sherry. If the mixture seems a little dry, add some of the reserved pork stock. Simmer, uncovered, until the liquid has almost evaporated. Allow to cool. Add the egg, mixing well.

Variation: Chile has a turnover very similar to the Venezuelan one. It may be fried or baked. Make the pastry in the same way. Use chopped sirloin steak or top round instead of pork, omit the green bell pepper, the capers, and the *aliño*, and add 1 tablespoon sweet paprika, ½ tablespoon hot paprika, and ½ teaspoon ground cumin (or to taste). Cut the pastry into 5-inch rounds using a small bowl or plate as a guide, stuff with about 1½ tablespoons of the mixture, paint the edges with a little egg mixed with ½ teaspoon water, fold over, and seal firmly, pressing the edges with a fork. Cut 2 or 3 slits in the top, brush with the egg mixture. To bake, place the turnovers on an ungreased cookie sheet in a preheated hot 400° F. oven for 10 minutes, then reduce the heat to 350° F. and cook for about 20 minutes longer, or until golden brown. The turnovers may be fried in the same way as the Venezuelan and Colombian ones.

A great many different fillings are used for turnovers in Chile; a piece of cheese, such as Münster or Monterey Jack, very thick béchamel sauce, highly flavored and mixed with grated Parmesan cheese, or with chopped cooked green vegetables such as green beans, spinach, Swiss chard, or with shrimp, fish, or any of the marvelous shellfish that the coast of Chile is blessed with. The seafood is often mixed with a thick béchamel seasoned with tomato.

Some turnovers are even simpler. Just a little chopped onion, salt and pepper, the shellfish, and its natural juices, baked in a pastry shell. There is no end to the inventiveness of Chilean cooks when it comes to *empanadas*.

Pastelitos Rellenos de Cerdo   COLOMBIA
Pork-Filled Turnovers

Makes about 100

FOR THE PASTRY

2 cups all-purpose flour	*½ teaspoon lemon juice*
½ teaspoon salt	*½ cup lukewarm water*
¼ pound (½ cup) butter	*Vegetable oil for deep frying*

Sift the flour and salt into a large bowl. Cut the butter into small pieces and rub into the flour with the fingertips to form a coarse meal. Mix the lemon juice with the water. Using a fork, stir in the water quickly to make a soft dough. Gather into a ball and refrigerate, covered with wax paper, for 30 minutes. Roll out the pastry on a floured surface to a thickness of 1/16 inch and cut into 2½-inch circles with a cookie cutter or glass. Put ½ tablespoon of filling in the center of each pastry circle, fold the pastry in half to make a turnover, and seal the edges by pressing with the tines of a fork. The turnovers may be frozen at this point until ready to use. Let them thaw for 3 hours at room temperature before cooking.

To fry: Pour enough vegetable oil in a fryer or saucepan to reach a depth of 2 to 3 inches. Heat to moderate, 350° F. on a frying thermometer. An easy way to check the temperature is to stir the oil with wooden chopsticks, then wait to see if tiny bubbles form on the sticks. If they do, the temperature is right. Fry the turnovers, a few at a time, until golden brown, turning once, about 5 minutes. Drain on paper towels and keep warm.

If preferred the *pastelitos* may be baked. Brush with egg yolk beaten with a little water in a preheated hot (400° F.) oven for 5 minutes. Reduce the heat to 350° F. and bake for 15 minutes longer, or until golden brown. Serve as an accompaniment to drinks.

They may also be cooked and later reheated in the oven just before serving.

FOR THE FILLING

½ pound ground pork
1 large onion, grated
4 tablespoons capers
1 hardboiled egg, finely chopped

½ cup deviled ham, or ¼ pound
   finely chopped boiled ham
Salt, freshly ground pepper to taste

Thoroughly mix all the ingredients together. Instead of pork, ground beef, chicken breast, or drained, canned tuna fish may be used. If using tuna, omit the ham and use 2 hardboiled eggs instead of 1.

ABOUT TORTILLAS

If one were to compile all the recipes that are in existence for tortilla-based appetizers, one would end up with an encyclopedia that would dizzy the reader. So I am giving here only my favorites, though I confess the choice has not been easy.

The Spaniards named them *antojitos*, little whims or fancies, and to me they are perhaps the most exciting aspect of pre-Columbian Mexican cooking. We have some very good descriptions of the markets of old Tenochtitlán, now modern Mexico City, before the Conquest was completed, when the city was virtually untouched by the invaders. In his *Historia General de las Cosas de Nueva España* Fray Bernardino de Sahagún, a Spanish priest, tells, among other things, of the types of tortilla on sale in the market; it is enough to make one's head spin — with envy. That marvelous early war correspondent, Bernal Díaz del Castillo, a captain who was with Cortés before and during the campaign, gives in his memoirs, *Historia de la Conquista de Nueva España*, a remarkable picture of dining in Mexico, so we do know that there was a great deal more, now alas lost, of this cuisine. However, loss was soon balanced by gain, as post-Conquest Mexicans made good use of the foods the Spanish brought from Europe and Asia, and their *antojitos* were enhanced by beef, pork, chicken, olives, almonds, raisins, and so on.

With the exception of *arepas*, the corn bread of Venezuela, tortillas are unique among breads in being made from a cooked, not a raw, flour. Dried corn is boiled with lime until the skins are loosened and the cooked, skinned kernels are then dried and ground to make the *masa harina*, dough flour, that is used for tortillas. Happily for anyone wanting to make them, it is sold packaged by the Quaker Company. The flour is mixed with water to a fairly soft dough, pressed on a tortilla press or patted into a flat pancake by hand, and baked on a *comal*, an ungreased griddle, for a minute or so. It is not possible to speak of a raw tortilla, only of an unbaked one. Tortillas for those who don't want to make them are available frozen.

Arepas are also made from a cooked flour, and since it was in the Valley of Mexico in 5000 B.C. that corn was first cultivated, not arriving in South America until about 1500 B.C., it is a safe bet that the technique of cooking the corn before making it into flour was established in Mexico long before Venezuela invented *arepas*. In any event they are quite different.

Tortillas for *antojitos* are made in a variety of shapes and sizes and with a variety of fillings. Sternly traditional cooks parcel the fillings out among the shapes with some rigidity. However, when we make such things in the States, we should have the freedom to follow our own whims and fancies.

A selection of *antojitos* makes a fine buffet lunch when accompanied by a dessert.

Tortillas

Mexican cooks pat out tortillas by hand. They take a small ball of tortilla dough and with quick, deft movements pat the dough from one hand to the other, transforming it in no time at all into a thin pancake, which is then baked. I have managed to produce a recognizable tortilla by this method, though most of my hand-patted ones were a little on the thick side. I am pretty sure that if I had spent two or three years at it I could have mastered the art of making tortillas by hand! However, since colonial Spain had faced the problem and come up with the solution in the form of a tortilla press, I gave up trying and bought myself a press. The old colonial ones were made of wood. Mine is cast iron. It works extremely well and many Mexican cooks who can hand-pat a tortilla use it for convenience. I use a plastic liner on the press — a plastic bag cut in half is ideal. However, some people prefer to use wax paper.

Makes about eighteen 4-inch tortillas

2 *cups* masa harina	1⅓ *cups lukewarm water*

Put the *masa harina* into a bowl, pour in 1 cup of the water, and stir to mix to a soft dough. Add the remaining water if necessary, as it probably will be. It is impossible to be absolutely precise about the amount of water needed. If the *masa harina* is very fresh it will need less water, and I have even found that an extremely humid day has its effect. The corn flour picks up moisture from the air. The dough should be flexible and hold together nicely. If it is too wet, it will stick to the tortilla press, in which case simply scrape it off the plastic sheet or wax paper, and add it to the dough with a little more flour. The dough is not hurt by being handled. If the dough is too dry, floury bits will show up on the cooked tortilla. Sprinkle the dough with a little more lukewarm water. Traditionally salt is not added to tortillas. However, a teaspoon of salt may be added to the flour by those who find the unsalted tortilla insipid.

Divide the dough into balls the size of small eggs and flatten on the tortilla press between 2 sheets of plastic or wax paper to thin pancakes about 4 inches across. Peel off the top piece of plastic or paper. Put the tortilla, paper side up, in the palm of the left hand, peel off the paper, then flip the tortilla onto a moderately heated, ungreased *comal* or griddle. It's a knack, but very easily learned. Cook until the edges begin to curl, about 1 minute, then, using a spatula or the fingers, turn the tortilla over and cook for about a minute longer. It should be very lightly flecked with brown. The side that is cooked first is the top. Pressing the first side with a spatula while the second side is cooking will turn it into an *inflado* — meaning something swollen with air; it subsides on being taken off the *comal* — which is said to be good luck. It certainly makes the stuffing of *panuchos* easier.

As they are done, stack the tortillas in a cloth napkin. When a dozen are stacked up, wrap them, napkin and all, in foil and put them into a preheated barely warm (150° F.) oven, where they will stay warm for hours. If it is necessary to reheat cold tortillas, dampen the hands and pat the tortillas between them. Place the tortillas over direct heat, fairly low heat, turning constantly for about 30 seconds.

For appetizers use a piece of dough about the size of a walnut and flatten it out to about 2 inches. Even smaller tortillas may be made if desired, using a piece of dough about the size of a large grape.

Variations

Tacos. Make 4-inch tortillas, stuff them with any filling, roll them into a cylinder, and eat by hand, or secure them with a toothpick and fry them in shallow oil or lard until crisp. Usually called soft and fried tacos.

Sopes. Pinch off a piece of tortilla dough about the size of a walnut, roughly 2 teaspoons, and pat or press it into a pancake about 2 inches in diameter. Bake it on an ungreased griddle, iron skillet, or *comal* until it is lightly flecked with brown on both sides, about 1 minute a side. Pinch up a ¼-inch border all round the *sope*, then fry in vegetable oil or lard on the flat side. Stuff with any filling, the most usual of which is *Frijoles Refritos* (Refried Beans), page 242, topped with a little grated cheese, a little chopped white onion, and a hot chili sauce with a radish slice for a garnish. The basic tortilla dough for *sopes* is often mixed with another ingredient. Half a cup of cottage cheese may be added to the dough, or 2 or 3 *ancho* chilies, soaked and ground, or 2 or 3 *serrano* chilies, seeded and ground in a blender or food processor.

Chalupas (little canoes). These are oval tortillas with a pinched-up rim. Pinch off a piece of tortilla dough, about 2 tablespoons, and roll it into a cylinder about 4 inches long. Flatten it into an oval on a tortilla press or pat it into shape by hand. Bake on a *comal* or griddle in the usual way, then pinch up a ¼-inch rim all the way round. Fry in vegetable oil or lard on the flat side. Some cooks spoon a little hot fat into the *chalupa* when frying it. Use any filling, but the most usual is shredded chicken or pork, crumbled or grated cheese, and a red or green chili sauce.

Totopos. Ordinary tortillas cut into 4 or 6 wedges, fried until crisp in lard or vegetable oil, and used for dips or with *Frijoles Refritos* (Refried Beans) are usually called *tostaditas*. However, in Mexico's Federal District they are often called *totopos*. This leads to some confusion as there is an entirely different *antojito* also called a *totopo*. To make *totopos* remove the seeds from 3 *ancho* or *pasilla* chilies, soak them in hot water, and purée them in a blender. Mix the chilies with the *masa harina* and ½ cup cooked, mashed red kidney beans. Season with salt and make into rather thicker than usual tortillas using about 2 teaspoons of dough for each *totopo*. Fry the *totopos* in hot lard or vegetable oil on both sides. Drain on paper towels and spread with *guacamole* topped with grated Parmesan cheese, or use any topping.

Tostadas. These are 6- or 4-inch tortillas fried until crisp in hot lard or vegetable oil and topped with various combinations of poultry, meat, fish, or shellfish and various garnishes, lettuce, chili sauce, and so on. Use 2-inch tortillas for appetizers.

FILLINGS

The most popular fillings are shredded chicken, shredded pork, or *Picadillo* (Chopped Beef), combined with various sauces such as *Salsa Cruda* (Uncooked Tomato Sauce), *Salsa de Tomate Verde* (Green Tomato Sauce), and *Salsa de Jitomate* (Cooked Tomato Sauce); chilies such as *serrano* or *jalapeño*, available canned; shredded lettuce, romaine or iceberg; grated cheese such as Parmesan or Münster; and *Frijoles Refritos* (Refried Beans). *Guacamole* can be added to almost any *antojito* to advantage. Radishes, sliced or cut into radish roses, and olives are a popular garnish.

Chorizo. Skin chorizos (hot Spanish sausage) and chop coarsely. Sauté in vegetable oil with a little chopped onion, and tomato if liked. Drain any excess fat. Mix with a little grated Parmesan or Romano cheese (in Mexico *queso de Chihuahua* or *queso añejo* would be used). If not using tomato, add a little tomato sauce, red or green. Garnish with shredded lettuce.

Sardine. Sauté a medium onion, chopped, in 1 tablespoon vegetable oil, add 2 medium tomatoes, peeled, seeded, and chopped, and chopped *serrano* or *jalapeño* chilies to taste. Cook until thick and well blended. Mash in 1 cup *Frijoles Refritos* (Refried Beans), page 242, mixing well. Fold in 1 can sardines packed in olive oil, drained, boned, and chopped. Sprinkle with Parmesan cheese.

Cream cheese. Mash 3 ounces cream cheese with 3 tablespoons heavy cream and combine with 1 cup shredded pork or chicken. Top with a tomato sauce or a bottled chili sauce and garnish with shredded lettuce.

Panuchos
MEXICO

Fried Stuffed Tortillas

Panuchos are one of the most popular appetizers in the Mayan cuisine of the Yucatán peninsula. The garnish may vary slightly, but black beans are always used. They make a fine snack or light meal, and I have found that if I make my tortillas a little thicker than usual, they are easier to stuff. Pressing down lightly on the tortilla with a wooden spoon, or a spatula, when it is baking makes it puff up and this puffed-up layer is easy to lift up to insert the stuffing.

Serves 4 to 6

1 cup black beans
1 teaspoon epazote *(see page 9)*,
   if available
Salt
1 medium onion, thinly sliced
½ cup mild white vinegar
Twelve 4-inch tortillas
½ cup lard or vegetable oil

Shredded lettuce, romaine or
   iceberg
1 whole cooked chicken breast,
   boned and shredded
12 slices tomato

Wash the beans and pick them over. Put into a saucepan with cold water to cover by about ½ inch, add the *epazote*, crumbled, and simmer, covered, until tender, adding a little hot water from time to time if necessary. Add salt when the beans are tender and continue cooking, uncovered, until almost all the liquid has evaporated. Mash to a thick paste. Keep warm.

Chop the onion and soak it in salted water for 5 minutes. Drain. Transfer the onion to a small saucepan, pour in the vinegar, bring to a boil, remove from the heat and cool. Strain, discard the vinegar, and set the onion aside.

Using the point of a small sharp knife, lift up the top skin of the tortilla, leaving the skin still attached to the tortilla on one side. Carefully spread a layer of beans inside each little pocket. Replace the tortilla layer. Heat the lard or oil in a skillet and fry the tortillas, bottom side down, until lightly browned. Drain on paper towels. Place a layer of lettuce, chicken, and onion on each tortilla, and top with a slice of tomato.

Variation: If liked, a slice of hardboiled egg may be put on top of the beans. Use 2 eggs for 12 tortillas. Cooked shredded pork may be used instead of chicken breast.

Sambutes
Stuffed Miniature Tortillas

MEXICO

Sambutes, sometimes spelled *salbutos*, are another Yucatán specialty —
they taste just as good no matter how they are spelled.

Makes about 18

FOR THE FILLING

2 tablespoons vegetable oil
½ pound lean ground pork
1 medium onion, chopped

2 medium tomatoes, peeled and
   chopped
Salt, freshly ground pepper

Heat the oil in a skillet and sauté the pork until it is lightly browned. Purée
the onion and tomatoes in a blender or food processor and add to the pork.
Season to taste with salt and pepper and simmer, uncovered, until the
mixture is thick and fairly dry. Set aside.

FOR THE TORTILLAS

2 *cups* masa harina
1 teaspoon salt

4 tablespoons all-purpose flour
Vegetable oil for deep frying

Mix the *masa harina*, salt, and flour together. Add enough water (about a
teaspoon) to make a fairly stiff dough. Pinch off pieces of the dough about
the size of walnuts and roll into balls. Flatten on the tortilla press into
miniature tortillas not more than 2 inches across. Do not bake. Holding
one tortilla in the palm of the hand, place a tablespoon of the filling on it.
Cover with another tortilla and pinch the edges together. Continue until
all the tortillas and the fillings are used up.

Into a fryer or saucepan pour enough oil to reach a depth of 2 to 3
inches. Heat to about 375° F. on a frying thermometer. Fry the stuffed
tortillas, a few at a time, turning once, until they are golden brown, about 3
minutes. Drain on paper towels and eat hot.

If liked, these can be made even smaller, an inch across, pinching off a
piece of dough not much bigger than a good-sized grape. Fill with 1 teaspoon of the stuffing.

Sambutes are often served as an appetizer accompanied by the same
pickled onion as in *Panuchos* (page 47) and with a tomato sauce made by
peeling and chopping ½ pound tomatoes and reducing them to a purée in a
blender or food processor with 1 fresh hot seeded pepper, or 1 canned
serrano chili. The sauce is not cooked and is spooned on top of the stuffed
tortilla, which is then topped with a little onion. They make a marvelous
accompaniment to drinks.

Soups
Sopas

Soup is extremely popular in Latin America, and most people there would regard a main meal without soup as a poor thing indeed. Soups were not part of the indigenous cooking but were introduced in the colonial period and range from the bowl of richly flavored amber chicken consommé, so highly esteemed at the beginning of Sunday or holiday midday dinner in Mexico, to the hearty soup-stews, the pot-au-feu dishes that Colombia, particularly, excels in, and that are a meal in themselves.

From a very large array of soups, I have made a small selection of those I have particularly enjoyed. The varied soup repertoire evolved from local ingredients, chayote, zucchini, squash blossoms, sweet red peppers, corn, coconut, winter squash, yams, yucca, hearts of palm, and from the marvelous fish and shellfish of the region's coasts. They are not run-of-the-mill soups, of which Latin America has its full share — the soups one could call universal — vegetable, onion, cream of tomato, celery, watercress, green pea. No matter how good these may be, their Latin American cousins have not changed enough from the versions with which we are all familiar to make it worthwhile including them. My choice has been soups that will introduce new combinations of flavors, refreshing to any palate that is pleased with change.

Nowadays, with excellent canned beef or chicken stock available, one need not go to the trouble of making one's own stock. But Latin American cooking methods do have a pleasant bonus. Many dishes are cooked on top of the stove because, in the past, cooking was done mostly over charcoal, and ovens were not greatly used. As a result, when poaching a flank steak for a Venezuelan *Pabellón Caraqueño*, or a chicken for a Mexican *mole*, I get stock as an extra. I seldom freeze it, just refrigerate it, though I make a point of boiling it up and simmering it for 3 or 4 minutes if it hasn't been used in 2 or 3 days, which doesn't happen often as one always seems to need stock in the kitchen. And a nice thing is that stock does not sneer at leftovers or bits of this and that but welcomes them. When I boil up a refrigerated stock, I take the opportunity of adding any extras I may have around. The good rich stock comes in very handy for soup making.

Sopa de Aguacate
Avocado Soup

MEXICO

Avocado soup is popular in Latin America from Mexico all the way south to Chile. I don't think I've ever had an avocado soup I didn't enjoy. The beautiful pale green color and the buttery richness of the flavor are seductive, yet one of my favorite avocado soups is also one of the simplest. It comes from Mexico and is good hot, marvelous chilled. It is vitally important when making the soup not to let the avocado cook, as cooked avocados tend to develop a bitter taste. I like the soup garnished with chopped fresh coriander leaves as this adds a very special flavor.

Serves 6

2 large, ripe avocados
4 cups rich chicken stock
1 cup heavy cream
Salt, freshly ground white pepper
1 tablespoon fresh green coriander
    (cilantro), finely chopped
    (optional)

6 tortillas, quartered and fried
    crisp in lard or oil

Peel and mash the avocados and put them through a sieve. Place them in a heated soup tureen. Heat the chicken stock with the cream. Pour the stock into the avocados, stirring to mix, or beat lightly with a wire whisk. Season to taste with salt and pepper. Sprinkle with the coriander, if desired. Serve immediately with the crisp tortillas.

For summer dining the soup is splendid chilled. In which case do not heat the tureen and make sure that the chicken stock has been skimmed of all fat. Combine the avocados, stock, cream, salt, and pepper in a blender or food processor and blend until it is smooth. Chill quickly and serve as soon as possible, as the soup tends to darken on top if left for long. If it darkens, simply stir it before serving. The flavor is not affected and the small amount of darkening won't show. Keeping air from the soup helps to minimize darkening, so it is useful to cover it with plastic wrap while it is chilling.

Variation: This *Sopa de Paltas* (Avocado Soup) from Chile is an interesting example of a culinary combination from the opposite ends of the earth. The avocado and the Béchamel go very well together, producing a soup that is subtly flavored. In a fairly large saucepan heat 4 tablespoons butter and sauté 1 medium onion, finely chopped, until it is soft. Add 4 tablespoons flour, and cook, stirring, for about 2 minutes over low heat without letting the flour take on any color. Gradually add 2 cups milk, stirring constantly until the mixture is smooth and thick. Stir in 2 cups chicken stock and continue to cook over low heat, stirring from time to time, for about 5 minutes. Cut 2 large, ripe avocados in half and remove the pits. Mash them in their shells, turn them into a warmed soup tureen, season with a little lemon juice, and continue to mash until they are quite smooth. Pour the hot béchamel mixture over the avocados, stirring to mix, or beat with a wire whisk. Season to taste with salt and pepper. Serves 4 to 6.

Variation: For *Sopa de Aguacate y Papas* (Avocado Vichyssoise) from Colombia, peel and dice 1 pound potatoes and put into a large saucepan with the white part of 2 leeks, washed and sliced, and 1 medium onion, sliced. Pour in 4 cups chicken stock, cover, and simmer until tender. Put the vegetables and broth through a sieve, return the mixture to the saucepan, stir in a cup of heavy cream, and heat just to a boil. Peel and mash 2 large avocados and put them into a heated soup tureen. Add the hot soup and stir to mix thoroughly. Season to taste with salt and white pepper. The soup is also very good served chilled. Serves 6.

Variation: For *Sopa de Aguacate* (Avocado Soup) from Venezuela, scoop out the flesh of 2 large avocados and put into a blender with 1½ cups clam juice, 1½ cups chicken stock, 1 cup light cream, and salt and white pepper to taste. Blend until smooth, chill, and serve garnished with a little chopped parsley and a little sweet paprika. If preferred, omit the cream and use 2 cups each chicken stock and clam juice. Serves 6.

Sopa de Creme de Palmito
BRAZIL

Creamed Hearts of Palm Soup

Hearts of palm are a commonplace in Brazil, where their delicate flavor and texture is taken for granted. I will always think of them as a luxury, even though most supermarkets have them canned. I particularly like to serve this soup when I am having a beef dish as a main course and want something elegantly light in contrast to the robust flavor of the meat. The soup can be prepared ahead of time and finished at the last minute. It is simplicity itself with a lovely, unusual, delicate flavor.

Serves 6

2 tablespoons rice flour
1 cup milk
A 14-ounce can hearts of palm

5 cups chicken stock
Salt, white pepper
2 egg yolks

In a small bowl mix the rice flour with the milk. Drain and chop the hearts of palm and purée in a blender or food processor with 1 cup of the chicken stock. Pour the mixture into a saucepan and stir in the rice flour mixture and the rest of the chicken stock. Season to taste with salt and pepper and cook, stirring, over low heat until the soup is smooth and thickened slightly. In a bowl beat the egg yolks. Beat in a little of the hot soup, then pour the egg yolk mixture into the soup, and cook, stirring, for about 1 minute. Do not let the soup boil as it will curdle.

Antonia's Sopa de Chayote
MEXICO

Chayote Soup

This soup from Cuernavaca in the state of Morelos has a lovely light texture and delicate flavor. The main ingredient, chayote, the pale green pear-shaped vegetable, is worth looking out for in tropical markets.

Serves 6

2 large chayotes, peeled and sliced
Salt
1 medium onion, finely chopped
1 clove garlic, chopped

2 tablespoons butter
1 tablespoon flour
4 cups chicken stock
White pepper

Put the chayotes in a saucepan with salted water to cover and simmer, covered, until they are tender, about 20 minutes. Transfer the chayotes to a blender or food processor with 2 cups of the cooking liquid and blend until smooth. Discard any remaining cooking liquid.

In a saucepan sauté the onion and garlic in the butter until the onion is soft. Stir in the flour and cook, stirring, for a minute without letting it brown. Add the chicken stock and cook, stirring, until the mixture is smooth. Combine the stock with the chayote mixture, season to taste with salt and white pepper, and simmer, covered, for 5 minutes longer, stirring from time to time. If liked, the soup may be put through a sieve for a finer texture.

Variation: I found an interesting variation of this soup in Nicaragua. It is made in exactly the same way except that just before serving, 1 cup (about ½ pound) cooked, shredded chicken breast is added and heated through, and the soup when served is garnished with croutons.

Sopa de Jitomate
Tomato Soup

MEXICO

This is a very fresh, simple tomato soup from Mexico, where the tomato originated and where it is sold large and ripe and sweet. I wait until the tomato season reaches its peak before cooking this, or better still until some home-grown tomatoes are ripe on the vine. I sometimes add a tablespoon of dry sherry to each serving, but mostly I prefer the unadorned flavor of tomato.

Serves 6

2 tablespoons butter or vegetable
   oil
1 large onion, finely chopped
1 clove garlic, chopped
6 large ripe tomatoes, peeled and
   coarsely chopped

4 cups chicken or beef stock
Salt, freshly ground pepper
6 tablespoons dry sherry
   (optional)

Heat the butter in a fairly large saucepan and sauté the onion and garlic until the onion is soft. Add the tomatoes and cook, stirring, for 2 or 3 minutes. Pour in the stock and simmer the mixture for 10 minutes. Cool slightly and purée in two or three batches in a blender or food processor. Reheat, add salt and pepper to taste, and serve in bouillon cups with the sherry, if liked.

Sopa de Pimientos Morrones
Sweet Red Pepper Soup   MEXICO

When I was first married and my husband was transferred to Mexico for some years, my mother-in-law found me a cook who had long associations with the family. Her name was Francisca and she was a Zapotecan Indian from Oaxaca, a tiny woman with a beautiful tranquil high-cheekboned face, framed by long plaits, quite gray. This soup was one she made for me, using bell peppers for their rather more robust flavor. It is important that they be smooth and shiny, as even slightly wrinkled peppers will have less flavor and the texture of the finished soup will not be so smooth. This is a beautiful soup to look at with its deep, rich color and I love its pleasantly unusual flavor. The addition of hot peppers to the pot is a matter of taste — I prefer it without.

Serves 6

2 tablespoons vegetable oil
1 medium onion, finely chopped
3 large ripe red bell peppers
4 cups chicken or beef stock
1 cup tomato juice

1 fresh hot red or green pepper,
    whole and with stem left on
    (optional)
Salt, freshly ground pepper

Heat the oil in a small skillet and sauté the onion until it is soft. Set aside. Peel the peppers according to the instructions on page 15. Seed and chop coarsely. Purée the peppers with the onion and a little stock in a blender or food processor. Transfer the purée to a saucepan, add the rest of the stock, the tomato juice, and if liked the hot pepper. Season to taste with salt and pepper. Simmer, covered, for 15 minutes. Remove and discard the pepper.

Sopa de Flor de Calabaza
Squash Blossom Soup   MEXICO

Squash, one of the oldest vegetables in the world, originated in Mexico. The flowers used in this recipe are usually from zucchini, although blossoms from any type of squash or pumpkin can be used. A popular Italian dish consists of the flowers dipped in batter and fried, so that Italian as well as Latin American markets are good places to go looking for squash blossoms. These are the male flowers, which produce no fruit. It is the female flower that gives us the zucchini, so one may eat the blossoms with a clear conscience. The male blossoms are attached to short, thin stems; the female flowers are attached to miniature squashes. *Epazote*, which adds a slight but distinctive flavor to the soup, is not often available in local markets, but the soup, with its subtle flavor, is still very good without it.

Serves 6

1 pound squash blossoms	5 cups chicken stock
4 tablespoons butter	Salt, freshly ground pepper
1 medium onion, finely chopped	1 sprig epazote, page 9 (optional)

Remove and discard the stems from the squash blossoms and chop the flowers coarsely. Heat the butter in a saucepan and sauté the onion until it is soft. Add the flowers and sauté for 3 or 4 minutes longer. Pour in the stock, season to taste with salt and pepper, cover, and simmer until the blossoms are tender, about 5 minutes. Purée in a blender or food processor, in more than one batch if necessary. Return to the saucepan and reheat with the sprig of *epazote* if it is available. Discard the *epazote* before serving.

Variation: For *Sopa de Flor de Calabaza con Crema* (Cream of Squash Blossom Soup), a rather richer soup, whisk 2 egg yolks with 1 cup of heavy cream, then whisk 1 cup of the hot soup into the egg mixture, beat this into the soup, and cook, without letting it boil, until the soup is lightly thickened. Mexican cooks always use only egg yolks. I find whole eggs do a much better job, and I use them even though this is a departure from tradition.

Variation: For *Sopa de Flor de Calabaza con Jitomate* (Squash Blossom and Tomato Soup), add 2 medium tomatoes, peeled, seeded, and chopped, to the onion with the squash blossoms. This makes a very pleasantly different soup with an interesting blend of flavors.

Caldo de Zapallo Tierno   PARAGUAY
Zucchini Soup

This lovely simple recipe was given me by a friend, Josefina Velilla de Aquino, when I visited her in Asunción, Paraguay. She is a gifted cook and teacher of cooking, with a great feeling for traditional cuisine. Another version of it, from a family cook in Cuernavaca, is even more simple, and I often make that one when I am alone, or in a hurry, and the more elaborate one when I have guests. I often leave the rice out of the Paraguayan recipe for a more purely vegetable flavor.

Serves 6

2 tablespoons vegetable oil
1 medium onion, finely chopped
1 clove garlic, chopped
5 cups chicken stock
3 tablespoons raw rice
1 pound zucchini, grated

Salt, freshly ground pepper
1 egg
3 tablespoons freshly grated
    Parmesan cheese
1 tablespoon finely chopped
    parsley

Heat the oil in a fairly large saucepan and sauté the onion and garlic until the onion is soft. Add the chicken stock and the rice and simmer, covered, for 10 minutes. Add the zucchini. Season to taste with salt and pepper and simmer until the zucchini is very tender, about 15 minutes. In a soup tureen beat the egg with the cheese and parsley, then whisk in the soup, mixing well.

Variation: Antonia Delgado's *Sopa de Calabacita* (Zucchini Soup) from Cuernavaca, Mexico. In a saucepan sauté 1 medium onion, finely chopped, and 1 large scallion, using the white and green parts, coarsely chopped, in 2 tablespoons butter until the onion is soft. Add 1 pound zucchini, coarsely chopped, and stir for a minute. Pour in 5 cups chicken stock and simmer, covered, until the zucchini is tender, about 15 minutes. Purée in two or three batches in a blender or food processor. Pour the soup back into the saucepan, season to taste with salt and pepper, and reheat. Remove from the heat and stir in ½ cup heavy cream. Serve immediately. Serves 6.

Sopa de Crema de Coco COLOMBIA
Cream of Coconut Soup

This is a subtle and unusual soup from Cartagena in coastal Colombia, where coconut plays a large role in the kitchen. I like it especially as the beginning to a summer lunch or dinner.

Serves 6

1 coconut
5 cups chicken stock
2 tablespoons butter

1 medium onion, grated
2 tablespoons flour
Salt, freshly ground white pepper

Follow the instructions for extracting the thick milk from a coconut (page 7), and set it aside. There will be ¾ to 1 cup. Heat 1 cup of the chicken stock and pour it over the grated coconut, from which the thick milk has been squeezed, and let it stand about 30 minutes. Squeeze out the liquid through a double layer of dampened cheesecloth. Repeat the process two or three times to extract as much flavor from the coconut as possible. Set aside. Do not mix the two lots of milk. Discard the grated coconut.

Heat the butter in a saucepan and sauté the onion until it is very soft. Stir in the flour and cook, stirring, over low heat for 2 minutes. Gradually whisk in the thin coconut milk made with the stock, and the rest of the stock. Add a little more stock if there is only ¾ cup of the thick coconut milk, to make 6 cups in all. Season to taste with salt and pepper, cover, and simmer for 15 minutes. Stir in the thick coconut milk and heat the soup through but do not let it boil. Serve in bouillon cups.

Sopa de Repollo
Cabbage Soup

CHILE

Chile's temperate, sunny climate produces lovely fruits and vegetables and the cabbages are no exception, firm and heavy in the hand. Green cabbage is the best kind for this delicious, fresh-tasting soup.

Serves 6

1 small green cabbage, weighing about 1 pound
1 large or 2 medium potatoes
1 large leek
3 tablespoons butter
4 cups beef or chicken stock

Salt, freshly ground pepper
1 cup coarsely grated Münster or similar cheese

Wash and finely shred the cabbage. Peel the potato, slice thinly, then cut each slice into 3 or 4 fingers. Trim the leek and split it lengthwise. Wash thoroughly, then slice finely. Heat the butter in a saucepan large enough to hold all the ingredients. Add the cabbage, potatoes, and leek and cook, stirring with a wooden spoon, until the vegetables have absorbed the butter and the cabbage and leek are wilted, about 3 or 4 minutes. Pour in the stock, season to taste with salt and pepper, and simmer, covered, over moderate heat for 30 minutes, until the cabbage is tender. Stir in the cheese, and serve in soup bowls.

Sopa de Lima
Lime Soup

MEXICO

This soup is one of Mexico's great regional dishes. It comes from Yucatán, where the Mayan kitchen predominates, and it owes its unique flavor to a local species of lime that is seldom available, even in Mexico, outside the Yucatán peninsula. I have sometimes found these limes in the great Mexico City markets, but even then not regularly or often. Fortunately I've found that the soup loses very little of its authentic — and marvelous — flavor when made with our limes. In Mérida, Yucatán's capital, I had an interesting and very pleasant variation of the soup. Instead of the chicken gizzards and livers, a whole chicken breast, boned, poached, and shredded, was added. The chicken breast was cut in half, then simmered very gently in the stock for 10 minutes, allowed to cool, then skinned, boned, and shredded with the fingers. It was added to the soup just long enough to heat through before serving.

Serves 6

Lard or vegetable oil
1 medium onion, finely chopped
1 medium tomato, peeled and
 chopped
½ green bell pepper, seeded and
 chopped
2 or 3 canned serrano chilies,
 chopped
6 cups chicken stock
Juice of ½ lime and the shell

3 chicken gizzards
6 raw chicken livers, chopped
Salt, freshly ground pepper
6 tortillas, cut into thin strips
1 lime, thinly sliced

Heat 2 tablespoons of lard or vegetable oil in a saucepan and sauté the onion until it is softened. Add the tomato and sweet pepper and sauté for 2 or 3 minutes longer. Add the chilies, the chicken stock, the lime juice, and lime shell. Simmer for 2 minutes. Remove and discard the lime shell.

Put the chicken gizzards into a small saucepan with water to cover. Bring to a boil, reduce the heat, cover, and simmer gently until the gizzards are tender, about 30 minutes. Drain, remove the gristle, chop, and set aside. Add the gizzards to the soup with the chicken livers. Simmer until the livers are done, about 5 minutes. Season to taste with salt and pepper. Have ready the tortillas, fried until crisp in lard or vegetable oil and drained on paper towels. Serve the soup garnished with the tortilla strips and thin slices of lime.

Quibebe

BRAZIL

Winter Squash Soup

This is a Bahian specialty but it is a safe bet to say that winter squash soup in one form or another is popular throughout Latin America, reflecting the New World origin of the vegetable. The *calabaza* (West Indian pumpkin) available in many tropical markets is closer in flavor to the varieties used in Latin America but I have had successful results using Hubbard, butternut, and crookneck squashes. Our American pumpkin won't do. It is both too strongly flavored and too sweet.

Serves 6

4 tablespoons (¼ cup) butter
1 medium onion, chopped
1 medium tomato, peeled, seeded,
    and chopped
1 clove garlic, minced
1 or 2 fresh hot red peppers, seeded
    and chopped
2 pounds winter squash,
    preferably calabaza (West
    Indian pumpkin), peeled and
    cut into ½-inch cubes

4 cups beef stock
Salt
¼ teaspoon sugar
Parmesan cheese (optional)

Melt the butter in a large saucepan; add the onion, tomato, garlic, and hot peppers; and cook until the onion is softened and the mixture thick and well blended. Add the squash and the stock to the saucepan, season to taste with salt, stir in the sugar, and simmer, covered, for 20 minutes or until the squash has disintegrated and thickened the soup, which should retain some texture and not be completely smooth. If liked, the soup may be sprinkled with 1 tablespoon Parmesan cheese for each serving.

Variation: In Chile the squash is cooked in stock or water, mashed until smooth, and combined with a sautéed onion and an amount of milk equal to the stock, 3 cups of each to 1 pound of squash. At the last minute a well-beaten egg is stirred into the soup.

Variation: In Colombia 2 pounds of squash are cooked in beef stock until the squash is tender. The soup, which should be thick, is put through a sieve or reduced to a purée in a blender or food processor. A little butter is added just before serving.

Variation: In Argentina, as in Chile, the soup is a thinner one, using 1½ pounds of squash to 3 cups each beef stock and milk. It is served with croutons. At the last minute 2 egg yolks beaten with a tablespoon or so of Parmesan cheese are stirred into the soup.

Variation: In Paraguay ¼ cup raw rice is cooked with the squash. At the last minute a whole egg is beaten with a tablespoon or so of grated Münster or Parmesan cheese together with a tablespoon of chopped parsley and stirred into the soup.

Variation: In Ecuador the squash is put on to cook with 1 sliced onion, 1 medium sliced tomato, peeled, 1 clove garlic, chopped, and water barely to cover, about 3 cups. When the squash is tender, purée it in a blender with all the liquid and return the soup to the saucepan. Add 2 cups milk and season to taste with salt and pepper. Mix 2 tablespoons butter with 2 tablespoons flour, and add, bit by bit, to the soup. Simmer gently, stirring, over low heat until the soup is thickened. Serve with grated Münster cheese.

Locro
Potato Soup

ECUADOR

This is a highlands dish. There is a coastal version in which 1 teaspoon ground annatto is used instead of the paprika.

Serves 6 to 8

4 tablespoons (¼ cup) butter
1 teaspoon sweet paprika
1 medium onion, finely chopped
4 pounds potatoes, peeled and
    sliced

1 cup each milk and light cream
½ pound Münster cheese, grated
Salt

In a large, heavy saucepan heat the butter and stir in the paprika. Add the onion and sauté over moderate heat until the onion is softened. Pour in 4 cups water, bring to a boil, add the potatoes, and simmer over low heat, uncovered, stirring occasionally. When the potatoes are almost done, add the milk and cream and continue to cook, stirring from time to time, until the potatoes begin to disintegrate. Stir the cheese into the potatoes, season to taste with salt, and serve immediately. Avocado slices are sometimes served with the *Locro*, on separate plates but to be eaten at the same time.

Variation: In coastal Ecuador shrimp fritters are sometimes added to the potato soup. Peel 2 dozen medium shrimp and set them aside. In a skillet heat 1 tablespoon butter and sauté the shrimp shells until they turn pink. Put the shells into a small saucepan with 1 cup water, cover, and simmer for 5 minutes. Strain, discard the shells, and stir the stock into the *Locro*. Chop the shrimp. Grate a medium ear of corn — there should be ½ cup. In 1 tablespoon butter sauté 1 medium onion, very finely chopped, with 1 medium tomato, peeled, seeded, and chopped, until the onion is tender and the mixture very thick and well blended. Allow the mixture to cool. Season to taste with salt and pepper, add the shrimp, the corn, and 1 egg, lightly beaten. Fry by the tablespoon in hot lard or vegetable oil until lightly browned on both sides. Add to the soup when serving.

Sopa de Elote
Corn Soup

CUBA

Serves 6

4 cups corn kernels, preferably fresh; if frozen, thoroughly defrosted	1 cup light cream
	Salt, freshly ground white pepper
	2 eggs, lightly beaten
2 cups chicken stock	2 tablespoons chopped parsley

Put the corn into a blender or food processor with the chicken stock and blend to a purée. Do this in two batches. Pour the purée into a saucepan, stir in the cream, and simmer over very low heat, stirring from time to time, for 5 minutes. Work the purée through a sieve, return it to the saucepan, and season it to taste with salt and pepper. If it is very thick, thin it with a little more chicken stock, and bring to a simmer. Stir ½ cup of the soup into the eggs, then stir the egg mixture into the soup and cook, stirring, for 1 or 2 minutes. Serve garnished with a little chopped parsley.

Sopa de Maní
Peanut Soup

ECUADOR

Peanut soup turns up all over Latin America, each version a little different from the others, though not very much so. My favorite is this creamy, delicate soup from Ecuador.

Serves 6

2 tablespoons butter
1 medium onion, finely chopped
1 cup toasted peanuts, finely
    ground
1 pound fresh potatoes, cooked
    and chopped

4 cups chicken or beef stock
1 cup light cream
Salt, freshly ground pepper
2 tablespoons chopped chives

Heat the butter in a skillet and sauté the onion until it is soft. In a blender or food processor combine the onion and any butter in the skillet, the peanuts, potatoes, and a little of the stock. Blend to a smooth purée, pour into a saucepan, stir in the rest of the stock, and simmer gently, covered, for 15 minutes. Stir in the cream, season to taste with salt and pepper, and simmer just long enough to heat through. Pour into soup bowls and garnish with the chopped chives.

Sopa de Topinambur   CHILE
Jerusalem Artichoke Soup

Chile was the only country in South America where I encountered this soup. Though differently made, it reminded me of my mother's artichoke soup, a family favorite. Autumn is the season for Jerusalem artichokes and I have found the soup comforting on a blustery evening, though it is richly delicate rather than hearty.

Serves 4

¾ pound Jerusalem artichokes
1 large onion, finely chopped
3½ cups chicken stock
Salt, freshly ground white pepper
1 cup heavy cream
2 tablespoons fresh coriander
    (cilantro) or parsley, chopped

Wash and scrape the artichokes and slice thinly. Put into a saucepan with the onion and the chicken stock, bring to a boil and simmer, covered, until the artichokes are soft, about 20 minutes. Reduce to a purée in a blender or food processor and pour back into the saucepan. Season to taste with salt and pepper, stir in the cream, and heat through. Pour the soup into bowls and garnish with the chopped coriander or parsley.

Sopa de Plátano Verde
Green Plantain Soup

Traditionally the plantains for this soup, which I first had in Puerto Rico, are grated on a grater but I find a blender or food processor does the job admirably. Recipes vary from country to country though not in essentials.

Serves 6

1 green plantain (see page 15)
6 cups chicken or beef stock
Salt, freshly ground pepper

Grate the plantain on the second finest side of a grater, or chop it and purée it in a blender or food processor with a little stock if necessary. Pour the cold stock into a saucepan, add the plantain, and cook over moderate heat, stirring with a wooden spoon, until the soup is thick. Season to taste with salt and pepper and simmer, covered, for 10 minutes.

Sopa de Batata Doce   BRAZIL
Sweet Potato Soup

This is one of the most delicious soups I have ever had, whether as *sopa de camote* in Spanish-speaking Latin America or as *sopa de batata doce* in Brazil. It is a beautiful golden-yellow color with a lovely tart hint of tomato flavor balancing the slight sweetness of the potato. The type of sweet potato used is the delightful *boniato*, which has a pink or brownish skin and white flesh and is available in Caribbean markets — it is well worth looking for.

Serves 6

1 pound boniatos (white sweet
    potatoes)
Salt
4 tablespoons butter
1 medium onion, finely chopped
4 medium tomatoes, peeled and
    chopped
4 cups beef stock

Freshly ground pepper
2 tablespoons chopped parsley or
    fresh coriander (cilantro),
    optional

Peel the sweet potatoes, slice thickly, and put into a saucepan with cold salted water to cover. Bring to a boil, reduce the heat, and simmer, covered, until tender, about 20 minutes. Drain thoroughly and chop coarsely.

Heat the butter in a skillet and sauté the onion until it is soft. Add the tomatoes and cook for about 5 minutes longer. Put the mixture into a blender or food processor with the sweet potatoes and 1 cup of the stock and reduce to a smooth purée. Pour into a saucepan with the rest of the stock. Season to taste with salt and pepper and reheat. I have sometimes had the soup garnished with chopped parsley or coriander, and though it looks pretty I feel this really adds very little to the incomparable flavor of the soup.

So'O-Yosopy   PARAGUAY
Beef Soup

This is a wonderfully comforting soup and needs little more than dessert to make a light supper. Its name in Guaraní, an official language in Paraguay, translates in Spanish into *sopa de carne*. It is easy to make if the simple rules are followed.

Serves 6

2 pounds ground lean sirloin or
     round steak
2 tablespoons vegetable oil
2 medium onions, finely chopped
1 green bell pepper, seeded and
     finely chopped, or 1 or 2 fresh
     hot peppers, seeded and
     chopped

4 medium tomatoes, peeled and
     chopped
½ cup rice or vermicelli
Salt
Grated Parmesan cheese

Have the butcher grind the meat twice, then mash it in a mortar to make sure it is completely pulverized, or use a food processor. Set the meat aside together with any juices.

Heat the oil in a skillet and sauté the onions and pepper until the onions are softened. Add the tomatoes and cook until the mixture is thick and well blended, about 5 minutes longer. Cool the mixture slightly. Put the beef and its juices into a saucepan. Stir in the sautéed onions, pepper, and tomatoes, known as the *sofrito*, and 8 cups cold water, mixing well. Bring to a boil over moderate heat, stirring with a wooden spoon. Add the rice or noodles and simmer, still stirring, until tender, about 15 minutes. At this point, season to taste with salt. If salt is added earlier, the meat and liquid, which should be completely blended, may separate. Some cooks believe that constant stirring is the most important step, others that the point at which the salt is added is the vital factor. Superstition has it that if anyone who does not enjoy cooking is present in the kitchen they may cause the *So'O-Yosopy* to separate and spoil the dish.

Serve with a baked sweet potato or a thick slice of boiled yucca (cassava), or both, and *Sopa Paraguaya*, Paraguayan Corn Bread despite its misleading name. Sprinkle, if liked, with grated cheese. Water biscuits may also be served with the soup.

Variation: Omit the rice or noodles and add 2 thinly sliced carrots to the onion and tomato mixture with a teaspoon of oregano and freshly ground pepper.

Variation: *Chupi* (Meat Soup) from Argentina is a very simple but traditional soup, easy to make and grand in winter weather. It is obviously related to Paraguay's exotically named *So'O-Yosopy*. Heat ¼ cup vegetable oil in a saucepan and sauté 1 large onion, finely chopped, and 1 red bell pepper, seeded and chopped (or use 2 canned pimientos, chopped), until onion and pepper are both tender. Add 1 pound lean beef, round or sirloin, coarsely chopped in a food processor, or by hand, and sauté, stirring to break up the beef for a few minutes. Add 3 medium potatoes, peeled and cubed, 1 tablespoon chopped parsley, ⅛ teaspoon of cayenne (optional), 6 cups beef stock or water, and salt and pepper to taste. Bring to a simmer and cook, covered, for 30 minutes, stirring once or twice during the cooking time. Serves 6.

Sopa de Garbanzo   MEXICO
Chickpea Soup

Though this is a regional Mexican dish from Oaxaca, its overtones are very Middle Eastern with its union of chickpeas and mint. It is clearly an old colonial dish. The fried egg is an interesting addition.

Serves 6

4 tablespoons vegetable oil
1 medium onion, finely chopped
1 clove garlic, minced
1 tablespoon fresh mint leaves,
    chopped, or ½ tablespoon
    dried
3 cups beef or chicken stock

2 cups cooked chickpeas
    (1¼-pound can), or ½ pound
    dried chickpeas, soaked
    overnight in cold water
Salt, freshly ground pepper
6 eggs

Heat 2 tablespoons of the oil in a skillet and sauté the onion and garlic until the onion is soft. Transfer the contents of the skillet to a blender or food processor, add the mint leaves, and ½ cup of the stock, and reduce the mixture to a purée. Pour the mixture into a medium-sized saucepan.

Put the cooked chickpeas in the blender or food processor with the liquid from the can. If using dried chickpeas, cook these in water to cover until tender, about 1 hour. Purée the chickpeas in a blender with 1 cup of the water in which they have cooked. Add the chickpea purée to the onion mixture and stir in the remaining stock. Season to taste with salt and pepper, bring to a simmer, and cook, stirring from time to time, until the flavors are blended, about 5 minutes.

Heat the remaining 2 tablespoons of oil in a skillet and fry the eggs. Pour the soup into bowls. Slide a fried egg into each bowl.

FISH SOUPS

The fruits of the sea, with which Latin America is so lavishly endowed, are used in some very fine soups, robust enough to be the main course of lunch or dinner. They may be enriched with corn, tomatoes, sweet peppers, or beans, with root vegetables like yams, yucca (cassava) root, or potatoes, with okra, zucchini, or other green vegetables, with coconut milk as well as stock, sometimes enlivened with a touch of hot pepper, and always with well-orchestrated seasonings, a symphony of flavors.

Sopa de Almejas   COLOMBIA
Clam Soup

This clam soup is a coastal favorite in Colombia, which is richly blessed in having both the Caribbean and the Pacific wash its shores. I had it with Colombian friends at a family gathering when there were twelve of us to lunch. The day was hot, the sun brilliant, and the soup hearty, but this did not stop even more substantial dishes following. At home I like it as a winter soup and make it the central dish of a family lunch or dinner, serving larger helpings; this recipe would serve 3 or 4 as a main dish, 6 as a soup.

In Colombia the large Spanish mackerel sierra (see page 16) is used. The stronger flavored Atlantic mackerel won't do for this dish, so substitute red snapper if Spanish mackerel is not available.

Serves 6

¼ cup olive oil
1 medium onion, finely chopped
1 clove garlic, chopped
1 red and 1 green bell pepper, or
    use 2 red or 2 green peppers,
    seeded and chopped
3 medium tomatoes, peeled,
    seeded, and chopped
1 pound (about 3 medium)
    potatoes, peeled and sliced
Salt, freshly ground pepper
1 bay leaf

Pinch ground cloves
⅛ teaspoon cumin
½ teaspoon sugar (optional)
3 dozen clams, well washed
2 pounds fillets of Spanish
    mackerel, red snapper, or
    similar fish, cut into 12 pieces
2 cups clam juice
2 cups water
2 tablespoons finely chopped
    parsley

Heat the oil in a fireproof casserole and sauté the onion, garlic, and peppers
until the onion is soft. Add the tomatoes and sauté for a minute or two
longer. Add the potatoes. Season to taste with salt and pepper. Add the bay
leaf, cloves, cumin, and sugar (if desired). Cover and simmer until the
potatoes are almost tender, about 15 minutes. Add the clams, pieces of
fish, clam juice, and water. Cover and simmer for 5 minutes longer, or
until the clams have opened and the fish has lost its translucent look.
Sprinkle with parsley and serve in soup bowls.

Chupe de Camarones   PERU
Shrimp Stew

More like a bouillabaisse, this soup is really a meal in itself. The word
"chupe" actually means a savory stew containing potatoes, cheese, eggs,
etc. Peru, Ecuador, and Chile all have magnificent *chupes*.

Serves 6

¼ cup vegetable oil
2 medium onions, finely chopped
2 cloves garlic, chopped
2 medium tomatoes, peeled and
    chopped
1 or 2 fresh hot red or green
    peppers, seeded and chopped
½ teaspoon oregano
Salt, freshly ground pepper
3½ quarts fish stock, or half clam
    juice, half water
2 medium potatoes, peeled and
    cut into 1-inch cubes
2 pounds jumbo shrimp

½ cup rice
3 large potatoes, peeled and
    halved
1½ pounds peas, shelled, or use
    one (10-ounce) package frozen
    peas, thawed
2 ears corn, each cut into 3 slices
3 eggs
1 cup light cream
2 tablespoons finely chopped fresh
    green coriander (cilantro), or
    use parsley, preferably flat
    Italian

Heat the oil in a large saucepan and sauté the onions and garlic until the onions are softened. Add the tomatoes, hot peppers, oregano, salt and pepper to taste, and cook for a few minutes, stirring to mix well. Add the fish stock and the diced potatoes. Peel the shrimp and add the shells to the saucepan. Set the shrimp aside. Bring to a boil, reduce the heat, and simmer gently, covered, for about 30 minutes. Strain through a sieve, pressing down on the solids to extract all the juices. Rinse out the saucepan and return the broth to it.

Add the rice, halved potatoes, and peas, cover, and simmer until the potatoes are tender, about 20 minutes. Add the corn and the shrimp and cook for 5 minutes longer. Break the eggs into the soup, one at a time, stirring, so that the eggs coagulate in strips. Pour in the cream and cook just long enough to heat through. Pour into a warmed soup tureen and sprinkle with the coriander or parsley. Ideally this is served in large, deep, old-fashioned rimmed soup plates. Serve in large bowls holding about 2 cups.

Variation: Use only 1 pound of shrimp. Add six 1-inch slices of fillet of bass, fried in oil at the last minute. Leave out the stirred-in eggs and top each soup plate with a poached egg and, if liked, a strip of lightly sautéed sweet red or green pepper. Serves 6.

Variation: In Chile, that paradise of fish and shellfish, there is a simple, very pleasant version of these hearty fish soup-stews, *Chupe de Pescado* (Fish Stew). It is light enough to serve as a soup, not as a meal in itself. Peel, quarter, and boil in salted water 6 fairly small potatoes. Set aside. In a saucepan sauté 2 finely chopped onions in 3 tablespoons vegetable oil and 1 tablespoon sweet paprika until the onions are soft. Add 2 cups freshly made breadcrumbs, 1 finely grated carrot (optional), 3 cups milk, 1½ cups fish stock or clam juice or water, salt and pepper to taste, ½ teaspoon oregano, and 1 pound mackerel fillets or hake or cod, cut into 1-inch pieces. Add the potatoes. Cover and simmer gently until the fish is done, about 5 to 8 minutes. The *chupe* should be about as thick as a medium Béchamel sauce. If it seems too thick, add a little more milk. Serve sprinkled with finely chopped hardboiled egg, using 2. Serves 6.

Sopa de Candia con Mojarras COLOMBIA
Okra and Pompano Soup

The foods of the Andean countries, Venezuela, Colombia, Ecuador, and Peru, have more distinctive regional characteristics because the countries, until recently, were so cut off from one another. Though now with modern transportation they enjoy one another's foods, the old regional kitchens have, happily, retained their identity. This is a typical coastal dish from Cartagena, which has a very lively cuisine. I first enjoyed it high up in Bogotá.

Serves 6

2 quarts fish stock
2 medium onions, finely chopped
2 cloves garlic, chopped
1 large tomato, peeled, seeded, and chopped
2 fresh hot peppers, seeded and chopped
¼ teaspoon each ground cumin and allspice
Salt
4 tablespoons lemon juice

½ pound small, fresh okra, quartered
1 pound small yams, peeled and cut into 1-inch pieces
2 ripe plantains, peeled and sliced
2 tablespoons butter
6 fillets pompano
2 tablespoons tomato paste
1 tablespoon Worcestershire sauce
Salt, freshly ground pepper

In a kettle combine the fish stock, onions, garlic, tomato, hot peppers, and cumin and allspice. Bring the mixture to a boil and simmer it, covered, for 15 minutes over low heat. To a saucepan of boiling salted water add the lemon juice and okra. Bring back to a boil, remove from the heat, drain the okra, and rinse it in cold water. Add the okra to the kettle with the yams and plantains and cook, covered, over very low heat for 1 hour.

In a skillet heat the butter and sauté the fish until the fillets are golden. Cut the fish into 1-inch pieces and add to the soup with the tomato paste, Worcestershire sauce, and salt and pepper to taste. Simmer for 30 minutes longer.

Variation: Coconuts are used a great deal in coastal cooking. Instead of the fish stock, use 3 cups thin coconut milk (see page 7), increase the cumin to ½ teaspoon, and omit the allspice. Add 1 pound yucca (cassava) root, peeled and cut into 1-inch pieces, when adding the okra. Omit the tomato paste and Worcestershire sauce. When the soup is ready, pour in 1 cup thick coconut milk and simmer for a few minutes longer.

Chupe de Corvina y Camarones   ECUADOR
Striped Bass and Shrimp Stew

This is Ecuador's version of the Peruvian *Chupe de Camarones* (Shrimp Stew), but a distinctively different dish.

Serves 6

1 ½ pounds striped bass fillets, cut into 1 ½-inch slices
Flour
Salt, freshly ground pepper
¼ cup vegetable oil
1 pound small or medium shrimp
4 tablespoons butter
1 teaspoon sweet paprika

1 large onion, finely chopped
2 pounds potatoes, peeled and sliced
2 cups milk or half milk, half light cream
½ pound Münster cheese, grated
3 hardboiled eggs, sliced

Rinse the fish and pat dry with paper towels. Season the flour with salt and pepper. Dredge the fish in the flour. Heat the oil in a skillet and sauté the fish slices until lightly browned on both sides. Set aside.

Shell the shrimp, reserving the shells. Cut the shrimp into ½-inch pieces and set aside. Melt a tablespoon of the butter in a saucepan, add the shrimp shells, and cook, stirring, until the shells turn pink. Add 3 cups water, bring to a boil, cover, and simmer for 5 minutes. Strain, discard the shells, and measure the stock. Bring it up to 3 cups with a little water if necessary. Set the stock aside.

Heat the rest of the butter in a large saucepan. Add the paprika and the onion and sauté until the onion is softened. Add the potatoes and the shrimp stock, cover, and simmer until the potatoes are tender, about 20 minutes. Add the milk, or milk and cream, to the saucepan and continue to cook the potatoes, stirring from time to time, until they are partly disintegrated. Add the cheese and stir to mix thoroughly. Season to taste with salt and pepper, then fold in the fish and the shrimp. Cook over low heat for about 3 minutes, or until the shrimp are cooked. Serve in bowls topped with slices of hardboiled egg. This should be thick, but still recognizable as a soup. Thin with a little milk if necessary.

Variation: This is also Ecuadorian, a simpler version, *Chupe de Corvina* (Striped Bass Stew). Heat 4 tablespoons butter in a large saucepan. Add 1 tablespoon sweet paprika; 1 large onion, finely chopped; 2 cloves garlic, chopped, and sauté until the onion is soft. Add 2 pounds potatoes, peeled and sliced, and 3 cups water. Cover and simmer until the potatoes disinte-grate. Season to taste with salt and pepper, stir in 1 cup light cream and ½ pound grated Münster cheese or, if available, Spanish *queso blanco*, crumbled. Cut 1 pound striped bass fillets into 1-inch slices. Dust with flour and fry in vegetable oil until golden brown on both sides. Drain and fold into the potato soup. Serve garnished with slices of hardboiled egg, using 2 eggs. Serves 4 to 6.

Caldillo de Congrio
Fish Soup

CHILE

Congrio is a magnificent firm-fleshed fish found in Chilean waters. I have found cod to be the most acceptable substitute.

Serves 4

2 pounds cod, cut into 4 steaks
Salt
¼ cup lemon juice
2 carrots, scraped and thinly
    sliced
2 pounds small potatoes, peeled
    and thinly sliced
2 medium onions, halved and
    thinly sliced

2 cloves garlic, chopped (optional)
Freshly ground pepper
½ teaspoon oregano
1 cup dry white wine
4 cups fish stock
4 tablespoons olive oil

Put the fish steaks into a casserole, preferably earthenware, large enough to hold them in a single layer. Season with salt and the lemon juice. Cover with a layer of carrots, then a layer of half the potatoes, then the onions and garlic, and the rest of the potatoes. Season with salt, pepper, and oregano. Pour in the wine, fish stock, and olive oil. Bring to a boil, reduce the heat, and simmer until the potatoes and carrots are tender, about 30 minutes. Serve in soup bowls accompanied by crusty bread and butter. With the addition of dessert, or cheese, this makes a splendid lunch or dinner.

Fanesca
Spring Soup

A traditional dish for Lent, when spring vegetables — peas, green beans, and so on — are first available, this soup is a meal in itself.

Serves 8 to 10

1 pound salt cod
4 tablespoons (¼ cup) butter
2 medium onions, finely chopped
1 clove garlic, minced
¼ teaspoon oregano
¼ teaspoon ground cumin
1 bay leaf
Freshly ground pepper
1 cup long-grain rice cooked in 1 cup milk and 1 cup water
1 cup cooked corn kernels
2½ cups cooked shredded cabbage
2 cups cooked, mashed winter squash

2 cups cooked, chopped zucchini
1 cup cooked baby lima beans or broad (fava) beans
1 cup cooked green peas
1 cup cooked green beans, cut into ½-inch pieces
½ cup peanuts, ground
4 cups milk
1 cup light cream
1 cup Spanish fresh cheese (queso fresco or queso blanco) or Münster, chopped
Salt
3 hardboiled eggs, sliced
Grated Parmesan cheese

Soak the cod in cold water to cover for 12 hours or more, changing the water frequently. Drain the fish and put it into a saucepan with fresh water to cover. Bring to a boil, lower the heat, and simmer until the fish is tender, about 15 minutes. Drain, and reserve the fish stock. Remove any skin and bones from the fish and cut it into ½-inch pieces. Set aside.

Heat the butter in a large saucepan and sauté the onions and garlic until the onions are soft. Add the oregano, cumin, bay leaf, and several grinds of black pepper and sauté for a minute or two longer. Add 1 cup water, bring to a boil, and add the cooked rice, corn, cabbage, squash, zucchini, lima or fava beans, peas, green beans, ground peanuts, the fish and fish stock, the milk, and the cream. Stir to mix and simmer very gently for about 5 minutes to blend the flavors. Add the chopped cheese and salt to taste. The soup should be about as thick as a minestrone. If it seems too thick, thin it with a little more milk and simmer for a few minutes longer.

Pour the soup into a tureen and serve in soup plates. Garnish the servings with sliced hardboiled egg. Have the grated Parmesan cheese in a bowl on the table to be used as liked.

Sopa de Frijol Negro con Camarones   MEXICO
Black Bean Soup with Shrimp

This is a recipe from Oaxaca, where avocado leaves are often used in cooking. Since I find it hard to prune my potted avocado trees, lost as I am in affectionate admiration for their beautiful glossy foliage, I am grateful to recipes like this, which urge me to pluck a couple of leaves. The flavor they add is less pronounced than bay leaf, which is also often used. The leaves may be toasted lightly before they are added to the pot. Some cooks insist this is a vital step, but from experience I do not think it matters a great deal, if at all. The soup is absolutely delicious with a most exciting flavor, the richness of the black beans contrasting unexpectedly with the fresh flavor of the shrimp.

Serves 4

¾ cup black beans, washed and
   picked over
⅛ teaspoon ground cumin
¼ teaspoon oregano
1 bay leaf, or 2 avocado leaves
2 tablespoons olive oil
1 medium onion, finely chopped
1 clove garlic, chopped
1 medium tomato, peeled and
   chopped

Salt, freshly ground pepper
2 cups chicken stock
½ pound peeled raw shrimp, cut
   into ½-inch pieces
4 tablespoons dry sherry

In a medium saucepan combine the beans, cumin, oregano, bay leaf or avocado leaves, with 3 cups water. Bring to a boil over moderate heat, reduce the heat to low, cover, and simmer until the beans are very tender, about 2½ hours. Cool a little, remove, discard the bay leaf or avocado leaves, and pour the beans and liquid into a blender or food processor.

Heat the oil in a skillet and sauté the onion and garlic until the onion is soft. Add the tomato and simmer until the mixture is well blended, 2 or 3 minutes. Season to taste with salt and pepper and add to the blender or food processor. If necessary do this in two batches. Reduce the mixture to a smooth purée and pour it into the saucepan. Stir in the chicken stock and bring to a simmer over moderate heat. Add the shrimp and cook for 2 minutes longer. Serve immediately, as overcooking toughens shrimp. Stir 1 tablespoon of sherry into each serving.

Fish
and Shellfish
Pescados y Mariscos

As I have noted, fish and shellfish in Latin America are superb, with the cold Humboldt Current that runs up the coasts of Chile and Peru being responsible for some of the most magnificent seafood in the world. *Erizos*, the sea urchins of Chile, which often measure as much as 4 and 5 inches across, provide an unrivaled gastronomic experience. I remember having *erizos al matico*, raw sea urchins served with a sauce of chopped onion, parsley, oil, and lemon juice, a soup spoon, and a pile of thin, hot buttered toast, at the Hotel Crillon's dining room in Santiago, and marveling not only at their exquisite flavor but at their astonishing size.*

It is the same with *locos* (abalone), which also reaches wildly generous proportions yet loses nothing in delicacy and flavor. At a beach club near Lima, Peru, I had huge scallops with their coral served on the half shell and accompanied only by the small tropical lemon-lime that I am sure is indigenous to tropical America, its flavor more lemon than lime, but muted, delicate. Shrimp, crabs, oysters, lobsters, clams, and scallops are found in abundance, and there are also strange shellfish like the *picoroccos*, beaked

---

Erizos (sea urchins) are sometimes available canned from specialty stores. Serve them with *Salsa de Perejil* (Parsley Sauce).

creatures that live in colonies of rocklike tubes and taste like crabs when cooked. Among the fish, *congrio* with its large head and tapering body is unique, and *corvina*, sea bass, is very fine. Mexico's waters produce excellent shrimp, conch, red snapper, and other fish and shellfish, and the same is true of the waters off Ecuador, Colombia, Argentina, and Brazil.

Perhaps because of this abundance of good seafood, recipes are not as numerous, or as varied, as for meat and poultry dishes, since the best way to cook splendid fish and shellfish is often the simplest. But there are a number of very good, original recipes, especially those from Brazil, suitable for fish usually available in any fish store. And there are the *seviches*, fish and shellfish "cooked" in a marinade of lime or lemon juice, and the *escabeches*, lightly pickled fish.

Salt cod is as popular in South America as it is in Spain and Portugal, with cooks combining indigenous and introduced foods to create exciting new dishes. Mexico cooks salt cod with a sauce of the mild but richly flavored *ancho* pepper and almonds. The north of Brazil marries coconut milk with tomatoes and sweet peppers for its salt cod Bahia style, in great contrast to the cod of Minas Gerais to the south, where tomatoes, sweet peppers, and cabbage are included.

Pescado a la Veracruzana   MEXICO
Fish, Veracruz Style

Pescado a la Veracruzana (Fish in the Style of Veracruz) is Mexico's best-known fish dish and rightly so for it is admirable. There are a great many versions of it, each one differing in minor details. This is the one I prefer and I never tire of it. When I first visited Venezuela, I realized I was meeting its culinary, and almost certainly younger, cousin, *Corbullón Mantuano*, made with striped bass, and in Buenos Aires the *Corvina a la Porteña*, also with bass, seemed to be the Argentine cousin. Subtle variations make all three worth trying; they come to table surprisingly different.

Serves 4

2 pounds red snapper fillets
Salt, freshly ground pepper
Juice of a small lemon or lime
⅓ cup olive oil
2 medium onions, finely chopped
2 cloves garlic, chopped
6 medium tomatoes, peeled and
    chopped
3 tablespoons capers

20 small pimiento-stuffed green
    olives
2 or 3 canned jalapeño chilies,
    seeded and cut into strips
12 small new potatoes, freshly
    cooked, or 6 medium
    potatoes, halved
3 slices firm white bread
Butter for frying

Season the fish with salt and pepper and the lemon or lime juice. Set aside.
Heat the oil in a skillet and sauté the onions and garlic until the onions are
soft. Reduce the tomatoes to a purée in a blender or food processor and add
to the skillet with the capers, olives, *jalapeño* chilies, and the fish. Season
with a little more salt and pepper and cook over very low heat until the fish
is tender and the sauce slightly thickened, about 10 to 15 minutes. Transfer to a warmed platter and garnish with the potatoes. Cut the bread into 6
triangles, sauté in butter until golden, and arrange as a border round the
edge of the platter.

Variation: *Corbullón Mantuano* (Striped Bass in Sweet Pepper Sauce) from
Venezuela. Remove the head and tail from a 2½-pound striped bass and cut
it into 1½-inch slices. Season with salt and freshly ground pepper. Heat 4
tablespoons butter and 1 tablespoon olive oil in a large skillet and sauté the
fish until it is lightly browned on both sides. Transfer the fish to a platter
and keep it warm. In the fat remaining in the pan sauté 2 medium onions,
thinly sliced, and 1 green and 1 red bell pepper, seeded and thinly sliced,
until the onions are soft. Add 6 medium tomatoes, peeled and chopped, ½
small fresh hot red pepper, or ¼ teaspoon ground hot red pepper (cayenne),
2 tablespoons capers, and 20 small pimiento-stuffed green olives, and
simmer for 2 or 3 minutes. Add 1 cup dry red wine and ¼ cup olive oil and
simmer until the sauce is well blended, about 10 minutes. Add the fish and
cook just long enough to heat it through. Arrange on a warmed platter. Peel
and slice 1½ pounds potatoes and boil, covered, in salted water until tender, about 15 to 20 minutes. Drain and arrange around the edge of the
platter with the fish. Serves 4.

Variation: *Corvina a la Porteña* (Striped Bass, Buenos Aires Style) is an
Argentine cousin of both dishes. Cut a 2½- to 3-pound striped bass with
head and tail removed into 1½-inch slices and dredge them in flour. Pour
½ cup olive oil in a baking dish and arrange the fish slices in it. In a skillet
heat another cup of olive oil and sauté 2 medium onions, chopped, until

softened. Add 2 tomatoes, peeled and chopped, 2 sliced green bell peppers, a bay leaf, ½ teaspoon oregano, and salt and freshly ground pepper to taste. Simmer the mixture until it is thick and well blended. Pour the sauce over the fish and bake in a preheated moderate (350° F.) oven for 20 minutes, or until the fish is done. Discard the bay leaf. Transfer to a warmed platter and sprinkle with a tablespoon of chopped parsley. Serves 4.

Corvina a la Chorrillana   PERU
Striped Bass with Vegetables

This is bass in the style of Chorrillos, a resort 10 miles out of Lima. The annatto oil gives a distinctive flavor to this robust and satisfying dish. Chorrillos means literally "the little streams," which flow down from the Andes creating a green patch on this desert coast so that the town can exist — and hence the dish.

Serves 6

1 tablespoon annatto oil (see page 324)
2 large onions, finely sliced
2 cloves garlic, chopped
2 large tomatoes, peeled and sliced
2 large or 4 small fresh hot red or green peppers, seeded and sliced
½ teaspoon oregano
Salt, freshly ground pepper

3 pounds striped bass, cut into 6 steaks
2 tablespoons peanut oil
Juice of 1 lemon

Pour the annatto oil into a heavy casserole so that it covers the bottom evenly. Make a layer of half the onions, garlic, tomatoes, and peppers. Sprinkle with half the oregano and season to taste with salt and pepper. Arrange the fish on top of the vegetables and cover with the remaining vegetables. Season with the rest of the oregano, salt and pepper, the peanut oil, and the lemon juice. Cover the casserole and cook over low heat for 20 to 30 minutes, or until the vegetables are tender. Serve with *Arroz Graneado* (Peruvian Style Rice).

Variation: Omit the oregano and use 2 tablespoons finely chopped fresh green coriander (cilantro) instead.

Corvina Rellena
Stuffed Striped Bass

ARGENTINA

Serves 4

A 3- to 3½-pound striped bass,
    cleaned and boned, with head
    and tail left on
Salt, freshly ground pepper
1 medium onion, finely chopped
2 cloves garlic, finely chopped or
    crushed

½ cup finely chopped parsley
1 cup fresh breadcrumbs
Milk
1 tablespoon butter
1 tablespoon olive oil
1 cup dry white wine

Rinse the fish and pat dry with paper towels. Season the inside of the fish
with salt and pepper. In a bowl combine the onion, garlic, parsley, breadcrumbs, and salt and pepper to taste. Moisten the mixture with a little
milk and stuff the fish with the mixture. Fasten with toothpicks. Butter a
shallow, heatproof casserole that will hold the fish comfortably, and arrange the fish in it. Dot the fish with the butter and pour the olive oil over
it, then pour the white wine over it. Bake in a preheated hot (400° F.) oven
for 40 minutes, or until the fish feels firm when pressed with a finger. The
wine will have reduced, combining with the butter and oil to form a sauce.
Serve directly from the casserole. Accompany with rice or potatoes and a
green vegetable or salad.

Mero en Mac-Cum
Striped Bass in Sauce

MEXICO

This dish with achiote (annatto), cumin, and Seville orange juice is typical
of the Mayan kitchen of Yucatán.

Serves 4

2 pounds striped bass, or any
    firm-fleshed, non-oily white
    fish, cut into 4 steaks
4 large cloves garlic, crushed
Black pepper
¼ teaspoon ground cumin
½ teaspoon oregano

1 teaspoon achiote (annatto),
    ground
Salt
½ cup Seville (bitter) orange juice,
    about, or a mixture of
    two-thirds orange juice to
    one-third lime juice

½ cup olive oil
1 large onion, thinly sliced
2 cloves garlic, minced
2 tomatoes, sliced
2 medium red bell peppers, seeded
    and sliced, or 2 canned
    pimientos, cut into strips

1 fresh hot pepper, seeded and
    chopped (optional)
2 tablespoons chopped parsley

Put the fish steaks on a platter in a single layer. Make a dressing of the garlic, 6 or more grinds black pepper, cumin, oregano, achiote (annatto), salt to taste, and enough orange juice to make a thin paste. Coat the steaks on both sides with the mixture and let stand for 30 minutes. Pour a little of the olive oil into a shallow baking dish large enough to hold the fish steaks. Use only enough oil to coat the bottom of the dish. Arrange the fish steaks, with any remaining marinade, in the dish. Top the steaks with the onion, minced garlic, tomatoes, and peppers. Pour the rest of the oil over the fish, cover, and cook over low heat until the fish loses its translucent look, about 15 minutes. Sprinkle with the parsley and serve with rice. Fresh hot tortillas may also be served.

Peixe em Môlho de Tangerina   NORTHERN BRAZIL
Fish in Tangerine Sauce

Serves 4

A 3-pound red snapper or bass,
    cleaned, with head and tail
    left on
2 tablespoons lemon juice
Salt, freshly ground pepper
Butter
1 tablespoon olive oil

1 tablespoon melted butter
¼ pound mushrooms, sliced
1 tablespoon chopped parsley
1 scallion, chopped, using green
    and white parts
1 cup dry white wine
½ cup tangerine juice

Season the fish with lemon juice, salt, and pepper. Put the fish in a buttered baking dish just large enough to hold it and pour over it the olive oil and melted butter. Sprinkle the fish with the mushrooms, parsley, and scallion. Pour the wine and tangerine juice over it and bake in a preheated hot (400° F.) oven for 25 to 30 minutes, or until it flakes easily when tested with a fork.

Pescado con Cilantro
MEXICO
Fish with Coriander

Fresh coriander leaves give this dish a delectable flavor, especially for addicts of the herb, of which I am one. It is a colonial dish, and very easy to make, which is unusual as many of the older recipes are rather long-winded. Plain White Rice (*Arroz Blanco*), cooked in the Mexican style, is the perfect accompaniment.

Serves 6

3 pounds fillets of red snapper,
    striped bass, flounder, or any
    firm white-fleshed fish
Salt, freshly ground pepper
¼ cup lemon juice
5 tablespoons vegetable oil

1 medium onion, finely chopped
½ cup chopped fresh coriander
    (cilantro)
3 canned jalapeño chilies, rinsed,
    seeded, and chopped

Season the fish with salt and pepper and sprinkle with the lemon juice. Heat 4 tablespoons of the oil in a skillet and sauté the onion until it is soft. Lightly film with oil the surface of a shallow ovenproof casserole large enough to hold the fish comfortably, in more than one layer if necessary. Arrange the fish fillets, with any liquid they may have yielded, in the casserole, cover with the onion and the oil, and sprinkle with the coriander and chilies. Drizzle with the remaining tablespoon of oil. Bake in a preheated moderate (350° F.) oven for 20 minutes, or until the fish has lost its translucent look.

Pescado Frito
con Salsa de Vino Tinto
COLOMBIA
Fried Fish with Red Wine Sauce

The red wine and tomatoes combine here to make a full-flavored sauce with the subtle pinch of allspice that I find very attractive and out of the ordinary.

Serves 4

2 pounds fish steaks, cut into 4
    pieces, using any firm-fleshed
    white fish such as red
    snapper, striped bass, tile fish,
    etc.
Salt, freshly ground pepper
Flour
4 tablespoons vegetable oil

2 medium onions, finely chopped
2 cloves garlic, minced
4 medium tomatoes, peeled and
    chopped
1 bay leaf
Pinch each cayenne pepper and
    ground allspice
1 cup dry red wine

Season the fish steaks with salt and pepper and coat lightly with flour, shaking to remove the excess. Heat the oil in a skillet and sauté the fish until lightly browned on both sides. Transfer to a platter and keep warm. In the oil remaining in the pan (add a little more if necessary), sauté the onions and garlic until the onions are soft. Add the tomatoes, bay leaf, cayenne pepper and allspice, and salt and pepper to taste, and sauté, stirring from time to time, until the mixture is thick and well blended, about 5 minutes. Stir in the wine and bring to a simmer. Add the fish and simmer for 2 or 3 minutes. Transfer the fish to a warmed serving dish and pour the sauce over it. Serve with rice, potatoes, or any starchy accompaniment.

Pargo al Horno
Baked Red Snapper

VENEZUELA

Serves 4

A 3- to 3½-pound red snapper,
    cleaned and boned, with head
    and tail left on, or striped or
    black bass
Salt, freshly ground pepper

4 tablespoons butter
¼ cup lime or lemon juice
1 cup fish stock or clam juice
½ cup heavy cream
1 teaspoon Worcestershire sauce

Rinse the fish and pat dry with paper towels. Season the fish inside and outside with salt and pepper. Using 1 tablespoon of the butter, grease a shallow, heatproof casserole that will hold the fish comfortably and arrange the fish in it. Combine the lime or lemon juice and fish stock and pour over the fish. Dot the fish with 1 tablespoon of the butter and bake in a preheated hot (400° F.) oven for 30 minutes, or until the fish feels firm when pressed with a finger. Using 2 spatulas, lift the fish out onto a serving platter and keep warm. Pour the liquid from the casserole into a small saucepan. Stir in the heavy cream and bring it to a simmer over moderate heat. Cut the remaining 2 tablespoons of butter into small pieces and stir in. Taste for seasoning and add more salt and pepper if necessary. Spoon a little of the sauce over the fish and serve the rest separately in a sauceboat. Accompany with potatoes or rice and a green vegetable.

Congrio en Fuente de Barro   CHILE
Fish with Tomatoes and Onions

Congrio, that very splendid large fish found in Chilean waters, is considered by Chileans to be the finest of all their food fishes. There are three kinds, *congrio colorado*, *congrio negro*, and *congrio dorado*, red, black, and gold fish. They made a fine sight when I saw them hanging up in a Santiago fish market, looking rather like eels with their big heads and tapering bodies — which explains their equivocal common name, for *congrio* is the Spanish word for eel. Eels these are not. They are *Genypterus chilensis*, living in the waters off Chile's long Pacific coast and existing as far north as Peruvian waters. Their only known relatives are a New Zealand fish known as ling, but not to be confused with the European ling to which it is not related.

The fish is firm-fleshed and when cooked breaks into large flakes. In my experience cod is the best substitute, though any firm-fleshed non-oily fish can be used successfully. The term *"fuente de barro"* simply means cooked in earthenware. Though any casserole may be used, the dish is better when cooked in earthenware. A lovely, satisfying, full-flavored dish.

Serves 4

2 pounds fillets of scrod or cod, cut
    into 4 pieces
Salt, freshly ground pepper
2 tablespoons lemon juice
3 tablespoons butter
1 teaspoon sweet paprika
1 large onion, finely chopped
4 medium tomatoes, peeled and
    chopped

4 slices firm white bread, fried in
    butter, or 1 pound potatoes,
    boiled and sliced
2 hardboiled eggs, sliced
1 sweet red pepper, seeded and
    cut into strips
½ cup milk (optional)
1 tablespoon chopped parsley

Season the fish with salt, pepper, and lemon juice, and set aside. Heat the butter in a skillet, stir in the paprika, add the onion, and sauté over moderate heat until it is soft. Add the tomatoes and sauté for a few minutes longer. Butter an earthenware casserole and put a layer of the tomato mixture, then the fish, more tomato, the fried bread or potatoes, and more tomato. Repeat until all these ingredients are used up. Or you may have a casserole large enough to hold the fish in a single layer. Top with the sliced hardboiled eggs and pepper strips. Cover and bake in a preheated moderate (350° F.) oven for 30 minutes. If the dish seems to be drying out during cooking, add up to ½ cup milk. This should not be necessary if the tomatoes are fully ripe and juicy. Sprinkle with parsley and serve.

Variation: I was quite astonished one day in Asunción, capital of land-locked Paraguay, to be given a dish remarkably like *Congrio en Fuente de Barro* from Chile, which is more seacoast than anything else and has a most remarkable harvest of fish and shellfish. The fish in this *Guiso de Dorado* was from the Paraguay River, a great, noble waterway. It seemed to me in flavor and texture very like the Spanish *dorado*, dolphin fish, and so it turned out to be, though not, of course, to be confused with the mammalian dolphin. *Dorado* is a famous fish of Paraguayan rivers and wholly delectable. Any firm-fleshed white fish would make a suitable substitute.

For *Guiso de Dorado* (Fish Stew), put 2 pounds fish, cut into 4 steaks, into a flat dish and season them with salt and pepper. Pour ¼ cup lemon juice over the steaks and let them stand 1 hour, turning once or twice. Lift out, pat dry with paper towels, and dust with flour. Heat ½ cup olive or vegetable oil in a casserole and sauté the fish steaks until golden on both sides. Arrange half the fish steaks in the casserole. Have ready 2 medium onions, thinly sliced, 2 cloves garlic, minced, 2 tomatoes, peeled and sliced, 2 red or green bell peppers, seeded and sliced, and 2 medium potatoes, peeled and thinly sliced. Arrange half of the onions, garlic, tomatoes, peppers, and potatoes over the fish. Top with a bay leaf, a sprig of thyme, and 2 or 3 sprigs of parsley. Season to taste with salt and pepper and top with the rest of the fish and the remaining vegetables. Season again with salt and pepper. Pour ½ cup each dry white wine and fish stock, or clam juice, or water, over the fish, cover tightly, bring to a simmer, and cook for 20 to 30 minutes, or until the potatoes and fish are both tender. Check to see if the fish is drying out during the cooking time and add a little more stock or wine if necessary. Serves 4.

Pescado en Escabeche
Fish in Oil and Vinegar Sauce

PERU

Pescado en Escabeche is very popular throughout Latin America. The cooking technique is of Spanish origin, but cooks have changed recipes adding an herb or vegetable, altering things a little, so that there is a whole group of New World *escabeche* dishes that make splendid appetizers or main courses.

Serves 6

3 pounds of any firm-fleshed white
  fish such as red snapper or
  striped bass, cut into 6 fillets
  or 6 steaks
Salt, freshly ground pepper
Flour
3 tablespoons butter or lard

1 cup olive oil or vegetable oil
3 medium onions, thickly sliced
1 or 2 fresh hot red or green
  peppers, seeded and cut into
  strips
¼ teaspoon oregano
4 tablespoons white vinegar

Season the fish with salt and pepper and dredge in flour, shaking to remove the excess. Heat the butter or lard in a skillet and sauté the fish until lightly browned on both sides. Transfer the cooked fish to a shallow serving dish and keep warm. Heat the oil in a medium-sized saucepan, add the onions and pepper strips, and cook over low heat until the onions are soft and very lightly browned. Stir in the oregano and cook for a minute longer. Pour in the vinegar, stir, and pour over the fish. Serve immediately.

For a more robust dish, garnish with 3 ears of freshly cooked corn, each cut into 4 slices, 3 hardboiled eggs, halved, lettuce leaves, and olives.

Variation: This Argentine version, *Merluza a la Vinagreta* (Hake in Vinaigrette Sauce), is quite different from the Peruvian one. Wash and pat dry 3 pounds of hake fillets, cut into 12 pieces, or use cod or any firm-fleshed white fish. Sprinkle the fish with salt, preferably coarse salt, and let stand for 1 hour. Rinse and dry. Dredge in flour, shaking to remove the excess, and sauté in 3 tablespoons olive oil until the fish has lost its translucent look. A good rule is to measure the thickness of the fish and give it 10 minutes to the inch, 5 minutes on each side. Arrange the cooked fish in a shallow dish and pour on a sauce made by mixing 1 clove garlic, peeled and finely chopped, 4 cornichons, chopped, 2 hardboiled eggs, chopped, 2 tablespoons capers, 2 tablespoons finely chopped parsley, salt, freshly ground pepper, 1 cup wine vinegar, and 1 cup olive oil. Let the fish stand for at least an hour before serving. Serve, garnished with lettuce leaves, at room temperature. Serves 12 as a first course.

Variation: *Pescado en Escabeche* from Mexico can be made with a variety of fish including pompano, mackerel, red snapper, or snook. Cut 2 pounds of fish fillets into 8 pieces and sprinkle them with 3 tablespoons lemon juice. Let the fish stand for 15 minutes, turning the pieces once. Rinse gently in cold water and pat dry. In a skillet heat 4 tablespoons of olive oil and sauté the fish until it has lost its translucent look and is lightly browned on both sides. Lift the fish out of the skillet and place in a dish.

In a saucepan combine 2 whole cloves, a 1-inch piece of stick cinnamon, 6 peppercorns, 2 cloves garlic, ⅛ teaspoon ground cumin, ¼ teaspoon thyme, ½ teaspoon oregano, 2 bay leaves, 2 whole fresh hot green peppers, preferably *serrano*, with stems left on, 6 sliced scallions, using white and green parts, salt to taste, and 1 cup white vinegar. Bring to a boil, lower the heat, and simmer, uncovered, for 2 or 3 minutes, or until the scallions are soft. Set aside. In another small saucepan or skillet heat 1 cup olive oil with 2 cloves garlic and fry the garlic over low heat until browned. Lift out and discard the garlic. Pour the oil into the saucepan with the vinegar mixture, heat to a simmer, and pour the mixture over the fish. Allow to cool, cover, and refrigerate for 24 hours. To serve, lift out the fish onto a shallow serving platter and sprinkle with a little oregano crumbled between the fingers, if liked. Garnish the platter with shredded lettuce tossed in vinaigrette sauce (page 326), 2 tablespoons capers, 2 canned *jalapeño* chilies, cut into strips, 1 bunch radishes, cut into flowers, and about 24 small pimiento-stuffed green olives. Serve with tortillas as an appetizer for 8. This makes a pleasant light lunch for 4.

Variation: For *Pescado en Escabeche* from Cuba, sauté 2 pounds fillets of red snapper or similar fish, cut into 8 pieces, in 1 cup olive oil until the fish has lost its translucent look and is lightly browned on both sides. Lift out the fish and arrange it in a shallow casserole or serving dish. Sauté 3 medium onions, thinly sliced, and 2 cloves garlic, chopped, in the oil remaining in the skillet until the onion slices are soft. Pour the onions, garlic, and oil over the fish. In a small saucepan heat ½ cup wine vinegar with 1 bay leaf, 6 peppercorns, ¼ teaspoon each thyme and marjoram, and 1 teaspoon paprika. Pour the mixture over the fish, allow to cool, and refrigerate for 24 hours. Serve as a first course garnished with lettuce leaves, small pitted green olives, and cornichons. Serves 8.

Variation: For *Escabeche de Atún* (Fresh Tuna in Oil and Vinegar Sauce), put a 1-pound slice of tuna in a skillet with ¼ cup olive oil, 4 tablespoons lemon juice, and a bay leaf and simmer, turning once, until the fish is done, 10 minutes for each inch of thickness. Lift out, remove any bones and skin, and cut into 4 pieces. Rinse out and dry the skillet. Heat ¼ cup olive oil in the skillet and sauté 2 medium onions, thinly sliced, and 2 red bell peppers, seeded and sliced, until the onions are tender. Add ½ pound cooked, sliced carrots, ½ pound cooked green beans cut into 1-inch pieces, and ½ pound cooked potatoes, peeled and sliced. Sauté for 2 or 3 minutes. Add the tuna, 2 tablespoons vinegar, and salt and pepper to taste. Remove from the heat, cool, and serve on a bed of lettuce. Mustard pickles are sometimes served with this. Serves 4 as an appetizer, 2 as a main course.

Sábalo Guisado con Coco   COLOMBIA
Shad Fillets in Coconut Milk

Coconut milk is used a great deal in the cooking of coastal Colombia, giving dishes an interestingly different flavor, rich yet delicate.

Serves 6

3 pounds boned shad fillets, cut into 6 pieces
3 medium tomatoes, peeled, seeded, and chopped
1 medium onion, finely chopped
1 or 2 fresh hot red or green peppers, left whole with stem on

Salt, freshly ground pepper
4 cups thin coconut milk, about (see page 7)
1 cup thick coconut milk (see page 7)

Arrange the fish fillets in a shallow flameproof casserole and cover with the tomatoes and onion. Lay the hot peppers on top. Season to taste with salt and pepper. Pour in the thin coconut milk, and simmer for about 10 minutes or until the fish is no longer translucent. A simple rule is to measure the thickness of the fish and cook it 10 minutes to the inch. Carefully lift out the fish onto a serving platter and keep warm. Discard the hot peppers. Reduce the liquid in the casserole to about 1 cup over brisk heat. Add the thick coconut milk and simmer just long enough to heat the sauce through. Strain the sauce but do not push the solids through the sieve. Pour the sauce over the fish. Serve with rice.

The fish may be cooked in a preheated moderate (350° F.) oven. In this case bring the liquid just to a simmer on top of the stove, transfer the casserole to the oven, and cook for 10 minutes to the inch, which will be about 10 minutes for fillets. Make the sauce in the same way. Any firm-fleshed white fish can be used for this dish when shad is not in season, making it *Pescado Guisado con Coco* (Fish Cooked in Coconut Milk).

If the peppers are very hot (nibble a tiny bit to check), the sauce may be too *picante* for some tastes. A simple solution is to take the peppers out of the sauce after 2 or 3 minutes instead of leaving them there for the full cooking time.

MOQUECAS

The mixture of indigenous Indian, African, and Portuguese cooking that makes up Bahian cuisine is particularly apparent in the *moquecas*, which I translate as stews for want of a better word. According to that great authority on the Bahian kitchen Darwin Brandão, *moquecas* were originally Indian *pokekas* — dishes wrapped in banana leaves and cooked over charcoal. Africans brought over as slaves and working as cooks for the Portuguese in the great houses of the sugar plantations around Bahia modified the indigenous dishes, and today *moquecas*, whether of shrimp, fish, crab, or whatever, are cooked in a saucepan on top of the stove. Coconut milk, *dendê* oil, and hot peppers are typical ingredients in these flavorful dishes.

Moqueca de Peixe
Fish Stew

BRAZIL

Serves 6

3 pounds fillets of sole or any
   white fish
2 medium onions, chopped
1 or 2 fresh hot peppers, seeded
   and chopped
3 medium tomatoes, peeled and
   chopped

1 clove garlic, chopped
2 tablespoons fresh coriander
   (cilantro)
Salt
4 tablespoons lime or lemon juice
¼ cup dendê (palm) oil

Cut the fish into 2-inch pieces and place in a large bowl. In a blender or food processor combine the onions, hot peppers, tomatoes, garlic, coriander, salt to taste, and the lime or lemon juice, and reduce to a purée. Pour the purée over the fish, mixing lightly, and allow to stand for 1 hour. Transfer the fish and the marinade to a saucepan. Add ½ cup cold water and ⅛ cup of the *dendê* oil. Cover and simmer until the fish is done, about 8 minutes. Pour in the remaining ⅛ cup *dendê* oil and cook just long enough to heat the oil through. Transfer the stew to a heated serving platter and surround with a border of plain white rice.

Variation: *Moqueca de Camarão* (Shrimp Stew). This is a very interesting *moqueca*. Substitute 2 pounds raw shrimp, shelled and deveined, for the fish. Shorten the cooking time to about 3 minutes, or just long enough for the shrimp to turn pink and lose their translucent look. Stir in 1 cup thick coconut milk with the shrimp. Omit the water. Serves 6.

Moqueca de Camarão   BRAZIL
Bahian Shrimp Stew

Serves 6

¼ cup olive oil
1 large onion, finely chopped
2 small carrots, scraped and thinly
    sliced
1 green bell pepper, seeded and
    chopped
1 red bell pepper, seeded and
    chopped

4 medium tomatoes, peeled,
    seeded, and chopped
Salt, freshly ground pepper
2 pounds large shrimp, shelled
    and deveined
2 tablespoons dendê *(palm) oil*

Heat the olive oil in a large, heavy skillet and sauté the onion, carrots, and green and red peppers until the onion is soft. Add the tomatoes and salt and pepper to taste, and cook for a few minutes longer over moderate heat. Stir in the shrimp and the *dendê* oil and cook, turning the shrimp once or twice, until the shrimp are pink and have lost their translucent look, about 3 minutes. Serve on a warmed platter surrounded by white rice. Serve separately with *Môlho de Pimenta e Azeite de Dendê* (Hot Peppers in Palm Oil), page 313, or *Môlho de Pimenta e Limão* (Hot Pepper and Lime Sauce), page 313.

SHRIMP DISHES

Shrimp in Latin America are magnificent in quality and abundant in quantity and in my experience almost always beautifully cooked, juicy, and well flavored. It takes discipline in Bahia to eat anything *but* shrimp, they are so delicious. Tomatoes and peppers, both sweet and hot, are used a great deal with shrimp, but because each country uses different seasoning, or different ways of preparing them, the finished dishes are quite varied in flavor. Perhaps the most unusual is the *Vatapá de Camarão e Peixe* (Shrimp and Fish in Coconut, Nut, and Shrimp Sauce), which illustrates the exuberance of this extraordinarily imaginative kitchen, where improbable combinations, such as dried and fresh shrimp, almonds and cashew nuts, *dendê* oil and coconut milk, marry in an exciting way — a lovely dish for a party (and fortunately a food processor simplifies the work).

Vatapá de Camarão e Peixe   BRAZIL
Shrimp and Fish in Coconut, Nut, and Shrimp Sauce

Serves 6 to 8

1 cup dried shrimp
¼ cup dendê *(palm) oil or olive oil*
2 medium onions, grated
2 cloves garlic, crushed
1 cup cashew nuts, ground
1 cup blanched almonds, ground
1 cup fresh breadcrumbs
4 cups thin coconut milk (see
    page 7)

2 or more tablespoons dendê
    (palm) oil
2 tablespoons olive oil
2 pounds see bass fillets, or other
    white fish
1 pound shrimp, shelled and
    deveined

Soak the dried shrimp in warm water to cover for 15 minutes. Drain the shrimp, then purée in a blender or food processor, or put through a food mill, using the fine blade. Set aside.

Heat ¼ cup *dendê* or olive oil in a heavy skillet and sauté the onions, garlic, cashew nuts, almonds, and the puréed shrimp for 5 minutes. Stir in the breadcrumbs and the coconut milk, and simmer, stirring occasionally, until the mixture has the consistency of a thick béchamel sauce. Add more breadcrumbs if necessary. Remove from the heat and stir in 2 or more tablespoons of *dendê* oil to taste.

Heat 2 tablespoons olive oil in a skillet and sauté the fish lightly. Add the fresh shrimp, and sauté for about 2 minutes, or until the shrimp turn pink. Fold the shrimp and fish mixture into the coconut milk sauce. Serve with *Angú de Arroz* (Molded Rice) and a hot pepper sauce (see page 311), if liked.

Camarones Acapulqueños
Shrimp, Acapulco Style

MEXICO

Serves 4

1 pound medium to large shrimp
4 tablespoons butter
2 cloves garlic, minced
¼ cup parsley, finely chopped
3 medium tomatoes, peeled and
    chopped

3 tablespoons tomato paste
Salt, freshly ground pepper
⅓ cup brandy

Peel and devein the shrimp and set aside. Put the shrimp shells into a small saucepan with 2 cups water, bring to a boil, reduce the heat, and simmer, uncovered, for 20 minutes. Strain and discard the shells. Measure the liquid. There should be 1 cup. If necessary, reduce it over brisk heat or make up the quantity with water. Reserve.

Heat the butter in a casserole and add the garlic and parsley, and sauté for 2 minutes, taking care not to let the garlic burn. Add the tomatoes and simmer until the mixture is thick, about 10 minutes. Add the reserved shrimp stock and the tomato paste, stir to mix, season with salt and pepper, and add the brandy. Bring to a simmer, add the shrimp, cover, and cook for 2 to 3 minutes, according to the size of the shrimp, until they are pink, taking care not to overcook. Serve on a bed of rice.

Camarão com Leite de Côco

Shrimp in Coconut Milk

A Bahamian dish that I find enticing.

Serves 6

1 ½ *pounds large shrimp*
3 *cloves garlic, crushed*
6 *tablespoons lime or lemon juice*
Salt, freshly ground pepper
¼ *cup vegetable oil*
1 *large onion, grated*

3 *scallions, chopped, using white*
  and green parts
3 *medium tomatoes, peeled,*
  seeded, and chopped
1 ½ *cups thick coconut milk (see*
  page 7)

Peel and devein the shrimp, saving the shells. Put the shrimp in a bowl with the garlic, lime or lemon juice, and salt and pepper to taste. Set aside.

Place the reserved shrimp shells in a saucepan with 3 cups water and simmer briskly, uncovered, for 30 minutes, or until the liquid is reduced to ¾ cup. Strain, discard the shells, and set the stock aside.

Heat the oil in a skillet and sauté the onion and scallions for 3 minutes, or until the onion is softened. Add the tomatoes and the shrimp stock to the skillet and simmer until the mixture is well blended and quite thick, about 5 minutes. Stir in the thick coconut milk and the shrimp with their liquid, and cook, uncovered, until the shrimp are pink and have lost their translucent look, about 3 minutes. Turn the shrimp over once or twice during the cooking. Be careful not to overcook the shrimp as they toughen very quickly. Taste for salt and pepper and add a little more if necessary. Serve on a bed of plain white rice.

Cuajado de Camarones

Shrimp and Potato Omelet

Cuajado means a dish made in a skillet with meat, fish, or fruit, and eggs to hold it together. "Omelet" seems the best word to describe it but the eggs do not play as large a role as they would in a French omelet, pushed off center stage by the onions, tomatoes, potatoes, and shrimp. Though not a heavy dish, this is robust and satisfying and served with a green salad makes an excellent lunch or dinner.

Serves 4

3 tablespoons butter
1 teaspoon sweet paprika
2 medium onions, finely chopped
3 large tomatoes, peeled, seeded,
    and chopped
Salt, freshly ground pepper
2 medium-sized new potatoes,
    cooked and cubed

4 large eggs, separated
1 pound small or medium-sized
    raw shrimp, peeled and cut
    into ½-inch pieces

Heat the butter in a large (10-inch) skillet, stir in the paprika and the onions and sauté over moderate heat until the onions are soft. Add the tomatoes and salt and pepper to taste and cook until the mixture is thick and well blended, about 5 minutes. Add the potatoes and cook for a few minutes longer. Beat the egg yolks until they are thick and lemony. In a separate bowl beat the egg whites until they stand in firm peaks. Fold the whites and yolks together with a spatula. Return the skillet to the heat, fold the shrimp into the sauce, cook 2 minutes for small shrimp, 3 for medium-sized ones. Then fold in the eggs, mixing thoroughly. Cook until the eggs are lightly set.

Arroz con Mariscos   PERU
Rice with Shellfish

This is a really festive dish with its shrimp-flavored rice and rich mixture of shellfish. The secret is in cooking the shellfish just until they are done and not a second longer as they toughen very quickly with overcooking.

Serves 4 to 6

4 tablespoons olive oil, about
1 large onion, finely chopped
2 cloves garlic, minced
2 fresh hot peppers,* preferably
    red, seeded and cut into strips
2 cups long-grain rice
4 cups shrimp stock
1 or 2 tablespoons fresh coriander
    (cilantro), chopped

½ pound medium-sized shrimp,
    about 18
½ pound scallops — if small, left
    whole; if large, halved
12 cherrystone or littleneck clams
12 oysters

---

*Peruvians for the most part like their food hot and are lavish in their use of *ajíes*, hot peppers, which in fact lend flavor as well as heat. A wicked Peruvian friend of mine says that his compatriots like *picante* food as it gives them an excuse to quench the fire with *pisco* sours, a lovely local drink, or with anything else alcoholic. However, use just as much, or as little, of the hot pepper as suits your personal taste.

Heat the oil in a skillet and sauté the onion, garlic, and pepper strips until the onion is soft. Using a slotted spoon, transfer the onion mixture to a casserole. There should be about 2 tablespoons oil left in the skillet. Add a little more if necessary. Add the rice and sauté until the rice has absorbed the oil, taking care not to let it brown. Transfer the rice to a casserole. Add the shrimp stock, bring to a boil over high heat, reduce the heat to low, and cook, covered, until the rice is tender and all the liquid absorbed, about 20 minutes. Add the coriander and the shrimp, scallops, and clams, folding them well into the rice. Cook, covered, over low heat for about 3 to 5 minutes, or until the shrimp have turned pink and lost their translucent look. Add the oysters, folding them into the rice and cook just long enough to plump them, about 1 minute. Serve immediately.

To make shrimp stock: In a small saucepan heat 1 tablespoon olive oil and toss the shrimp shells in this until they turn pink. Add 1 sprig parsley, 1 slice onion, or a sliced scallion, using white and green parts, 1 sprig thyme or ⅛ teaspoon dried, 3 or 4 peppercorns, and 4 cups water. Bring to a boil, reduce the heat, and simmer, covered, for 30 minutes. Strain and measure. There should be about 3 cups. Measure the liquid from the oysters and clams. If there is more than 1 cup, reduce the shrimp stock, uncovered, over brisk heat so that there will be 4 cups stock. Cool the stock and stir in the oyster and clam liquid. Season to taste with salt.

Moqueca de Siri Mole   BRAZIL
Softshell Crabs in Coconut Milk

Serves 2

6 softshell crabs, cleaned and ready for cooking
2 tablespoons dendê *(palm)* oil or olive oil
1 small onion, finely chopped
2 medium tomatoes, peeled and chopped
1 tablespoon fresh coriander (cilantro), chopped

1 or 2 fresh hot red peppers, seeded and chopped
1 tablespoon lime or lemon juice
¾ cup thin coconut milk *(see page 7)*
Salt, freshly ground pepper

Rinse the crabs, pat them dry with paper towels, and set aside. In a skillet heat the oil and add the onion, tomatoes, coriander, hot peppers, and lime or lemon juice. Cook, stirring from time to time, over moderate heat for 5 minutes. Add the coconut milk and the crabs and cook for about 8 minutes, turning the crabs once or twice. Serve with plain rice or *Pirão de Arroz* (Rice Flour Pudding).

Variation: Omit the coconut milk and use 4 tomatoes.

SALT COD DISHES

Many fish stores, some supermarkets, and most Latin American markets and specialty stores sell salt cod, so that it will be easy to duplicate these typical Latin American dishes. It is sold packaged by the pound, sometimes in a box, sometimes as a piece cut from a whole fish, often very large. There is no important difference between the two except that the packaged fish is usually boneless while pieces from the whole fish may be quite bony, involving a little extra work.

Bacalao en Salsa de Chile Ancho y Almendra   MEXICO
Salt Cod in Mild Red Chili and Almond Sauce

Serves 4 to 6

2 pounds salt cod
1 medium onion, chopped
1 whole clove garlic

1 recipe Salsa de Chile Ancho y
    Almendra *(Mild Red Chili
    and Almond Sauce)*, page 315
1 teaspoon red wine vinegar

Soak the cod in cold water to cover for 12 hours or more, changing the water 5 or 6 times. Drain the fish and put into a saucepan with the onion and garlic and cold water to cover. Bring to a boil, reduce the heat, and simmer, covered, for 15 minutes, or until the fish is tender. Drain the fish. Strain and reserve the stock. Remove any skin and bones from the fish and cut into 2- to 3-inch pieces.

Make the sauce and thin it with 2 cups of the reserved fish stock, stir to mix, and simmer for a minute or two. Add the fish and the vinegar and simmer for 5 minutes. Serve with rice.

Bacalhau a Baíana
BRAZIL

Salt Cod, Bahia Style

This Brazilian dish of salt cod cooked in a tomato mixture is the most original of these popular dishes, but other versions are good, too.

Serves 4

1 pound salt cod
3 tablespoons vegetable oil
1 medium onion, grated
1 clove garlic, crushed
2 sweet peppers, 1 red, 1 green, seeded and chopped
3 tomatoes, peeled and puréed

1 cup hot water
Salt, freshly ground pepper
1 tablespoon dendê (palm) oil
1 cup thick coconut milk (see page 7)
1 cup scallions, chopped, using white and green parts

Soak the cod in cold water to cover for 12 hours or more, changing the water frequently. Drain the fish and remove any skin and bones. Pat the fish dry with paper towels and cut it into 2-inch pieces. Heat the oil in a saucepan and sauté the onion, garlic, and peppers until the onion and peppers are soft, about 5 minutes. Add the tomatoes, fish, and hot water. Cover and simmer for 15 minutes, or until the fish flakes easily when tested with a fork. Season to taste with salt, if necessary, pepper, and *dendê* oil. Stir in the coconut milk and the scallions and heat through without letting the mixture boil.

Variation: *Bacalao a la Criolla* (Salt Cod, Creole Style), from Venezuela. Prepare the cod as for *Bacalhau a Baíana.* Heat 4 tablespoons of olive or vegetable oil in a casserole and sauté 1 large onion, finely chopped, with 3 cloves garlic, minced, until the onion is tender. Add 3 large tomatoes, peeled and chopped, ½ teaspoon cumin, ½ teaspoon oregano, pepper to taste, and a bay leaf, and simmer for 5 minutes. Add the fish, 1 cup dry white wine, 2 tablespoons lemon juice, and salt if necessary. Simmer until the fish is tender, about 15 minutes. Accompany with rice. Serves 4.

Bacalhau a Mineira   BRAZIL
Salt Cod and Cabbage, Minas Gerais Style

Serves 4

1 pound salt cod
3 tablespoons olive oil
1 onion, finely chopped
1 clove garlic, crushed
1 sweet red pepper, seeded and
   chopped, or 1 green pepper
3 medium tomatoes, peeled and
   chopped

¼ cup chopped parsley
½ cup dry white wine
Freshly ground pepper
1 pound (5 cups) shredded
   cabbage
Salt

Soak the cod in cold water to cover for 12 hours or more, changing the water frequently. Drain the fish and remove any skin and bones. Pat the fish dry with paper towels and cut it into 2-inch pieces. Heat the oil in a large skillet and sauté the onion, garlic, pepper, tomatoes, and parsley for 5 minutes, stirring occasionally. Add the fish, wine, pepper to taste, and cabbage. Stir to mix and simmer, partially covered, until the cabbage is tender and the fish flakes easily when tested with a fork, about 15 minutes. Season with salt, if necessary.

Pudim de Bacalhau com Ovos   BRAZIL
Salt Cod with Eggs

This is an unusual and delicious first-course or breakfast dish. The salt cod in the tomato-flavored white sauce makes a rich topping for the egg.

Serves 6 as a first course, 3 as a breakfast

½ pound salt cod fillets
2 tablespoons cornstarch
2 cups milk
4 tablespoons (¼ cup) butter plus
   1 tablespoon
1 medium onion, grated
2 medium tomatoes, peeled,
   seeded, and chopped

2 tablespoons drained capers
Salt, freshly ground pepper
Butter for ramekins
6 eggs
3 tablespoons grated Parmesan
   cheese

Soak the cod in cold water to cover, changing the water several times, for 24 hours. Drain and rinse the fish. Put it into a saucepan with water to cover and poach it for 15 to 20 minutes, or until it flakes easily when tested with a fork. The water should just simmer. Drain and flake the fish and set it aside.

Mix the cornstarch with a little of the milk, add the rest of the milk, and pour the mixture into a small saucepan. Add 1 tablespoon of butter and cook, stirring, over moderate heat until the mixture is smooth and lightly thickened. Set aside.

In another saucepan heat the 4 tablespoons of butter, add the onion, and cook, stirring, for a few minutes. Add the tomatoes and cook until the mixture is thick and well blended. Stir in the Béchamel sauce and the capers. Fold in the codfish and add a little salt if necessary. Season generously with pepper. Cool slightly.

Butter six ⅔-cup-size ramekins and break an egg into each. Pour the codfish mixture over the eggs and sprinkle each ramekin with ½ tablespoon grated Parmesan cheese. This may also be cooked in a single shallow Pyrex dish. Bake in a preheated hot (400° F.) oven for 8 minutes.

Meats

Carnes

Nowhere in Latin American cooking is there such a coming together of introduced and indigenous foods and cooking methods as there is in the meat and poultry dishes. All of South and Central America, as well as Mexico, was poorly supplied with animals for meat. There were no sheep, goats, or cattle, all of which had been domesticated thousands of years before in the Middle East, and no domestic pigs or chickens, which had been supplying meat for a long while in Asia.

But the Aztecs did cultivate turkeys, ducks, quails, and doves among other birds, and they hunted a type of wild boar. Yucatán was known as the land of *Faisán y Venado* (the curassow pheasant and deer). From Mexico on south there were many rabbitlike animals from the small *agouti* to the *ñeque* or *paca*, the *viscacha*, and the huge *capybara*, weighing up to 150 pounds; this may explain why modern Latin America has so many splendid rabbit recipes. The *cuy* (pronounced kwee), a type of guinea pig, is still popular in Peru and tastes like young rabbit. The Incas bred the llama, vicuna, and alpaca from *guanacos*, small camel-like animals that still roam wild in herds in the Andean highlands. They supplied milk, meat, and soft, fleecy wool, while the llama did extra duty carrying loads as well.

The Spanish introduced sheep, goats, cattle, pigs, and chickens quite soon after the Conquest, and these were welcomed with varying degrees of enthusiasm into the Aztec, Inca, and Chibcha kitchens, among others. Pork and chicken were the favorites, reflected in the cooking of today. The new meats were incorporated into existing local dishes and, as the colonial kitchens evolved, new dishes were created, some with echoes from Spain's own colonial past, when the country had been dominated for nearly eight centuries by the Arabs. The Middle Eastern influence can still be seen in meat dishes cooked with almonds, raisins, cinnamon, and cloves, or with fruits, either dried or fresh. In Brazilian meat dishes, once again you find the contributions of the rich Portuguese cuisine, the indigenous foods of Africa like yams, nuts, and palm oil, blending with the local produce of the Indians. Dried shrimp and nuts may be ground together and mixed with coconut milk and rice flour to form a sauce colored gold with *dendê* oil — as luscious to the palate as to the eye.

The meeting of conqueror and conquered produced astoundingly rich and varied results, new food and old combined in a harmony of contrasting flavors, exuberant often, but never bland or dull. Chili peppers join chocolate to make an exotic sauce for Mexico's national dish, *Mole Poblano de Guajolote* (Turkey in Chili and Chocolate Sauce). Peppers and tomatoes used with nuts, and the herbs of both Old and New Worlds make aromatic sauces. In Peru, Brazil, and Ecuador shellfish, especially shrimp, make fascinating combinations with both meats and poultry. Fruits, fresh as well as dried, enhance beef or veal stews in Argentina and may be cooked in a large, hollowed-out squash, the vegetable itself becoming the cookpot. Tropical root vegetables, yams, taros, and sweet potatoes, transform everyday dishes into something unctuous, attractive, and different, and beans make all sorts of unusual combinations in dishes ranging from grand affairs like Brazil's *Feijoada Completa* (Black Beans with Mixed Meats) to simple ones like their *Tutú a Mineira* (Black Beans, Minas Gerais Style), where the vegetable dominates. Annatto and allspice, very much New World spices, enliven meat dishes.

Many traditional meat dishes in Latin America are types of stew, cooked on top of the stove, largely because reliable ovens are a comparatively new feature in kitchens where until recently tiled charcoal stoves were commonplace. Also much of the continent is mountainous and altitude is an important feature in cooking. It was discovered early that long, slow cooking gives very flavorful results, making meat tender and juicy. An advantage is that dishes can be prepared ahead of time and need little watching.

Argentina, which is famous for its beef, and Brazil, whose south is great cattle country, both have wonderful outdoor feasts, the *asado criollo* and the *churrasco*.

On this diverse continent there is a whole new world of flavors to be explored.

MEAT STEWS
WITH VEGETABLES AND WITH FRUIT

There is a seemingly inexhaustible range of meat stews — made from beef, veal, pork, lamb, kid — with vegetables and with fruits in the Latin American kitchen. Taste, texture, and aroma are balanced in excitingly different combinations, gentle, pungent, fiery, earthy, or elegant. Unusual ingredients are put together in subtle partnerships to produce a wonderful array of dishes, splendid for everyday eating, grand for guests as all the work can be done ahead of time. And despite a rich complexity of ingredients, cooking is straightforward. Long, slow simmering makes even the cheaper cuts of meat juicy and tender. Orange juice, wine, or vinegar is used to flavor and tenderize, nuts are used for flavor and to thicken the already richly flavored cooking liquid, and fruits, fresh and dried, lend a hint of acid blended with sweetness to the robustness of meat.

Seco de Carne   PERU
Beef Stew

This stew is very curiously named, since *seco* means dry. Once upon a time stews were very much more soupy than they are now and the *seco* here is simply to indicate that this is not a soupy stew like a pot-au-feu.

The ingredients are not exotic but the flavor of the finished stew is far from ordinary, as the garlic, hot pepper, fresh coriander, and lemon juice combine to give the sauce a fine flavor.

A similar stew made with kid, *Seco de Cabrito*, is a great favorite. Kid is more strongly flavored than beef and Peruvian cooks take advantage of this, adding extra coriander and white wine or *chicha*, a sort of corn beer, as well as stock to the dish, with very savory results. *Seco de Carnero* (Lamb Stew) and *Seco de Chancho* (Pork Stew) belong to the same family.

In Peru the potatoes used would be ones with yellow flesh, not to be confused with sweet potatoes. Though they are delicious as well as pretty, they taste the same as ordinary white potatoes.

Serves 6

4 tablespoons lard or vegetable oil
4 cloves garlic, finely chopped
1 medium onion, finely chopped
1 teaspoon ground hot pepper or
    cayenne
3 pounds beef chuck, cut into
    1-inch cubes

2 cups beef stock
Salt, freshly ground pepper
2 tablespoons fresh coriander
    (cilantro), chopped
Juice of 1 lemon
2 pounds potatoes, boiled and
    halved

Heat the lard or oil in a casserole and sauté the garlic, onion, hot pepper, and beef cubes until the beef is lightly browned. Add the beef stock, salt and pepper to taste, and the coriander. Cook, partially covered, over low heat until the beef is tender, 1½ to 2 hours. The liquid should be reduced so that the sauce is quite thick and not very abundant. Just before serving stir in the lemon juice and cook a minute or two longer. Heap the stew onto a warmed serving platter and surround with the freshly cooked, hot potato halves.

Variation: *Seco de Cabrito.* Make the stew as for the beef stew above, using 3 pounds boneless kid cut into 1-inch pieces instead of the beef. Use 1 fresh hot red or green pepper, seeded and finely chopped, instead of cayenne pepper, and increase the amount of fresh coriander to 1 cup. Use equal amounts of dry white wine and stock for the cooking liquid but use only enough barely to cover the meat. An authentic Peruvian touch would be to use 1 cup of *chicha* (corn beer). When the stew has been simmering, partially covered, for 2 hours, or when the kid is almost tender, add 6 medium-sized potatoes, peeled and halved, and cook for 20 minutes longer, or until both kid and potatoes are tender. Omit the lemon juice and add 1 cup cooked green peas just before serving. The stew is cooked partially covered to reduce the liquid as the gravy should not be abundant. Serves 6.

Carne en Jocón   GUATEMALA
Beef in Tomato and Pepper Sauce

This is called *Carne en Adobo* in some parts of Guatemala.

Serves 6

¼ cup peanut oil
1 medium onion, finely chopped
2 cloves garlic, chopped
2 red or green bell peppers, seeded
    and chopped
1 fresh hot red or green pepper,
    seeded and chopped
3 pounds lean, boneless beef
    chuck, cut into 1-inch cubes
A 10-ounce can Mexican green
    tomatoes and liquid from the
    can

4 medium tomatoes, peeled and
    coarsely chopped
1 bay leaf
2 cloves
½ teaspoon oregano
Salt, freshly ground pepper
½ cup beef stock, more or less
2 stale tortillas, or 2 tablespoons
    masa harina, or 2 tablespoons
    cornmeal

Heat the oil in a heavy saucepan or casserole and sauté the onion, garlic, and peppers until the onion is soft. Add the meat and all the other ingredients except the tortillas. The liquid should barely cover the meat. Add a little more stock, if necessary. Cover, and simmer gently until the beef is tender, about 2 hours. If using tortillas soak them in cold water, squeeze them out, and crumble like breadcrumbs. Add to the casserole and simmer, uncovered, until the sauce is thickened. If using *masa harina* or cornmeal, mix it with a little cold water and stir into the stew, cooking just until the sauce is thickened (cornmeal will take a few minutes longer to thicken). Serve the stew on a bed of *Arroz Guatemalteco* (Rice, Guatemalan Style).

Tomaticán   CHILE
Beef and Tomato Stew

Serves 4

4 tablespoons paprika oil (Color
    Chilena), see page 324
1½ pounds lean, boneless beef,
    cut into 1½-inch cubes

1 large onion, chopped
1 clove garlic, chopped
½ teaspoon oregano

1 tablespoon parsley, finely
    chopped
Salt, freshly ground pepper
8 medium tomatoes, peeled and
    chopped

4 medium potatoes, peeled and
    quartered
1 cup corn kernels

Heat the paprika oil in a heavy casserole and add the beef, onion, garlic, oregano, parsley, and salt and pepper to taste, and sauté, stirring frequently, for about 5 minutes. Add the tomatoes, cover, and cook over very low heat until the meat is almost tender, about 1½ hours. Add the potatoes and cook until both meat and potatoes are tender, about 30 minutes longer. Stir in the corn and cook for 5 minutes longer. If liked, the dish may be garnished with slices of hardboiled egg. Some cooks fry the potatoes in oil before adding to the casserole.

Ternera en Pipián Verde   MEXICO
Veal in Pumpkin Seed Sauce

Pipián is a stew of meat or poultry where the liquid is thickened with ground nuts or seeds — pumpkin, sesame, peanuts, almonds — whatever the cook chooses. It may be red or green according to the type of peppers and tomatoes used. This one has a delicious flavor and is a lovely color. It looks truly elegant accompanied by rice, and green beans for their contrastingly darker green.

Serves 6

3 pounds boneless veal, shoulder
    or shank, cut into 2-inch
    pieces
2 cups chicken or veal stock,
    about
¾ cup pepitas (pumpkin seeds)
1 medium onion, chopped
1 clove garlic, chopped
3 fresh hot green peppers, seeded
    and chopped (serrano or
    jalapeño peppers, if available)

½ cup chopped fresh coriander
    (cilantro) leaves
A 10- or 12-ounce can of Mexican
    green tomatoes, drained
6 romaine lettuce leaves,
    preferably the darker green
    outside leaves, chopped
2 tablespoons lard or vegetable oil
Salt, freshly ground pepper

Put the veal into a heavy casserole and pour in the stock, adding a little more if necessary barely to cover. Simmer over low heat, covered, until the meat is tender, about 1½ hours. In an ungreased skillet toast the pumpkin seeds for a few minutes. Cool slightly and pulverize in a blender or food processor fitted with a steel blade. Add to the blender or food processor the onion, garlic, hot peppers, coriander, green tomatoes, and romaine, and reduce to a pastelike purée. If necessary add a little of the stock.

In a skillet heat the lard or vegetable oil and cook the pumpkin seed mixture, stirring, for about 3 minutes. Thin the pumpkin seed mixture with about 2 cups of the stock, or until it is the consistency of heavy cream. Season to taste with salt and pepper. Drain the veal and set the meat aside. Return the veal to the casserole, pour on the sauce, and cook just long enough to heat through.

Ternera con Zanahorias   PERU
Veal with Carrots

I have often admired the great heaps of small, deep orange carrots in markets throughout Latin America, exquisitely clean and glowing with color. They make a great contribution to this veal stew.

Serves 6

3 pounds shank or shoulder of
    veal, cut into 2-inch pieces
Salt, freshly ground pepper
⅛ teaspoon grated nutmeg
2 large cloves garlic, crushed
1 cup dry white wine

4 tablespoons butter
1 medium onion, finely chopped
1 pound small young carrots,
    scraped and thinly sliced
1 cup beef stock, about

Season the veal pieces with salt, pepper, nutmeg, and garlic and put into a large bowl. Pour the wine over them. Cover and marinate in the refrigerator for about 4 hours, turning once or twice.

Heat the butter in a heavy casserole and sauté the onion and carrots until the onion is very soft, about 10 minutes. Add the veal and the marinade and enough beef stock barely to cover. Simmer, covered, over very low heat until the veal is tender, about 1½ hours. The carrots should be very soft, almost disintegrating in the sauce. Serve with a green vegetable.

Chancho Adobado

Spicy Pork

Serves 6

1 whole head garlic
2 tablespoons ground annatto
    (achiote)
2 teaspoons ground cumin
Salt, freshly ground pepper
1 cup white vinegar

3 pounds shoulder of pork, cut
    into 2-inch cubes
2 tablespoons lard or vegetable oil
Juice of 1 Seville (bitter) orange, or
    ¼ cup orange juice
1 ½ pounds sweet potatoes

Peel the garlic cloves and reduce them to a purée in an electric blender with the annatto, cumin, salt and pepper to taste, and vinegar. Put the pork pieces into a large bowl and pour the garlic marinade over them, mixing well. Marinate overnight in the refrigerator, covered. Strain, reserving the marinade. Pat the pork cubes dry with paper towels. Heat the lard or oil in a large skillet and sauté the pork pieces until golden brown all over, trans- ferring them to a casserole as they are done. Pour the reserved marinade over the pork, add the orange juice, cover, and cook over very low heat until the meat is tender, 1½ to 2 hours. If the meat seems to be drying out, add a little water; 3 or 4 tablespoons will probably be enough. There should be very little gravy when the dish is finished.

    Peel the sweet potatoes and cut them into slices about ¾ inch thick. Cook in boiling salted water until tender, 15 to 20 minutes. Drain.

    To serve, heap the pork in the center of a large warmed platter and surround with the sweet potato slices moistened with a little of the meat gravy. White rice is another traditional accompaniment to this dish.

Seco de Chancho
Pork Stew

Serves 6 to 8

2 tablespoons annatto oil or lard
   (see page 324)
3 pounds lean pork shoulder, cut
   into 2-inch cubes
1 large onion, finely chopped
2 large cloves garlic, minced
1 large tomato, peeled, seeded,
   and chopped
1 red bell pepper, seeded and
   coarsely chopped, or 2 canned
   pimientos, chopped

1 fresh hot red or green pepper,
   seeded and finely chopped
1 tablespoon fresh coriander
   (cilantro), chopped coarsely
½ teaspoon ground cumin
½ teaspoon oregano
Salt, freshly ground pepper
Pinch sugar (optional)
2 cups beer

Heat the oil or lard in a heavy skillet and lightly sauté the pork cubes. With a slotted spoon remove the pork pieces to a heavy flameproof casserole. Remove all but 2 tablespoons of fat from the skillet, add the onion and garlic, and sauté the mixture until the onion is soft. Add the tomato, the sweet and hot peppers, coriander, cumin, and oregano, and simmer until the mixture is well blended, about 10 minutes. Season to taste with salt and pepper and, if liked, the pinch of sugar. Pour over the pork, add the beer, cover, and cook over very low heat until the pork is tender, about 2 hours. The sauce should be quite thick. If it seems at all watery, partially uncover the casserole during the second hour of cooking. Serve with rice.

Jamón del País
Peruvian Fresh Ham

Though this is called ham (*jamón*), it is really fresh pork spiced and cooked in a most unusual way — marinated, simmered until tender, then browned in hot fat. Very different and marvelous for a buffet either hot or trans-formed when cold into a delicious dividend, *Butifarras*, special Peruvian sandwich rolls. It can be made with a boned leg of pork but I find the shoulder a more manageable size. Incidentally, though the meat is strictly speaking stewed, the finished dish is more like a baked meat.

Peruvian and Mexican garlic have quite enormous cloves, which comes in handy when one has to peel a number of them. I have specified large cloves of garlic but if these are not available, a whole head of garlic should be used. It will not overpower the other flavors.

Serves 12 or more

12 large cloves garlic, peeled, or 1
    whole head
2 tablespóons annatto (achiote)
    seeds, ground
1 teaspoon cumin, ground

Salt, freshly ground pepper
About 6 pounds pork shoulder
    (cali), boned and rolled
4 tablespoons lard

Crush the garlic cloves and mix to a paste with the annatto, cumin, and salt and pepper to taste. Spread this on the pork, put the pork into a baking dish, cover loosely with foil, and refrigerate overnight. Put the pork, and any liquid in the pan, into a very large saucepan or kettle and pour in enough water to cover it. Cover, bring to a boil, reduce the heat to low, and simmer gently until the meat is tender, 2½ to 3 hours. When it is cool enough to handle, remove it from the cooking liquid and pat it dry with paper towels. Heat the lard in a very large skillet or baking dish and sauté the pork until it is browned all over. Transfer the pork to a serving platter and serve hot, sliced with rice or potatoes, a green vegetable or a salad, or allow to cool and use to make *Butifarras* (Peruvian Ham Sandwiches).

Variation: For *Butifarras*, put thinly sliced onions into a bowl with an equal amount of thinly sliced radishes; fresh hot peppers, seeded and sliced; and salt and pepper to taste. Pour in enough white vinegar to cover the vegetables and let them stand at room temperature for 2 hours before using. The amount of hot peppers will depend on taste. Strain and discard the vinegar. Have ready crusty rolls, cut three-quarters of the way through. Butter the rolls if desired and place a lettuce leaf, a slice of ham, and a layer of the pickled vegetables in each roll. Serve as a snack.

Cordero Criollo
Lamb, Creole Style

PERU

Lamb and kid are used interchangeably in Latin America, though kid requires a little longer cooking time. There are not a great many recipes calling for these meats, but the few that exist are very good indeed. Annatto (achiote) lends a marvelous fragrance to this Peruvian roast leg of lamb. The herbs and spices in the dressing are the same as those in *aliño criollo* (Venezuelan creole style seasoning powder), and I find the prepared version exactly right for this dish, though I add a large clove of crushed garlic to the mixture. Shoulder of lamb or kid can also be used successfully.

Serves 6

A 4-pound leg or shoulder of lamb
    or kid
2 tablespoons aliño criollo *(see*
    page 325)
¼ cup red wine vinegar
1 large clove garlic, crushed

½ cup olive oil
3 large potatoes, peeled and
    halved lengthwise
Lettuce leaves, preferably romaine
1 canned pimiento, cut into strips

Trim the lamb of all but a thin layer of fat. Mix the seasoning powder with the vinegar, add the garlic, then beat in the oil with a fork. Rub this marinade into the lamb and let it stand for at least 2 hours, turning the meat from time to time and spooning the marinade over it. When ready to cook scrape off and reserve the marinade. Put the lamb into a baking pan brushed over with oil and surround with the potatoes. Bake in a preheated moderate (325° F.) oven for 1 hour (15 minutes to the pound), for rare lamb, 130° to 135° F. on a meat thermometer. Cook for 15 minutes longer if medium rare lamb is preferred. Baste every 20 minutes with the reserved marinade and any pan juices. Turn the potatoes halfway through the cooking time.

Remove the lamb to a carving board and let it stand 15 minutes before carving. Arrange the potatoes round the edge of a serving platter and keep warm in the turned-off oven. Slice the lamb and arrange it on the platter. Garnish the edge of the dish with lettuce leaves and strips of pimiento. Spoon the fat off the pan juices and put into a gravy boat with the juices from the meat as it is carved. Either spoon over the meat or serve as gravy. There will not be a great deal.

Variation: A most delicious variation, which has overtones of the Middle East in its use of mint, is *Carnero o Cabrito al Horno* (Roast Lamb or Kid). Make a dressing of 3 tablespoons butter creamed with 8 large cloves crushed garlic, salt, freshly ground pepper, and 4 tablespoons finely chopped fresh mint. Spread over the lamb or kid and roast as above. Baste with 1 cup dry white wine instead of the marinade.

Cazuela de Cordero
Lamb Casserole

CHILE

This lamb stew is a Chilean standby, a family favorite, both rich and simple at the same time. The winter squash slightly thickens the sauce, and the final whisking in of beaten eggs finishes it.

Serves 6

2 pounds boneless lamb for stew,
   cut into 2-inch pieces
1 onion, coarsely chopped
1 leek, sliced
1 carrot, scraped and sliced
Small stalk of celery with leaves
½ teaspoon oregano
Pinch of ground cumin
1 sprig parsley
1 bay leaf
6 small potatoes, peeled, or 3 large
   potatoes, peeled and halved
½ pound winter squash, peeled
   and cut into 1-inch cubes

Salt, freshly ground pepper
3 small zucchini, cut into 1-inch
   slices
½ pound green beans, cut into
   1-inch pieces
2 cups fresh corn kernels
2 eggs, lightly beaten

Put the lamb, onion, leek, carrot, celery, oregano, cumin, parsley, and bay leaf into a large saucepan or casserole. Pour in enough water to cover, about 6 cups, bring to a boil, skim off any froth that rises to the surface, lower the heat, cover, and simmer until the meat is almost tender, about 1½ hours. Lift out the pieces of lamb onto a plate and set aside. Strain the stock, pressing down to extract all the juices. Discard the solids. Rinse out and dry the casserole.

Return the lamb pieces to the casserole and add the potatoes and winter squash. Pour in the strained stock, adding a little water if necessary to cover the lamb and vegetables. Season to taste with salt and pepper and simmer 15 minutes. Add the zucchini, beans, and corn, and simmer until the beans are tender, about 10 minutes.

Whisk a cup of the hot stock gradually into the eggs, then pour the mixture into the saucepan, stirring to mix. Do not let the liquid boil, as the eggs will curdle. Cook over very low heat until the eggs have thickened the sauce. The winter squash will have disintegrated, also thickening the sauce slightly. Serve in soup plates, making sure that each serving has a little of everything.

Arvejado de Cordero   CHILE
Lamb Stew with Green Peas

This Chilean lamb stew is characterized by the interesting use of paprika oil (*Color Chilena*).

Serves 6

3 tablespoons paprika oil (Color
   Chilena), *see page 324*
2 pounds boneless lamb for stew,
   cut into 1-inch pieces
1 large onion, finely chopped

1 tablespoon flour
Salt, freshly ground pepper
2 cups fresh green peas
2 eggs, lightly beaten
¼ cup chopped parsley

Heat the paprika oil in a casserole or large saucepan. Add the lamb pieces and the onion, and sauté until the onion is soft. Add the flour and cook for a minute or two longer, stirring with a wooden spoon to mix thoroughly. Add 2 cups water, season to taste with salt and pepper, cover, and simmer until the lamb is almost done, about 1½ hours. Add the peas, bring back to a simmer, and cook for 15 minutes longer, or until the peas are tender. Transfer the meat and peas to a serving dish and keep warm. Stir the eggs and parsley into the liquid in the casserole and cook over very low heat, stirring constantly with a wooden spoon, until the sauce has thickened lightly. Do not let it boil, as it will curdle. Pour the sauce over the lamb and serve with boiled potatoes or any puréed root vegetable or plain rice.

Carnero en Adobo   MEXICO
Lamb in Chili and Vinegar Sauce

Lamb and kid are very popular in the north of Mexico, much of it mountain country well suited to these animals. Julia, the cook of my husband's uncle, General Procopio Ortiz Reyes, who lives in Torreón, Coahuila, cooked this for me and gave me her recipe. It is easy yet exotic. *Ancho* chili is mild and full flavored, *mulato* chili a little *picante*. Using both gives a sauce full of character.

Serves 6

3 pounds boneless lamb (shoulder
   or leg), cut into 1½-inch
   pieces

2 medium onions, chopped
2 cloves garlic, chopped
3 or 4 sprigs fresh coriander

Salt
3 ancho *and* 3 mulato *chilies*
⅛ *teaspoon ground cumin*
½ *teaspoon oregano*

2 *tablespoons red wine vinegar*
3 *tablespoons lard or vegetable oil*

Put the lamb into a heavy saucepan or casserole with 1 onion, 1 clove garlic, the coriander sprigs, salt, and water barely to cover. Bring to a boil, lower the heat, and simmer, covered, over moderate heat until the meat is tender, about 1½ hours. Drain the lamb, strain the stock, and set aside. Rinse out and dry the casserole and return the lamb to it.

Prepare the chilies (page 13) and put them with the soaking water into a blender or food processor fitted with a steel blade. Add the remaining onion and garlic, the cumin, oregano, vinegar, and salt, and blend until fairly smooth. The mixture should be more of a paste than a purée. Heat the lard or oil in a skillet and cook the mixture, stirring constantly with a wooden spoon, for about 5 minutes, over moderate heat. Thin with 1½ cups of the reserved lamb stock. The mixture should be the consistency of a medium white sauce. Add more stock if necessary. Pour the sauce over the lamb and simmer over very low heat for 20 minutes. Serve with rice, beans, and a green vegetable. Tortillas are good with this.

Variation: Mexican friends who like their food hot and very highly flavored suggest adding a canned *chipotle* or *morita* chili to the blender when making the sauce. It makes a delicious change.

Variation: For *Carnero en Salsa de Chile Ancho* (Lamb in Mild Red Chili Sauce) from Mexico, sauté the lamb in 2 tablespoons olive oil in a skillet and transfer to a casserole. Prepare 6 *ancho* chilies (page 13) and put them with the soaking water into a blender or food processor fitted with a steel blade. Add 1 chopped onion, 1 clove garlic, and 4 medium tomatoes, peeled and chopped, and reduce to a purée. If necessary, add enough oil to the skillet to make the quantity of fat up to 2 tablespoons. Add the chili mixture and cook, stirring constantly, for about 5 minutes over moderate heat. It has a tendency to splutter. Pour over the lamb, season to taste with salt and freshly ground pepper, a pinch of cinnamon, and ⅛ teaspoon of cloves. Cover and simmer over low heat until the lamb is tender, about 1½ hours. Soak ¼ cup small, pimiento-stuffed olives, about 12, in cold water for 15 minutes to get rid of the brine, drain and halve them. Put the lamb in a serving dish and garnish with the olives and ⅛ cup slivered, toasted almonds. Serve with rice and a green vegetable. Depending on the juiciness of the tomatoes, it may be necessary to add a little more liquid to the lamb, though the sauce should not be abundant. Add tomato juice, stock, or water. Serves 6.

Seco de Carnero
Lamb Stew

PERU

Don't be afraid of the amount of garlic used here. The flavor will not be at all aggressive, indeed it will be quite gentle as the pungent oils cook out. The coriander, garlic, fruit juices, and hot peppers combine into a most delicious sauce.

Serves 6 to 8

1 cup fresh coriander (cilantro), chopped

2 or 3 fresh hot red or green peppers, seeded and chopped

1 whole head garlic, peeled and chopped

½ cup olive oil

2 medium onions, finely chopped

4 pounds lean, boneless lamb (shoulder or leg), cut into 1-inch cubes

Salt, freshly ground pepper

½ cup bitter (Seville) orange juice, or use two-thirds fresh orange juice and one-third lime or lemon juice

2 pounds potatoes, peeled and sliced

1 pound green peas, or 2 packages frozen peas

In a blender or food processor combine the coriander leaves, hot peppers, and garlic, and reduce to a purée. Set aside. Heat the oil in a casserole and sauté the onions until they are soft. Stir in the coriander mixture and cook for a minute or two longer. Add the lamb pieces and cook for about 5 minutes, turning the pieces to coat them with the sauce. Season to taste with salt and a generous amount of pepper. Add the bitter (Seville) orange juice or the orange and lime (or lemon) juice mixture and enough water to cover, about 1½ cups. Cover and simmer until the lamb is tender, about 1½ hours. The stew may be cooked to this point a day ahead and refrigerated so that any fat may be removed. Let the casserole stand until it reaches room temperature before reheating.

Boil the potatoes in salted water until they are tender. Drain and add to the casserole. Boil the peas in salted water until they are tender, drain, and add to the casserole. Bring the casserole to a simmer and cook just long enough to heat it through.

Posta en Frutas Secas
Beef and Dried Fruit Stew

COLOMBIA

This is one of the Latin American meat and fruit stews that have links, via Spain when it was a Moorish colony, to ancient Persia, where these delectable dishes were first concocted. Interestingly there are also links with the cooking of present-day Morocco, where dishes very similar to those of ancient Persia survive. Most Colombians take advantage of modern marketing and use an 11-ounce package of dried mixed fruit, but you can make the mixture yourself.

Serves 6

An 11-ounce package mixed dried
    fruit (prunes, dried apricots,
    peaches, and pears)
3 tablespoons olive or vegetable
    oil
3 pounds lean beef, preferably top
    round, cut into 1-inch cubes
1 medium onion, finely chopped
1 clove garlic, minced
1 medium carrot, scraped and
    chopped
Salt, freshly ground pepper

1 cup dry red wine
1 tablespoon soft butter (optional)
1 tablespoon flour (optional)

Put the mixed dried fruit into a bowl with 1½ cups warm water and leave to soak for 1 hour, turning the fruit from time to time. Drain, reserve the soaking water, and set the fruit aside.

Heat the oil in a heavy casserole or saucepan and sauté the beef, onion, garlic, and carrot for about 5 minutes. Season with salt and pepper. Pour in the wine and the reserved soaking water from the fruit. Bring to a boil, reduce the heat to low, and simmer, covered, for 2 hours, or until the beef is almost tender. Add the fruit. The prunes and apricots should be left whole, the pears and peaches halved or quartered. Cover and simmer 30 minutes longer. If the sauce is too thick, add a little more wine. If you want a slightly thicker sauce, mix the butter and flour together and drop a few smooth pieces into the casserole, blending well. Serve with rice.

Carne con Salsa de Frutas
Beef in Fruit Sauce

ECUADOR

A particularly delicious beef stew, with the flavors of the fruits and the tomatoes subtly blended and enriched by the cream, though still nicely tart.

Serves 6

6 tablespoons vegetable oil
1 large onion, finely chopped
3 pounds boneless beef chuck, cut into 1-inch cubes
1 cup dry white wine
1 cup beef stock
Salt, freshly ground pepper
2 quinces, peeled, cored, and chopped, or 2 peaches, peeled, pitted, and chopped

2 apples, peeled, cored, and chopped
2 pears, peeled, cored, and chopped
2 large tomatoes, peeled and chopped
Sugar to taste
1 cup heavy cream

Heat 4 tablespoons of the oil in a skillet and sauté the onion until it is soft. Using a slotted spoon transfer the onion to a casserole. In the oil remaining in the skillet sauté the beef until it is browned on all sides. Add it to the casserole with the wine, stock, and salt and pepper to taste. Cover and simmer until the meat is tender, about 2 hours. Arrange the meat on a serving platter and keep warm. Reserve the stock.

Heat the remaining 2 tablespoons of oil in a saucepan and add the fruit, including the tomatoes. Cook for a few minutes, stirring. Add a little sugar, if liked. The sauce should be quite tart. Add enough of the reserved stock barely to cover, and simmer, stirring from time to time, until the mixture is thick and well blended. In the old days cooks had to work the mixture through a sieve, a tedious procedure; today a blender or food processor does the job. Return the purée to the saucepan and taste for seasoning, adding a little salt if necessary. Stir in the cream and cook just long enough to heat through. Pour the sauce over the meat. Serve with rice.

Variation: Guava shells or nectarines may be used instead of quinces or peaches. Boneless pork loin may be used instead of beef. The sauce is also pleasant served with grilled lamb chops. If preferred, serve with *Llapingachos* (Potato Cakes) instead of rice.

Chuletas de Cerdo con Frutas
DOMINICAN REPUBLIC

Pork Chops with Dried Fruit

The use of dried fruits, especially apricots, in meat dishes is very much a Middle Eastern thing. In Iran lamb and dried apricots are used together in a most delectable dish. A lot of old dishes have survived in the Dominican Republic and this one was obviously brought over by the Spanish, using pork instead of lamb. It works beautifully.

Serves 4

¼ pound, about 1 cup, pitted prunes
¼ pound, about 1 cup, dried apricots
¼ pound, about 1 cup, dried pears
4 pork loin chops, weighing 2 pounds

Salt, freshly ground pepper
2 tablespoons vegetable oil
1 medium onion, finely chopped
1 clove garlic, chopped
1 cup chicken stock, about
1 cup dry white wine, about

Put the prunes in a bowl with the apricots, halved, and the pears, quartered. Pour in enough cold water barely to cover and let soak for 30 minutes.

Season the chops with salt and pepper. Heat the oil in a skillet and sauté the chops until golden on both sides. Transfer the chops to a casserole. In the fat remaining in the pan sauté the onion and garlic until the onion is softened. Add to the casserole. Arrange the fruit over and around the pork chops. Pour in the chicken stock and wine, adding a little more of each if necessary to cover. Cover the casserole with aluminum foil, then the lid, and bake in a preheated moderate (350° F.) oven for about 1½ hours or until the pork is tender.

Chirmole de Puerco

MEXICO

Pork Stew with Peppers and Greengage Plums

Serves 6

3 pounds lean, boneless pork, cut
   into 2-inch cubes
6 ancho chilies
3 fresh or canned hot green serrano
   peppers, seeded
2 cloves garlic, chopped
1 large onion, chopped
¼ teaspoon ground cinnamon
Salt, freshly ground pepper
1 pound greengage plums

4 medium tomatoes, sliced
½ teaspoon crumbled, dried
   epazote *(optional)*
¼ cup masa harina
¼ cup Seville (bitter) orange juice,
   or use two-thirds orange juice
   and one-third lime juice
2 tablespoons lard or vegetable oil
   (optional)

Put the pork into a large, heavy saucepan or casserole, add water barely to cover, and simmer, covered, until almost tender, about 1½ hours.

Pull off the stems and shake out the seeds from the peppers and tear them into pieces. Rinse and put into a bowl with ½ cup hot water. Let the peppers soak for 1 hour, turning them frequently. Combine the *ancho* chilies, the water in which they were soaked, the *serrano* peppers, garlic, onion, and cinnamon in an electric blender or food processor and reduce to a coarse purée. Drain the pork, reserving the stock, and return the meat to the saucepan. Add enough of the stock to the purée to make a thin sauce. Season to taste with salt and pepper and pour over the pork, mixing well. Pit the greengages and cut each plum into 4 pieces. Add them to the pork. Add the tomato slices, and if it is available the *epazote*. Simmer, covered, until the pork is tender. Mix a little of the remaining stock with the *masa harina*. Stir the orange juice into this mixture and add to the pork stew. The lard or vegetable oil may be added at this time, if liked. Simmer, stirring gently, for a minute or two longer.

Ternera en Salsa de Ciruelas Pasas

MEXICO

Veal in Prune Sauce

This is an old colonial dish that I particularly like to serve when friends are coming to dinner. The prunes give the dark sauce a rich, subtle flavor.

Serves 6

1 ½ cups large, pitted prunes,
    chopped
1 cup dry red wine
4 tablespoons lard or vegetable oil
2 ½ to 3 ½ pounds boneless veal
    roast, preferably top round

2 medium onions, finely chopped
2 cloves garlic, chopped
3 medium tomatoes, peeled,
    seeded, and chopped
2 cups beef or veal stock, about
Salt, freshly ground pepper

Put the prunes to soak in the wine for at least 2 hours.

Heat the lard or oil in a heavy casserole and sauté the veal until it is golden brown all over. Lift out of the casserole and set aside. In the oil remaining in the casserole sauté the onions and garlic until the onions are soft. Add the tomatoes and cook until the mixture is well blended. Add the prunes and wine. Add the veal and pour in just enough stock to cover. Simmer, covered, over low heat until the veal is tender, about 2 hours. Lift out the veal to a serving platter, slice, and keep warm. Season the sauce to taste with salt and pepper. During cooking the prunes should have disintegrated, thickening the sauce. If necessary, cook the sauce over fairly brisk heat, stirring, for a few minutes to amalgamate the solids and reduce the sauce a little. It should be thick but not completely smooth. Spoon a little sauce over the veal slices and serve the rest in a sauceboat. Serve with rice or any starchy root vegetable.

Ternera con Aceitunas   MEXICO
Veal with Olives

The stuffed green olives add a distinctive flavor to this dish.

Serves 4 to 6

4 tablespoons olive or vegetable
    oil
2 pounds shank or shoulder of
    veal, cut into 1-inch cubes
2 ounces boiled ham, coarsely
    chopped
1 medium onion, finely chopped
1 clove garlic, chopped

½ cup chopped parsley
36 small pimiento-stuffed green
    olives
1 cup dry white wine
1 cup beef stock
Salt, freshly ground pepper
2 eggs

Heat the oil in a skillet and sauté the veal with the ham. Lift out into a casserole. In the oil remaining in the skillet sauté the onion and garlic until the onion is soft. Add to the casserole with the parsley. Soak the olives in cold water for 10 minutes, drain, and add to the casserole. Pour in the wine and stock, season to taste with salt and pepper, cover, and simmer until the veal is tender, about 1½ hours. Lightly beat the eggs, then whisk ½ cup of the hot liquid into them. Pour the mixture back into the casserole and cook, stirring, until the sauce is lightly thickened. Do not let the sauce boil, as it will curdle. Serve with rice or a starchy root vegetable and a green vegetable or salad.

FLANK STEAK DISHES

South Americans hold flank steak in high esteem for its fine flavor and adaptability. It may be braised, stewed, and broiled, stuffed, baked, or shredded. And it may be served hot or cold. It is used for the national dish of Venezuela with the traditional accompaniments of rice, black beans, and fried plantains. It is stuffed with spinach, or even more exotically with an omelet, asparagus tips, and strips of pimiento to make a party dish that is not only satisfyingly hearty but elegant in appearance. It has the added merit of being a lean and tender cut that is also economical.

Pabellón Caraqueño   VENEZUELA
Steak with Rice, Black Beans, and Plantains

This national dish of Venezuela is said to look like a flag (*pabellón*) because of the different colors of meat, rice, beans, and plantains. It is a robust and satisfying dish.

Serves 6

1½ pounds flank steak or skirt steak	1 recipe Arroz Blanco (White Rice), page 248
1½ cups beef stock, about	6 eggs, fried in olive oil
1 medium onion, finely chopped	1 recipe Caraotas Negras (Black Beans), page 243
1 clove garlic, minced	
2 medium tomatoes, peeled, seeded, and chopped	1 ripe plantain, or 2 underripe bananas
Salt	2 tablespoons vegetable oil
2 tablespoons olive oil	

Cut the steak into 2 or 3 pieces to fit conveniently into a saucepan, and add the stock to cover. If necessary add a little more. Bring to a simmer and cook, covered, over very low heat until the meat is tender, 1½ to 2 hours. Allow to cool in the stock, drain, reserve the stock for another use, and shred the meat with the fingers. Combine the meat with the onion, garlic, and tomatoes. Season to taste with salt. Heat the oil in a skillet and sauté the meat mixture until the onion is cooked and the mixture is quite dry. Put the rice in the center of a large, warmed platter and heap the meat on top of it. Arrange the fried eggs on top of the meat. Surround the rice with the black beans and decorate the edge of the platter with the fried plantains or bananas.

To fry the plantains or bananas: Peel the plantains and cut them in half lengthwise, then crosswise into thirds. If using bananas, peel and cut into thirds. Heat the oil in a skillet and fry the plantains or bananas until golden brown on both sides, about 2 or 3 minutes.

Matambre ARGENTINA
Stuffed Rolled Flank Steak

This translates literally as "kill hunger" and it is indeed a very satisfying dish whether eaten hot as a main course, or cold with salads, ideal for a picnic. In more modest amounts, it makes an unusual first course.

Serves 4

1 teaspoon oregano
2 cloves crushed garlic
1½ pounds flank steak
Salt, freshly ground pepper
1 cup spinach leaves, about

1 small carrot, thinly sliced
1 hardboiled egg, thinly sliced
Cayenne pepper (optional)
8 cups beef stock, about

Mix the oregano and garlic and spread over the steak. Season the steak with salt and pepper to taste, then cover with the spinach leaves, leaving about a ½-inch margin. Top the spinach with the carrot and egg and sprinkle with a little cayenne pepper, if liked. Roll up with the grain and tie with kitchen string at about 1-inch intervals. Place in a casserole into which it fits comfortably but quite snugly. Pour in the beef stock. There should be enough to cover the steak. Bring to a boil, skim off any froth that rises, reduce the heat, and simmer gently for 1½ to 2 hours, or until the beef is tender. Lift out, remove the strings, slice, and serve hot, moistening the steak with a little of the stock. Serve with potatoes or rice. Or allow the steak to cool in the stock and serve cold, sliced, with salad. Reserve the leftover stock for another use. Serve with *Salsa Criolla* (Creole Sauce), page 320.

Variation: For *Matambre al Horno* (Baked Flank Steak), put the stuffed steak into the casserole with 3 cups stock. Bring the stock to a boil on top of the stove, cover the casserole, and transfer to a preheated moderate (350° F.) oven for about 1 hour, or until the steak is done.

Variation: In Uruguay, where this dish is also popular, the steak is sometimes just seasoned and stuffed with spinach.

Variation: *Matambre a la Cacerola* (Casseroled Flank Steak). Heat 2 tablespoons butter in a skillet, add 1 small onion, finely chopped, ½ cup finely chopped celery, and 1 small carrot, scraped and finely chopped. Sauté until the onion is soft, about 5 minutes. Remove from the heat and stir in 2 tablespoons finely chopped parsley and 2 cups cubed bread. Season with salt and pepper. Stir in 2 tablespoons beef stock, mix well, and spread over the steak, leaving a ½-inch margin. Roll up with the grain and tie at 1-inch intervals with kitchen string. Heat 2 tablespoons vegetable oil in a casserole large enough to hold the steak, and brown the steak all over. Pour in enough stock, about 8 cups, to cover, and simmer for 1½ to 2 hours. Or cook in a preheated moderate (350° F.) oven for 1 hour or so, in which case add only enough stock to come about one-third of the way up the steak, about 3 cups. If liked, thicken about 2 cups of the stock with a beurre manié (see page 328). Serve with carrots and potatoes and a green vegetable.

Variation: *Malaya Arrollada* (Rolled Flank Steak) is a Chilean version of *Matambre*, and why this particular cut of steak is called a *malaya* in Chile is entirely beyond me. Admittedly, women in Malaya wear sarongs and sarongs are wrapped around ladies, while the *malaya* is wrapped around a filling, but this is surely stretching a linguistic point too far. Season the steak with salt, pepper, and 1 teaspoon oregano. Cover it with 1 onion, finely chopped, 1 stalk celery, finely chopped, 1 carrot, scraped and finely sliced, and 1 hardboiled egg, thinly sliced. Roll up with the grain, tie with string, and place in a flameproof casserole that holds it snugly. Pour in enough stock to cover and simmer until it is tender, 1½ to 2 hours. Let it cool in the stock. Lift out, remove the string and slice. Serve as a first course with any salad. Serves 8.

Sobrebarriga

Flank Steak

Serves 4 to 6

A 2-pound flank steak, with layer
   of fat left on
1 medium onion, chopped
2 cloves garlic, chopped
2 medium tomatoes, chopped
1 carrot, scraped and chopped
1 bay leaf
2 or 3 sprigs parsley

½ teaspoon thyme
½ teaspoon oregano
Salt, freshly ground pepper
Beef stock or water
1 or 2 tablespoons butter, softened
   at room temperature
1 cup fresh breadcrumbs

Put the steak into a large saucepan with the onion, garlic, tomatoes, carrot, bay leaf, parsley sprigs, thyme, oregano, and salt and pepper to taste. Add enough stock or water to cover the meat and cook it, covered, over low heat for about 2 hours, or until it is tender. Remove the meat from the liquid, pat it dry with paper towels, and place it in a broiling pan, fat side up. Spread the butter over the meat and cover with breadcrumbs. Broil until the crumbs are golden brown. Slice the steak and arrange it on a heated platter. Strain the hot seasoned liquid into a sauceboat. Serve with *Papas Chorreadas* (Potatoes with Cheese, Tomato, and Onion Sauce) and *Ensalada de Aguacate* (Avocado Salad).

Sobrebarriga Bogotana

Flank Steak, Bogotá Style

Serves 4 to 6

1 medium onion, finely chopped
2 cloves garlic, chopped
2 medium tomatoes, peeled and
   chopped
1 tablespoon parsley, chopped
½ teaspoon thyme
1 bay leaf, crumbled
1 teaspoon prepared mustard
1 teaspoon Worcestershire sauce

Salt, freshly ground pepper
A 2-pound flank steak, trimmed of
   all fat
2 cups beef stock or water, about
2 cups dark beer, about
2 tablespoons butter, softened at
   room temperature
1 cup fresh breadcrumbs

Mix together the onion, garlic, tomatoes, parsley, thyme, bay leaf, mustard, Worcestershire sauce, and salt and pepper to taste. Spread the mixture on the steak. Roll the steak up with the grain and tie securely with string. Place in a flameproof casserole, cover, and refrigerate until the following day. Cover with equal quantities of beef stock or water, and dark beer. Bring to a boil, reduce the heat to a bare simmer, and cook, partially covered, until the steak is tender and the liquid reduced, about 2 hours. Remove the steak from the casserole, brush it with the butter, and roll it in the breadcrumbs. Arrange the steak in a baking tin and bake in a preheated hot (400° F.) oven until the crumbs are lightly browned, about 15 minutes. Heat the sauce remaining in the casserole and serve in a sauceboat. Slice the steak and arrange on a warmed platter. Serve with *Papas Chorreadas* (Potatoes with Cheese, Tomato, and Onion Sauce) and *Ensalada de Aguacate* (Avocado Salad).

Roupa Velha   BRAZIL
Old Clothes

This is the Brazilian version of the Spanish dish *Ropa Vieja* (Old Clothes). Ideally flank steak is used since the cooked meat should be shredded, as old clothes can be said to shred into rags and tatters. The dish is infinitely more appetizing than its name, and occurs very widely in Spanish- and Portuguese-speaking countries, varying from place to place. The Brazilian version, though it is not as rich as, for example, the Cuban version, is very good. Traditionally leftover beef from a *cozido* (pot-au-feu), or similar dish, is used, and if you have some, by all means use it.

Serves 4 to 6

A 2-pound flank steak, or 2 pounds cooked boiled beef	1 sprig parsley
	1 bay leaf
1 medium onion, stuck with a clove	1 clove garlic
	6 peppercorns
1 carrot, scraped and halved	1 tablespoon salt
1 stalk celery	

Put the steak into a flameproof casserole with the onion, carrot, celery, parsley, bay leaf, garlic, peppercorns, and salt and enough cold water to cover. Bring to a boil, simmer for 5 minutes, and skim the froth that rises to the surface. Cover, lower the heat, and simmer for 1½ hours, or until the steak is tender. Leave the steak in the stock until it is cool enough to handle. Lift it out of the stock onto a chopping board. Strain the stock into a jar and refrigerate for another use. Cut the steak in half crosswise, then shred it along the grain into strips. Set aside.

FOR THE SAUCE

¼ cup olive oil
2 medium onions, thinly sliced
2 medium tomatoes, peeled and
    sliced
½ cup finely chopped parsley

Salt, freshly ground pepper
Pinch of sugar
2 tablespoons vinegar
Tabasco sauce (optional)

Heat the oil in a skillet and sauté the onions until they are lightly browned. Add the tomatoes, parsley, salt and pepper to taste, and the sugar. Cook the mixture for 5 minutes longer, stirring occasionally. Add the steak, vinegar, and a little Tabasco sauce, if liked, and cook, stirring, until the steak is heated through. Transfer to the center of a heated platter and surround it with plain white rice.

PORK LOIN DISHES

Pork is one of the best-liked meats in Latin America, and pork loin one of the favorite cuts. In my view pork shoulder is just as attractive and much more economical though it will need a little longer cooking time. Recipes are quite varied, ranging from an Ecuadorian dish where the meat is larded with raw shrimp and braised, reminding one of the flavors of Chinese food, to an Argentine dish where the meat is baked in milk and emerges deliciously tender with a creamy sauce, to pork simmered in orange juice, tender and delicate, to pork loin, Chilean style, served with a fiery pepper sauce to be taken with discretion.

Lomo con Camarones   ECUADOR
Pork Loin with Shrimp

The combination of pork and shrimp braised in wine is unusual and exciting — the flavor exquisite. This is one of my party favorites.

Serves 6

A 3-pound boned loin of pork
½ pound raw shrimp, peeled and
*   coarsely chopped*
1 hardboiled egg, chopped
Salt, freshly ground pepper
2 cloves garlic, crushed
4 tablespoons butter
2 cups dry white wine
1 tablespoon flour
White wine or chicken stock

With a steel, or with a sharp, narrow knife, make holes about the thickness of one's thumb all over the loin, almost to the center of the meat. Season the shrimp and egg with salt and pepper. With your fingers, stuff half the holes with the shrimp, the other half with chopped egg, or mix the shrimp and egg together and use as a stuffing. Season the loin with salt, pepper, and the crushed garlic. Heat 3 tablespoons of the butter in a flameproof casserole large enough to hold the loin comfortably (an oval casserole is best) and sauté the meat until it is golden all over. Pour in the wine and bring to a simmer. Remove from the heat. Cover with aluminum foil and the casserole lid and bake in a preheated moderate (325° F.) oven for 2 hours, or until the pork is tender. Lift the pork onto a warmed serving platter and remove the string. Slice the pork and keep warm. Mix the flour with the remaining tablespoon of butter and stir it, over moderate heat, into the casserole, stirring until the sauce is lightly thickened. If the liquid has reduced a great deal during cooking and the sauce is too thick, add a little wine or chicken stock to thin it to medium consistency. Taste, and season with more salt and pepper, if necessary. Spoon a little of the sauce over the pork slices, and pour the rest into a sauceboat. Serve with shoestring potatoes, sliced tomatoes, and *Ensalada de Habas* (Fresh Broad Bean Salad).

Lomo de Cerdo a la Caucana   ARGENTINA
Pork Loin Baked in Milk

This is an unusual version of a meat cooked in milk. The lemon juice clabbers the milk slightly and also tenderizes the pork. At the end of the cooking time there are about 3 cups of slightly thickened milk in the baking dish. This makes a very light and attractive sauce when reduced. Boned shoulder of pork, a more economical cut, can also be used, in which case increase the cooking time by about half an hour.

Serves 6

2 pounds boneless pork loin or
*   boned shoulder*
4 cups milk
¼ cup lemon juice
Salt, freshly ground pepper
2 tablespoons butter

Put the pork into an oblong Pyrex or other flameproof baking dish that will just hold it comfortably. Mix the milk with the lemon juice and pour it over the pork. Cover the dish lightly and leave overnight in a cool place. When ready to cook, lift the pork out of the milk mixture and pat it dry. Season with salt and pepper. Heat the butter in a skillet and brown the pork lightly all over. Put the pork back into the dish with the milk together with the pan drippings, and bake it, uncovered, in a preheated moderate (350° F.) oven for 1½ to 2 hours, or until the pork is tender. Lift the pork out onto a warmed serving platter and remove the string tying it up. Skim the fat from the sauce and pour the sauce into a saucepan. Reduce it over brisk heat to 1½ cups. Pour it into a sauceboat and serve separately. Slice the meat and serve hot with rice or potatoes and a green vegetable.

This is also good served cold with *Guasacaca* (Avocado Sauce) from Venezuela (page 317) or *Guacamole* (Avocado Sauce) from Mexico (page 316) and salad.

Lomo en Jugo de Naranja   ECUADOR
Pork Loin in Orange Juice

Serves 6

3 tablespoons butter
1 large onion, finely chopped
1 clove garlic, minced
A 3-pound loin of pork, boned
Salt, freshly ground pepper
1 tablespoon grated orange rind
1 fresh hot red or green pepper,
    seeded and ground, or 1
    teaspoon hot pepper sauce
    such as Tabasco
2 cups orange juice
Chicken stock
2 teaspoons cornstarch

Heat the butter in a skillet and sauté the onion and garlic until the onion is
soft. With a slotted spoon transfer the onion and garlic to a flameproof
casserole large enough to hold the pork loin. Season the pork with salt and
pepper and brown all over in the fat remaining in the skillet. Add the pork
to the casserole with the grated orange rind, the hot pepper or hot pepper
sauce, orange juice, and enough stock barely to cover. Bring to a bare
simmer and cook, covered, over very low heat for about 2 hours, or until
the meat is tender. Put the meat on a serving platter, slice it, and keep it
warm. Measure the liquid in the casserole and reduce it over brisk heat to 2
cups. Mix the cornstarch with a little water and stir it into the sauce.
Cook, stirring, over moderate heat until the sauce is lightly thickened.
Spoon a little of the sauce over the pork and serve the rest separately in a
sauceboat. Accompany the pork with a salad made of cooked sliced beets,
carrots, and potatoes in a vinaigrette sauce made with a teaspoon of Dijon
mustard. If liked, toss the vegetables separately in the vinaigrette sauce
and arrange them in heaps on a bed of lettuce leaves on a platter. Or serve
with plain rice and a green vegetable.

Chancho a la Chilena
Pork Loin, Chilean Style

Serves 6 to 8

¼ cup vegetable oil
4 pounds boneless pork loin
2 medium onions, sliced
2 cloves garlic, chopped
1 carrot, scraped and sliced
1 stalk celery, cut into 1-inch
    pieces

1 bay leaf
½ teaspoon oregano
½ teaspoon thyme
¼ teaspoon ground cumin
Salt, freshly ground pepper
½ cup red wine vinegar

Heat the oil in a large flameproof casserole and brown the meat lightly all over. Add all the other ingredients to the casserole with enough water to cover. Bring to a boil, cover, reduce the heat, and simmer gently until the meat is tender, about 3 hours. Allow the meat to cool completely in the stock, then remove to a serving platter. Reserve the stock for another use.

Serve the pork sliced with *Salsa de Ají Colorado* (Red Pepper Sauce), page 311, separately. In Chile the pork slices would be covered with the sauce. But since it can be quite incendiary if the peppers used are very hot, it is wiser to test one's palate with a little at a time.

GROUND MEAT DISHES

Albóndigas
Meatballs

Albóndigas enjoy great popularity in Latin America and are obviously inspired by the Middle East, where the range and variety of delicious meatballs seem inexhaustible. The countries of Latin America, adding their own very special touches, make their meatballs with beef, veal, or pork or a combination. They are usually lightly sautéed first, then cooked in a broth or sauce, seasoned quite differently from the meatballs themselves, thus creating a counterpoint of flavors that is very intriguing. Often there is the added richness that wine gives to the sauce. In Mexico the full-flavored yet mild *ancho* chili or the peppery, exotic *chipotle* adds unusual flavor to the sauces. With such variety in seasonings it would be hard to tire of them.

Makes about 18 meatballs, serves 4 to 6

5 tablespoons vegetable oil
1 medium onion, finely chopped
1 medium tomato, peeled and
    chopped
1 fresh hot red pepper, seeded and
    chopped
1 teaspoon sugar
Salt, freshly ground pepper
1 pound veal, finely ground

1 cup fresh breadcrumbs
4 tablespoons grated Parmesan
    cheese
¼ cup seedless raisins
¼ teaspoon grated nutmeg
2 eggs
Milk, if necessary
Flour

FOR THE BROTH

1 tablespoon vegetable oil
1 medium onion, finely chopped
1 ½ cups beef stock
1 ½ cups dry red wine
¼ teaspoon thyme

¼ teaspoon oregano
1 bay leaf
Salt, freshly ground pepper
Additional stock and wine, if
    necessary

In a skillet heat 2 tablespoons of the oil and sauté the onion until it is soft. Add the tomato, hot pepper, sugar, and salt and pepper to taste. Cook, stirring from time to time, until the mixture is thick and quite dry. Let the mixture cool. In a bowl mix together the veal, breadcrumbs, Parmesan cheese, raisins, nutmeg, and the tomato mixture. Add the eggs, mixing thoroughly. If the mixture is too dry to hold together, add a very little milk. Form into balls, about 2 inches in diameter, and flour them lightly. Heat the remaining 3 tablespoons of oil in the skillet and sauté the meatballs until lightly browned. As they are done, lift them out and set aside.

To make the broth: Heat the tablespoon of oil in a saucepan and sauté the onion until it is very soft. Add the stock, wine, thyme, oregano, and bay leaf, and simmer for a few minutes to blend the flavors. Season to taste with salt and pepper. Add the meatballs, cover, and cook over low heat until they are done, about 30 minutes. If necessary to cover the meatballs, add more stock and wine in equal amounts.

Serve the meatballs with rice or any starchy vegetable, using the broth as gravy. The broth may be a little thin, or too abundant, in which case lift out the meatballs to a serving dish and keep them warm. Reduce the broth over brisk heat until it is slightly thickened. If any is left over, I find it comes in handy for use in other sauces. *Ensalada de Habas* (Fresh Broad Bean Salad) from Ecuador makes a very pleasant accompaniment.

Variation: For *Albóndigas* from Chile, use ground beef instead of veal and mix the beef with 1 finely chopped onion, 1 cup fresh breadcrumbs, salt, pepper, and 2 eggs, adding a little milk if the mixture is too dry. Form into balls, and poach in beef stock until tender, about 30 minutes. While the meatballs are poaching, make a sauce: In a saucepan heat 2 tablespoons butter and sauté 1 onion, finely chopped, until it is soft. Add 1½ cups each beef stock and dry red wine, 1 very finely grated carrot, ¼ teaspoon ground cumin, 1 bay leaf, and salt and pepper to taste. Bring to a boil and simmer, covered, for 30 minutes, then strain. Return the sauce to the pan and thicken with a beurre manié. Mix 2 teaspoons flour with 2 teaspoons butter and stir it into the hot sauce bit by bit. Reserving the poaching stock for another use, remove the meatballs to a serving dish and pour the sauce over them. Serve with rice. Serves 4 to 6.

Variation: For *Albóndigas en Caldo* (Meatballs in Stock) from Paraguay, thoroughly mix together 1 pound ground beef, 1 cup cornmeal or fresh breadcrumbs, 1 onion, finely chopped, 1 clove garlic, minced, 2 tablespoons finely chopped parsley, 1 fresh hot red pepper, minced, ¼ teaspoon oregano, salt and pepper to taste, and 2 eggs. Add a little stock if the mixture seems too dry. Form into balls, about 2 inches in diameter, putting a piece of hardboiled egg in the center of each ball. Set aside. Heat 1 tablespoon vegetable oil in a saucepan and sauté 1 onion, finely chopped, 2 medium tomatoes, peeled and chopped, 1 fresh hot red pepper, seeded and chopped, and salt and pepper, until the onion is soft. Add 3 cups beef stock and bring to a boil. Add the meatballs and simmer until they are done, about 30 minutes. Serve with rice. Serves 4 to 6.

If liked the meatballs may be made small, 1 inch in diameter, and the amount of stock increased to 8 cups. Cook the meatballs with 3 tablespoons well-washed rice for 20 minutes and serve in soup plates, with the stock, as a soup. The cornmeal will give this version a slightly drier texture, the breadcrumbs a very soft one. Both are good. Serves 4 to 6.

Variation: For *Albóndigas Picantes* (Peppery Meatballs) from Paraguay, put 1½ pounds lean beef, ground twice, in a bowl with 2 cloves garlic, minced, 1 cup fresh breadcrumbs, ½ teaspoon each ground oregano and cumin, salt and pepper to taste, and a beaten egg. Mix very thoroughly, adding a little milk or stock if the meat mixture seems too dry. Make into balls 1½ inches in diameter and roll lightly in flour. Sauté the balls in vegetable oil until lightly browned all over and set aside.

Next make a sauce: Heat 3 tablespoons vegetable oil in a saucepan and sauté 2 medium onions, finely chopped, 1 bell pepper, seeded and chopped, preferably red (if red peppers are not available, use 2 canned pimientos, chopped). Add 2 fresh hot red or green peppers, seeded and chopped, or use 1 teaspoon cayenne pepper or 1 teaspoon hot pepper sauce such as Tabasco. (If using cayenne or Tabasco, add these later with the tomato purée.) When the onion is soft, add 1 bay leaf, 1 teaspoon sugar, and salt and pepper to taste. Stir in 2 cups beef stock and 6 cups tomato purée and simmer, covered, for 15 minutes. Remove and discard the bay leaf and purée the liquid in a blender or food processor. Return to the saucepan and bring to a simmer, add the meatballs and simmer, uncovered, for 15 minutes longer, or until the meatballs are done. Serve with white rice. There should be a generous amount of sauce to go over the rice. It may be reduced over brisk heat or thickened with a little flour if it is too abundant. Serves 4 to 6.

Variation: Perhaps of all the meatballs in Latin America, the Mexican ones are the most exotic. There is one version with a choice of sauces — either a gentle *ancho* chili sauce or a hot *chipotle* or *morita* chili sauce, so that all tastes are accommodated happily.

For *Albóndigas Mexicanas*, in a bowl thoroughly mix together ½ pound each twice-ground beef, pork, and veal. Add ½ cup fresh breadcrumbs, 1 medium onion, finely chopped, ½ teaspoon oregano or ground cumin, according to preference, salt, freshly ground pepper, and 1 egg, lightly beaten. Mix thoroughly, adding a little milk if necessary. Form into 1½-inch balls, roll lightly in flour, and set aside. If liked, a little cooked rice, a little hardboiled egg, or a slice of green olive, or a combination of all three, may be put in the center of each meatball. Makes 24 meatballs.

For the Ancho Chili Sauce: Pull the stems off 3 dried *ancho* chilies, shake out the seeds, and tear the peppers into pieces. Rinse and put to soak in a bowl with ½ cup warm water. Leave to soak for about 1 hour, turning from time to time. Put into a blender or food processor with the liquid and reduce to a purée. Set aside. In a skillet heat 3 tablespoons vegetable oil and sauté 1 medium onion, finely chopped, with 1 clove garlic, minced, until the onion is soft. Add the puréed *ancho* chili and 2 cups peeled, seeded, and finely chopped tomato, and sauté, stirring frequently, for 5 minutes over moderate heat. Pour the mixture into a fairly large saucepan, add 1 cup or more of beef stock to thin the mixture to a souplike consistency. Season to taste with salt, pepper, and ¼ teaspoon sugar. Bring to a simmer, add the meatballs, and simmer, uncovered, until the meatballs are tender, about 20 minutes. Serve with rice. Serves 4 to 6.

For the Chipotle or Morita Chili Sauce: Follow the instructions for the preceding sauce, but omit the *ancho* chili. Put the 2 cups peeled, seeded, and chopped tomato in a blender or food processor with 1 *chipotle* or 2 *morita* chilies, coarsely chopped, and blend to a purée. Sauté with the onion and thin with the beef stock, adding more stock if necessary. The sauce will be quite hot, and very much thinner than the mild but full-flavored *ancho* sauce.

Variation: For *Albóndigas* from Venezuela, in a bowl combine 1 pound finely ground lean beef, ¼ pound boiled ham, ground, 1 finely chopped onion, ½ cup fresh breadcrumbs, 2 lightly beaten eggs, and salt and freshly ground pepper to taste. Mix thoroughly and form into balls about 1 inch in diameter. Heat 4 tablespoons vegetable oil in a skillet and sauté the meatballs, in batches, until they are browned all over. Transfer to a flameproof casserole or saucepan. In a blender or food processor combine 1 onion, chopped, 1 tablespoon chopped parsley, 4 medium tomatoes, peeled and chopped, salt and freshly ground pepper to taste, and 1 cup dry white wine. Blend until the mixture is smooth. Pour over the meatballs, adding a little beef stock if necessary to barely cover. Simmer, covered, over low heat until the meatballs are cooked, about 20 minutes. Serve with rice or potatoes, and a green vegetable or salad as a main course. Serves 6.

The meatballs may be made half size, speared with toothpicks and served as an accompaniment to drinks. Drain them thoroughly and reserve the sauce for another use.

Picadillo
Seasoned Chopped Beef

MEXICO

Picadillo is a great favorite throughout Latin America and every country has its own version. In Mexico it is much appreciated as a filling for tacos, *empanadas*, tamales, and green peppers. In the north of the country it is popular on its own and is eaten as a main dish, accompanied by rice, beans, *guacamole*, and tortillas.

Serves 6

3 tablespoons olive or vegetable
    oil
2 pounds lean ground beef
1 large onion, finely chopped
1 clove garlic, finely chopped
3 medium tomatoes, peeled and
    chopped
2 tart cooking apples, peeled,
    cored, and chopped
1 or more fresh hot green peppers,
    seeded and chopped, or 2 or 3
    canned jalapeño chilies,
    seeded and chopped

½ cup raisins, soaked 10 minutes
    in warm water
½ cup pimiento-stuffed olives,
    halved crosswise
½ teaspoon oregano
½ teaspoon thyme
Salt, freshly ground pepper
1 tablespoon butter
½ cup slivered almonds

Heat the oil in a large, heavy skillet. Add the beef and sauté until it is lightly browned, stirring to break up any lumps. Add the onion and garlic and sauté for 5 minutes longer. Add all the remaining ingredients except the butter and the almonds. Mix well and simmer, uncovered, over moderate heat, stirring from time to time, for 20 minutes. In a small skillet heat the butter and sauté the almonds until they are golden brown. Mound the beef onto a serving platter and sprinkle with the almonds. Surround it with a border of *Arroz Blanco* (White Rice).

Variation: Instead of oregano and thyme, use a pinch or two of cinnamon and ⅛ teaspoon ground cloves. This makes an interesting difference in flavor, giving the dish an almost Middle Eastern taste.

Variation: In Chihuahua, the apple is left out and 4 medium potatoes, cooked and cubed, and 2 cups cooked green peas are added to the beef at the end of the cooking time for just long enough to heat them through. This makes a nice one-dish meal.

Variation: *Picadillo de la Costa* from the state of Guerrero, best known for the beach resort of Acapulco, uses the tropical fruits in which the region abounds, and instead of beef uses an equal mixture of ground pork and veal. The method is the same but the meats, with the onion, garlic, tomatoes, hot peppers, salt, and pepper, are cooked, uncovered, for 15 minutes. Then 1½ cups pineapple chunks, 2 pears, peeled, cored, and cut in chunks, and 2 bananas, peeled and sliced, are added and the mixture simmered for 15 minutes longer over low heat. Sprinkle with almonds just before serving. This is a delicious summer dish, good with plain rice.

Picadinho de Porco
Pork Hash

BRAZIL

Serves 6

1 tablespoon butter
1 medium onion, grated
2 large tomatoes, peeled, seeded,
    and chopped
2 pounds ground pork
½ pound chorizo or other spiced,
    smoked pork sausage,
    skinned and chopped

4 tablespoons lemon juice
Salt, freshly ground pepper
¼ cup chopped parsley
2 hardboiled eggs
3 large bananas, peeled
Butter

Heat the butter in a skillet and sauté the onion for 2 minutes. Add the tomatoes and cook, stirring occasionally, until the mixture is thick and well blended. Add the pork and the sausage and continue cooking for 20 minutes until the pork is cooked through, breaking up the meat with a fork. Add the lemon juice and salt and pepper to taste and cook for a few minutes longer. Transfer the hash to a warmed serving dish and sprinkle with the parsley, the egg whites, finely chopped, and the egg yolks, sieved. Keep warm.

Halve the bananas crosswise, then lengthwise, and sauté in butter until lightly browned. Surround the hash with the bananas.

If preferred, omit the bananas and serve with *Angú de Farinha de Milho* (Molded Cornmeal), or include with both accompaniments.

RABBIT DISHES

Rabbit, with its lean, flavorful meat, is very adaptable, taking happily to a wide variety of seasonings. In Latin America, where it is a favorite, having superseded its indigenous relatives like the *agouti* or *paca* in modern markets, it may be cooked with white wine in the simplest of ways, or exotically with sweet peppers and thick coconut milk, with annatto, with orange juice, or even more exotically with ground peanuts. A friend of mine uses peanut butter, but I prefer the texture of the sauce when home-ground nuts are used. Excellent quality frozen rabbit cut up in ready-to-cook pieces is available in supermarkets. However, a whole rabbit is very easy to cut up.

Usually the head has already been removed. If not, cut it off using a sharp, heavy knife. Split it in two and use it to enrich the dish. There is a small amount of meat on it and the brains can be eaten separately. Cut off the forelegs — easy, as they are not jointed. Cut across the rabbit just under the rib cage, then cut the rib cage in half. Cut across the section with the hind legs, then split it in two, separating the legs. Cut the part remaining, the saddle, into two pieces crosswise. One piece will contain the kidneys. There will be eight pieces in all but the two rib pieces have very little meat.

Guiso de Conejo
Rabbit Stew

PERU

Serves 4

6 cloves garlic
1 teaspoon each cumin, oregano,
    and rosemary
Salt, freshly ground pepper
½ cup vegetable oil
¼ cup white wine vinegar

A 2½-pound rabbit, or 2½ pounds
    of kid, cut into serving pieces
3 slices bacon, chopped
2 cups dry white wine
12 small white onions, peeled

Grind the garlic, cumin, oregano, and rosemary together with a mortar and pestle or in a small blender jar. Add salt to taste and a generous amount of pepper. Mix with ¼ cup of the oil and all the vinegar. Put the rabbit pieces in a bowl and pour the mixture over them. Cover with plastic wrap and marinate overnight in the refrigerator, turning once or twice. Lift out the rabbit pieces, pat dry. Reserve the marinade.

In a skillet heat the remaining ¼ cup of oil and sauté the bacon until it is crisp. Push it to one side of the skillet and sauté the rabbit pieces in the fat until they are golden. Transfer the rabbit and the contents of the skillet to a flameproof casserole or heavy saucepan. Add the marinade, the wine, and the onions. Cover and simmer until the rabbit is tender, about 1½ hours. Arrange the rabbit and the onions in a serving dish and keep warm. Reduce the sauce over brisk heat until it is slightly thickened. Pour over the rabbit. Garnish if liked with black olives and parsley sprigs and serve with boiled potatoes.

Conejo con Leche de Coco
Rabbit in Coconut Milk

COLOMBIA

In Colombia this is made with *ñeque* or *paca*, an animal like a hare, but rabbits are enough like hares for the substitution to succeed. It is a coastal dish and uses both annatto and coconut milk, typical of the cooking of this region. *Conejo Guisado con Coco* (Rabbit Stew with Coconut Milk), also from the coast, uses coconut milk too, but the flavors of the two dishes are very different and demonstrate the versatility of this attractive cuisine.

Serves 4

6 large cloves garlic
1 teaspoon salt
¼ teaspoon cayenne pepper
½ teaspoon ground cumin
12 grinds black pepper, about
3 tablespoons white vinegar
A 2½-pound rabbit, cut into
    8 serving pieces

1 tablespoon annatto oil or lard
    (see page 324)
1 medium onion, chopped
1 large tomato, peeled, seeded,
    and chopped
1 tablespoon tomato paste
½ cup thick coconut milk (see
    page 7)

In a mortar crush the garlic with the salt, cayenne pepper, cumin, and black pepper. Stir in the vinegar. Spread this mixture over the pieces of rabbit in the casserole in which they are to be cooked and marinate at room temperature for about 4 hours, turning the pieces once or twice.

Heat the annatto oil or lard in a skillet and sauté the onion until it is softened. Add it to the rabbit with the tomato and tomato paste and enough water barely to cover. Bring to a boil, cover, and cook over low heat until the rabbit is tender, about 1½ hours. Lift the rabbit pieces onto a serving dish and keep warm. Over brisk heat reduce the liquid in the casserole to about 1 cup, stirring frequently. Stir in the coconut milk and heat it through. Do not let it boil. Pour the sauce over the rabbit. Serve with rice.

Conejo Guisado con Coco   COLOMBIA
Rabbit Stew with Coconut Milk

Serves 4

3 tablespoons butter
A 2½-pound rabbit, cut into
    8 serving pieces
1 large onion, finely chopped
2 cloves garlic, chopped
1 green bell pepper, seeded and
    chopped
1 fresh hot red or green pepper,
    seeded and chopped

1 large tomato, peeled and
    chopped
1 pimiento, chopped
Salt, freshly ground pepper
2 cups beef or chicken stock
½ cup thick coconut milk (see
    page 7)

Heat the butter in a skillet and sauté the rabbit pieces until they are lightly browned. Transfer the rabbit to a flameproof casserole. In the fat remaining in the skillet sauté the onion, garlic, and the sweet and hot peppers. Add to the casserole with the tomato, pimiento, salt and pepper to taste, and the stock. Bring to a boil, cover, and cook over very low heat until the rabbit is tender, about 1½ hours. Remove the rabbit pieces to a serving dish and keep warm. Over brisk heat reduce the liquid in the casserole to about half. Lower the heat and stir in the coconut milk. Cook, stirring, for a few minutes, then pour the sauce over the rabbit. The sauce should be quite thick. Serve with rice.

Variation: Omit the coconut milk, and reduce the amount of stock to 1 cup and add 1 cup red wine instead. Reduce the liquid in the casserole in the same way, as the sauce should not be abundant.

Conejo con Maní   CHILE
Rabbit in Peanut Sauce

Serves 4

¼ cup vegetable oil
1 tablespoon sweet paprika
A 2½-pound rabbit, cut into
    serving pieces
2 large onions, finely chopped
1 clove garlic
1 cup roasted peanuts, finely
    ground

Salt, freshly ground pepper to taste
½ teaspoon ground cumin
1 tablespoon white wine vinegar
1½ cups chicken stock
1½ cups dry white wine

Heat the oil in a heavy casserole and stir in the paprika, taking care not to let it burn. Add the rabbit pieces and sauté lightly. Lift out and set aside. Add the onions and garlic to the casserole and sauté until the onions are softened. Return the rabbit pieces to the casserole. Add all the other ingredients, mix well, cover, and simmer until the rabbit is tender, about 1½ hours. Serve with rice and a salad.

Variation: Peru has a *Conejo con Maní* using the very hot yellow peppers that are a feature of this kitchen. It can however be made with fresh hot red or green peppers instead. Sauté the rabbit pieces in a mixture of 2 tablespoons vegetable oil and 2 tablespoons butter. Transfer the rabbit to a casserole. In the fat remaining in the skillet sauté 3 medium onions, cut into thick slices, and add to the casserole with 1 or 2 hot peppers ground in a blender with 2 cloves garlic and 1 teaspoon salt. Cover with chicken stock or water, 2 to 3 cups, and simmer for 1 hour. Add 1 cup roasted ground peanuts and simmer until the rabbit is tender, about 30 minutes longer. Just before serving, add 8 small whole cooked potatoes. The peanuts will thicken as well as flavor the stew.

Conejo en Salsa de Naranja CHILE
Rabbit in Orange Sauce

Serves 4

2 tablespoons vegetable oil
A 2½-pound rabbit, cut into
    serving pieces
2 medium onions, finely chopped
1 clove garlic, chopped
1½ cups dry white wine
1½ cups orange juice

Salt, freshly ground pepper
1 tablespoon flour
1 tablespoon butter
2 eggs, lightly beaten
1 hardboiled egg, finely chopped
1 tablespoon chopped parsley

Heat the oil in a skillet and sauté the rabbit pieces until they are lightly browned. Transfer to a flameproof casserole. In the oil remaining in the pan, adding a little more if necessary, sauté the onions and garlic until the onions are softened. Add to the casserole. Pour the wine into the skillet and scrape up all the brown bits. Pour into the casserole. Add the orange juice to the casserole and season to taste with salt and pepper. Cover and simmer until the rabbit is tender, about 1½ hours. Transfer the rabbit pieces to a serving dish and keep them warm.

Work the flour and butter into a paste. Add it to the liquid in the casserole and cook over low heat, stirring, until it is lightly thickened. Beat ½ cup of the sauce into the eggs, then pour the eggs into the casserole, stirring constantly. Do not let the sauce come to a boil, as it will curdle. Pour the sauce over the rabbit and sprinkle with the egg and parsley. Serve with rice, potatoes or noodles, and a green vegetable.

INNARDS, OR VARIETY MEATS

❋ Tripe Dishes

Of all the *interiores* (innards) none is so popular in Latin America as tripe, understandably so since few dishes are as appetizing when well prepared from an imaginative recipe. Tripe, which generally means the first and second stomach of beef, comes to the market from the packing house, ready prepared and partially cooked. The best kind is honeycomb, but plain tripe is also good. Pig and sheep tripe are also sometimes sold. Tripe is quite tough and needs to be simmered 2 or more hours to tenderize it, but a word of warning must be sounded — much depends on how long the tripe has been precooked before being sold. It is wise to test from time to time during the cooking process so as not to overcook it. It should be tender but with a good, firm texture, a nice bitey resistance. Overcooked tripe has no character.

I have chosen a group of recipes that come from Mexico and all over South America — all deliciously appetizing, easy to cook, earthy dishes to be enjoyed at any time of the year. They need little in the way of accompaniment, potatoes if they are not already included in the recipe, or perhaps rice, a green vegetable, or a salad. And your excellent dish of tripe has the added merit of being inexpensive.

Mondongo Serrano   MEXICO
Tripe, Mountain Style

This is quite a fancy dish from northern Mexico, with a wonderful blending of flavors and a fine aroma. I like to serve it to close friends or family.

Serves 6 to 8

3 pounds honeycomb tripe, cut into 1-inch squares
¼ cup lemon juice
3 cups beef stock, about
½ cup vegetable oil
1 large onion, finely chopped
4 chorizos (hot Spanish sausages), coarsely chopped
A ½-pound piece boiled ham, cut into ½-inch dice
A 1-pound can cooked garbanzos (chickpeas), or ½ pound dry chickpeas, soaked overnight and boiled until tender (about 2 hours)
⅓ cup seedless raisins

⅓ cup blanched almonds, ground
⅔ cup orange juice
2 fresh hot green peppers, seeded and chopped, or canned Mexican serrano or jalapeño chilies
½ cup small pitted green olives, halved
Pinch each ground cloves and cinnamon
¼ teaspoon thyme
¼ teaspoon oregano
1 bay leaf
Salt, freshly ground pepper
Freshly grated Parmesan cheese

Wash the tripe in water mixed with the lemon juice, rinse, and put into a heavy saucepan or casserole with the beef stock, adding a little more if necessary to cover. Cover and simmer over low heat until the tripe is barely tender, about 1 to 2 hours. Test often for doneness, as the cooking time for tripe varies greatly. Lift the tripe out of the stock with a slotted spoon and pat dry with paper towels. Reserve the stock.

Heat the oil in a skillet and sauté the onion and chorizos until the onion is soft. Lift out with a slotted spoon and put into the casserole. In the fat remaining in the pan sauté the tripe and add to the casserole with all the remaining ingredients except the cheese. Pour in the reserved stock, cover, and simmer over very low heat for 30 minutes, or until the tripe is tender. Add a little more stock if necessary as the sauce should be quite abundant. Serve in rimmed soup plates with the cheese served separately. Accompany with crusty bread and a green salad.

Tripa de Vaca a Brasileira BRAZIL
Tripe with Vegetables, Brazilian Style

This is another rather fancy dish made special by the fresh coriander and the dry Madeira, which lend a lovely flavor.

Serves 6

3 pounds honeycomb tripe
4 tablespoons lime or lemon juice
3 cups beef broth
3 tablespoons olive oil
1 large onion, finely chopped
1 large clove garlic, chopped
1 sweet red pepper, seeded and
    chopped

3 medium tomatoes, peeled and
    chopped
1 bay leaf
3 tablespoons fresh coriander
    (cilantro), chopped
¼ cup dry Madeira
18 small pitted black olives
½ cup grated Parmesan cheese

Wash the tripe in cold running water and cut it into strips about ¾ inch by 2 inches. Put the tripe into a flameproof casserole and add the lime or lemon juice, stir to mix, and leave for 5 minutes. Add the beef broth to the casserole. Cover and simmer over low heat until the tripe is tender. Drain the tripe and set it aside. Reserve the broth. Rinse out and dry the casserole. Heat the oil in the casserole and sauté the onion, garlic, and sweet pepper until the onion is soft. Add to the casserole the tomatoes, bay leaf, fresh coriander, Madeira, tripe, and 2 cups of the reserved stock. Simmer, partially covered, until the tripe is tender and the sauce slightly thickened, about 1 hour. Stir from time to time with a wooden spoon to prevent the tripe from sticking. Add the olives and cook for a minute or two longer. Stir in the cheese. Serve with *Angú de Farinha de Milho* (Molded Cornmeal).

Chupe de Guatitas   CHILE
Tripe Stew

A very flavorful stew with a modestly fiery accent from the hot pepper combined with the richly subtle flavor of sweet red peppers. Chileans often use breadcrumbs, as is done here, to thicken sauces.

Serves 4 to 6

2 pounds honeycomb tripe
½ cup paprika oil (Color Chilena),
    page 324, made with olive or
    vegetable oil
1 medium onion, finely chopped
1 red bell pepper, seeded and
    chopped, or 2 canned
    pimientos, chopped
¼ cup parsley, chopped

½ teaspoon oregano
1 fresh hot red pepper, seeded and
    chopped, or ½ teaspoon
    cayenne
Salt, freshly ground pepper
1 cup fresh breadcrumbs
1 cup milk
½ cup grated Parmesan cheese
1 hardboiled egg, sliced

Put the tripe into a large saucepan or flameproof casserole with cold, unsalted water to cover, bring to a boil, lower the heat, and simmer, covered, until the tripe is barely tender, about 1 to 2 hours. Test during the cooking period as tripe varies greatly. Drain, cut the tripe into strips about ½ inch by 2 inches, and set aside. Reserve the stock.

Heat the paprika oil in the saucepan and add the onion and bell pepper. If using pimientos, add later with the parsley. Sauté until the onion and pepper are soft. Add the parsley, oregano, hot pepper or cayenne, salt and freshly ground pepper to taste, and the pimientos, if using. Stir to mix, and simmer, uncovered, for about 5 minutes, or until well blended.

Put the breadcrumbs and milk into a small saucepan and cook, stirring from time to time, for about 5 minutes. Purée in a blender or food processor. This step is not absolutely necessary but it does give a finer textured sauce. Add the breadcrumb sauce to the casserole, stirring to mix. Add the tripe. If the sauce is very thick, thin with ½ cup or more of the reserved tripe stock. Simmer, uncovered, over very low heat, stirring from time to time, for 20 minutes to blend the flavors. Pour into a heated serving dish. Sprinkle with the grated cheese and garnish with the hardboiled egg slices. Serve with crusty bread and a green salad.

Variation: For *Guatitas con Tomates* (Tripe with Tomatoes), cook the tripe in the same way but omit the bell pepper in the first sauce, and omit the breadcrumb sauce altogether. Sauté the onion and garlic, then add 6 medium tomatoes, peeled and chopped, and 2 carrots, scraped and grated. When the tomato sauce is well blended, add 6 medium potatoes, peeled and quartered, the tripe, and enough of the reserved tripe stock to cover. Simmer, covered, over low heat until the potatoes are tender. Thicken the sauce with 1 tablespoon flour mixed with a little stock to a paste, stirred into the casserole, and simmered until the sauce is lightly thickened. Omit the hardboiled egg garnish, and sprinkle the dish with grated Parmesan cheese.

Variation: A simple dish, great as a meal in itself, *Mondongo a la Criolla* (Tripe, Creole Style) is popular throughout Latin America. This is an Argentine recipe. Soak ½ pound dried lima beans overnight, drain, and put into a saucepan with salted water to cover. Simmer until the beans are tender, 1 to 1½ hours. Drain and set aside. In a flameproof casserole heat ½ cup olive oil and sauté 1 large onion, finely chopped, 1 large stalk celery, chopped, and 1 red bell pepper, seeded and chopped, until the onion is soft. Add 2 large tomatoes, peeled and chopped, and simmer for a few minutes to blend the flavors. Add 2 pounds honeycomb tripe cut into 1½- by ½-inch strips, 1 bay leaf, ¼ teaspoon each thyme and oregano, 2 cups beef stock, 1 tablespoon tomato paste, and salt and pepper to taste. Simmer, covered, over low heat for 1 to 2 hours, or until the tripe is barely tender. Test often, as the cooking time for tripe varies greatly. Add 1 cup well-washed long-grain rice and simmer until the rice is tender, about 20 minutes. If necessary add a little more stock as there should be plenty of sauce. Add the beans and heat through. Serve in rimmed soup plates with plenty of freshly grated Parmesan cheese, crusty bread, and a green salad.

Two 1-pound cans of *cannellini* (white kidney beans), rinsed and drained, and 2 canned pimientos, chopped, can be used instead of lima beans and bell pepper. Add just before serving and heat through.

Variation: The ground peanuts used in this Ecuadorian recipe for *Guatita* (Tripe) may seem a little startling at first. They add a delightful nutty taste, not at all overwhelming, and thicken the sauce at the same time. The annatto adds a subtle grace note of flavor, light and fragrant, while giving the dish an attractive yellow color. This is a most imaginative recipe yet the flavor of the finished dish is in no way bizarre.

Cook the tripe in the same way as for *Chupe de Guatitas* (Tripe Stew, see page 140). In a skillet heat 4 tablespoons annatto oil or lard (see page 324) and sauté 1 large onion, finely chopped, 2 cloves garlic, minced, 1 green bell pepper, seeded and chopped, until the onion is soft. Add 1 large tomato, peeled, seeded, and chopped, season with salt, and cook until the mixture is well blended. Stir in 1 cup ground peanuts and enough of the reserved tripe stock to thin to a medium thick sauce. Add the tripe and 1 pound potatoes, cooked and cubed, and simmer until heated through. Serve sprinkled with chopped coriander or parsley. Accompany with a green vegetable or a salad. Serves 4.

Variation: For *Caucau a la Limeña* (Tripe, Lima Style), Peruvian cooks would use hot yellow peppers, but I find fresh hot red or green peppers a perfect substitute, and where Peruvians would use 1 tablespoon of ground *palillo*, a yellow herb, I use 1½ teaspoons of turmeric, with fine results. Cook the tripe in the same way as for *Chupe de Guatitas* (Tripe Stew, see page 140). In a large, heavy skillet that has a lid, heat 1 cup vegetable oil and add 1 or more, according to taste, fresh hot red or green peppers, seeded and pounded in a mortar or puréed in a blender, 4 medium onions, finely chopped, and 6 cloves garlic, chopped. Sauté over moderate heat until the onions are soft and beginning to brown. Add the tripe and 2 pounds potatoes, peeled and cut into ½-inch cubes. Sauté for 2 or 3 minutes, then add 1½ teaspoons ground turmeric mixed with ½ cup tripe stock, a sprig of mint or parsley, and salt and freshly ground pepper to taste. Cover and simmer over low heat until the potatoes are almost done. Cook, uncovered, until the dish is quite dry. If necessary add a little more tripe stock during cooking, but only enough to cook the potatoes. Before serving pour a tablespoon of oil over the tripe, folding it into the mixture. Serves 4.

✳ Tongue

Lengua en Salsa Picante
Tongue in Hot Pepper Sauce   CHILE

Fresh beef tongue is popular as a main dish in all of Latin America. This dish from Chile is not very peppery. There is just enough hot chili in the sauce to justify the name, but only enough to give a pleasant piquancy.

Serves 6 to 8

A fresh beef tongue, weighing
    about 3 pounds
1 onion, sliced
1 sprig each parsley and coriander
    (cilantro)

1 small stalk celery
1 bay leaf
2 teaspoons salt

Wash the tongue and put into a large saucepan or flameproof casserole with all the remaining ingredients and enough cold water to cover. Bring to a boil, skim as necessary, reduce the heat, cover, and simmer until the tongue is tender, about 3 hours. Uncover and leave in the stock until it is cool enough to handle. Lift out onto a platter, remove skin and any bones or fat, and cut into ½-inch slices. Strain the stock into a jug. Rinse out and dry the casserole and return the tongue to it.

FOR THE SAUCE

2 shallots, finely chopped
½ cup red or white wine vinegar
2 tablespoons butter or vegetable
　oil
2 tablespoons flour

2 cups tongue stock
1 or more fresh hot peppers,
　preferably red, seeded and
　finely chopped
2 tablespoons chopped parsley

Put the shallots into a small saucepan with the vinegar and simmer until the shallots are tender, about 3 minutes. Set aside. Heat the butter or oil in a saucepan and add the flour. Cook, stirring constantly with a wooden spoon, for 2 minutes over low heat without letting the flour brown. Stir in the stock and simmer over low heat for 10 minutes. Stir in the vinegar and shallot mixture, the hot pepper, and parsley, and pour over the tongue. Simmer just long enough to heat the tongue through. Arrange on a platter and serve surrounded by halved cooked potatoes, or with rice served separately.

Variation: Ecuador has a similar recipe. Also called *Lengua en Salsa Picante*, the tongue is cooked in the same way but the sauce differs, and I find it makes an interesting change from the Chilean version. In 2 tablespoons vegetable oil or butter, sauté 1 medium onion, finely chopped, with 1 clove garlic, chopped, until the onion is soft. Stir in 1 tablespoon dry mustard, mixing well. Add 1½ cups stock from the cooked tongue and simmer for 5 minutes. Add 1 tablespoon capers, 2 tablespoons chopped parsley, 1 pimiento, coarsely chopped, 1 tablespoon lemon juice, and salt and pepper to taste. Pour the sauce over the sliced tongue and simmer just long enough to heat through.

Variation: The very first Mexican dish I learned to cook was *Lengua en Salsa de Tomate Verde* (Tongue in Green Tomato Sauce), using the little green husk tomatoes that have such a special, and delicious, flavor. The tongue is cooked in the same way as in the previous recipes. In a blender or food processor combine 1 medium onion, coarsely chopped, 2 cloves garlic, chopped, ½ cup coriander (cilantro) sprigs, chopped, 1½ cups canned Mexican green tomatoes, drained, and 3 or 4 canned *serrano* chilies, or 1 or 2 fresh hot green peppers, seeded and chopped, and reduce to a coarse purée. Heat 3 tablespoons lard or vegetable oil in a skillet, pour in the purée, and cook, stirring, for about 4 minutes. Add 1 cup stock from the cooked tongue, season to taste with salt, and pour over the tongue. Simmer just long enough to heat through. Serve with small new potatoes.

If fresh Mexican green tomatoes are available, peel off the brown outer husk and chop coarsely before adding to the blender or food processor.

Variation: Another favorite Mexican recipe is *Lengua en Salsa de Chile Ancho y Almendra* (Tongue in Mild Red Chili and Almond Sauce). Simply heat the tongue through in 2 cups of the sauce (see page 143).

Variation: There is usually quite a lot of stock left over from cooking a tongue, and Latin American cooks frequently use it to make soup, saving the trimmings of the tongue for garnish. Recipes are not very formal. Vegetables such as carrots, turnips, potatoes, Swiss chard, or cabbage are cubed or chopped and may be cooked in a little butter for a few minutes before being added to the stock, or just added and simmered until tender, about 25 minutes. A little sherry is sometimes added to the finished soup, and sometimes it is sprinkled with grated cheese. Rice, vermicelli, or cornmeal is also sometimes added, in short whatever is on hand. The result is a very pleasant unpretentious soup augmented by a feeling of virtue for having avoided waste.

✱ Pig's Feet

Patitas de Cerdo   ARGENTINA
Pig's Feet

Pig's feet, with their bland flavor and delicious gelatinous quality, are a favorite wherever pork is eaten. Latin America has some excitingly different recipes for this splendidly economical dish. I sometimes like to serve the pig's feet whole, instead of boned and cut up. I have borrowed a trick from James Beard, a dear friend always generous with help. I wrap the feet in cheesecloth and tie them with string before cooking them. It gives them a neat and tidy look, prevents broken skin, and makes for a much more attractive presentation.

Serves 4

8 pig's feet   2 cloves garlic
1 ripe red bell pepper, seeded and
  chopped

FOR THE DRESSING

1 teaspoon Spanish (hot) paprika
    or cayenne
1 cup red wine vinegar
Salt

1 cup vegetable oil
1 ripe red bell pepper, peeled (page
    15) and seeded
Lettuce leaves

Wrap each of the pig's feet tightly in cheesecloth and tie with string. Put into a large saucepan with the pepper and garlic and enough water to cover. Bring to a boil, reduce the heat, and simmer, covered, for 3 to 4 hours, or until tender. Let the pig's feet stand in the pan until cool enough to handle. Lift out and remove cheesecloth wrapping. Put into a shallow dish and pour on the dressing. Let stand at room temperature, turning once or twice, for at least an hour before serving.

To make the dressing mix the ground hot paprika or cayenne with the vinegar and salt to taste. Beat in the oil. Cut the pepper into strips and add. Serve the pig's feet on plates garnished with lettuce leaves, 2 per person, as a main course, or serve 1 per person as an appetizer. Accompany with crusty bread and butter.

Patitas de Cerdo con Chile Poblano   MEXICO
Pig's Feet in Poblano Pepper Sauce

In Mexico the flavorful dark green *chile poblano* would be used for this recipe. Green bell pepper is a good substitute.

Serves 4

8 pig's feet
1 medium onion, coarsely
    chopped
⅛ teaspoon thyme

⅛ teaspoon oregano
1 bay leaf
1 sprig parsley or coriander
    (cilantro)

FOR THE SAUCE

1 medium onion, chopped
2 cloves garlic, chopped
6 medium tomatoes, peeled and
    chopped
4 tablespoons vegetable oil

3 green bell peppers, peeled (page
    15), seeded, and cut into
    strips
Pinch of sugar
Salt, freshly ground pepper

Wrap each of the pig's feet tightly in cheesecloth and tie with string. Put into a large saucepan with the onion, thyme, oregano, bay leaf, and parsley or coriander, and enough water to cover. Bring to a boil, reduce the heat, and simmer, covered, for 3 to 4 hours, or until tender. Let the pig's feet stand in the pan until cool enough to handle. Lift out and remove the cheesecloth wrapping. Return to the saucepan.

To make the sauce put the onion, garlic, and tomatoes into a blender or food processor fitted with a steel blade and reduce to a purée. Heat the oil in a skillet and add the tomato mixture and the pepper strips. Add the sugar and season to taste with salt and pepper. Simmer, uncovered, stirring from time to time, until the mixture is thick and well blended. Pour over the pig's feet and simmer until they are heated through. Serve with tortillas.

Variation: Leftover sauce from dishes like *Ternera en Pipián Verde* (Veal in Pumpkin Seed Sauce), *Pollo Verde Almendrado* (Chicken in Green Almond Sauce), *Pollo en Pipián de Almendra* (Chicken Stew with Almonds), *Mole Coloradito de Oaxaca* (Chicken in Red Sauce, Oaxaca Style), or *Salsa de Chile Ancho y Almendra* (Mild Red Chili and Almond Sauce), page 315, can be used with pig's feet.

Patitas de Chancho a la Criolla   PERU
Pig's Feet, Creole Style

Served at room temperature, this is more a salad for a luncheon main course or an hors d'oeuvre.

*Serves 4 as luncheon dish,
8 as first course*

2 pig's feet, about 2 pounds
Salt
2 medium onions, very thinly
    sliced
2 medium tomatoes, peeled and
    sliced
1 fresh hot red or green pepper,
    seeded and sliced lengthwise

2 cooked medium-sized potatoes,
    halved and sliced
6 tablespoons vegetable oil
2 tablespoons white vinegar or
    lemon juice, or a mixture
Salt, freshly ground pepper
Lettuce leaves for garnish

Wash the pig's feet and put them into a saucepan with salted water to cover, bring to a boil, reduce the heat, and simmer, covered, for 3 hours, or until tender. Cool in the stock, lift out, bone, and cut into 1-inch pieces, about. Discard the stock.

In a large bowl combine the pig's feet, onions, tomatoes, hot pepper strips, potatoes, oil, vinegar or lemon juice, salt and pepper to taste, and mix lightly. Allow to stand for about 15 minutes, then place in a serving dish garnished with lettuce leaves and serve at room temperature.

Picante de Pata Arequipeña
Spicy Pig's Feet, Arequipa Style

PERU

Serves 4

3 pig's feet
3 sprigs fresh mint
1 or more fresh hot red or green
    peppers, seeded and ground
2 tablespoons lard or vegetable oil
2 medium onions, finely chopped
3 cloves garlic, minced

½ teaspoon oregano
½ cup roasted peanuts, finely
    ground
Salt, freshly ground pepper
3 medium potatoes, about 1
    pound, cooked and cut into
    1-inch cubes

Wash the pig's feet and put them into a saucepan large enough to hold them comfortably, preferably in a single layer. Add the mint and enough water to cover by about 1 inch. Cover and simmer until the pig's feet are tender, about 3 hours. Let them cool in the stock, then lift out, remove the bones, and cut into 1-inch pieces. Set aside. Strain and reserve the stock.

Grind the peppers with a mortar and pestle or in a small blender jar.

Heat the lard or oil in a flameproof casserole and sauté the onions, garlic, oregano, and hot peppers until the onions are soft. Stir in the peanuts and sauté for 1 or 2 minutes longer. Season to taste with salt and pepper. Stir in 1 cup of the reserved stock and simmer for a few minutes to blend the flavors. Add the pig's feet and the potatoes and simmer just long enough to heat them through. The sauce should be thick and highly spiced but one's own taste should determine the number of hot peppers used. If the sauce is too thick, add a little more of the reserved stock. In Peru this would be served with rice. I prefer it with a green vegetable or a salad.

Coração Recheado
Stuffed Beef Heart

BRAZIL

Stuffed beef heart has been a favorite dish of mine since childhood, so I was delighted when a Brazilian friend gave me her recipe, which is quite grand. I was also pleased to be given a Chilean version of this old favorite in a new guise, a simpler recipe than the Brazilian one. I like both. Calf's heart is also good. It usually weighs about 1 pound so use about one-quarter of the stuffing and reduce the cooking time to 1½ hours. It would serve 2 or 3.

Serves 8

1 beef heart, weighing about 4 pounds
4 tablespoons butter
1 medium onion, finely chopped
1 cup corn kernels
½ cup freshly made breadcrumbs
2 hardboiled eggs, chopped
½ sweet red pepper, peeled (see page 15), seeded and chopped
8 pimiento-stuffed olives, halved

1 small fresh hot red or green pepper, seeded and chopped
2 tablespoons chopped parsley
Salt, freshly ground pepper
1½ cups dry red wine
1½ cups beef stock
1 clove garlic, chopped
2 teaspoons cornstarch or arrowroot

Thoroughly wash the heart and remove the membrane inside that divides the two chambers if the butcher has not already done this. Trim away any fat. In a skillet heat 2 tablespoons of the butter and sauté the onion until it is soft. Purée the corn in a food processor or blender and stir into the onion off the heat. Add the breadcrumbs, the eggs, sweet pepper, olives, hot pepper, parsley, and salt and pepper to taste, mixing well. Stuff the heart with the dressing. Sew it up or skewer it and lace with string. In a flame-proof casserole large enough to hold the heart comfortably, heat the remaining 2 tablespoons of butter and brown the heart all over. Pour in the wine and stock, add the garlic, and bring the liquid to a boil. Cover the casserole with foil, then with the lid, and cook in a preheated moderate (350° F.) oven for about 3½ hours, or until tender. Lift the heart out onto a serving platter and remove the sewing thread or the skewers and string. Cut the heart into crosswise slices and keep warm. Reduce the cooking liquid over brisk heat to 2 cups. Mix the cornstarch or arrowroot with a little cold water, stir into the sauce, and cook, stirring, for a few minutes until the sauce is thickened. Pour a little sauce over the sliced heart and serve the rest in a sauceboat. Serve with mashed potatoes and green beans or peas.

Variation: For *Corazon Relleno* (Stuffed Heart) from Chile, prepare the heart in the same way. For the stuffing soak 4 slices firm white bread in milk, then squeeze out and mix with 1 medium onion, finely chopped, 2 tablespoons parsley, finely chopped, 4 slices of bacon, chopped, salt and pepper to taste, and 1 egg, lightly beaten. Stuff the heart with the mixture and sew or skewer it closed. Heat 2 tablespoons vegetable oil in a flame-proof casserole and brown the heart all over. Add to the casserole 1 onion, coarsely chopped, 1 carrot, scraped and sliced, ½ teaspoon thyme, 1 sprig parsley, 1 bay leaf, and 1½ cups each beef stock and dry red wine. Cook as for *Coração Recheado*.

❋ Brains

Brains are popular in Latin America, particularly French Calf's Brains in Black Butter, which sounds very splendid in Spanish as *Sesos con Salsa de Mantequilla Quemada*. But there are several interesting recipes common to a number of countries that provide us with some new ways to cook this delicacy. A preliminary soaking and peeling are always necessary, followed by a simmering in seasoned liquid, except when the brains are to be stewed as in the first of these recipes.

Sesos Guisados   COLOMBIA
Stewed Brains

This recipe is as appetizing as it is simple.

Serves 6

1½ pounds brains
1 medium onion, finely chopped
1 clove garlic, chopped
3 medium tomatoes, peeled and
    chopped

1 tablespoon butter
Salt, freshly ground pepper

Soak the brains in several changes of water for about 2 hours. Carefully pull off the thin membrane that covers the brains. This is not difficult but requires patience. Rinse the brains in fresh cold water. Then simmer in enough water to barely cover, with the onion, garlic, tomatoes, butter, and salt and pepper to taste for 30 minutes. Lift out the brains and cut each one into 4 to 6 slices. Arrange in a warmed serving dish. Reduce the liquid in the saucepan over brisk heat until it is slightly thickened, then pour over the brains. Serve with rice or potatoes or any other starchy vegetable.

Variation: For *Sesos Rebozados* (Sautéed Brains), soak 1½ pounds brains and remove the membranes in the usual way. Then simmer, in enough water to cover, with 1 small chopped onion, 1 clove garlic, and ½ teaspoon salt for 30 minutes. Cool in the cooking liquid, lift out, and pat dry with paper towels. Cut each brain into 4 to 6 slices. Beat 2 egg whites until they stand in peaks. Fold the whites into 2 egg yolks beaten with ½ teaspoon salt. Dip the brain slices in flour, then in the beaten egg, and sauté in 4 tablespoons butter until golden brown on both sides. Serve with rice or potatoes and a fresh Hot Pepper Sauce (page 311), or lemon wedges.

Variation: For *Sesos en Vino* (Brains in Wine Sauce), soak and simmer 1½ pounds brains as for *Sesos Rebozados*. Cut into cubes and put into a buttered casserole. Heat 2 tablespoons butter in a skillet and sauté 1 medium onion, finely chopped, and 1 clove chopped garlic until the onion is soft. Add to the casserole. Season to taste with salt and pepper. Fold 3 cups diced cooked potatoes into the brains and pour 1½ cups dry white wine over the mixture. Simmer very gently for 15 minutes to blend the flavors, sprinkle with 2 tablespoons chopped parsley, and serve surrounded by 12 triangles of white bread fried in butter.

Variation: For *Sesos con Jamón* (Brains with Ham), soak and simmer 1½ pounds brains as for *Sesos Rebozados*. Halve the brains, dip in flour seasoned with salt and pepper, and fry in butter, about 4 tablespoons, until golden on both sides. Sauté 6 thin slices of ham in butter and arrange on a warmed platter. Put the halved brains on top of the ham and mask with 1½ cups *Môlho ao Tomate* (page 318).

✳ Liver

Hígado en Salsa de Hongos   CHILE
Calf's Liver in Mushroom Sauce

Chile's excellent wine turns an ordinary dish into a fine one in this simple recipe. Either a dry white or red wine, which I prefer, may be used.

Serves 4

6 tablespoons butter
2 tablespoons oil
1 medium onion, finely chopped
¼ teaspoon oregano
½ pound mushrooms, sliced
1 ½ cups dry red wine
Salt, freshly ground pepper
1 pound calf's liver, cut into
    ¼-inch slices

Heat 3 tablespoons of the butter and 1 tablespoon of the oil in a skillet and sauté the onion and oregano until the onion is soft. Add the mushrooms and cook over fairly high heat, stirring from time to time with a wooden spoon, until the mushrooms are lightly browned, about 5 minutes. Pour in the wine and cook, stirring, until the wine is reduced to half and the sauce is slightly thickened.

In another skillet heat the remaining 3 tablespoons butter and 1 tablespoon oil and sauté the liver over moderate heat for 2 minutes. Turn the pieces and sauté for 1 minute longer. Add the liver and the juices in the pan to the skillet with the mushrooms, stir to mix, and simmer for about 1 minute. Be careful not to overcook the liver — it should be pink inside. Transfer to a warmed serving dish and serve with potatoes or rice and a green vegetable.

Hígado con Vino   COLOMBIA
Calf's Liver in Red Wine Sauce

The red wine marinade gives this calf's liver a special delicate flavor.

Serves 2

½ pound calf's liver, cut into
    ½-inch slices
Salt, freshly ground pepper

1 large clove garlic, crushed
¾ cup dry red wine
3 tablespoons butter

Arrange the liver slices in a large shallow dish, season with salt and pepper
and the garlic. Pour the wine over them. Leave at room temperature for 2
hours, turning the slices from time to time. When ready to cook, lift out
the liver slices and pat them dry with paper towels. Reserve the marinade.
In a large skillet heat the butter and sauté the liver slices over moderate
heat for about 2 minutes on the first side and 1 minute on the second side.
The liver should remain pink inside. Pour the marinade into a small saucepan and reduce to half its volume. Arrange the liver on a warmed platter.
Pour any liquid from the skillet into the wine sauce, stir to mix, and pour
over the liver.

❄ Kidneys

Riñones con Vino   CHILE
Kidneys in Wine Sauce

I love to make this simple, quick Chilean kidney dish just for myself with
two lamb kidneys or one pork. It is a fine dish for a hurried supper.

Serves 3 to 4

1 beef kidney
Salt, freshly ground pepper
4 tablespoons butter
1 medium onion, finely chopped

4 tablespoons parsley, chopped
1 cup dry white wine
4 medium potatoes, freshly
    cooked and cubed

Trim the surplus fat from the kidney, and cut the kidney into thin slices.
Season with salt and pepper. Heat the butter in a skillet and sauté the
kidney slices for about 5 minutes, turning frequently. Lift out and set aside

in a covered dish. In the butter remaining in the pan sauté the onion until it is soft. Add the parsley and sauté for a minute longer. Add the wine and the potatoes. Add the kidney slices and cook just long enough to heat them through without further cooking, which would toughen them. Serve immediately.

If cooking this for one and using lamb or pork kidneys, remove the thin skin and any fat from the kidneys and slice them thinly. Use one-quarter of the remaining ingredients, and cook as above.

Variation: In Argentina cooks use a similar recipe for *Riñones a la Porteña* (Kidneys, Buenos Aires Style) except that veal kidney, chopped instead of sliced, is used and is sautéed in oil instead of butter.

Variation: For the Brazilian *Rim de Vitela* (Veal Kidney) or *Rims de Carneiro* (Lamb Kidneys), the kidneys are cleaned and sliced, and sautéed in 2 tablespoons olive oil. They are then heated through in the following sauce: Sauté 1 chopped onion and ½ green bell pepper, seeded and chopped, in 2 tablespoons olive oil until the onion is soft. Add 1 chopped tomato, ¼ cup chopped parsley, and salt and pepper. Simmer until well blended. Stir in ⅛ cup dry sherry and the kidneys. Reheat the kidneys without letting the sauce boil. For those who like a fiery touch, 1 small fresh hot pepper may be added with the bell pepper, or a dash of Tabasco with the sherry.

BARBECUES

The great cattle countries of Argentina and Brazil have marvelous outdoor feasts, elaborate and sophisticated barbecues that are superb for informal, warm weather entertaining, and easy to copy in the United States.

The *asado criollo*, the Argentine spit-roasted barbecue, originated with the gauchos — the cowboys of the *pampas*, those wide, rolling plains that stretch like a sea of grass for thousands of miles. The cowboys tended cattle, and later sheep, and when they were hungry killed an animal, spit-roasted it, and had dinner. In comparison, today's barbecue is a very grand affair. In addition to barbecued meats there are salads, sauces, bread, and wine, as well as the cowboy's favorite beverage, *mate*, the green herb tea popular in many parts of South America for its refreshing, slightly bitter flavor. But the essentials are the same — meat, salt, and a fire.

The word "barbecue" comes from the Spanish *barbacoa*, derived from a Haitian word in the Taino Indian language. It meant a rude framework either for sleeping or for drying meat over a fire, and reached the United States with that meaning by 1697. By 1809 its American meaning had changed to an outdoor social entertainment at which animals were roasted whole. Because of the growing popularity of outdoor cooking, grills of various kinds can easily be bought, and it is not difficult to build a do-it-yourself grill in the Argentine or Brazilian style provided there is yard space.

To make a *parrilla* (grill) for an Argentine *asado* (roast), dig a pit about 1 foot deep and about 3 feet long by 2 feet wide. Make sure the fire bed is level and cover it with a layer of sand. Surround it with bricks at ground level or, for a more luxurious grill, extend them to waist level, and cover with an iron grate. Also needed are a long three-pronged fork, a small work table to cut up the cooked meat, canvas work gloves, an asbestos oven mitt for hot jobs, tongs for turning meats and lifting them from the grill, a bowl for the *salmuera* (brine) to baste the meats, a brush or bunch of twigs for basting, and a bottle with a sprinkler top, filled with water, to discipline unruly flames.

It takes about an hour for a fire of wood and charcoal to burn down to embers that are ready to be used, and whoever looks after the grill has to put the meats on in sequence so that they are served hot and crispy brown on the outside, red and juicy inside. It is a considerable art and one that can be mastered only by experience, common sense, and a watchful eye. Meats are not basted with a barbecue sauce. Brine is used, usually a simple solution of salt and water. When the meat is seared on one side it is basted with brine and turned, and the other side seared and basted. After that the meat is turned and basted frequently until done.

Argentine hosts are generous in their estimate of how much meat is enough. They work it out roughly as a pound a person. The *asado* always begins with grilled sausages, either a halved chorizo, or 2 or 3 slices of grilled *longaniza*, nothing else, served with a glass of dry red wine. The sausages are just to hold off starvation, not to destroy appetite, while guests wait for the meats on the grill to cook. For ten people the traditional meats for the *parrillada* (barbecue) would be 2 pounds short ribs, 2 pounds rump or chuck steak, 1½ pounds flank steak, 1 pound blood sausage, 1 or 2 beef kidneys or a whole calf's liver, 1½ pounds sweetbreads, and 1½ pounds tripe, cut into strips about 1 inch wide. Traditionally intestines, udders, and prairie oysters are part of the roast. Intestines are grilled, then sliced. Udders are grilled, then cut into ½-inch slices. And prairie oysters are peeled, halved, grilled, and sliced.

After the sausages, the "innards" are served, and then the meats. Guests go to the grill to be served, then eat informally at simple wooden tables set with baskets of French bread and bottles or carafes of red wine. There are bowls of salad — lettuce, tomatoes, and sliced onions or scallions in a garlic-flavored oil and vinegar dressing, or a more robust one of potatoes, beets, hardboiled eggs, chopped celery, and radishes, also in a vinaigrette dressing. *Crudités* are sometimes served, raw carrot sticks, celery, and radishes. And there is always a bowl of hot pickled peppers as well as the traditional bowls of sauces — *Salsa Criolla* (Creole Sauce), a really fiery one to be taken with discretion, or sauce *Chimichurri*, an untranslatable name, hardly any milder. There is another less lethal sauce, *Salsa para Asados* (Barbecue Sauce) from nearby Uruguay, where barbecues are also popular.

The barbecue pit with a grate over it is really a sophisticated refinement. Whole animals, a lamb, kid, suckling pig, or a side of beef, can be spit-roasted in the true gaucho manner. The animals are split and impaled on iron rods that have a crosspiece to keep them flat. The rods are thrust firmly into the ground at an angle of about 20 degrees, toward a wood fire and about a foot away. They too are basted with brine and with their own fat and turned as they brown so that both sides cook evenly.

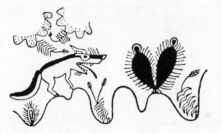

It is difficult to give more than approximate times for barbecuing as the heat of the fire and the thickness of the meats vary, as well as the degree of doneness preferred. Sausages will take about 10 minutes a side. A 2½- to 3-pound chicken, split down the back, will take about 1 hour. A medium-sized suckling pig will take 3 to 3½ hours, and baby lamb and kid about the same time. A 3-pound piece of short ribs should be cooked 10 to 15 minutes, rib side down, then turned, salted, and cooked for about 30 minutes longer. Rump or sirloin takes 20 to 30 minutes according to size. Flank steak, over high heat, starting fat side down, takes about 7 minutes a side.

The Brazilian barbecue, *Churrasco a Gaucha* from the cattle state of Rio Grande do Sul, has its own refinements and sophisticated extras. Originally the meat was spitted on long iron skewers and stuck in the ground at an angle to the fire much as the gauchos of Argentina did. It is still done for a traditional *churrasco*, but more and more people find a barbecue pit with a grate on top much more convenient for backyard barbecues. Short ribs and rump are the preferred meats. Though traditionally beef is the only meat used, many people temporarily tired of beef, like to have a *galeto*, a chicken, instead. This is split down the back and grilled whole. A whole parsley plant is used as a baster to apply the brine, seasoned sometimes with chopped onion and parsley, or crushed garlic cloves.

Slices of grilled *linguiça* (Portuguese sausage) may be served with a *Caipirinha* or a *batida* (Brazilian cocktails), page 333, as a first course. The meats are accompanied by *Farofa de Ouro* (Cassava Meal with Hardboiled Eggs) or *Farofa de Manteiga* (Cassava Meal with Butter). A nice variation is to add 4 bananas, cut into ½-inch slices and fried in 2 tablespoons of butter, to the cassava meal and mixed together. There is always a lettuce and tomato salad in an oil and vinegar dressing, and *Môlho de Tomates* (Tomato Sauce). Brazil's excellent beer is the popular drink to serve.

❋ Sauces for the Barbecues

Salsa Criolla   ARGENTINA
Barbecue Sauce, Creole Style

Makes about 5 cups

1 tablespoon hot paprika or
   cayenne pepper
½ tablespoon dry mustard
½ cup red wine vinegar
½ cup olive oil

Salt, freshly ground pepper
2 green bell peppers, seeded and
   finely chopped
1 medium onion, finely chopped
3 medium tomatoes, chopped

Mix the paprika or cayenne and mustard to a paste with a little of the vinegar, then stir in the rest of the vinegar. Beat in the oil. Season to taste with salt and a generous amount of freshly ground pepper. Add the remaining ingredients and stir to mix. The sauce has a lot of liquid. The solids should float in the bowl, so add a little more oil and vinegar if necessary. This is very hot.

Variation: Brazilian *Môlho ao Tomate* (Tomato Sauce). In a bowl combine 4 medium tomatoes, coarsely chopped, 2 medium onions, chopped, 2 cloves garlic, chopped, ½ cup each chopped parsley and coriander, salt, pepper, 1 cup olive oil, and ½ cup red wine vinegar. Mix lightly and serve at room temperature. Makes 4 to 5 cups.

Chimichurri
Vinegar Sauce

ARGENTINA

This is a popular sauce with barbecued meats or with any broiled or roasted meat or poultry.

Makes about 1 ½ cups

4 tablespoons olive oil
1 cup red wine vinegar
4 tablespoons hot paprika or
    cayenne pepper
4 cloves garlic, crushed

1 teaspoon black peppercorns
1 teaspoon oregano
1 bay leaf, crumbled
½ teaspoon salt

Combine all the ingredients in a bottle, shake well to mix, and put in a cool place, or refrigerate, for 4 or 5 days for the flavor to develop. Shake a few drops on meat or poultry.

Brine

½ cups coarse salt

2 cups water

Mix the salt and water thoroughly and use to baste meats.

Salsa Para Asados
Barbecue Sauce

URUGUAY

Makes about 3 cups

1 cup olive oil
½ cup red wine vinegar
8 cloves garlic, chopped
1 cup finely chopped parsley
1 teaspoon oregano

1 teaspoon thyme
2 teaspoons hot paprika or
    cayenne pepper
Salt, freshly ground pepper

Combine all the ingredients and mix thoroughly. Allow to stand for 2 or 3 hours before serving. Serve with barbecued meats. This sauce may also be used as a marinade.

POT-AU-FEUS

The pot-au-feu (literally, pot on the fire) is one of the earliest cooking methods and probably goes back to the Bronze Age. Bronze cauldrons from 3500 B.C. are not very much different from the casseroles and kettles in use today, and there is hardly a country on earth that does not have a pot-au-feu in its repertoire. In Latin America this type of stew may be called a *sancocho* (literally parboiled, a dish where foods are added to the pot after some have already been partially cooked), a *pozole* (from an Aztec word meaning beans boiled with other things), a *puchero* (a glazed earthenware pot for cooking meat and vegetables together), a *carbonada* (a meat stew from the New World), a *cocido* (a cooked meat dish), and an *ajiaco* (a dish made of boiled meat and vegetables from South America). Essentially, as elsewhere, it is a whole meal cooked in a single pot on top of the stove.

In Latin America over the years versions of the pot-au-feu have served as plantation meals, useful for feeding large numbers of people. There is often an enormously long list of ingredients including the marvelous root vegetables, the yams, taros, and cassava, that flourish in this region, where many of them originated; they vary in texture and flavor and lend variety to any stew they grace. Plantains are another widely used ingredient, as are the winter squashes and, of course, that greatest of all Inca achievements, the potato. Meats introduced by Spain and Portugal — beef, kid, lamb, chicken, and pork — are all used. So are beans, both the indigenous beans (*Phaseolus vulgaris*, kidney, Navy, pea, lima, turtle, etc.) and such exotics as chickpeas (*garbanzos, hummus*), brought by Spain from the Middle East. In addition there are all the green vegetables, and onions, scallions, and garlic — a grand assemblage, needing only a degree of selection, and a knowledge of when to add them to the pot.

These dishes are still very popular in Latin America for parties and family gatherings, since it is not really possible to cook them for small numbers like two or four. They are usually presented in a grand manner with various meats on one platter, vegetables on another, the soup in a large tureen, sauces on the side, and the table set with generous-sized rimmed soup plates. With a little planning, they are easy and you don't have to spend time at the last minute in the kitchen, since the ingredients can all be prepared ahead of time, the work being mostly the peeling and cutting up of vegetables. What is essential is a large enough pot; I have often solved this problem by using two fairly big casseroles and dividing the ingredients equally between them. Since such a dish comprises the entire meal, the whole stove is available for its cooking. Permutations and combinations of ingredients have resulted in a group of wonderfully diverse dishes.

Carbonada en Zapallo ARGENTINA
Veal Stew in Baked Pumpkin

West Indian pumpkin (*calabaza*) is available in many Caribbean and Latin American markets and is ideal for this colorful and quite spectacular dish, as it is usually possible to get just the size needed. However, any large winter squash can be used, the Hubbard shape probably being the best. U.S. pumpkins won't do; they are too watery. The stew is served from the squash itself, which plays a dual role as both container and ingredient. The squash will be very soft and mashes into the sauce, thickening it. It has a lovely flavor, which mingles with the stew.

Serves 6 to 8

A 10- to 12-pound West Indian
    pumpkin (calabaza) or other
    large winter squash, such as
    Hubbard
¼ cup vegetable oil
2 pounds boneless veal, cut into
    1-inch cubes
1 large onion, finely chopped
1 green bell pepper, seeded and
    chopped
1 or 2 fresh hot peppers, seeded
    and chopped (optional)
1 large tomato, peeled and
    chopped
1 ½ cups chicken stock
1 ½ cups dry white wine

1 pound potatoes, peeled and cut
    into 1-inch cubes
1 pound sweet potatoes,
    preferably boniatos (white
    sweet potatoes), peeled and
    cut into 1-inch cubes
2 ears corn, cut into 1-inch slices
2 large pears, peeled and sliced
3 large peaches, peeled, pitted,
    and sliced
1 tablespoon chopped chives
1 tablespoon sugar
Salt, freshly ground pepper
½ cup long-grain rice, soaked for 1
    hour and drained

Scrub the pumpkin. Cut a slice off the top to make a lid, then scrape out the seeds and stringy fibers from the pumpkin and lid. Bake the pumpkin on a baking sheet in a preheated moderate (350° F.) oven for 45 minutes.

Meanwhile, heat the oil in a heavy skillet and sauté the veal pieces until they are golden all over. Lift them out into a flameproof casserole with a slotted spoon. In the fat remaining in the pan sauté the onion, pepper, and hot peppers, if using, until the onion is soft. Add the tomato and cook until the mixture is well blended, about 5 minutes. Add to the casserole with the chicken stock and wine. Bring to a boil, reduce the heat, and simmer, covered, for 40 minutes. Add the potatoes and sweet potatoes and cook 15 minutes. Add the corn and cook 5 minutes longer. Remove from the heat and add the pears, peaches, chives, and sugar. Season to taste with salt and pepper. Add the rice. Transfer the contents of the casserole to the pumpkin. Replace the lid and bake in a preheated moderate (350° F.) oven for 30 minutes or until the rice is cooked. Transfer the pumpkin to a large serving platter and serve directly from it, taking care when scooping out the cooked pumpkin not to break the shell.

Variation: If liked, 2 quinces, peeled and sliced, may be added when the potatoes and sweet potatoes are put into the casserole.

Variation: Lean beef chuck may be used instead of veal.

Variation: Six dried apricots, soaked for 20 minutes in cold water, drained, and quartered, may be used instead of the peaches.

Carbonada Criolla
Beef Stew, Argentine Style

ARGENTINA

This is a simpler, less spectacular version of *Carbonada en Zapallo* (Veal Stew in Baked Pumpkin). Once more it demonstrates the Argentine flair for combining meat and fruit.

Serves 6

¼ cup olive oil
2 pounds lean beef, cut into 1-inch
    cubes
1 large onion, finely chopped
1 clove garlic, chopped
3 medium tomatoes, peeled and
    chopped
½ teaspoon oregano
1 bay leaf
1 teaspoon sugar
1 tablespoon tomato paste
Salt, freshly ground pepper
1 cup beef stock, about
1 cup dry red wine, about
1 pound sweet potatoes,
    preferably boniatos (white
    sweet potatoes), peeled and
    sliced
1 pound potatoes, peeled and
    sliced

1 pound West Indian pumpkin
    (calabaza) or any winter
    squash, peeled and sliced
6 small peaches, peeled
4 ears corn, each cut into 3 slices

Heat the oil in a large, heavy casserole and sauté the beef until it is lightly browned all over. Push it to the side and add the onion and garlic. Sauté the onion until it is soft. Add the tomatoes and cook for 5 minutes longer. Add the oregano, bay leaf, sugar, tomato paste, salt and pepper to taste, the stock, and the wine. Cover and simmer for 1½ hours, or until the meat is almost tender. Add the sweet potatoes and potatoes and a little more stock and wine if necessary to cover. Simmer for 10 minutes, then add the pumpkin or squash and peaches, and simmer for a further 10 minutes. Add the corn and cook 5 minutes longer, or until all the ingredients are tender. Some cooks add ½ cup rice or vermicelli during the last 20 minutes of cooking.

Cozido à Brasileira   BRAZIL
Stew, Brazilian Style

This is a dish from São Paulo that was taken by Paulistas to Minas Gerais. I have met it both in the new capital, Belo Horizonte, and the old one, Ouro Prêto. This recipe was given me by the mother of a good friend, Gilberto Rizzo, a Paulista.

Serves 12

2 pounds top round of beef, cut
    into 1-inch cubes
6 pork chops, boned
4 medium onions, grated
4 cloves garlic, crushed
4 scallions, including the green
    tops
2 or 3 sprigs each parsley and fresh
    coriander (cilantro)
Beef broth
A 3-pound chicken, cut into 6
    pieces
A 2-pound linguiça sausage, or use
    a similar sausage such as
    Spanish longaniza or Polish
    kielbasa
6 small whole carrots, scraped
1 small bunch celery, with stalks
    cut into 3- to 4-inch pieces

1 small whole cabbage
6 small whole potatoes, peeled or
    scraped
3 small sweet potatoes, peeled
    and halved
1 ½ pounds cassava root (manioc,
    yucca), peeled and cut into
    2-inch slices
2 pounds West Indian pumpkin
    (calabaza) or any winter
    squash, peeled and cut into
    2-inch cubes
2 ears corn, each cut into 3 slices
Salt, freshly ground pepper
3 medium slightly underripe
    bananas, or 2 half-ripe
    plantains
1 cup cassava meal (manioc,
    mandioca)

In a kettle or saucepan large enough to hold all the ingredients put the beef, pork chops, onions, garlic, scallions, parsley and coriander sprigs, and enough beef broth to cover. Simmer, covered, over low heat for 1 hour. At the end of that time add the chicken, sausage, and more beef broth as necessary to cover, and cook for 30 minutes longer. Add to the kettle the carrots, celery, cabbage, potatoes, sweet potatoes, cassava root, pumpkin or winter squash, corn, salt and pepper to taste, and more beef broth to cover.

In a separate saucepan put the bananas or plantains, cover with cold water, and simmer, covered, for 20 minutes. If using plantains, cook them for 30 minutes. When cool enough to handle, lift out and peel. Halve the bananas, or cut the plantains into thirds, and add to the ingredients in the kettle just long enough to heat through. Have ready two large, deep, warmed platters. Arrange the meats on one of the platters. Place the cabbage in the center of the second platter and cut it into wedges. Arrange the other vegetables on the platter in decorative groups.

Remove and discard the parsley and coriander sprigs from the broth in the kettle. Moisten the meats and vegetables with some of the broth. Measure 4 cups of the broth and pour it into a saucepan. Stir in the cassava meal, then simmer, stirring constantly, over moderate heat until the cassava has thickened the liquid to a porridgelike consistency. Pour this *pirão* into a bowl and serve it as a sauce with the *cozido*.

Sancocho Especial
Special Boiled Dinner

COLOMBIA

The Spanish verb *sancochar* means to parboil and has come to be applied to a number of South American dishes of the pot-au-feu family in the sense of adding new ingredients to already parboiled ones in the pot. The more ingredients there are in a *sancocho*, the more of a party dish it becomes. This one is very festive. It has to be done ahead of time, as it takes about a week. Simplified by the omission of some of the vegetables and meats, it will still be very good indeed. The salted beef gives a distinctive, though not pronounced, flavor to this special *sancocho*.

Serves 6 to 8

1 pound beef chuck, cut into
    1½-inch cubes
1 pound lean pork, cut into
    1½-inch cubes
1 pound salted beef, well washed
    and cut into 1½-inch cubes
    (see below)
2 large onions, sliced
3 cloves garlic, chopped
2 large tomatoes, peeled, seeded,
    and chopped
1 pound yucca root (cassava),
    peeled and sliced
1½ quarts beef stock
1½ quarts chicken stock
A 3½-pound chicken, cut into
    serving pieces
1 pound sweet potatoes, peeled
    and sliced

1 pound yams, peeled and sliced
1 pound winter squash, peeled
    and cubed
1 pound potatoes, peeled and
    sliced
2 green plantains, peeled and cut
    into 2-inch slices
2 ripe plantains, peeled and cut
    into 2-inch slices
3 ears corn, each cut into 3 slices
Salt, freshly ground pepper
3 or 4 limes, quartered

Put the beef, pork, salted beef, onions, garlic, tomatoes, yucca, and the beef and chicken stock into a soup kettle or pot large enough to hold all the ingredients. Bring to a boil over moderate heat, skim off the froth, and reduce the heat so that the liquid barely moves. Cook, covered, for 1¼ hours. Add the chicken pieces, sweet potatoes, yams, winter squash, potatoes, and green and ripe plantains and simmer until the chicken is tender, about 45 minutes longer. Add the corn, season to taste with salt and pepper, and cook for 5 minutes longer.

Arrange the meats on a warm platter, the vegetables on another warm platter, and pour the broth into a soup tureen. Serve in large soup plates with side dishes of quartered limes, and *Salsa de Ají* (Hot Pepper Sauce).

Salted beef, Colombia style. The salted beef, which is a special feature of this dish, is easy to do, and once done keeps indefinitely in the refrigerator. It is well worth the effort.

Cut a 3- to 4-pound piece of bottom round of beef into horizontal slices about ½ inch thick, stopping short of the far side of the meat so that it opens like a book. Pour 1 pound salt over the beef, between the slices, and on the top and bottom. Place on a large platter and cover lightly with cheesecloth. Leave it to stand in a cool place overnight and in the morning pour off the liquid that has accumulated. There will be a lot of it the first day. Check that the meat is still heavily coated with salt, adding more if necessary. Repeat the process, leaving the beef to stand for another 24 hours and again pouring off the liquid. If necessary add more salt. Place on a piece of heavy aluminum foil, or on a platter, cover with cheesecloth, and put in the sun to dry, turning the meat over daily. It will take about a week. Shake out the excess salt, wrap the beef in foil, and store in the refrigerator. Wash well before using. I have found that Brazilian *carne sêca* (sun-dried salt beef, or jerked beef) works very well. If plantains are not available, use unripe (green) bananas for green plantains and barely ripe bananas for the ripe plantains. Reduce the cooking time to about 20 minutes for green bananas, 5 minutes for the barely ripe ones.

Pozole Tapatío
MEXICO
Pozole, Guadalajara Style

Tapatío is an affectionate term for the people of Guadalajara, the capital of Jalisco, and is also used for special dishes from the city. It comes from a colonial dance from Guadalajara, the *Jarabe Tapatío* (The Hat Dance), those who danced it being *tapatíos*. In Mexico the hominy used here would not always be bought canned but is very often prepared at home. Whole, large white corn kernels are soaked overnight, then boiled with lime. The skins are then rubbed off and the *"cabecita,"* little head, at the base removed. The corn is then ready to be cooked. It is a long and time-consuming process and I have found canned whole hominy an excellent substitute.

Serves 8 to 10

6 ancho *chilies*
3 *pig's feet*
1 *head garlic, peeled*
3 *quarts chicken stock*
1 *pound boneless pork loin, cut into 1-inch cubes*

A 3½- to 4-pound chicken, cut into serving pieces
Salt
2 *cups canned whole hominy*

FOR THE GARNISH

1 *large onion, finely chopped*
½ *head iceberg lettuce, shredded*
1 *bunch radishes*
½ *pound Spanish fresh cheese* (queso fresco *or* quesco blanco), *optional*
Oregano

Ground hot pepper, or hot pepper sauce such as Tabasco
Fresh hot tortillas, or tortillas cut into triangles and fried in hot lard or vegetable oil
3 *limes or lemons, cut into wedges*

Break off the stems and shake the seeds out of the chilies. Rinse the chilies and tear them into pieces. Put them into a bowl with 1 cup hot water and leave to soak for 1 hour, turning them from time to time. Put them into a blender or food processor and reduce to a purée. Set aside.

Put the pig's feet into a large saucepan or kettle with the garlic and chicken stock. Bring to a boil, reduce the heat, cover, and simmer for 3 hours. Add the pork loin and simmer for 1 hour, then add the chicken pieces and the puréed chilies. Add a little salt if necessary. Simmer for 40 minutes, add the hominy, and cook for 5 minutes longer. By this time all the ingredients should be tender. Simmer for a little longer if necessary.

To serve put the meats and broth into a large soup tureen and set the table with large-rimmed soup plates. Put the onion, lettuce, radishes, and crumbled cheese into bowls, and the oregano and ground hot pepper or hot pepper sauce into small bowls. Serve the tortillas, in a straw basket, wrapped in a napkin. To eat, add the garnishes to each serving of meat and broth, with squeezes of lime or lemon juice.

Cocido a la Dominicana

DOMINICAN REPUBLIC

Spanish Stew, Dominican Style

Serves 6 to 8

½ pound dried chickpeas, or a
   1-pound can
4 tablespoons vegetable oil
A 4-pound chicken, cut into
   serving pieces
½ pound beef, cut into 1-inch
   cubes
A ½ pound slice of smoked ham,
   such as prosciutto or Spanish
   Jamon Serrano, cut into
   1-inch cubes
½ pound chorizo (hot Spanish)
   sausages, sliced, or use hot
   Italian sausages
1 medium onion, chopped
4 cloves garlic, chopped
2 pounds potatoes, peeled and
   sliced

1 large carrot, scraped and sliced
1 small cabbage, cut into 8
   wedges
½ pound West Indian pumpkin
   (calabaza) or winter squash,
   peeled and cubed
1 fresh hot red or green pepper, left
   whole with stem on
1 bay leaf
1 tablespoon white vinegar
8 cups beef stock
Salt
6 small pitted green olives, sliced
1 tablespoon finely chopped
   parsley

If using dried chickpeas, soak them overnight in cold water to cover. Drain, cover with fresh water, and simmer, covered, for 1 hour. Drain, measure the liquid, and use it to replace some of the beef stock. Set aside. If using canned chickpeas, drain, rinse in cold water, and set aside.

Heat the oil in a skillet and sauté the chicken pieces until golden on both sides. Transfer to a large saucepan or soup kettle. In the oil remaining in the skillet sauté the beef cubes, ham, and sausages, and add them to the saucepan. In the remaining oil, adding a little more if necessary, though the sausages will give off quite a lot of fat, sauté the onion and garlic until the onion is soft. Add the mixture to the kettle with the potatoes, carrot, cabbage, pumpkin or winter squash, whole hot pepper, bay leaf, vinegar, the chickpeas and liquid or the canned, drained, chickpeas, the stock, and salt to taste. Cover and simmer until all the ingredients are tender, about 1 hour. The pumpkin or squash will have disintegrated, slightly thickening the broth. Remove and discard the bay leaf and hot pepper. Transfer the stew to a warmed tureen or serving dish, add the olives, and sprinkle with the parsley.

Variation: There is an interesting variation, *Sancocho de Longaniza y To-cino* (Sausage and Bacon Stew), also from the Dominican Republic. Soak 1½ pounds bacon, in a single piece, for 15 minutes in cold water, rinse, drain, and cut into 1-inch cubes. Slice 2 pounds *longaniza* (Spanish garlic) sausages, or *linguiça* or *kielbasa*, into 1-inch slices. Heat 4 tablespoons vegetable oil in a skillet and sauté the bacon cubes and sausage slices until lightly browned. Transfer to a flameproof casserole. In the fat remaining in the skillet sauté 1 large onion, finely chopped, 3 cloves garlic, chopped, and 1 green bell pepper, seeded and chopped, and add to the casserole with 1 tablespoon red wine vinegar and 2 tablespoons Seville (bitter) orange juice, or two-thirds orange juice and one-third lime or lemon juice. Add 3 quarts beef stock, and simmer, covered, for 1½ hours, then add 1 pound cassava

(yucca) root, peeled and sliced, 1 pound taro (*yautía*), peeled and sliced, 1 pound yam (*ñame*), not orange sweet potatoes, and 1 pound West Indian pumpkin (*calabaza*) or winter squash, peeled and cubed. Season to taste with salt, freshly ground pepper, 1 teaspoon oregano, and hot pepper sauce (such as Tabasco) to taste. Simmer, covered, until all the ingredients are tender. In a separate saucepan, in water to cover, boil 2 green plantains in their skins for 30 minutes, cool, peel, slice, and add to the casserole just long enough to heat them through. The plantains may be omitted, if preferred, or green (underripe) bananas may be used instead, in which case boil them for 20 minutes. Put the meats and vegetables on a heated serving platter, pour the broth into a tureen, and serve in soup plates. Serves 6 to 8.

Puchero Estilo Mexicano

MEXICO

Mexican Pot-au-Feu

If you want to present everything in this pot-au-feu at the same time, serve the soup in bowls, the meats and vegetables on plates. The green vegetables may be varied to suit the cook. Cabbage and turnips may be added, chayotes may be used instead of zucchini.

Serves 8 to 10

½ pound dried chickpeas, or a
  1-pound can
1 pound lean boneless beef chuck,
  cut into 1-inch cubes
1 pound boneless lamb, cut into
  1-inch cubes
½ pound raw ham, cubed
½ pound chorizo (hot Spanish
  sausages), sliced
1 large onion, chopped
2 cloves garlic, chopped
⅛ teaspoon peppercorns
1½ quarts chicken stock
1½ quarts beef stock
Salt
A 3½- to 4-pound chicken, cut
  into serving pieces
4 carrots, scraped and sliced
4 zucchini, sliced
1 pound green beans, cut into
  ½-inch pieces

1 pound sweet potatoes, peeled
  and sliced
3 ears corn, cut into 1-inch slices
4 tablespoons lard or vegetable oil
1 pound potatoes, peeled and
  sliced
2 green plantains, or 2 large green
  (underripe) bananas, peeled
  and cut into 1-inch slices
3 large peaches, peeled, pitted,
  and quartered
3 large pears, peeled, cored, and
  quartered
1 tablespoon chopped fresh
  coriander (cilantro)
Fresh hot tortillas
Guacamole *(Avocado Sauce)*, page
  316
2 limes or lemons, cut into wedges
Hot pepper sauce *(Tabasco or any of
  the sauces on pages 311–13)*

Soak the chickpeas overnight, drain, and rinse. Put them into a large soup kettle. If using canned chickpeas, drain, rinse, and set aside until later. Add to the kettle the beef, lamb, ham, chorizo, onion, garlic, peppercorns, chicken and beef stock, and salt to taste, if necessary. Bring to a boil, skim any froth that comes to the surface, reduce the heat, cover, and simmer gently for 45 minutes. Add the chicken pieces and simmer for 30 minutes longer. Add the carrots, zucchini, green beans, sweet potatoes, and canned chickpeas, if using, and cook for 15 minutes longer. Add the corn and cook for 5 minutes.

Heat the lard or vegetable oil in a skillet and sauté the potatoes and plantains or green bananas until tender. Lift out onto a platter and keep warm. Take a cupful of stock from the kettle and gently poach the peaches and pears, between 10 and 15 minutes. Add to the kettle with the stock.

Check that all the ingredients are tender. Arrange the meats in the center of a large platter and surround with the vegetables and fruits. Moisten with a little stock and keep warm. If liked, the chickpeas may be left in the soup, or put on the platter. Pour the soup into a tureen and sprinkle with the chopped coriander. Serve the soup in bowls. Serve the meats, fruits, vegetables, and the fried potatoes and plantains as a second course accompanied by hot tortillas, *Guacamole*, lime or lemon wedges, and hot pepper sauce.

Sancocho de Gallina   VENEZUELA
Chicken Pot-au-Feu

Tropical markets carry an astonishing variety of root vegetables so if *apio* (*arracacha*) is not available, use taro (*yautía, dasheen*), or white sweet potato (*boniato*), or more than one type of yam. None of the vegetables has a dominating flavor, and all cook in about the same time so it is easy — and perfectly acceptable — to make substitutions. It is also a good way to get to know more about these delicious vegetables.

Serves 8 to 10

Two 3½-pound chickens, cut into serving pieces
3 quarts chicken stock
1 leek, well washed and halved lengthwise
1 large onion, chopped
1 head garlic, peeled
3 white turnips, peeled and quartered

3 carrots, scraped and cut into 4 slices
1 large tomato, peeled, seeded, and chopped
2 or 3 sprigs fresh coriander (cilantro)
Salt, freshly ground pepper

THE VEGETABLES

1 pound cassava root (yucca), peeled and cut into ½-inch slices
1 pound West Indian pumpkin (calabaza) or any winter squash, peeled and cut into ½-inch slices
1 pound yam (ñame, not orange sweet potatoes), peeled and cut into ½-inch slices

1 pound apio (arracacha), peeled and cut into ½-inch slices
1 pound potatoes, peeled and cut into ½-inch slices
1 small cabbage, blanched and cut into 8 wedges
3 ears corn, each cut into 4 slices
2 green plantains (optional), or 3 large green bananas

Put all the ingredients except those listed under vegetables into a large saucepan or soup kettle. Bring to a boil, reduce the heat to a bare simmer, and cook, covered, for 30 minutes. Add all the vegetables except the corn and plantains, and continue cooking until the chicken and vegetables are tender, 20 to 30 minutes. Add the corn in the last 5 minutes of cooking. In a separate saucepan boil the unpeeled green plantains in water to cover for 30 minutes. When they are cool enough to handle, lift out, peel, and cut into 1-inch slices. Add to the chicken and vegetables just long enough to heat through. If using green bananas, cook for 15 minutes, peel, slice, and add to the kettle. Arrange the chicken pieces on a large, heated serving platter and surround with the vegetables. Strain the soup into a soup tureen. Serve in soup plates with *Guasacaca* (Avocado Sauce) or *Salsa de Ají* (Hot Pepper Sauce), separately.

Traditionally a large stewing hen (*gallina*) is used for this dish, but stewing hens are no longer readily available and require long, slow cooking. I find 3½-pound chickens very satisfactory. The dish can also be made with beef, using 4 pounds lean, boneless beef such as chuck, cut into 1-inch cubes. It is then called *Hervido*.

Ajiaco   CUBA
Meat and Vegetable Stew

Serves 8 to 10

3 pounds lean, boneless pork, cut into 2-inch cubes

1 pound corned beef, cut into 2-inch cubes

2 quarts beef stock

2 quarts water

1 pound cassava root (yucca), cut into ½-inch slices

1 pound taro (yautía), peeled and cut into ½-inch slices

1 pound yam (ñame, not orange sweet potatoes), peeled and cut into ½-inch slices

1 pound sweet potatoes, preferably white (boniatos), peeled and cut into ½-inch slices

1 pound West Indian pumpkin (calabaza) or winter squash, peeled and cubed

2 ears corn, cut into 1-inch slices

2 chayotes, peeled and sliced, or use zucchini

2 ripe plantains, peeled and cut into 1-inch slices

4 tablespoons olive oil

2 medium onions, finely chopped

2 cloves garlic, minced

1 green bell pepper, seeded and coarsely chopped

2 or more fresh hot red or green peppers, seeded and finely chopped

3 medium tomatoes, peeled and
*   coarsely chopped*
Salt, freshly ground pepper

2 green plantains (optional)
Juice of 2 limes

Put the pork and corned beef into a large saucepan or soup kettle with the stock and water. Bring to a boil, boil for a minute or two, and skim the froth that rises to the surface. Reduce the heat to a bare simmer, and cook, covered, for 1 hour. Add the cassava root, taro, and yam, and cook 15 minutes longer. Add the sweet potatoes, pumpkin or winter squash, corn, chayotes, and ripe plantains, and continue to simmer gently. If using zucchini do not add until later.

Heat the oil in a skillet and sauté the onions, garlic, and sweet and hot peppers until the onions are soft. Add the tomatoes, season to taste with pepper and salt, if necessary (the corned beef may have added enough saltiness), and cook until well blended, about 5 minutes longer. Add to the kettle with the zucchini, if using, and continue cooking at a gentle simmer until everything is done, which should be about 2 hours from starting. The pumpkin or winter squash will disintegrate, slightly thickening the broth.

Boil the green plantains in a separate saucepan in water to cover for 30 minutes. Cool, peel, and cut into 1-inch slices. Add to the kettle just long enough to heat through. Add the lime juice, stir, and serve. Arrange the meat and vegetables on a large heated serving platter, or if preferred, on two separate, smaller platters. Pour the broth into a soup tureen. Serve in soup plates with a hot pepper sauce on the side. This is wonderful with crusty rolls and butter.

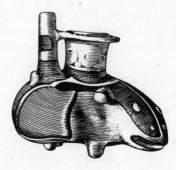

Poultry
Aves

CHICKEN

There is no doubt that chicken — inexpensive and extremely versatile — is the favorite bird in the kitchens of Latin America. It is impossible to tire of chicken with so many delectable ways to cook it.

Most Latin American recipes are variations on a poaching theme. Chicken is gently simmered with herbs and spices and vegetable flavorings like onion and garlic, and deliciously sauced in a great variety of ways. Also, corn plays a special role in dishes like *Cuscuz de Galinha* (Garnished Steamed Chicken and Cornmeal) and *Pastel de Choclo con Relleno de Pollo* (Chicken Pie with Corn Topping) — see Substantial Dishes.

Out of a vast array of recipes I have chosen dishes that I have enjoyed, not just once, but time and again.

Pollo con Naranja

Chicken in Orange Sauce

Serves 4

A 3- to 3½-pound chicken,
   quartered
Salt, freshly ground pepper
3 tablespoons butter
1 cup chicken stock

1 cup orange juice
Grated rind of 1 orange
1 tablespoon flour
2 eggs
1 tablespoon heavy cream

Season the chicken pieces with salt and pepper. Heat the butter in a heavy casserole and sauté the chicken pieces, one or two at a time, until golden on both sides. Set aside as they are done. Pour off the fat from the casserole into a small bowl and reserve. Return the chicken pieces to the casserole, putting the legs in first with the breasts on top, as the breasts cook more quickly. Add the chicken stock, orange juice, and grated orange rind. Cover and simmer for 30 to 45 minutes, or until the chicken is done. Lift out the chicken onto a serving dish and keep warm. Mix the flour with a tablespoon of the reserved fat and stir it into the liquid in the casserole. Bring to a boil and cook, stirring, for a minute or two. Reduce the heat to low. Beat the eggs with the cream. Stir 1 cup of the thickened liquid from the casserole, 1 tablespoon at a time, into the egg mixture, then pour the mixture into the casserole and cook, stirring with a wire whisk, until the sauce is lightly thickened, a minute or two. Do not let the sauce boil, as it will curdle. Pour some of the sauce over the chicken and serve the rest in a sauceboat. Serve with rice or mashed or French fried potatoes.

Frango com Bananas

Chicken with Bananas

This chicken dish from Brazil's Mato Grosso is simmered with white wine and tomatoes, then topped with lightly fried bananas; a most attractive and unusual combination of flavors, slightly sweet, slightly sour.

Serves 4

A 3-pound chicken, quartered
¼ cup lemon juice
2 teaspoons salt
3 tablespoons butter
1 medium onion, grated
2 tomatoes, peeled, seeded, and
   chopped

⅛ teaspoon sugar
1 cup dry white wine
¼ cup vegetable oil
6 ripe bananas, peeled and halved
   lengthwise
1 cup grated Parmesan cheese
1 tablespoon butter

Season the chicken with the lemon juice and salt. Heat the butter in a flameproof casserole and stir in the onion, tomatoes, and sugar. Add the chicken pieces and any of their liquid. Simmer for 5 minutes, uncovered, turning the chicken pieces once. Add the wine, cover the casserole, and simmer until the chicken is tender, about 45 minutes.

Heat the oil in a skillet and sauté the bananas until they are lightly browned on both sides. Arrange the bananas, cut side down, on top of the chicken pieces and sprinkle them with the grated cheese. Dot with the butter, cut into little bits. Place the casserole in a preheated hot (400° F.) oven and bake until the cheese is lightly browned, about 10 minutes. Serve with white rice.

Pollo en Piña
Chicken in Pineapple

GUATEMALA

Serves 4 to 6

A 3½- to 4-pound chicken, cut
   into serving pieces
1 ripe pineapple, weighing about
   1½ pounds, peeled, cored,
   and coarsely chopped, or a
   1-pound can unsweetened
   pineapple, in its own juice
2 medium onions, finely chopped
2 cloves garlic, chopped
2 whole cloves

A 1-inch piece of stick cinnamon
2 bay leaves
½ cup olive oil
½ cup white vinegar
½ cup dry sherry
2 medium tomatoes, peeled and
   coarsely chopped
Salt, freshly ground pepper
Chicken stock, if necessary

Put the chicken pieces into a heavy saucepan or casserole. If using fresh pineapple, be careful to save and use all the juice. If using canned pineapple, use the juice. Add all the rest of the ingredients, including salt and pepper to taste. If using fresh pineapple, it may be necessary to add a little chicken stock to cover the chicken pieces, as the fresh fruit will not have as much juice as the canned. Cover and simmer over low heat until the chicken is tender, about 45 minutes. If the sauce is very abundant, cook partially covered for the last 15 minutes. Serve with rice.

Ají de Gallina
Chicken in Pepper Sauce

PERU

Serves 6

A 3½- to 4-pound chicken, quartered	8 fresh hot red or green peppers, seeded
3 cups chicken stock, about	2 medium tomatoes, peeled and seeded
¼ cup vegetable oil	
2 medium onions, finely chopped	4 ounces walnuts, ground
2 cloves garlic, minced	Salt, freshly ground pepper
2 cups fresh breadcrumbs	½ cup grated Parmesan cheese
2 cups milk	

Put the chicken pieces into a large saucepan or flameproof casserole with the stock, adding a little more if necessary to cover, and poach until the chicken is tender, about 45 minutes. Let the chicken cool in the stock. Remove the skin and bones and shred the meat into pieces about 1½ inches long and ¼ inch wide. Set the shredded chicken aside and reserve the stock.

Heat the oil in a flameproof casserole and sauté the onions and garlic until the onions are golden. Soak the breadcrumbs in the milk and mash to a paste. Add the breadcrumb mixture to the casserole. In a blender or food processor reduce the peppers and tomatoes to a purée and stir into the casserole. Add the ground walnuts. Season to taste with salt and pepper, and cook, stirring, over moderate heat for about 5 minutes. Add the chicken, 1 cup of the stock, and the cheese, and cook just until heated through. The sauce should be thick. Serve the chicken and sauce on a heated platter surrounded by halved, boiled potatoes, hardboiled eggs, sliced lengthwise, and black olives.

Cecilia Blanco de Mendoza's Ajiaco

Chicken Stew   COLOMBIA

This is a very special *ajiaco* (chicken stew) with subtle seasonings that include *guascas* or *huascas*, a Colombian herb whose botanical name is *Galinsoga parviflora Lineo*. It is sold, dried and ground, in jars in Colombian markets and has a mild flavor vaguely reminiscent, to my palate, of Jerusalem artichokes, to which, I am assured by a Colombian botanist, it bears no relationship whatsoever. It might one day appear in a specialty food shop and will enhance any soup or stew, as the flavor is delicate and unobtrusive. However, though *guascas* is an attractive extra, it is not essential to the deliciousness of this dish, which depends on a combination of flavors including scallions and coriander.

Also in the stew are three types of potatoes: Idahos or any similar potato, small red potatoes, and *papas criollas*. These last are delicious small Colombian potatoes that are sometimes available in Latin American markets. They have yellow flesh and stay whole through prolonged cooking. Small white new potatoes make a very good substitute, perhaps not as pretty to look at, but equal otherwise.

Serves 6

A 3½- to 4-pound chicken, left
    whole
4 whole scallions
6 sprigs fresh coriander (cilantro)
1 teaspoon ground guascas
3 cups chicken stock or water
Salt, freshly ground pepper
4 small ears corn, cut into 1-inch
    slices
2 pounds Idaho or similar
    potatoes, peeled and cut into
    ¼-inch slices

2 pounds small red potatoes,
    peeled and cut into ¼-inch
    slices
1 pound papas criollas or small
    white new potatoes, unpeeled
2 cups milk
1 small can Vienna sausages,
    sliced
½ cup cooked baby peas
1 or 2 tablespoons capers
2 hardboiled eggs, sliced
6 tablespoons heavy cream

In a soup kettle or large saucepan combine the chicken, scallions, coriander, *guascas* (if available), chicken stock or water, and salt and pepper to taste. Bring to a boil and skim off any froth that rises to the surface, reduce the heat, cover, and simmer gently until the chicken is tender, about 45 minutes. Let the chicken cool in the broth, lift it out, cut it into 6 serving pieces, and set it aside, covered. Strain the broth and add the corn to it.

Bring the broth to a simmer over moderate heat and add all the potatoes. Simmer until the broth thickens. The Idaho potatoes will disintegrate and thicken the broth, the red potatoes will retain some texture, and the *papas criollas* or new potatoes will remain whole. Add the milk and the chicken pieces and cook just long enough to heat them through. To serve, have ready six large, deep soup plates. Put a piece of chicken in each, 2 or 3 slices of Vienna sausage, 1 tablespoon peas, a few capers, a slice of egg, and the broth, making sure each gets a *papa criolla* or new potato. Pour a tablespoon of heavy cream over each serving. Serve with knife, fork, and soup spoon.

Ajiaco de Pollo Bogotano   COLOMBIA
Bogotá Chicken Stew

Serves 6

4 tablespoons (¼ cup) butter
A 3½-pound chicken, cut into
    serving pieces
2 large onions, finely chopped
8 small potatoes, peeled and thinly
    sliced
8 cups chicken stock

12 whole, peeled papas criollas, if
    available (otherwise 6 new
    potatoes halved)
Salt, fresh ground pepper
2 ears corn, each cut into 3 slices
3 tablespoons capers
1 cup heavy cream

Heat the butter in a heavy casserole and sauté the chicken pieces with the onions until the chicken is golden on both sides. Add the thinly sliced potatoes and the stock, cover, and cook over very low heat until the chicken is about half done and the potatoes are beginning to disintegrate, about 25 minutes. Add the 6 halved new potatoes and continue cooking until both chicken and potatoes are tender. With a slotted spoon, remove the chicken pieces and potatoes from the casserole and keep warm. Work the stock through a sieve. It will have been thickened by the sliced potatoes. Return the stock to the casserole, season to taste with salt and pepper, add the chicken and potatoes, the corn and capers, and simmer for 5 minutes longer. Add the cream and continue cooking just long enough to heat it through. Serve in deep soup plates with *Ají de Huevo* (Avocado Sauce) on the side.

Carapulcra   PERU
Chicken, Pork, and Potatoes in Peanut Sauce

When I decided to test *carapulcra* in New York, having enjoyed it in Peru, I was told I could regard one of its ingredients, *chuño* or *papaseca* (freeze-dried potato) as optional, to be replaced with fresh potatoes, since I couldn't buy the commercially packaged article here. I decided that what the Inca women could do I could do. When the Inca, who were the first people to cultivate the potato back in 2500 B.C., faced crop storage problems, they invented freeze-drying, and there is every reason to believe that they were the first people to do so. Raw, unpeeled potatoes were put outside their houses at night in the icy cold of the Andean highlands, where they froze solid. In the morning they thawed in the sun and the water was trampled out of them by Inca women, and the process repeated until they were thoroughly dry.

The sixteenth floor of a New York high-rise is not to be compared with the Andes, whose soaring peaks topple the imagination, so I put my potatoes, 3 large Idahos, in the freezer overnight. In the morning, since I have a small terrace with a southern exposure, I put them in the sun to thaw. One cannot trample the water out of 3 potatoes — it takes a whole crop to make that possible — so I squeezed the water out of my potatoes by hand. At the end of three days they were like stone, strange skinny objects. The flesh had turned quite dark, almost black. I kept one for two years before I used it, just to see, and it was as good as ever. The others I used in this *carapulcra*. I had a lot of fun making *chuño*, but I can honestly say my Peruvian friends were right when they said it was all right to substitute fresh potatoes for it.

Serves 6

2 freeze-dried Idaho potatoes, or 2 fresh potatoes
A 2½-pound chicken, cut into serving pieces
1 pound boneless loin of pork, cut into ¾-inch cubes
2 cups chicken stock, about
4 tablespoons lard or vegetable oil
1 large onion, finely chopped
4 cloves garlic, minced
½ teaspoon Spanish (hot) paprika or cayenne

⅛ teaspoon ground cumin
Salt, freshly ground pepper
½ cup roasted peanuts, finely ground
6 small potatoes, freshly cooked
3 hardboiled eggs, sliced
20 medium-sized pitted black or green olives

Put the dried potatoes on to soak in warm water to cover for about 2 hours. If using the fresh potatoes instead of the dried ones, add them to the stew, peeled and diced at the same time the dried potatoes would be added. When the dried potatoes have been soaked, drain them, and chop coarsely. Set aside.

Put the chicken and pork pieces into a saucepan and add enough chicken stock to cover. Cover and simmer until tender. Drain and set the stock aside. Bone the chicken and cut the meat into cubes about the same size as the pork. Set aside with a little stock to moisten the meats.

Rinse out and dry the saucepan or use a flameproof casserole, and heat the lard or oil in it. Add the onion, garlic, hot paprika or cayenne, and cumin, and sauté until the onion is soft. Add the potato and about a cup of the reserved stock, cover, and simmer gently until the potato has disintegrated, thickening the mixture, about 1 hour. Season to taste with salt and pepper and stir in the ground peanuts. Cook for a minute or two, then add the chicken and pork pieces. The sauce should be thick, but add a little more stock if necessary. Simmer just long enough to heat through and blend the flavors.

Arrange the chicken and pork mixture on a heated serving platter and garnish it with the fresh, hot potatoes, the hardboiled egg slices, and olives.

Pollo Borracho
Drunken Chicken

ARGENTINA

This is a typical *criollo* dish and with slight variations occurs all over Latin America.

Serves 4

1 tablespoon butter
½ pound boiled ham, cut into
    strips about 2 inches by ¼
    inch
A 3½-pound chicken, cut into 4
    serving pieces
Salt, freshly ground pepper
¼ teaspoon ground cumin
¼ teaspoon ground coriander

¼ cup white wine vinegar
2 cups dry white wine
1 cup chicken stock, about
3 cloves garlic, minced
12 medium pimiento-stuffed
    olives
3 tablespoons capers

Melt the butter in a flameproof casserole. Make a layer of one-third of the ham. Season the chicken pieces with the salt, pepper, cumin, and coriander, and add the chicken legs to the casserole with another third of the ham on top. Arrange the chicken breasts over the ham and sprinkle with the remaining ham strips. Pour in the vinegar, wine, and enough chicken stock to cover. Add the garlic, cover, and simmer over low heat for 45 minutes, or until the chicken is tender. Rinse the olives and soak them for 15 minutes in cold water. Drain. Rinse and drain the capers. Place the chicken pieces and ham strips in a serving dish and keep warm. Measure the liquid in the casserole and reduce it, over brisk heat, to 2 cups. Moisten the chicken with a little of the liquid and serve the rest in a gravy boat. Garnish the chicken with the olives and capers.

If liked, the sauce may be lightly thickened. Mix 1 tablespoon flour with 1 tablespoon butter, stir into the liquid, and simmer over low heat, stirring constantly, until the sauce is thickened. Serve with plain boiled potatoes or white rice and a green vegetable or salad.

Pollo en Pepián Dulce   GUATEMALA
Mayan Chicken Fricassee

Because Guatemala was the heart of the Mayan empire, with its capital city of Tikal, the kitchen of post-Columbian Guatemala is close to that of Yucatán in Mexico. This dish unites a medley of flavors, which the chicken absorbs during cooking. They blend harmoniously in the sauce, which is as thick as heavy cream and delicious with plain rice.

Serves 6

A 3½- to 4-pound chicken, cut into serving pieces
2 cups chicken stock, about
1 tablespoon sesame seeds
½ cup pepitas (Mexican pumpkin seeds)
3 red bell peppers, seeded and coarsely chopped, or 5 canned pimientos, chopped
3 medium tomatoes, peeled and coarsely chopped

1 medium onion, chopped
2 cloves garlic, chopped
2 tablespoons lard or vegetable oil
¼ cup Seville (bitter) orange juice, or use two-thirds orange juice and one-third lime juice
½ teaspoon ground allspice
Salt, freshly ground pepper
¼ cup seedless raisins
Butter
¼ cup chopped almonds

Put the chicken pieces into a heavy casserole, pour in the stock, adding a little more to cover, if necessary. Cover and simmer until almost tender, about 30 minutes. In a blender or food processor grind the sesame and pumpkin seeds as fine as possible and shake through a sieve. Set aside. Put the peppers, tomatoes, onion, and garlic into a blender or food processor and reduce to a coarse purée. Mix the purée with the ground sesame and pumpkin seeds. Heat the lard or vegetable oil in a skillet, add the purée, and cook, over moderate heat, stirring constantly with a wooden spoon, for 5 minutes. Drain the chicken, reserve the stock, and return the chicken to the casserole. Add to the purée 1 cup of the stock, the Seville (bitter) orange juice, allspice, and salt and pepper to taste. Stir to mix, and pour over the chicken. Cover and simmer gently until the chicken is tender, about 15 minutes. Add a little more stock if necessary. The sauce should be thick. Soak the raisins in cold water to cover for 15 minutes. Drain thoroughly. Heat a little butter in a skillet and sauté the almonds until they are golden. Drain. Transfer the chicken and sauce to a warmed serving dish and sprinkle with the raisins and almonds. Serve with rice.

Pollo Verde Almendrado
MEXICO
Chicken in Green Almond Sauce

I find all the Mexican green chicken dishes delicious; this one is enchanting, not only for its very subtle flavor but because the green sauce is downright pretty to look at.

Serves 6

A 3½-pound chicken, cut into
   serving pieces
2 cups chicken stock
1 medium onion, chopped
1 clove garlic, chopped
1 cup parsley sprigs, coarsely
   chopped
1 cup coriander (cilantro) sprigs,
   coarsely chopped
1 heart of romaine lettuce,
   coarsely chopped

1 or 2 fresh hot green peppers,
   seeded and chopped, or 2
   canned jalapeño or 3 canned
   serrano chilies, seeded and
   chopped
4 ounces ground almonds, about
   ¾ cup
3 tablespoons vegetable oil or lard
Salt

Put the chicken pieces into a heavy casserole with the stock, bring to a boil, reduce the heat, and simmer gently, covered, for 45 minutes, or until tender. Lift the chicken out onto a platter and set aside. Pour the stock into a jug. Rinse out and dry the casserole.

In a blender or food processor combine the onion, garlic, parsley, coriander, lettuce, hot peppers, and almonds, and reduce to a coarse purée. Do not overblend as the finished sauce should have some texture, not be entirely smooth. Heat the oil or lard in a large, heavy skillet and pour in the purée, which will be almost pastelike because of the almonds. Cook the mixture, stirring constantly with a wooden spoon, for 3 to 4 minutes over moderate heat. Transfer it to a casserole. Stir in 2 cups of the stock, season to taste with salt. Add the chicken pieces, cover, and simmer just long enough to heat the chicken through.

Arroz Blanco (White Rice) is good with this. For a completely Mexican meal, serve the chicken with the rice and with tortillas, *Frijoles* (Beans), and *Guacamole* (Avocado Sauce).

Pollo en Pipián de Almendra　　MEXICO
Chicken Stew with Almonds

Pipián is one of the best dishes in the Mexican kitchen and one of the hardest to define. The dictionary of the Spanish Royal Academy says it is an American stew made of meat, chicken, turkey, or other fowl with salt pork and ground almonds. Other dictionaries describe it as a kind of Indian fricassee. The *Nuevo Cocinero Méjicano*, a dictionary published in Paris in 1888, gives a more complete description. It says that *pipián* is a Mexican stew made with red or green peppers, pumpkin seeds, almonds, or oily seeds such as sesame or peanuts. The stew may be made with turkey, chicken, duck, or indeed any bird, as well as with meats or fish and shellfish. There are even vegetarian versions using fruits and vegetables. It should not be salted until the moment of serving, as salt is said to make the sauce separate.

Serves 4

A 3-pound chicken, cut into serving pieces	*½ cup (4 ounces) almonds, blanched*
2 or 3 scallions	*2 tablespoons lard or vegetable oil*
2 or 3 large sprigs fresh coriander (cilantro)	*⅛ teaspoon ground cloves*
1 carrot, scraped and halved	*¼ teaspoon ground cinnamon*
2 cups chicken stock, about	*¼ teaspoon oregano*
6 ancho *chilies*	*Salt*

Put the chicken pieces into a large, heavy casserole or saucepan with the scallions, coriander, and carrot. Pour in the chicken stock, adding a little more if necessary to cover. Bring to a boil, reduce the heat, and simmer, covered, for 45 minutes, or until the chicken is tender. Lift the chicken pieces out of the stock. Strain and reserve the stock, discarding the solids. Rinse out the casserole and put the chicken pieces back in it. Shake the seeds out of the chilies and rinse them. Tear them in pieces and put them to soak for 1 hour in about ½ cup hot water, turning them from time to time. If they absorb all the water, add a little more. Reduce the chilies to a paste in a blender or food processor, using a little of the soaking water. Put them into a bowl. Toast the almonds in a skillet and pulverize them in a nut grinder, blender, or food processor, shake them through a sieve, and add to the chilies, mixing thoroughly. Heat the lard or oil in a skillet, add the chili and almond mixture, and sauté, stirring constantly with a wooden spoon, for 4 or 5 minutes over moderate heat. Thin with about 2 cups of the reserved chicken stock to make a medium-thick sauce. Stir in the cloves, cinnamon, and oregano, and pour over the chicken pieces in the casserole. Cook at a bare simmer over very low heat for 15 minutes, or until the chicken is heated through and the flavors have blended. Season to taste with salt. Serve with rice, beans, tortillas, *guacamole* or other salad, and a green vegetable, if liked.

Despite the solemn warnings in ancient cookbooks and from experienced Mexican cooks, I must confess I have never found that salting the sauce earlier makes it separate, so I leave this question open.

Some cooks reserve the seeds of the *ancho* chilies, toast them, and grind them with the almonds. I have not found this a good idea. The seeds seem to coarsen the sauce and blur the delicate flavor of the almonds. Also more stock has to be added, making too much sauce.

Pollo en Salsa de Almendra
MEXICO

Chicken in Almond Sauce

Serves 4

4 tablespoons (¼ cup) butter
A 3- to 3½-pound chicken, cut
    into serving pieces
3 cups chicken stock, about
1 medium onion, finely chopped
1 fresh hot red or green pepper,
    seeded and finely chopped, or
    1 canned serrano or jalapeño
    chili, rinsed

½ cup toasted almonds, finely
    ground
2 hardboiled eggs, chopped
1 cup freshly made breadcrumbs
Salt, freshly ground pepper

Heat the butter in a large skillet and sauté the chicken pieces until lightly golden all over. Transfer the chicken to a heatproof casserole, add enough chicken stock to cover, bring to a boil, lower the heat, cover, and simmer gently until the chicken is tender, about 45 minutes. Lift out the chicken pieces and keep warm. Pour the stock into a container and set it aside. Rinse out and dry the casserole.

In the fat remaining in the skillet sauté the onion with the hot pepper until the onion is soft. Add the almonds, eggs, breadcrumbs, and salt and pepper to taste, and sauté for a minute or two longer. Stir in 2 cups of the reserved chicken stock, pour the mixture into a blender or food processor, and reduce it to a purée. Do not overblend. The sauce should have some texture. Return the chicken pieces to the casserole and pour the sauce over them. Simmer just long enough to heat the chicken through. Serve with rice.

Pollo Pibil
Chicken, Yucatán Style

MEXICO

This is an old dish from the distant past. It would have been wrapped in banana leaves and cooked in a *pib*, an earth oven, one of the earliest methods of cooking. A modern oven does well but not as well as the *pib*. Sometimes one still gets a chance to have *pollo pibil* cooked in the traditional way and it is a grand experience.

Serves 4

12 peppercorns
½ teaspoon oregano
¼ teaspoon cumin seeds
2 teaspoons achiote (annatto)
    seeds
1 teaspoon salt
4 large cloves garlic

1 cup Seville (bitter) orange juice,
    or use two-thirds orange juice
    and one-third lime juice
A 3½- to 4-pound chicken,
    quartered
Banana leaves (or kitchen
    parchment or aluminum foil)

Using mortar and pestle, a blender, or a food processor, grind together the peppercorns, oregano, cumin, achiote seeds, salt, and garlic. Transfer the mixture to a large bowl and mix thoroughly with the orange juice. Add the chicken pieces, mixing well to coat them with the marinade. Cover and refrigerate for 24 hours, turning two or three times.

Wrap each piece of chicken in a square of banana leaf, kitchen parchment, or aluminum foil, about 12 inches by 12 inches, dividing the marinade equally among the pieces. Arrange the packages in a casserole, cover, and bake in a preheated moderate (325° F.) oven for about 2 hours, or until the chicken is very tender. Serve with hot tortillas.

Pollo Ticuleño
Chicken, Ticul Style

This is a favorite Mayan dish from Yucatán. The delicate chicken breast makes a fine contrast to the robust flavor of black beans and tortilla, all enhanced by the very pure flavor of the tomato sauce. Put the beans on to cook about 3 hours ahead of time, so they will be ready when needed. The dish really needs no accompaniment other than the garnishes and, for lovers of the *picante*, *Ixni-Pec*, the hot pepper sauce from Yucatán (page 312).

Serves 4

FOR THE TOMATO SAUCE
3 *medium tomatoes*
1 *small onion*

Salt, freshly ground pepper

FOR THE CHICKEN
8 *tablespoons (½ cup) butter*
2 *whole chicken breasts, boned and halved*
Flour
1 *egg, lightly beaten*
2 *cups breadcrumbs, about*

4 *tortillas, fried crisp in vegetable oil*
1 *cup black beans cooked as for* Panuchos *(see page 47)*
4 *tablespoons freshly grated Parmesan cheese, about*

FOR THE GARNISH
1 *onion prepared as for* Panuchos *(see page 47), but thinly sliced instead of chopped*
1 *cup cooked green peas*
2 *ripe plantains, halved crosswise, then lengthwise, and fried until golden brown in vegetable oil*

8 *to 12 radish flowers*
1 *or 2 medium tomatoes, sliced (optional)*

To make the tomato sauce, peel and chop 3 medium tomatoes and add to a blender or food processor with 1 small onion, chopped. Reduce to a purée. Pour the mixture into a small saucepan and simmer, uncovered, over very low heat for 15 minutes, or until thick and well blended. Season with salt and freshly ground pepper to taste.

Chop the butter coarsely and put it into a small, heavy saucepan. Melt the butter over very low heat. Skim off the foam that rises to the top and carefully pour the butter into a heavy skillet, discarding the milky sediment. Roll the chicken breasts in flour, dip in the egg, then in breadcrumbs. Heat the clarified butter and sauté the breasts for about 4 minutes on each side, taking care not to overcook them. Spread the tortillas with the beans, place the chicken breasts on top of the tortillas, pour a little tomato sauce over them, and sprinkle with the grated cheese. Place 1 tortilla on each of four warmed serving plates and garnish with the onion, peas, plantains, radishes, and, if liked, sliced tomatoes.

Xinxim de Galinha   BRAZIL
Chicken with Shrimp and Peanut Sauce

This is a Bahian dish, as the use of *dendê* (palm) oil indicates. The mixture of flavors is unusual and exciting, but not difficult for the unaccustomed palate to accept.

Serves 6

A 3-pound chicken, cut into
  serving pieces
4 tablespoons lime or lemon juice
2 cloves garlic, crushed
Salt
2 tablespoons olive oil
1 medium onion, grated

1 cup dried shrimp, finely ground
½ cup dry roasted peanuts,
  ground
1 fresh hot red pepper, seeded and
  chopped (optional)
½ cup chicken stock, about
¼ cup dendè (palm) oil

Season the chicken with the lime or lemon juice, the garlic, and salt to taste. Set aside.

In a heavy saucepan heat the oil and sauté the onion, dried shrimp, peanuts, and hot pepper for 5 minutes, stirring from time to time. Add the chicken pieces and their liquid, and cook for a few minutes, turning the pieces once. Add the chicken stock, cover, and simmer gently until the chicken is tender, about 30 minutes, turning once during the cooking and adding a little more stock if necessary. When the chicken is tender, taste for seasoning, pour in the *dendê* (palm) oil, and cook for a minute or two longer. The sauce should be thick and not very abundant. Serve with white rice and *Farofa de Azeite de Dendê* (Cassava Meal with Palm Oil).

Vatapá de Galinha

BRAZIL

Chicken in Shrimp and Almond Sauce

Vatapá is one of the great dishes of the Bahian kitchen of Brazil, but it does take quite a lot of work. It is an exciting dish for guests and I find their pleasure in this truly exotic food makes it well worth the effort. The coconut milk can be made ahead of time and tedious jobs like grinding the dried shrimp are made easy with the help of a food processor. I so well remember the first time I had *vatapá* in Salvador, Bahia. It was a revelation, with so many unfamiliar and delicious flavors to beguile the palate.

Serves 6 to 8

3 tablespoons olive oil
2 medium onions, finely chopped
4 scallions, chopped, using white
    and green parts
2 large cloves garlic, chopped
4 medium tomatoes, peeled,
    seeded, and chopped
1 or 2 fresh hot peppers, seeded
    and chopped
Salt, freshly ground pepper
3 tablespoons lime or lemon juice
4 tablespoons fresh coriander
    (cilantro), or use flat-leafed
    Italian parsley

Two 2½-pound chickens,
    quartered
Chicken stock, if necessary
1¾ cups finely ground almonds
2 cups dried shrimp, finely ground
3 cups thin coconut milk (see
    page 7)
1 cup thick coconut milk (see
    page 7)
1 tablespoon rice flour
4 tablespoons dendê (palm) oil

In a large skillet heat the oil and sauté the onions, scallions, garlic, to-matoes, and hot peppers for 5 minutes. Season the mixture to taste with salt and pepper and stir in the lime or lemon juice and the coriander or parsley. Add the quartered chickens, cover, and cook until the chickens are tender, 30 to 35 minutes. Add a little chicken stock to the skillet if the mixture seems too dry. With a slotted spoon, transfer the chickens to a dish and let them cool. Skin and bone the chickens and chop the meat coarsely. Put the vegetable mixture through a sieve, pressing down hard on the vegetables to extract all the liquid. Discard the solids and reserve the liquid.

In a saucepan combine the almonds, ground shrimp, the thin coconut milk, and the reserved liquid from cooking the chicken. Bring to a boil and simmer for 15 minutes. Add the thick coconut milk and the rice flour mixed with a little water, and cook, uncovered, stirring frequently, until the mixture has the consistency of a thick béchamel. Add the chicken pieces and the *dendê* (palm) oil. Cook just long enough to heat through, about 5 minutes. Serve with *Pirão de Arroz* (Rice Flour Pudding).

Variation: To make *Vatapá de Camarão* (Shrimp and Fish in a Shrimp and Almond Sauce), in place of the chicken, substitute 1 pound raw shrimp, shelled and deveined, and 3 pounds fillets of any firm white fish, cut into 2-inch pieces. Add 1 tablespoon of finely chopped fresh ginger to the onion and tomato mixture, and cook the fish for 10 minutes, the shrimp only until they turn pink and lose their translucent look, about 3 minutes.

Pollo en Salsa de Huevos   ECUADOR
Chicken in Egg Sauce

Ecuador was once part of the great Inca empire, which had its center in Cuzco, Peru, and dominated the whole Andean region, stretching as far as northern Chile. Even today the dominant language of the Inca empire, Quechua, is still spoken in both countries. Coastal Ecuador was not gathered into the Inca fold, and with its vastly different climate and vegetation has a distinct regional kitchen, whose notable feature is the use of plantains, especially the *verde* (green, or unripe) plantain. The secret of the cooking lies in combining foods not usually put together, pork stuffed with shrimps, for example, or Seville (bitter) orange used for the *seviches* (marinated fish). Dry mustard is used interestingly in the chicken dishes — sautéed with chopped onion first so that it adds an elusive flavor to the finished dish. Elsewhere ground walnuts make a wonderfully rich sauce for chicken, with that hint of bitterness and sweetness peculiar to walnuts. Wine, vinegar, both orange and lemon juice, eggs, sweet red peppers, and nuts are all used one way or another with chicken, making for a very versatile yet simple cuisine, requiring no elaborate techniques.

Serves 4 to 6

4 tablespoons (¼ cup) butter or vegetable oil	1 clove garlic, minced
A 3½- to 4-pound chicken, cut into serving pieces	1 tablespoon dry mustard
	Salt, freshly ground pepper
1 large onion, finely chopped	2 cups chicken stock, about
	6 hardboiled eggs, finely chopped

Heat the butter in a skillet and sauté the chicken pieces until golden on both sides. Transfer them to a casserole. In the butter remaining in the skillet sauté the onion and garlic with the mustard, stirring to mix. When the onion is soft, transfer the contents of the skillet to a flameproof casserole. Season with salt and pepper to taste and pour in the stock, adding a little more barely to cover the chicken, if necessary. Cover and simmer until the chicken is tender, about 45 minutes. Transfer the chicken to a warmed serving platter and keep warm. Over brisk heat reduce the sauce until it is of medium thickness. Taste the sauce for seasoning and add a little salt and pepper if necessary. Stir in the eggs and cook just long enough to heat through. Pour the sauce over the chicken and serve, or serve the sauce separately in a sauceboat. Accompany with rice or potatoes, mixed vegetable salad, or a green vegetable.

Variation: For *Pollo en Salsa de Nuez* (Chicken in Nut Sauce), omit the hardboiled eggs and add 1½ cups ground walnuts to the sauce.

Variation: For *Pollo con Aceitunas* (Chicken with Olives), use 1 cup red wine in place of 1 cup of the stock, and omit the mustard. Instead of the hardboiled eggs, add 1½ cups sliced, green, pimiento-stuffed olives to the sauce. Rinse the olives in warm water before slicing.

Variation: For *Pollo a la Criolla* (Chicken, Creole Style), omit the mustard and the hardboiled eggs, adding with the stock, ½ cup oil, 2 tablespoons vinegar, and 1 bay leaf. Serve with fried potatoes.

Variation: For *Pollo con Pimientos* (Chicken with Sweet Red Peppers), omit the hardboiled eggs. Use 1 cup stock and 1 cup dry red wine. Increase the dry mustard to 2 tablespoons and add to the sauce one 8-ounce can of pimientos, drained and puréed in a blender. Simmer the sauce for a few minutes longer, and if necessary add enough fresh breadcrumbs to make it of medium consistency. It should not be thin.

Variation: For *Pollo al Limón* (Chicken with Lemon), omit the hardboiled eggs. Reduce the chicken stock to 1½ cups and add ½ cup fresh lemon juice. Traditionally the sauce is thickened by adding 1 cup fresh breadcrumbs and stirring over moderate heat until the sauce is smooth and thick. I prefer to reduce the sauce over brisk heat, or to thicken it with 1 tablespoon flour mixed with 1 tablespoon of butter. The flavor is not changed, it is simply a matter of texture.

Variation: For *Pollo en Salsa de Almendras* (Chicken in Almond Sauce), omit the mustard and reduce the hardboiled eggs to 3. When the chicken is cooked, transfer it to a platter and keep it warm. Reduce the stock to 1½ cups over brisk heat. Pulverize ¾ cup blanched almonds in a blender, add the eggs and stock, and reduce to a smooth purée. Heat the sauce, spoon a little over the chicken, and serve the rest separately. A deceptively simple dish. The eggs and almonds give the sauce a very subtle flavor.

Variation: For *Pollo en Jugo de Naranja* (Chicken in Orange Juice), omit the hardboiled eggs. Omit the mustard and use 1 tablespoon sweet paprika instead. In place of 2 cups chicken stock, use 1 cup stock and 1 cup orange juice. Add 6 ounces coarsely chopped boiled ham to the chicken in the casserole. Before serving, reduce the sauce over brisk heat to medium thick.

Variation: For *Pollo al Jerez* (Chicken with Sherry), omit the hardboiled eggs. Reduce the amount of dry mustard to 1 teaspoon, and instead of 2 cups chicken stock, use 1 cup stock, 1 cup dry sherry. Thicken the sauce with 1 cup of breadcrumbs, or reduce it over brisk heat.

Variation: For *Pollo con Queso* (Chicken with Cheese), omit the hardboiled eggs. When adding the stock to the casserole, add 1 bay leaf and ½ teaspoon each thyme and oregano. When the chicken is done, lift it out onto an ovenproof serving dish and sprinkle it generously with grated Parmesan cheese, about ½ cup, and dot with 2 tablespoons butter. Put it into a preheated moderate (350° F.) oven until the cheese is golden brown. Strain the sauce and reduce it to half over brisk heat. Serve in a gravy boat.

In Ecuador a fresh, or bottled, hot pepper sauce would be on the table to be taken with any of these dishes according to individual taste.

Pollo con Arroz   PARAGUAY
Chicken with Rice

It would be impossible to have a book of Latin American food without including recipes for *Arroz con Pollo*, a perennial favorite, almost always translated as Chicken with Rice though literally it is Rice with Chicken. This simplest of dishes is also somewhat of a paradox. Its ingredients are not, for the most part, native to Spain, and the dish there is sometimes called *Arroz a la Valenciana* (Rice, Valencia Style). It is also often thought of as a cousin of *paella*, Spain's famous rice, chicken, and shellfish dish. The dish is quintessentially international, for the chickens originally came from India, the saffron arrived with Phoenician traders, the Arabs brought the rice from Asia, and the tomatoes and peppers are the gift of Mexico. It is tremendously popular in the Spanish-speaking Caribbean and in Mexico, as well as in South America, and differs a little from country to country not only in ingredients and technique but in the name as well. One of my favorites, in which the name is reversed to *Pollo con Arroz* (Chicken with Rice), is perhaps the simplest of all the versions I've encountered.

Serves 4 to 6

2 tablespoons oil, preferably olive
   oil
A 3- to 3½-pound chicken, cut
   into serving pieces
1 medium onion, finely chopped
1 green or red bell pepper, seeded
   and chopped

3 tomatoes, peeled and chopped
Salt, freshly ground pepper
4 cups chicken stock or water
⅛ teaspoon saffron
2 cups long-grain rice

Heat the oil in a heavy skillet and sauté the chicken pieces until they are golden on both sides. Transfer the chicken to an earthenware or enameled iron casserole. In the oil remaining in the skillet sauté the onion and pepper until they are soft. Add to the casserole with the tomatoes, salt and pepper to taste, 2 cups of the chicken stock or water, and the saffron, crumbled. Simmer, covered, over low heat for 30 minutes.

Lift out the chicken pieces onto a dish or plate and set aside. Pour the liquid through a sieve, reserving the solids. Measure the liquid and make the quantity up to 4 cups with the rest of the chicken stock. Pour it into the casserole, add the rice and the reserved solids, stir to mix, and bring to a boil over fairly brisk heat. Arrange the chicken pieces on top of the rice, cover, and cook over very low heat until the rice is tender and all the liquid absorbed, about 20 minutes. Serve directly from the casserole. If liked, artichoke hearts, about 12, may be scattered through the chicken.

Variation: Venezuela has an interesting version of this dish. It is a little more elaborate and has raisins, olives, and capers mixed with the rice. In a blender purée 4 medium tomatoes, skinned and chopped, 2 medium onions, chopped, 1 green and 1 red bell pepper, seeded and chopped, 2 leeks, well washed and chopped, and 1 clove garlic. Season the mixture with salt and freshly ground pepper and pour it over a 3- to 3½-pound chicken, cut into serving pieces, in a flameproof casserole. Add ½ cup dry white wine and a little chicken stock to cover, if necessary, and simmer, covered, for 30 minutes. Lift out the chicken pieces onto a plate or dish, and measure the liquid. Make up the quantity to 4 cups, if more liquid is needed, with chicken stock. Rinse out and dry the casserole. Heat 4 tablespoons (¼ cup) butter in the casserole and stir in the rice. Stir constantly with a wooden spoon over moderate heat, taking care not to let the rice burn. Pour the chicken stock mixture over the rice. Add ½ cup seedless raisins, 12 pimiento-stuffed green olives, halved, and 2 tablespoons capers, and stir to mix. Bring to a simmer. Arrange the chicken pieces on top of the rice, cover, and cook over low heat until the rice is tender and the liquid absorbed, about 20 minutes. Serves 4 to 6.

Variation: Coastal Colombia uses annatto (achiote) in its version of *Arroz con Pollo*; interesting, since this was a favorite seasoning of the Maya, the Caribs, and the Arawaks as well as the Colombian coastal people of pre-Conquest times. It is still popular in Yucatán, coastal Colombia, and the Caribbean today. Put 2 tablespoons of *aceite de achiote* (annatto oil), see page 324, in a heavy casserole, and add a 3- to 3½-pound chicken, cut into serving pieces, 4 medium tomatoes, peeled and chopped, 2 medium onions, finely chopped, 1 large carrot, scraped and chopped, 2 stalks celery, chopped, 3 or 4 scallions, trimmed, 1 fresh hot pepper, seeded and chopped (optional), 1 bay leaf, ⅛ teaspoon ground cumin, 2 cloves, 1 tablespoon vinegar, and salt and pepper to taste. Cover and simmer over low heat for about 30 minutes, or until the chicken is barely tender. If more liquid is needed, add a little chicken stock. Lift out the chicken pieces onto a plate or dish. Remove and discard the scallions, bay leaf, and cloves. Strain the liquid and reserve the solids. Make up the quantity of liquid to 4 cups. Pour the liquid into the casserole, add 2 cups long-grain rice and the reserved vegetables, stir to mix, and bring to a boil. Arrange the chicken pieces on top of the rice, cover, and cook over low heat until the rice is tender and all the liquid absorbed, about 20 minutes. Serves 4 to 6.

Variation: The Dominican Republic has its own, very attractive *Arroz con Pollo*. In this version the chicken is marinated in a mixture containing hot pepper, and the marinade later mixed with the rice. Put a 2- to 2½-pound chicken, cut into serving pieces, into a bowl with 2 cloves garlic, crushed, 1 medium onion, finely chopped, 1 tablespoon parsley, chopped, 1 bay leaf, crumbled, 1 fresh hot red or green pepper, seeded and finely chopped, salt and freshly ground pepper to taste, and 2 tablespoons vinegar, and let it stand for about an hour. Some cooks like to add 2 ounces cubed boiled ham to the chicken. Lift the chicken pieces out of the marinade and pat them dry with paper towels. Reserve the marinade. Heat 4 tablespoons vegetable oil or lard in a heavy casserole and fry the chicken pieces until they are golden on both sides. Add the reserved marinade and cook for a minute or two. Add 2 cups rice and stir into the oil and vegetable mixture. Cook for 2 or 3 minutes. Pour in 4 cups chicken stock or water mixed with 2 tablespoons tomato purée and bring to a boil over fairly high heat. Cover and cook over low heat until the chicken and rice are both tender and all the liquid absorbed, about 30 minutes. Add ½ cup pimiento-stuffed green olives, sliced, 1 tablespoon capers, ½ cup cooked green peas or cut green beans, and 1 or 2 pimientos, cut into strips. Cook just long enough to heat through and serve from the casserole. Serves 4.

Variation: From Mexico I have a family recipe for *Arroz con Pollo* given me by my husband's maternal grandmother, Doña Carmen Sarabia de Tinoco.

She was a fabulous cook and when she made *tamales del norte* (tamales, northern style) for a party, all the world scrambled for an invitation. I think it is a dreadful pity that grandmothers are usually so much older than their granddaughters-in-law. I could have learned so much more from a very wonderful teacher. Her recipe is interesting for having both saffron and hot peppers.

For Mexican chicken with rice, season a 3- to 3½-pound chicken, cut into serving pieces, with salt and pepper. Heat 3 tablespoons olive oil in a skillet and sauté the chicken pieces until they are golden on both sides. Put the chicken pieces into an earthenware casserole heavy enough to go on direct heat, or any heavy casserole. In the oil remaining in the skillet sauté 1 medium onion, finely chopped, and 2 cloves garlic, chopped, until the onion is soft. Add to the chicken. Add 4 medium tomatoes, peeled and chopped, 1 or 2 canned *jalapeño* chilies, seeded and chopped, ¼ teaspoon ground cumin, and ⅛ teaspoon saffron, crumbled. Pour in 3 cups chicken stock or water, or enough to cover the chicken. Bring to a boil, reduce the heat to low, cover, and simmer gently for 30 minutes. Lift out and set aside the chicken pieces and measure the stock. Make up the quantity to 4 cups. In the oil remaining in the skillet sauté 2 cups rice until the rice grains are well coated. Do not let the rice brown. Add the rice to the casserole, pour in the stock, and stir to mix. Bring to a boil, add the chicken pieces, reduce the heat, cover, and cook over very low heat until the rice is tender and all the liquid absorbed. Garnish with 2 pimientos, cut into strips. Serve directly from the casserole.

Two ounces of dry sherry may, with advantage, be poured over the chicken and rice at the end of the cooking and the dish cooked for a minute or two longer. The *jalapeño* chilies may be left out, if preferred. Serves 4 to 6.

Pollo Escabechado
Pickled Chicken

CHILE

In this recipe the chicken literally stews in the oil, which is poured or spooned off the sauce at the end of the cooking time. It makes for a very delicate, moist, and tender bird. Though the name of the dish translates as pickled chicken, the small amount of vinegar used leaves just a pleasant echo on the palate. Since the chicken is served cold, it is done ahead of time, which makes it perfect for a family meal in summer. It is an attractive dish in its pale, translucent jelly, lovely for a cold buffet accompanied by salads such as *Ensalada de Aguacate* (Avocado Salad), *Ensalada de Habas* (Fresh Broad Bean Salad), or *Ensalada de Verduras* (Vegetable Salad).

Serves 6 to 8

A 4-pound roasting chicken, cut
   into serving pieces
1 cup vegetable oil
½ cup white wine vinegar
1 teaspoon salt

6 peppercorns
1 bay leaf
2 medium onions, thinly sliced
2 carrots, scraped and thinly
   sliced

Place all the ingredients in a large kettle or heavy casserole, cover, and cook over very low heat until the chicken is tender, about 1½ hours. Allow to cool. Place the chicken pieces on a serving platter with the vegetables arranged around them. Remove and discard the peppercorns and bay leaf. Pour the liquid in the casserole into a bowl, then spoon off all the oil (it is easier to do it this way). Save the oil, incidentally, for sautéing other meats and poultry. Pour the stock over the chicken pieces and refrigerate. The liquid will set into an aspic. If a firmer jelly is preferred, add to the stock ½ tablespoon unflavored gelatin softened in water and stir to dissolve, over low heat, before pouring it over the chicken. In very hot weather I find this is sometimes necessary. If any oil escapes being spooned off, it will separate out when the jelly sets. Just tip the dish and pour it off, or remove it with a piece of blotting paper or paper towel.

To serve, decorate a platter with lettuce leaves, sliced tomatoes, cooked green peas and beans, and sliced pimiento or other suitable vegetables such as artichoke hearts.

Variation: *Pollo a la Paisana* (Country Chicken), also from Chile, can, I suppose, be considered a variation of *Pollo Escabechado* (Pickled Chicken) though it is served hot not cold and is a much simpler dish. It is in fact simplicity itself and is most useful when one is both busy and hungry for delectable food. The chicken emerges from the pot wonderfully moist and tender and with a subtle flavor that the cook can vary by the use of different vinegars. Tarragon vinegar and Japanese rice vinegar both spring to mind and I have used them with great success, though I doubt whether Japanese rice vinegar is a commonplace in Chile. I claim cook's privileges for this departure from strict tradition.

For *Pollo a la Paisana* (Country Chicken), cut a 3½- to 4-pound chicken into serving pieces and put it into a heavy earthenware or enameled cast iron casserole with 4 scallions, cut into 1-inch pieces and using both white and green parts, 4 cloves garlic, left whole, salt and freshly ground black pepper to taste, 1 or 2 sprigs parsley, 6 tablespoons olive oil, and 2 tablespoons vinegar. Cover and cook over very low heat until the chicken is tender, 45 minutes to 1 hour. Serve with either shoestring potatoes or French fries and a lettuce or watercress salad or a green vegetable. Serves 4 to 6.

TURKEY

Pavo Relleno
Stuffed Turkey

MEXICO

Until recently when industrialization brought gas and electric stoves into the kitchens of Mexico to replace the charcoal stoves of the past, there was very little oven cooking done, except for the baking of breads and cakes. This roast turkey with its hearty meat stuffing is an exception. I was a little taken aback the first time I encountered it; it seemed such a double richness, meat and bird. But I very soon adopted it with enthusiasm, for it is delicious. In Mexico the bird would be served with a garnish of chopped lettuce, sliced tomatoes, and avocado, in oil and vinegar dressing, and olives and radish roses, but I prefer these garnishes served separately as a salad.

Serves 6 to 8

½ recipe Picadillo *(Seasoned Chopped Beef), page 131*
A 6- to 8-pound turkey, ready to cook

Butter
1 cup dry white wine
3 tablespoons flour
Salt, freshly ground pepper

Make the *Picadillo* stuffing and allow it to cool. Fill the cavities of the bird with the stuffing and close them with skewers. Truss the bird and place it breast side up on a rack in a roasting pan. Have ready a double thickness of cheesecloth large enough to cover the bird. Soak it in melted butter and drape it over the bird. Roast in a preheated moderately slow (325° F.) oven for 2 to 2½ hours, or until the bird is done, basting through the cheesecloth several times with pan drippings or melted butter. While the bird is roasting, make a stock by covering the neck, giblets, and liver with water and 1 cup white wine and simmer 45 minutes to 1 hour. Remove the cheesecloth 30 minutes before the bird is done so that it will brown, basting twice during this period. Lift the bird onto a platter and remove the trussing strings and skewers. Let it rest 15 minutes before carving. Skim all but 3 tablespoons of fat from the roasting pan and stir in the flour, blending thoroughly over moderate heat. Stir in 1 cup of the stock and blend well, adding a little more if the gravy is too thick. Season to taste with salt and pepper and serve separately in a sauceboat.

Variation: For another popular stuffing, substitute 2 pounds ground pork for the beef. Omit the oregano and thyme and add ⅛ teaspoon of cloves and half that amount of ground cinnamon. Ground cumin (⅛ teaspoon) may be added to either stuffing. This spice is very popular in Mexican cooking and I find it makes a pleasant change.

Pavita Rellena a la Criolla   ARGENTINA
Hen Turkey with Creole Stuffing

Quinces, when they are available, may be used instead of peaches in this delicious turkey stuffing.

Serves 10 to 12

8 slices firm white bread	3 tablespoons pitted green olives,
Milk	chopped
2 tablespoons butter	2 cups pitted, peeled, and chopped
1 medium onion, finely chopped	peaches
2 pounds sausage meat	Salt, freshly ground pepper
1 bay leaf, crumbled	3 eggs, lightly beaten
1 teaspoon oregano	A 10- to 12-pound turkey,
1 tablespoon parsley, finely	preferably a hen turkey
chopped	Olive oil
2 hardboiled eggs, finely chopped	Butter for basting

Soak the bread in milk, squeeze out, and fluff. In a saucepan heat the butter and sauté the onion until it is golden. Add the sausage meat and cook until it has lost all its color, mashing with a fork to break it up. Remove the saucepan from the heat. Add the bread, herbs, hardboiled eggs, olives, and peaches. Season to taste with salt and a generous amount of pepper. Stir in the lightly beaten eggs. Stuff the bird with the mixture and truss it in the usual way. Rub the bird all over with olive oil and bake in a preheated moderate (325° F.) oven for 3 to 3½ hours, or until it is done. Baste every 30 minutes with ½ cup melted butter and when this is used up, the drippings in the pan. If necessary, use a little more butter. If any dressing is left over, bake it separately in a foil-covered container. If liked, make a gravy by simmering the giblets and neck in water to make 3 cups of stock, stir 4 tablespoons flour into 4 tablespoons fat from the roasting pan, add the stock, and cook, stirring, until the gravy is thickened.

Pavo Guisado
DOMINICAN REPUBLIC
Turkey Stew, Dominican Style

Perhaps because it remained out of the mainstream, the cooking of the Dominican Republic has preserved some of the best dishes of the Spanish colonial period, when indigenous and introduced foods combined very happily in the stewpot.

Serves 8 to 10

An 8- to 8½-pound turkey, cut into serving pieces
4 cloves garlic, crushed
Salt, freshly ground pepper
2 tablespoons red wine vinegar
½ cup vegetable oil
1 cup tomato purée
1 green bell pepper, seeded and chopped
24 small pitted green olives
4 tablespoons capers
3 pounds potatoes, peeled and sliced
1 pound fresh peas, shelled, or a 10-ounce package frozen peas, thawed

Season the turkey pieces with the garlic, salt and pepper to taste, and the vinegar. Leave for 1 hour at room temperature. Heat the oil in a heavy casserole or Dutch oven large enough to hold the turkey pieces comfortably. Pat the turkey dry with paper towels, and reserve any marinade that remains. Sauté the turkey pieces, two or three at a time, until lightly browned on both sides. Arrange the turkey in the casserole and add the marinade. Add the tomato purée, the bell pepper, and enough water to cover. Cover and simmer over moderate heat for 1 hour. Add the olives, capers, and potatoes, and cook for 20 minutes longer. Add the peas, and cook for about 10 minutes longer, or until both the turkey and vegetables are tender. If using frozen peas, add only for the last 5 minutes of cooking. To serve arrange the turkey pieces on a warmed serving platter and surround with the potatoes. If the liquid is very abundant, reduce it over brisk heat and pour over the turkey.

MOLE DISHES
Turkey or Chicken

Mole Poblano de Guajolote   MEXICO
Turkey in Chili and Chocolate Sauce

This is Mexico's most famous dish and though it is native to the state of
Puebla, it is served all over the republic on truly festive occasions. It can be
absolutely sensational for a party when served with tortillas, Mexican rice
and beans, and *Guacamole* (Avocado Sauce). I always put a small bowl of
canned *serrano* or *jalapeño* chilies on the table for the bold souls who
claim no dish is hot enough for them. Actually *Mole Poblano* is not hot
though I have come across versions of it where a *chipotle* chili or two had
been added, introducing both heat and this chili's very exotic flavor. For a
more everyday dish, chicken or pork may be used instead of turkey.

There is a charming but apocryphal legend, that a group of nuns at the
convent of Santa Rosa in Puebla invented the dish in early colonial times
to honor a visiting viceroy and archbishop. But, in fact, it had long been a
royal dish of the Aztec court; since it contained chocolate, it was forbidden
to women, and among men it was reserved for royalty, the military nobility, and the higher ranks of the priesthood. It is on record that the Spanish
conquistador Hernán Cortés was served a version of the dish at the court of
Aztec Emperor Moctezuma. All the same I do think we owe the sisters a
debt. They recorded the recipe, which might otherwise have been lost, and
they substituted familiar ingredients for some of the more exotic herbs and
spices used in the emperor's day. I'd be prepared to swear that in the past
allspice (a native spice) was used instead of cloves and cinnamon brought
by Spain from the East, but since the flavor is much the same, why fuss?

Since *mole*, which comes from the Nahuatl word *molli*, means a sauce
made from any of the chilies, hot, pungent, or sweet, there are more *moles*
in Mexico than one can count. Out of the innumerable array, I have chosen
this one and some of the *moles* from the state of Oaxaca—known as the
land of the seven moles—where I am always aware of the mysteries of the
past and where the cooking of today brings the past very much to life.

Serves 10

An 8-pound turkey, cut into   2 cloves garlic, chopped
    serving pieces   Salt
1 medium onion, chopped   6 tablespoons lard

FOR THE SAUCE

6 ancho *chilies*
6 mulato *chilies*
4 pasilla *chilies*
2 *medium onions, chopped*
3 *cloves garlic, chopped*
3 *medium tomatoes, peeled,
    seeded, and chopped*
2 *tortillas, or 2 slices toast, cut up*
1 *cup blanched almonds*
½ *cup peanuts*
½ *cup raisins*

4 *tablespoons sesame seeds*
½ *teaspoon ground coriander seed*
½ *teaspoon ground anise*
2 *whole cloves*
A ½-inch *piece of stick cinnamon*
½ *cup lard, about*
1 ½ *squares (1 ½ ounces)
    unsweetened chocolate*
Salt, freshly ground pepper
1 *tablespoon sugar (optional)*

Put the turkey pieces into a large heavy saucepan or casserole with the onion, garlic, and water to cover. Season with salt, bring to a boil, lower the heat, and simmer, covered, for 1 hour, or until the turkey is barely tender. Drain off and reserve the turkey stock. Lift out the turkey pieces and pat them dry with paper towels. Heat the lard in a large skillet and sauté the turkey pieces until they are lightly browned on both sides. Set them aside.

To make the sauce, remove the stems and seeds from the *ancho*, *mulato*, and *pasilla* chilies. Tear them into pieces, put them in a bowl, and pour hot water over them barely to cover, about 2 cups. Let them stand for 30 minutes, turning the pieces from time to time. In a blender or food processor combine the chilies and the water in which they have soaked with the onions, garlic, tomatoes, and tortillas or toast, and blend the mixture until it forms a paste. Do this in two lots if necessary. Transfer the paste to a bowl. Rinse out and dry the container of the blender or food processor and add the almonds, peanuts, raisins, 2 tablespoons of the sesame seeds, the coriander seed, the anise, the cloves, and the cinnamon stick, broken up, and blend the mixture well. Mix thoroughly with the chili paste. Measure the lard left in the skillet from sautéing the turkey and add enough to bring the quantity up to 4 tablespoons. Add the chili paste and sauté over moderate heat, stirring, for 5 minutes. Transfer the mixture to the saucepan or casserole in which the turkey was cooked. Stir in 2 cups of the reserved turkey stock and the chocolate, cut into pieces. Season to taste with salt and pepper. Cook the mixture over low heat, stirring until the chocolate is melted and adding more turkey stock if necessary to make the sauce the consistency of heavy cream. Stir in the sugar, if liked. Add the turkey and simmer it, covered, for 30 minutes. Arrange the turkey and sauce in a serving dish. In a small skillet toast the remaining sesame seeds and sprinkle them over the turkey. Serve with Tortillas, *Arroz Blanco*, *Frijoles*, and *Guacamole*.

For an authentic Mexican fiesta meal, start with *Seviche de Sierra* (Mackerel Marinated in Lime Juice) and finish with *Chongos Zamoranos* (Custard Squares in Syrup).

Mole Negro Oaxaqueño   MEXICO
Chicken in Chili Sauce, Oaxaca Style

Though *Mole Poblano de Guajalote* (Turkey in Chili and Chocolate Sauce) is probably the most famous of all Mexican dishes, *mole* Oaxaca style is not far behind. Traditionally made with a hen turkey (*pípila*) weighing about 8 pounds, it is equally good with chicken, which I have used here. These are both very old dishes, served at pre-Conquest courts to emperors and kings. They are essentially royal dishes because of the chocolate, and they have obviously been modified since colonial times, using some ingredients not available before the Conquest — peppercorns, cinnamon, cloves, and almonds, for example. The chilies used in the Oaxacan *mole* include *chilhuacle*, a rather bitter pepper that gives the dish a very dark color. This is not available here and I have found *guajillo* chili, which is available, a very good substitute from the point of view of flavor, though the color is lighter. This is a very good party dish especially as the sauce is improved by being made a day ahead.

Serves 8

Two 3½-pound chickens, cut into
    serving pieces
Chicken stock
12 guajillo chilies (about 2 ounces)
4 ancho chilies
4 pasilla chilies
1 medium onion, chopped
2 cloves garlic, chopped
2 medium tomatoes, peeled and
    chopped
¼ cup dried apricots, soaked and
    chopped
¼ cup almonds, ground
¼ cup peanuts, ground
2 tablespoons sesame seeds
2 slices French bread or firm white
    bread, fried in lard or
    vegetable oil

⅛ teaspoon ground cloves, or 2
    whole cloves
4 peppercorns
1 teaspoon thyme
1 teaspoon oregano
⅛ teaspoon ground cinnamon, or
    a small piece of stick
    cinnamon
8 tablespoons lard or vegetable oil
2 squares (2 ounces) unsweetened
    chocolate
1 or 2 avocado leaves (optional)
Salt

Put the chicken pieces in a large flameproof casserole or saucepan and pour in enough chicken stock to cover. Bring the stock to a simmer, cover, and cook over low heat for 30 minutes. Set aside.

Shake the seeds out of the chilies, rinse them, and tear them into pieces. Put them in a bowl with 1 cup warm water, using a little more water if necessary. Let them soak for 1 hour, turning them from time to time. Combine the chilies, onion, garlic, tomatoes, apricots, almonds, peanuts, 1 tablespoon of the sesame seeds, the bread, broken into pieces, the cloves, peppercorns, thyme, oregano, and cinnamon, and reduce to a purée, bit by bit, in a blender or food processor. Heat the lard or oil in a large skillet and add the purée, which should be quite thick. Fry the mixture, stirring constantly with a wooden spoon as it tends to splatter, for 5 minutes.

Lift the chicken pieces out of the casserole or saucepan and set them aside in a dish. Pour out and measure the stock. Rinse out the saucepan or casserole and pour in the chili mixture. Stir in 3 cups of the chicken stock and the chocolate. Drop the avocado leaves briefly into boiling water and add to the saucepan. Season to taste with salt. Stir over low heat until the chocolate has melted. The sauce should be rather thicker than heavy cream; if it is too thick, add a little more chicken stock. Add the chicken pieces, cover, and simmer over very low heat for 30 minutes, or until the chicken is tender. Remove the avocado leaves. Put the chicken pieces and the sauce in a large serving dish. Toast the remaining sesame seeds in a skillet over moderate heat until they begin to pop, a minute or two, and sprinkle them over the *mole*. Serve with *Arroz Blanco* (White Rice), *Frijoles* (Beans), *Guacamole*, and Tortillas.

Variation: If using a turkey, cut an 8-pound bird into serving pieces and put into a large saucepan or kettle with water to cover. Season with salt, bring to a boil, reduce the heat, and simmer gently, covered, for 1 hour. Drain and pat dry with paper towels. Use the turkey broth to thin the chili mixture. Heat 4 tablespoons lard or vegetable oil in a skillet and sauté the turkey pieces until they are browned on both sides. Add them to the chili sauce and simmer over very low heat, covered, until the turkey is tender, about 30 minutes.

Variation: Cut 3 pounds lean, boneless pork into 2-inch pieces and put into a saucepan with water barely to cover. Season with salt and simmer gently, covered, for 1 hour. Drain. Use the pork broth to thin the chili mixture. Add the pork to the sauce and simmer gently, covered, until the pork is tender, about 30 minutes.

Mole Amarillo
Chicken in Yellow Sauce

MEXICO

Serves 6

A 3½- to 4-pound chicken, cut
    into serving pieces
4 cloves garlic
4 canned largo chilies, or use any
    fresh hot light green pepper,
    seeded
2 tablespoons lard or vegetable oil
1 medium onion, chopped
4 medium tomatoes, peeled and
    chopped

½ teaspoon oregano
⅛ teaspoon ground cumin
Salt, freshly ground pepper
1 pound zucchini, sliced
½ pound green beans, cut into
    1-inch pieces
Masa harina

Put the chicken into a saucepan with 2 of the cloves of garlic, crushed, and water barely to cover. Bring to a boil, lower the heat, cover, and simmer until the pork is tender, about 2 hours. Put the chilies into a blender or food processor and reduce them to a purée. If necessary add a tablespoon of the chicken stock. Heat the lard or oil in a skillet and sauté the chili purée, stirring constantly with a wooden spoon, for 3 or 4 minutes. Put the remaining 2 cloves garlic, the onion, and tomatoes in a blender or food processor and reduce them to a purée. Pour the mixture into the skillet with the chili and cook, stirring from time to time, until the mixture is thick and well blended, 3 or 4 minutes. Drain the pork but leave the meat in the saucepan. Pour 2 cups of the stock into the skillet, stir to mix, season with the oregano, cumin, salt and pepper, and pour the mixture over the pork. Cook the zucchini (about 8 minutes) and the beans (about 10 to 15 minutes) separately in boiling salted water, drain them, and add to the saucepan. Simmer over very low heat for 10 to 15 minutes to blend the flavors. I like to thicken the sauce with a little *masa harina* (tortilla flour) if it seems too thin; mix a tablespoon of the flour with a little of the stock and stir it into the saucepan and cook for a minute or so longer. Serve with rice.

Variation: Instead of the *largo* chilies use 6 *guajillo* chilies. Shake out the seeds and soak the chilies in ½ cup warm water for 30 minutes, then purée in the blender or food processor in the soaking water. Sauté the chili purée in the lard or oil. Instead of the tomatoes, use two 10-ounce cans Mexican green tomatoes, drained and puréed in a blender with 2 medium romaine lettuce leaves. The red tomatoes and green peppers give a yellow sauce, and here the green tomatoes and red peppers give the same color result though with a subtly different flavor. If liked, chayotes may be used instead of zucchini.

Variation: 3 pounds boneless pork, loin or shoulder, cut into 1-inch pieces may be used instead of chicken.

Variation: Traditionally *chochoyotes* are added to the stew in the last few minutes of cooking. These are small balls made by mixing 1½ cups *masa harina* (tortilla flour) with a little salt and 4 tablespoons lard with just enough water to hold them together. A little dent is made in each of the balls, which are about 1 inch in diameter. But I do not think these can be made successfully with the dried, packaged flour. The fresh, moist dough sold in local markets is what is needed. The dishes are distinguished by color. There is *mole negro* (black sauce), perhaps the most famous, as well as yellow, red, light red, green, and two others, *mancha manteles* (tablecloth stainer), and *chichilo*, made with the distinctive local chili, *chilhuacle*, which is also used in the *mole negro*. Versions of *mancha manteles* turn up all over the republic, but the others are exclusively Oaxacan. Not all of them can be reproduced faithfully outside Oaxaca, but some can and I have included them here: *negro, verde, amarillo,* and *coloradito*.

Mole Verde de Oaxaca
Chicken in Green Sauce, Oaxaca Style

MEXICO

Serves 6

1 cup Great Northern, Navy, pea beans, or lima beans
Salt
1 medium onion, finely chopped
3 cloves garlic, chopped
A 10-ounce can Mexican green tomatoes, drained
1 canned jalapeño chili, or 2 canned serrano chilies, rinsed and chopped
3 tablespoons lard or vegetable oil

1 pound boneless pork loin, cut into 1-inch cubes
2 cups chicken stock or water, about
A 3- to 3½-pound chicken, cut into serving pieces
1 cup parsley sprigs, fairly tightly packed
1 cup fresh coriander leaves, fairly tightly packed
2 tablespoons masa harina

Pick over and rinse the beans. Put them into a saucepan with cold water to cover, put the lid on, and bring to a boil over moderate heat. Let stand 35 to 40 minutes off the heat, covered. Drain, rinse, and put on to cook with cold water to cover. Simmer the beans, covered, until they are tender, about 1 hour. Season with salt to taste in the last 30 minutes of cooking. Drain, reserve the cooking liquid, and set the beans aside.

In a blender or food processor combine the onion, garlic, Mexican green tomatoes, and chilies, and reduce to a purée. In a skillet heat the lard or vegetable oil and sauté the tomato mixture for 3 or 4 minutes. Pour the mixture into a saucepan and add the reserved cooking liquid from the beans. Add the pork loin and a little chicken stock or water, if necessary, to cover. Cover and simmer for 1 hour. At the end of this time, add the chicken, and a little more stock, if necessary. Continue cooking until both chicken and pork are tender, about 1 hour. Add the cooked beans and simmer just long enough to heat them through.

Put the parsley and coriander into a blender or food processor with a little stock if necessary and reduce to a purée. Stir into the saucepan and cook without letting the mixture return to a boil for a minute or so. If the mixture boils, the sauce will lose its fresh green color. If the sauce is too thin, thicken with the *masa harina* mixed with a little stock. Serve with rice and *guacamole*.

Variation: Sometimes when Mexican green tomatoes are hard to find I have used a 7-ounce can of *Salsa Verde Mexicana* (Green Mexican Sauce) put up by Herdez. In this case, I omit the onion, garlic, green tomatoes, and chilies. The sauce does contain coriander (cilantro) but I do not find I need to alter the amount of fresh coriander. If liked, ½ pound cooked green beans and/or cooked, sliced zucchini may be added to the finished *mole*. I have a trick I sometimes use to make sure of the bright green color of the green dishes. Purée 2 or 3 leaves of romaine lettuce with the parsley and coriander if the color seems at all pallid. The lettuce also slightly thickens the sauce but does not alter the flavor to any perceptible extent.

Mole Coloradito de Oaxaca   MEXICO
Chicken in Red Sauce, Oaxaca Style

Serves 4 to 6

A 3½- to 4-pound chicken, cut
    into serving pieces
3 cups chicken stock, about
6 ancho *chilies*
1 *medium onion, chopped*
1 *clove garlic, chopped*
4 *medium tomatoes, peeled and
    chopped*

⅛ *teaspoon cinnamon*
¼ *teaspoon oregano*
2 *tablespoons sesame seeds,
    toasted and ground*
2 *tablespoons lard or vegetable oil*
Salt, freshly ground pepper

Put the chicken pieces into a large saucepan or heatproof casserole and pour in enough chicken stock to cover. Bring to a boil, lower the heat, cover, and simmer gently until the chicken is tender, about 45 minutes. Lift out the chicken pieces and set aside. Pour the stock into a container and set aside. Rinse out and dry the saucepan or casserole.

Pull off the stems and shake out the seeds of the *ancho* chilies. Tear the chilies into pieces, put them into a bowl with ½ cup warm water, and soak, turning them from time to time, for about 1 hour. Transfer the soaked chilies and any liquid to a blender or food processor. Add the onion, garlic, tomatoes, cinnamon, oregano, and sesame seeds and reduce to a coarse purée. Heat the lard or oil in a skillet and add the purée. Sauté, stirring constantly with a wooden spoon, until the mixture is thick and heavy, about 5 minutes. Turn the chili mixture into the casserole and stir in 2 cups of the reserved stock. Season to taste with salt and pepper. Add the chicken pieces and simmer, uncovered, until the chicken is heated through and the sauce slightly thickened. Serve with rice, tortillas, *guacamole*, and beans.

Variation: Pork may also be used for this *mole*. Instead of the chicken, use 3 pounds boneless pork loin, cut into 1-inch cubes, and cook, with 2 or 3 large cloves garlic, in water barely to cover until tender, about 2 hours. Strain the stock before using it for the sauce.

Many cooks in Oaxaca like to add an avocado leaf or two to the sauce in its final simmering. The leaves may be toasted lightly before they are added. They are discarded, like a bouquet garni, before the dish is served.

Variation: There is a pleasant vegetarian version of this *mole*. Instead of chicken or pork, add to the sauce ½ pound each cooked, cut-up potatoes, green beans, and peas. Any other vegetables such as zucchini, chayote, or cauliflower may be added. I particularly like cooked green bananas with this *mole* instead of rice. Choose very green (unripe) bananas and cut through the skin lengthwise in 2 or 3 places to peel off the skin. Boil the bananas in salted water for 10 to 15 minutes, or until tender, drain and add them to the vegetarian *mole*, or serve as a side dish.

DUCK

Arroz con Pato   PERU
Duckling with Rice

It is not surprising that this is Peru's favorite duckling dish. The coriander and cumin unite in a most subtle way with the dark beer in which the rice is cooked, and the rich flavor of the duckling permeates the whole.

Serves 6

A 4½- to 5-pound duckling, cut
    into 6 serving pieces
Vegetable oil
1 large onion, finely chopped
3 fresh hot red or green peppers,
    seeded, coarsely chopped, and
    puréed in a blender or food
    processor
6 large cloves garlic, crushed

2 tablespoons fresh coriander
    (cilantro), chopped
1 teaspoon ground cumin
Salt, freshly ground pepper
4 cups chicken stock, about
2 cups long-grain rice
2 cups dark beer
½ cup cooked green peas

GARNISH

Sliced tomatoes and fresh hot
    peppers, seeded and cut into
    flower shapes

Prick the skin of the duckling all over with the tines of a fork. Film the bottom of a heavy skillet with a small amount of oil and sauté the duckling pieces — about 10 to 15 minutes — until they are lightly browned all over in their own fat, which will run out during the cooking. Transfer the duckling pieces to a heavy casserole. Pour off all but 3 tablespoons of fat from the skillet in which the duckling was browned, and in the remaining fat sauté the onion, peppers, and garlic until the onion is golden. Add the vegetables to the casserole with the coriander, cumin, salt and pepper to taste, and the chicken stock, which should just cover the duckling pieces. Add a little more if necessary. Cover and simmer over low heat until the duckling is almost done, about 45 minutes. Drain off the stock and measure it. Add the rice to the casserole with 2 cups of the stock and the dark beer. Cover, bring to a boil, reduce the heat to low, and cook until the rice is tender and quite dry. Fold in the peas. Serve hot on a large platter garnished with tomato slices and fresh hot peppers.

Pato al Vino
Duckling in Wine

COLOMBIA

Spices from the New and Old Worlds — allspice, cinnamon, and cloves — combine to give this duckling a full, rich flavor. It may be cooked on top of the stove, but I find it much more satisfactory to use the oven as do many modern Latin Americans.

Serves 3 to 4

A 4½- to 5-pound duckling
Salt, freshly ground pepper
2 tablespoons butter
2 large onions, finely chopped
1 bay leaf
2 whole cloves
A 1-inch piece of stick cinnamon

4 allspice berries
1 whole fresh hot red or green pepper
1 cup dry red wine
1 cup duck stock, made by simmering giblets, neck, and liver for 1 hour

Pull the loose fat from inside the duckling and prick the bird all over with a fork to help release the excess fat. Season inside and out with salt and pepper. Heat the butter in a heavy casserole and sauté the duckling until it is golden brown all over. Lift out and set aside. Spoon off all but 4 tablespoons fat from the casserole. Add the onions and sauté until soft. Return the duckling to the casserole. Tie the bay leaf, cloves, cinnamon, allspice berries, and hot pepper in a square of cheesecloth and add to the casserole with the red wine and duck stock. Season to taste with more salt and pepper if necessary and bring to a boil on top of the stove. Cover with aluminum foil, then with the casserole lid, and cook in a preheated moderate (350° F.) oven for 1½ hours, or until the duckling is tender. Lift out onto a serving platter and keep warm. Remove and discard the cheesecloth bag. Spoon excess fat from the sauce, and if it is very abundant, reduce it over brisk heat for a few minutes. Spoon a little sauce over the duckling and serve the rest separately. Serve with *Arroz con Coco y Pasas* (Rice with Coconut and Raisins) and a green salad.

Variation: *Pato Borracho* (Drunken Duckling) is a popular duck dish all over Latin America. Cook as for *Pato al Vino* but use white wine instead of red. Omit the cloves, cinnamon, allspice, and hot pepper, and use instead a bouquet garni of parsley and thyme tied in a cheesecloth square with the bay leaf. Add 3 cloves of chopped garlic to the onions, and when they are soft, add 4 tomatoes, peeled, seeded, and chopped.

Variation: *Pato com Ameixas* (Duckling with Prunes), from Brazil, is a full-flavored, robust dish. Cook as for *Pato al Vino* but omit the cloves, cinnamon, allspice berries, and hot pepper. When sautéing the onions, add 2 cloves garlic, chopped. When the onions are soft, add 3 large tomatoes, peeled, seeded, and chopped, and ½ teaspoon thyme. Instead of 1 cup dry red wine, add 2 cups dry white wine and the cup of duck stock, and 1½ cups pitted prunes, quartered. Just before serving stir in ¼ cup dry Madeira.

Pato en Jugo de Naranja   MEXICO
Duck in Orange Juice

This is a very old colonial dish that has remained popular, with slight variations, throughout Latin America, though it seems to have originated in Mexico. I have chosen a modern version where the duck is braised in the oven, instead of on top of the stove.

Serves 4

1 duckling weighing about 4 pounds	¼ teaspoon thyme
2 tablespoons butter	¼ teaspoon marjoram
1 medium onion, finely chopped	1 bay leaf
2 cloves garlic, chopped	¼ cup raisins
3 medium tomatoes, peeled, seeded, and chopped, about 1 cup pulp	1 tablespoon white wine vinegar
	1 cup orange juice
	¼ cup toasted, slivered almonds

Pull out the loose fat from inside the duckling and prick the bird all over with a fork to help release the excess fat. Heat the butter in a large skillet and brown the duckling lightly all over. Transfer the duckling to a flame-proof casserole large enough to hold it comfortably. Spoon off all but 2 tablespoons of fat from the skillet and sauté the onion and garlic until the onion is soft. Add to the casserole with all the remaining ingredients except the almonds. Add the duck giblets to enrich the sauce. Bring the liquid in the casserole to a boil on top of the stove. Cover the casserole with foil, then with the lid, and cook in a preheated moderate (325° F.) oven for 1½ hours, or until the duckling is tender. Lift the bird out and carve it. Put it onto a serving platter and keep warm. Spoon off the fat from the sauce, take out and discard the giblets and bay leaf. If the sauce is very abundant, reduce it over brisk heat for a few minutes. Spoon a little of the sauce over the duckling and sprinkle with the almonds. Pour the rest of the sauce into a sauceboat and serve separately with rice and green peas or green beans.

SQUAB

Latin America has a marvelous way with pigeons (or what we call squab), which everyone loves. They range from the beautifully simple Mexican favorite *Pichones al Vino* (Squab with Wine) to the exotic *Pichones con Salsa de Camarones* (Squab in Shrimp Sauce) of Peru. They make an ideal dinner party dish, with each guest served a plumply elegant, full-flavored bird. You may also substitute fresh Rock Cornish game hens.

Pichones con Salsa de Camarones   PERU
Squab in Shrimp Sauce

The shrimp sauce turns this into an excitingly different dish, the apparently contradictory flavors deliciously complementing each other.

Serves 6

4 tablespoons clarified butter
　(page 328)
6 squab, each weighing about 8
　ounces
1 medium onion, finely chopped
1 clove garlic, chopped
2 tablespoons flour
1½ cups dry white wine

1½ cups chicken stock
Pinch of nutmeg
Salt, freshly ground pepper
½ pound raw shrimp, peeled and
　coarsely chopped
2 eggs, lightly beaten
2 tablespoons finely chopped fresh
　coriander

Heat the butter in a skillet and sauté the squab until they are golden on both sides. Transfer to a heavy casserole. In the butter remaining in the skillet sauté the onion and garlic until the onion is soft. Add the flour and cook, stirring, for a minute or two. Add the wine, stir, add the stock and the nutmeg, and simmer, stirring, until the mixture is smooth. Season to taste with salt and pepper and pour over the squab. Cover the casserole with foil, then with the lid, and simmer over moderate heat until the squab are tender, about 1½ hours. Lift out the squab and arrange on a serving dish. Keep warm. Add the shrimp to the liquid in the casserole and cook for about 2 minutes. Then stir in the eggs and the coriander and cook, stirring, over low heat until the sauce is lightly thickened. Do not let the sauce boil once the eggs are added, as it will curdle. Spoon a little of the sauce over the squab and serve the rest separately in a sauceboat. Serve with white rice or boiled potatoes and a green vegetable or a salad.

Pichones al Vino
MEXICO
Squab with Wine

Dry sherry is sometimes used in this recipe and though it is pleasant I prefer the equally traditional dry red wine. Baked *boniato* (white sweet potato) is a splendid accompaniment.

Serves 4

4 squab, each weighing about 8 ounces
2 cloves garlic, chopped
16 scallions, trimmed and cut into 1¼-inch pieces, using both green and white parts
4 medium-sized carrots, scraped and thinly sliced
½ teaspoon thyme
½ teaspoon marjoram
⅛ teaspoon freshly ground black pepper

⅛ teaspoon ground allspice
1 whole clove
Salt
1 small fresh hot pepper, seeded and chopped
¼ cup olive oil
2 tablespoons red wine vinegar
1 cup dry red wine or dry sherry
½ cup chicken stock, about

Arrange the squab in a flameproof casserole just large enough to hold them comfortably. Add all the ingredients except the chicken stock and mix well. Marinate in the refrigerator overnight, turning once or twice. When ready to cook, add the stock, using a little more if necessary barely to cover. Bring to a simmer on top of the stove, then cook, covered, in a preheated moderate (350° F.) oven until tender, about 1½ hours. Arrange the squab on a warmed serving dish, spoon a little of the sauce over them. Serve the rest of the sauce separately.

Pichones Saltados

PERU

Squab Stew

This is a deceptively simple dish, very easy to cook yet with a fine, rich flavor.

Serves 4

*4 squab, each weighing about 8
    ounces
Salt, freshly ground pepper
½ cup olive oil
1 large onion, finely chopped
1 fresh hot red or green pepper,
    seeded and chopped*

*2 tablespoons flour
2 teaspoons sweet paprika
1 cup dry white wine
1 cup chicken stock*

Season the squab inside and out with salt and pepper. Heat the oil in a flameproof casserole and sauté the squab over moderate heat until they are golden brown all over, about 15 minutes. Lift out and set aside. Add the onion and the hot pepper to the oil remaining in the casserole and sauté until the onion is soft. Stir in the flour and the paprika and cook, stirring, for a minute longer. Add the wine, stir to mix, then stir in the stock. Return the squab to the sauce, cover the casserole with a piece of foil, then with the lid, and simmer over low heat until the squab are tender, about 1½ hours. Lift out the squab onto a serving dish. Taste the sauce and add more salt and pepper if necessary. Pour a little sauce over the squab and serve the rest in a sauceboat. Serve with rice, mashed potatoes, or a purée of any starchy root vegetable such as sweet potato or yams, or with a purée of winter squash, and a green vegetable.

Pichones en Jugo de Naranja   COLOMBIA
Squab in Orange Juice

Orange juice and white wine combine to make a delicate sauce for the richness of the squab, a balancing of flavors that is typical of Colombian cooking.

Serves 6

4 tablespoons butter
6 squab, each weighing about 8
    ounces
1 medium onion, finely chopped
1 cup dry white wine

1 cup orange juice
Salt, freshly ground pepper
Pinch of cinnamon
2 teaspoons cornstarch

Heat the butter in a skillet and sauté the squab until golden brown all over. Transfer them to a heavy casserole. In the butter remaining in the skillet sauté the onion until it is soft. Pour in the wine and the orange juice, bring to a boil, and stir, scraping up all the brown bits. Season to taste with salt and pepper and add the cinnamon. Pour the mixture over the squab, cover, and simmer over low heat until the squab are tender, about 1½ hours. Transfer the squab to a serving dish and keep warm. Mix the cornstarch with a little cold water and stir into the casserole. Simmer, stirring, until the sauce is lightly thickened. If the sauce seems very abundant, reduce briskly over fairly high heat for a few minutes before adding the cornstarch. Serve with any root vegetable or rice and a green vegetable.

Substantial Dishes

Platillos Fuertes

Including Beans and Rice

There are a number of hearty dishes in the Latin American cuisine that combine fish, meat, or poultry with beans, rice, corn, potatoes, or other root vegetables. These once served as a course in a meal as soup or appetizers do now. To our modern appetites they are main dishes, so I have put them into a category of their own. I have included the festive dish *Feijoada Completa* (Black Beans with Mixed Meats) here because beans are such an important part of it. This is not a very sharply defined category but I think it is a useful one.

Feijoada Completa
BRAZIL
Black Beans with Mixed Meats

This exuberant mixture of black beans, meats, vegetables, and garnishes is Brazil's national dish. It was created in Rio de Janeiro but has now spread all over the country. It is magnificent for parties and well worth the work involved. And it is versatile as one can eliminate or substitute many of the meats if some are not available. Polish or Spanish sausage (*kielbasa* or *longaniza*) can substitute for *linguiça*, fresh pork hocks can be used instead of pig's feet, ears, and tail. Kale can be used for collard greens, and any fresh hot peppers can be used in the hot pepper sauce. To serve the *Feijoada*, the meats are sliced and arranged on one or more platters, the beans, which should be quite soupy with an almost saucelike consistency, are served in a tureen or large serving bowl with a soup ladle or generously sized serving spoon, and accompanied by *Arroz Brazileiro* (Brazilian Rice), *Couve a Mineira* (Kale or Collard Greens, Minas Gerais Style), *Farofa de Manteiga* (Cassava Meal with Butter) or *Farofa de Ouro* (Cassava Meal with Hardboiled Eggs), as well as 6 peeled and sliced oranges arranged in a serving dish, *Môlho de Pimenta e Limão* (Hot Pepper and Lime Sauce) and *Salada de Palmito* (Hearts of Palm Salad).

The table looks very splendid with this array of food. Guests put a serving of everything onto a single plate, then sprinkle *farofa* over the lot. The flavors blend delightfully, an orchestra of taste and texture. *Cachaça*, Brazilian rum, is traditionally served with *Feijoada* but to the uninitiated this can be traumatic. Ideally either *batidas* or *Caipirinhas*, two *cachaça* drinks made with lime or lemon juice, are served before the meal, and chilled beer with it.

Brazilian friends say *Feijoada* should be eaten for Saturday lunch so that one may sleep it off. I've done that but I find I prefer *Feijoada* for dinner, or for a festive Sunday luncheon party. It is a truly international dish since the beans and hot peppers come originally from Mexico, the cassava (manioc) meal from pre-Portuguese Brazil, the meats and sausages from Europe by way of Portugal, and the cooking genius that put it all together from Africa.

An admirable dessert to accompany this feast is *Quindins de Yáyá* (Coconut Cupcake Dessert), which is deliciously rich and sweet.

Serves 10 to 12

4 pig's ears
1 pig's tail
Salt
3 pig's feet, split
A 1-pound piece carne sêca
    (sun-dried salted beef or
    jerked beef), see page 6
A 3-pound smoked beef tongue
A ½-pound piece of lean bocon
4 cups black (turtle) beans
A 1-pound piece of lean beef
    chuck or bottom round
1 pound linguiça sausage (see page
    16), or use longaniza or
    kielbasa sausage

1 pound fresh pork sausages
2 tablespoons lard or vegetable oil
2 onions, finely chopped
2 cloves garlic, minced
2 tomatoes, peeled, seeded, and
    chopped
1 fresh hot pepper, seeded and
    minced, or ⅛ teaspoon
    Tabasco (optional)
Salt, freshly ground pepper

Two days ahead of time put the pig's ears and tail into a mixing bowl and sprinkle thoroughly with salt. Cover and refrigerate for 2 days. Lift out of the bowl, discard the liquid, and rinse the meats thoroughly in cold water. Put into a large saucepan with water to cover, bring to a boil, lower the heat, and simmer for 10 minutes. Drain. Set aside until ready to cook.

The night before put the pig's feet on to cook in cold water to cover and simmer, covered, for 1½ hours. Cool and refrigerate in a covered container in the cooking liquid until ready to use.

Also on the night before cut the jerked beef in half lengthwise. Put the jerked beef, the beef tongue, and the bacon to soak overnight in cold water to cover. Start soaking early in the evening and change the water 2 or 3 times if possible. Thoroughly wash and pick over the beans and put them to soak in cold water to cover.

When ready to cook, allowing 4 hours for the actual cooking time, put the beans and their soaking liquid into a kettle or casserole large enough to hold all the ingredients. Drain and add the pig's feet. Reserve the jellied liquid from the pig's feet for some other time to make stock. Add enough cold water to cover by 2 inches. Bring to a boil, then simmer over low heat, covered, for 1½ hours.

While the beans are cooking, put the tongue, jerked beef, and bacon into a large saucepan with fresh cold water to cover, bring to a boil over moderate heat, then simmer, covered, over low heat for 1 hour. When the beans have cooked for 1½ hours, add the bacon and jerked beef to the bean pot but continue to simmer the tongue separately. At the same time add the fresh beef, pig's ears and tail to the beans. Add hot water as necessary to cover and simmer, covered, for 2 hours longer. By this time the tongue will be tender. Remove from the heat and allow to cool. As soon as it is cool enough to handle, peel it and remove any gristle and bones. Add the tongue to the beans with hot water if necessary to keep the beans covered. Stir the pot with a wooden spoon from time to time to prevent the beans from sticking.

Fill the pot in which the tongue was cooked with fresh water, bring to a boil, and add the *linguiça* (or its substitute) and the fresh pork sausages. Bring back to a boil and simmer for 1 minute. Drain and add the sausages to the beans, which by now will have been cooking for 3½ hours.*

Heat the lard or oil in a skillet and sauté the onions and garlic until the onions are soft. Add the tomatoes and the hot pepper or Tabasco, if liked, and simmer until the mixture is well blended. Season to taste with salt and pepper. Remove 1 cup of the cooked beans and add, smashing them into the sauce. Stir the mixture back into the beans and simmer for 15 minutes longer, or until the beans have been cooking for 4 hours. The beans should be very soft, almost falling apart. Lift out the meats and continue to simmer the beans, uncovered, over low heat. Remove any bones from the meats. Slice the pig's ears and tail into 4 or 5 pieces. Slice all the meats and arrange on a platter with the tongue in the center, its traditional position. Use two platters if necessary. Moisten the meats with a little bean liquid and keep warm. Pour the beans into a tureen or large serving bowl.

*The *Feijoada* can be cooked ahead to this point and kept overnight in a cool place, or refrigerated, until half an hour before it is to be served. Bring it to room temperature before adding the onion, tomato, and mashed bean mixture.

Tutú a Mineira
Black Beans, Minas Gerais Style

This is a sort of junior *Feijoada*, much simpler than that grand feast but nonetheless a hearty dish. It is really a dish of mashed beans and cassava (manioc) meal generously garnished with meat and eggs. It is a very old dish going back to the days of slavery and was a great favorite with small children. Somehow the infants, lisping the word purée, converted the sound into *tutú* and that is what it has been called ever since.

Serves 6

1 *recipe* Feijão Preto *(Black Beans), page 243*
4 *large eggs*
A ¾-*pound* linguiça, *or similar sausage such as* longaniza *or* kielbasa

1 *tablespoon lard*
8 *slices bacon, chopped*
2 *medium onions, finely sliced*
⅓ *cup cassava (manioc) meal (farinha de mandioca)*

Have ready the black beans, freshly cooked. Put the eggs into a large saucepan and boil them for 8 minutes. Shell under cold running water. Halve the eggs and set them aside. Put the sausage in a saucepan with cold water to cover and simmer for 30 minutes. Drain and cut into ½-inch slices. Heat the lard in a skillet and sauté the sausage slices and bacon until the bacon is crisp. Transfer the sausage and bacon to a dish lined with paper towels and keep them warm. In the fat remaining in the skillet sauté the onions and keep them warm.

Put the beans into a large saucepan and mash over low heat. Stir in the cassava meal and cook, stirring, until the mixture has the consistency of rather heavy mashed potatoes, adding a little more cassava meal if necessary. Transfer the mashed beans to a deep, hot serving dish and pat them down lightly to an even layer. Pour the onion and bacon fat mixture over the beans. Arrange the sausage and bacon at opposite ends of the dish and put the hardboiled eggs in a row down the middle. Serve with *Couve a Mineira* (Kale, Minas Gerais Style) and, if liked, a hot pepper sauce.

Variation: Some cooks serve the *Tutú* with eggs fried in butter instead of hardboiled eggs. Roast pork, cut into small slices, may be substituted for the chopped bacon or the *Tutú* may be served with *Roupa Velha* (Old Clothes), a traditional Brazilian shredded beef dish.

Ocopa Arequipeña   PERU
Potatoes with Cheese, Walnut, and Hot Pepper Sauce

Having "invented" the potato, the Incas developed splendid recipes using this most versatile of all root vegetables. I am sure dishes like the *ocopas* and the *causas* are pre-Columbian, slightly changed, I think for the better, by food introduced by the Conquest — walnuts, for example. In colonial times (and still today for a really traditional Peruvian meal), these were considered dishes to have before the main course. As far as I am concerned, they make a complete meal with the addition of a light dessert. They are very useful when one wants a vegetarian meal or something a little different made with fish or shrimp. In Peru *mirasol* pepper would be used. Hot dried red peppers are an excellent substitute.

Serves 6

6 hot red dried peppers, about 1½
*   to 2 inches long*
½ cup peanut oil
1 medium onion, thickly sliced
2 cloves garlic, finely chopped
1 cup walnut meats, ground
¼ pound Spanish fresh cheese
*   (queso blanco or queso fresco),*
*   crumbled, or use grated*
*   Münster cheese*

1 cup milk
1 teaspoon salt, or to taste
Lettuce leaves
6 warm, freshly cooked medium
*   potatoes, peeled and halved*
*   lengthwise*
6 hardboiled eggs, halved
*   lengthwise*
12 black olives
Strips of pimiento for garnish

Shake the seeds out of the peppers and put them to soak in ¼ cup hot water for 30 minutes. Drain and set aside. Heat the oil in a small skillet and sauté the onion and garlic over very low heat until the onion is golden. Put the oil, onion, garlic, hot peppers, walnut meats, and fresh cheese in a blender or food processor. Add the milk and salt and blend to a smooth sauce, about the consistency of a heavy mayonnaise. Add milk and oil in equal quantities to thin the sauce if necessary.

Arrange a bed of lettuce leaves on a large, warmed platter. Arrange the potatoes, cut side down, on top of the lettuce. Mask the potatoes with the sauce, then garnish the dish with the eggs, cut side up, the black olives, and the strips of pimiento.

Variation: For *Ocopa de Camarones* (Shrimp and Potatoes with Cheese, Walnut, and Hot Pepper Sauce), reduce the walnut meats to ½ cup and add to the blender or food processor ½ pound cooked, chopped shrimp. In addition garnish the platter with ¼ pound cooked, peeled shrimp, preferably medium-sized.

Papas a la Huancaina   PERU
Potatoes with Cheese and Hot Pepper Sauce

This is from Huancayo, in the Peruvian highlands at 11,000 feet. It is a typical highlands dish, very Indian, especially in the use of the local herb *palillo*, which colors food a bright yellow. Turmeric, used sparingly, is an admirable substitute.

Serves 8 as a first course,
4 as a light luncheon dish

¼ cup lemon juice
⅛ teaspoon cayenne pepper
Salt, freshly ground pepper
1 medium onion, thinly sliced
8 medium potatoes
3 cups coarsely chopped Spanish
　　fresh cheese (queso blanco or
　　queso fresco), or use Münster
　　cheese
1 or more fresh hot yellow
　　peppers, seeded and chopped,
　　or use red or green peppers

1 teaspoon palillo, or ½ teaspoon
　　turmeric
1½ cups heavy cream
⅔ cup olive oil
Lettuce leaves
4 hardboiled eggs, halved
2 or 3 ears of corn, cooked and cut
　　into 8 slices
8 black olives

In a bowl combine the lemon juice, cayenne pepper, and salt and pepper to taste. Add the onion, separated into rings, and set it aside to pickle at room temperature.

Boil the potatoes in their skins until tender. Drain, peel, and keep warm. In a blender or food processor combine the cheese, hot peppers, *palillo* or turmeric, and the cream. Blend until smooth. Heat the oil in a skillet, pour in the cheese mixture, reduce the heat to low, and cook, stirring constantly with a wooden spoon, until the sauce is smooth and creamy.

Garnish a platter with the lettuce leaves. Arrange the potatoes on the platter and pour the sauce over them. Arrange the eggs, corn slices, and olives around and in between the potatoes. Drain the onion rings and arrange them over the potatoes.

Causa a la Chiclayana   PERU
Potatoes with Fish and Vegetables

This is a very decorative dish and looks lovely on a buffet with lettuce leaves framing the serving platter and the mound of mashed potatoes garnished with strips of hot red pepper, onion rings, wedges of cheese, and black olives, in the center surrounded by the fried fish, sliced green bananas, corn, and slices of tropical root vegetables. The potatoes are transformed into something quite exciting with the vinaigrette dressing. It makes a hearty and satisfying one-dish meal.

Serves 6

¼ cup finely chopped onion
½ cup lemon juice
⅛ teaspoon cayenne pepper
Salt, freshly ground pepper
3 pounds boiling potatoes, peeled and halved
1½ cups olive oil plus 4 tablespoons
1 pound sweet potatoes, peeled and cut into 6 slices
1 pound cassava (yucca) root, peeled and cut into 6 slices
3 green plantains or green bananas
2 ears corn
Flour
2 pounds striped bass fillets, cut into 2-inch pieces, or any firm white fish

3 fresh hot red peppers, about 4 inches long, or use hot green peppers
3 medium onions, cut into ⅛-inch slices
½ cup white vinegar
Lettuce leaves
½ pound Spanish fresh cheese (queso blanco or queso fresco) or Münster cheese, cut into 6 wedges
Lettuce leaves
Black olives

In a small bowl combine the finely chopped onion, lemon juice, cayenne pepper, and salt and pepper to taste. Set aside. Cook the potatoes in salted water until they are tender, but not mushy. Drain well and mash. Add 1 cup of the olive oil to the onion and lemon juice. Pour this dressing over the potatoes, mixing thoroughly. Make a mound of the potatoes in the center of a large round platter and keep warm, not hot.

Boil the sweet potatoes and cassava in salted water for 20 minutes, or until they are tender. Drain and keep warm. It does not matter if the cassava slices have broken up. In a separate saucepan boil the plantains, unpeeled but cut in half if necessary to fit the pan, until tender, about 30 minutes. Green bananas will take less time, about 15 minutes. Peel and cut into 12 slices. Keep warm with the sweet potatoes and cassava. Drop the corn into a large saucepan of boiling salted water and boil for 5 minutes. Cut each ear into 3 slices and put with the other vegetables.

Season the flour with salt and pepper. Dredge the fish pieces in the seasoned flour, shaking to remove the excess. In a skillet heat the 4 tablespoons of olive oil and fry the pieces of fish until they are golden brown on both sides, about 3 or 4 minutes. Drain on paper towels and keep warm.

Cut the peppers into ⅛-inch strips and put, with the sliced onions, into a saucepan of boiling water. Blanch for a few minutes then drain well. Add the remaining ½ cup olive oil, the vinegar, and salt and pepper to taste. Bring to a boil over low heat and cook, covered, for 2 or 3 minutes.

To serve, garnish the platter round the edge with lettuce leaves. Arrange the fish fillets, corn, sweet potato, cassava, and plantains or bananas on the lettuce leaves. Pour the onion and pepper mixture over the potatoes and garnish the mound with the wedges of cheese and black olives.

Variation: For *Causa a la Limeña* (Potatoes with Shrimp and Vegetables), add a seeded and finely chopped fresh hot red or green pepper to the chopped onion pickle. Omit the plantains and fish. Instead drop 6 jumbo shrimp (or more if using smaller shrimp) into boiling salted water and cook until just tender, 3 to 5 minutes. Hardboil 3 eggs and cut them in halves lengthwise. To serve arrange lettuce leaves round the edge of the mound of potatoes and arrange the cassava and sweet potato slices on the lettuce leaves. Make a circle on the edge of the mound of potatoes with the corn, then another circle on the potatoes with the cheese and shrimp alternately, and finally place the eggs and black olives on top of the potatoes. Serves 6.

Ocopa de Pichones   PERU
Potatoes and Eggs in Pigeon and Walnut Sauce

This is a most exotic and delectable dish, ideal for a summer lunch or dinner when hot food is unappetizing and the palate longs for something light yet substantial. The flavor of the pigeon is subtly enhanced by the walnuts, cheese, and oil-stewed onion, to make a most sumptuous sauce for the potato and hardboiled egg. Start with a corn or sweet red pepper soup and follow the *Ocopa* with *Mazamorra Morada* (Peruvian Fruit Compote) for dessert. A dry white wine or a rosé makes extremely pleasant drinking.

Serves 6

4 pigeons, each weighing about 8
   ounces
Salt, freshly ground pepper
6 medium onions
4 medium tomatoes
1 large hot dried red pepper, or 2
   small
4 tablespoons olive oil
1 cup walnut meats, about 8
   ounces

FOR THE GARNISH
Lettuce leaves
Black and green olives
4 fresh hot red peppers (optional)

8 ounces fresh cheese, or Spanish
   queso fresco or queso blanco,
   or use Münster or a similar
   cheese
Milk
6 eggs
6 medium potatoes

Split the pigeons in half and season on both sides with salt and pepper. Thinly slice 4 of the onions and put them in the bottom of a heavy casserole. Arrange the pigeons on top of the onions. Peel the tomatoes and cut them into thin slices, about ⅛ inch. Make a layer of the tomatoes over the pigeons. Cover the casserole with foil and then with the casserole lid. Cook over very low heat, using an asbestos mat if necessary to keep the contents from burning. Cook until the pigeons are tender, about 3 hours, shaking the casserole from time to time. Let the pigeons cool thoroughly in the casserole. Lift the birds out and bone them. Chop the meat coarsely and set aside. Reserve the pan juices. Rinse out and dry the casserole. Shake the seeds out of the hot dried pepper and put it to soak in warm water.

Cut the remaining 2 onions into thick slices, about ¾ inch. Heat the oil in the casserole and add the onion slices. Cook over low heat, turning once, until they are golden brown on both sides. Allow to cool slightly, then put into a blender or food processor fitted with a steel blade, with the oil, the pigeon meat, and the pan juices. Drain the pepper, chop, and add. Add the walnuts and cheese and reduce to a purée, adding milk as necessary to make the sauce the consistency of a thick mayonnaise. Purée in batches if necessary.

Hardboil the eggs, shell them, and halve them lengthwise. Boil the potatoes and drain them. Arrange the eggs, yolk side up, and the potatoes while still warm on a large warmed serving platter. Pour the sauce over them. Decorate the edge of the platter with lettuce leaves and arrange the olives on top of the potatoes and eggs. Slice the peppers from the tip to the stem and into 4 or 5 sections, which will then curl back, forming flowers.

Place them round the edge of the dish. This is optional but I like to do it, as there is always someone who really enjoys nibbling on hot peppers.

If serving this as an appetizer, halve the potatoes lengthwise and serve half a potato and half a hardboiled egg per person. Serves 12.

Cuscuz de Galinha   BRAZIL
Garnished Steamed Chicken and Cornmeal

This *Cuscuz* from São Paulo is made of cornmeal. The original *couscous* — the national dish of the Maghreb, the North African countries of Morocco, Tunisia, and Algeria — is made of wheat. There are other differences, which help to illustrate the Brazilian cook's ability to absorb foreign influences and to transform what is borrowed. This is a delicious dish, easy to make and wonderfully festive looking.

Serves 6 to 8

A 3½-pound chicken, cut into serving pieces	1 cup dry white wine
2 tablespoons lemon juice	½ cup chicken stock
4 tablespoons (¼ cup) butter	1 tablespoon olive oil
4 scallions, chopped, using white and green parts	½ pound chorizo or other spiced smoked pork sausage, cut into ¼-inch slices
2 medium tomatoes, peeled, seeded, and chopped	¼ cup chopped parsley
Salt, freshly ground pepper	1 or 2 fresh hot red peppers, seeded and chopped

Put the chicken pieces in a bowl with the lemon juice. Mix well and let stand 15 minutes. Lift out the chicken pieces, pat dry, and reserve the liquid. Heat the butter in a flameproof casserole and sauté the chicken pieces lightly. Add the scallions and tomatoes and season to taste with salt and pepper. Pour in the wine and chicken stock. Bring to a simmer, cover, and cook over low heat until the chicken pieces are tender. Let them stand, off the heat, until they are cool enough to handle. Lift them out of the stock, skin and bone them, and shred the meat into pieces about 1 inch by ¼ inch. Strain the stock and discard the solids. There should be 1½ cups. Make up the quantity if necessary with chicken stock. Return the chicken to the stock.

Heat the olive oil in a skillet and sauté the sausage until browned on both sides. Drain on paper towels and add to the chicken with the parsley and hot peppers. Set aside.

FOR THE CORNMEAL MIXTURE

4 cups white cornmeal
½ pound (1 cup) butter
2 medium tomatoes, thinly sliced
A 10-ounce can hearts of palm,
    drained and thinly sliced
3 hardboiled eggs, sliced

12 pitted black olives, halved
1 cup cooked fresh green peas or
    cooked frozen peas
2 oranges, preferably Seville
    (bitter) oranges, peeled and
    thinly sliced

Toast the cornmeal in a heavy skillet over moderate heat, stirring constantly with a wooden spoon, until it is golden, about 5 minutes. Sprinkle 1 cup boiling water over the cornmeal and stir to mix. Cook, stirring, for 2 minutes. Melt the butter in a small saucepan and pour it over the cornmeal, mixing well. Stir the cornmeal, little by little, into the reserved chicken, sausage, and stock mixture, combining it gently but thoroughly. Test the mixture to see if it holds its shape when pressed into a ball. If it is too crumbly, add a little warmed chicken stock and mix, testing again to see that the mixture keeps its shape.

If using a *cuscuzeiro* (*couscoussière*) butter the upper part. Otherwise, butter the inside of a fine-holed colander. Place a tomato slice in the center of the colander or *couscoussière*. Divide the remaining tomato, the hearts of palm, eggs, and olives into 3 equal parts. Divide the peas into 2 parts. Arrange one-third of the tomatoes, palm hearts, eggs, and olives in a decorative pattern around the bottom and sides of the colander. They will stay in place because of the butter. Put one-third of the cornmeal mixture into the colander and pat it down lightly. Sprinkle with half of the peas and another third of the garnish. Cover with another third of the cornmeal. Add the remaining ½ cup of peas and the remaining garnish and top with the remaining cornmeal. Cover with a cloth napkin, then cover the colander tightly with foil, tucking the foil firmly under the rim. Pour boiling water into a deep pot large enough to hold the colander comfortably (or into the bottom half of the *couscoussière*), taking care that the water is not deep enough to reach the bottom of the colander. Cover and steam over low heat for 1 hour, adding a little boiling water during the cooking period if necessary. Turn off the heat and let the colander stand for a few minutes. Remove the napkin and unmold the *Cuscuz* onto a serving dish. It will look like a steamed pudding decorated with the tomato, hearts of palm, and so on. Garnish the dish with the sliced oranges.

Pastel de Choclo
con Relleno de Pollo

BOLIVIA

Chicken Pie with Corn Topping

This is simply delicious, with a combination of flavors that is new to our palates though none of the ingredients is hard to find. As it can be prepared ahead of time, it makes an ideal party dish.

Serves 6

*A 3½-pound chicken, cut into
    serving pieces
2 cups chicken stock, about
¼ cup seedless raisins
3 tablespoons olive or vegetable
    oil
2 medium onions, finely chopped
3 medium tomatoes, peeled and
    chopped*

*Salt
1 or 2 pinches ground cinnamon
2 hardboiled eggs, coarsely
    chopped
12 small pimiento-stuffed olives,
    rinsed and halved*

FOR THE TOPPING

*½ cup butter or lard, or a mixture
    of both
4 cups corn kernels
1 tablespoon sugar, or less to taste
2 teaspoons salt, or to taste
4 eggs
Sweet paprika*

Put the chicken pieces into a large saucepan or casserole, pour in the stock, adding a little more if necessary to barely cover. Bring to a boil, cover, and simmer over low heat until the chicken is tender, about 45 minutes. Let it cool in the stock. When it is cool enough to handle, lift it out of the stock, remove the skin and bones, and cut the meat into 1-inch pieces. Set aside. Reserve the stock for another use. Put the raisins to soak in cold water to cover for 10 minutes. In a skillet heat the oil and sauté the onions until they are soft. Add the tomatoes and cook for about 5 minutes longer, or until the mixture is well blended. Season with salt, drain, and add the raisins, cinnamon, chopped eggs, olives, and chicken. Set aside.

To make the topping, melt the butter or lard in a small saucepan. Put the corn kernels in a blender or food processor and reduce to a purée. Pour into a saucepan and stir in the melted butter or lard. Stir in the sugar and salt. Cook over very low heat, beating the eggs in one by one. Cook, stirring with a wooden spoon, until the mixture has thickened. Allow to cool slightly.

Butter a 2-quart soufflé dish and spoon in about one-third of the corn mixture, patting it up to cover the sides of the dish. Carefully spoon in the chicken mixture, then cover with the rest of the corn. Sprinkle with sweet paprika. Bake in a preheated moderate (350° F.) oven for 1 hour, or until the topping is set and lightly browned. Serve hot.

The pie may be prepared ahead and refrigerated until ready to bake, in which case let it come to room temperature before baking.

Variation: There is a slightly simpler Chilean version of this dish in which cooked, boned chicken, either in small or large pieces, is put into a buttered earthenware casserole or soufflé dish and topped with slices of hardboiled egg, a few raisins, and pitted green olives. The corn topping is then spooned over the chicken. The topping is sprinkled with 1 tablespoon sweet paprika and 1 tablespoon of either superfine or confectioners' sugar, and the pie is baked as for *Pastel de Choclo con Relleno de Pollo*.

Variation: Another, and very popular, filling is *Pino de Carne* (Beef Hash), reminiscent of Mexican *Picadillo*. Sauté 1 pound lean beef, chopped by hand, with 4 finely chopped medium onions in 2 tablespoons oil until the beef and onions are both tender — 2 or 3 minutes. Season with salt, pepper, 1 tablespoon sweet paprika, ⅛ teaspoon cayenne, ½ teaspoon ground cumin, and ⅛ cup seedless raisins, soaked 15 minutes in warm water. Sauté for a few minutes, then put in an earthenware casserole or soufflé dish and top with 2 sliced hardboiled eggs. Cover with the corn topping and bake as for the *Pastel de Choclo con Relleno de Pollo*. If the meat mixture seems a little dry, it may be moistened with beef stock before adding it to the casserole.

Variation: Latin America is not only corn country, it is very much potato country, and the *Pino de Carne* turns up in a potato pie, *Pastel de Papas*. For this make the *Pino* as described above and set it aside. Peel and slice 3 pounds of potatoes and boil them in salted water until soft. Mash them with enough light cream, about 1 cup, to make a purée, then, over low heat, beat in 1 well-beaten egg. In a buttered earthenware casserole or soufflé dish make alternate layers of potato and beef hash, beginning and ending with potato. Bake in a preheated moderate (350° F.) oven until the potato pie is heated through and the top lightly browned. Serves 6. If liked, the amount of *Pino de Carne* may be doubled.

Pudín de Choclo   ECUADOR
Corn Soufflé

This is less like a French soufflé than like an American corn pudding. It is a
rich-tasting dish, but not heavy, nice for a light meal, or as the first course
of a grand one.

Serves 6

2 cups kernels of young corn, or 2 cups frozen corn, thawed	Salt, white pepper
½ pound Münster cheese, cubed	5 eggs, well beaten
4 tablespoons (¼ cup) butter, cut into small pieces	Butter

Combine the corn, cheese, and butter in a blender or food processor. Season
to taste with salt and pepper and pour in the eggs. Blend on high speed until
the mixture is smooth. Pour into a buttered 1½-quart soufflé dish and set
the dish in a pan of hot water in a preheated moderate (350° F.) oven. Bake
for 1 hour, or until a knife inserted in the soufflé comes out clean.

Chouriço, Brócolos, y Creme de Milho   BRAZIL
Sausage and Broccoli with Puréed Corn

This dish from the state of Minas Gerais is a fine one-dish family meal.
The corn purée makes a lovely sauce for the broccoli.

Serves 4

A 1½-pound bunch of broccoli	Oil
4 tablespoons (¼ cup) butter plus 1 tablespoon	¾ pound chorizo or other spiced smoked pork sausage
Salt, freshly ground pepper	4 cups raw corn kernels

Rinse the broccoli in cold water and cut off and discard the tough stems.
Chop the broccoli. In a saucepan heat the 4 tablespoons butter, add the
broccoli, stir, and cook for 2 minutes. Add 1 tablespoon water, cover, and
cook until the vegetable is tender, about 8 minutes. Season with salt and
pepper. Put in a serving dish and keep warm.

Film the bottom of a skillet with oil and sauté the chorizos until browned all over, about 5 minutes. They will cook in their own fat. Drain on paper towels and slice, or halve crosswise. Arrange the sausage around the broccoli and keep warm.

Purée the corn in a blender or food processor. In a saucepan melt the tablespoon of butter, add the corn, and cook stirring constantly with a wooden spoon for about 5 minutes over low heat. Season with salt and pepper. Pour the corn purée over the broccoli.

Chilaquiles de Estudiante   MEXICO
Student's Tortilla Casserole

My husband says this dish reminds him of his days at the university in Mexico, when he was perpetually hungry but often lacked the time to get home for the main meal at midday and found no one very interested in feeding him at night, when only *merienda*, a light supper, was served. *Chilaquiles* is essentially a leftover dish using anything the kitchen has to offer, usually leftover chicken, or turkey *mole*, or any pork. This one is very special indeed, quite approaching elegance. I suspect that only a very warm-hearted family cook, who understood that acquiring knowledge provokes appetite, would have gone to the trouble of preparing it for the evening meal of a hungry student and three of his friends, equally hungry, since it serves 4. I also suspect the cook must have overbought the pork for the midday meal to have had a pound left over. Made on purpose with no students around, it makes a fine lunch or supper dish.

Serves 4

FOR THE TORTILLAS
1 recipe tortillas (page 44)
4 tablespoons vegetable oil or
    lard, about

Make the tortillas the previous day, if possible, as they should have time to dry out a little. Simply wrap them in a cloth and leave them in the kitchen. If they are freshly made, dry them in the oven with the pilot light on for an hour or two. When ready to use, cut the tortillas with kitchen shears into strips about ½ inch wide. Heat the oil or lard in a skillet and fry the tortilla strips in batches, but do not let them brown. Drain on paper towels and set aside. Reserve the oil in the skillet.

FOR THE FILLING

1 pound pork, raw or cooked
   cut into 1-inch pieces
2 medium tomatoes, peeled and
   chopped
1 medium onion, chopped
2 cloves garlic, chopped

3 tablespoons seedless raisins
16 small pimiento-stuffed olives,
   halved
1 tablespoon red wine vinegar
½ teaspoon sugar
Salt and pepper to taste

Put raw pork into a heavy saucepan with water just to cover and simmer, covered, over low heat until tender, about 1½ hours. Allow the pork to cool in the stock. Lift out and shred. If using cooked pork, simply shred. Reserve the stock. Put the tomatoes, onion, garlic in a blender or food processor and purée. Measure the oil remaining in the skillet and if necessary make up the quantity to 2 tablespoons. Add the tomato mixture and cook, stirring, for 2 or 3 minutes. Add the pork, raisins, olives, vinegar, sugar, and salt and pepper to taste, and simmer over low heat until quite thick, about 5 minutes. Make a layer of half the tortilla strips in a greased ovenproof casserole, preferably earthenware, and spread the pork mixture on top. Cover with the remaining tortilla strips. Set aside.

FOR THE SAUCE

4 ancho *chilies*
1 medium onion
1 clove garlic
⅛ teaspoon cinnamon
Pinch of ground cloves
1 teaspoon sugar
Salt, freshly ground pepper

3 tablespoons vegetable oil or lard
2 medium tomatoes, peeled and
   chopped

Pull the stems from the *ancho* chilies, shake out the seeds, rinse in cold water, and tear into pieces. Put into a bowl with ½ cup warm water and soak, turning from time to time, for about 1 hour. Put the chilies and any soaking water into a blender or food processor with the onion and garlic and reduce to a purée. It should be quite thick and heavy. Do not over-blend, as it should have some texture. Add the cinnamon, cloves, sugar, salt, and pepper. Heat the oil or lard in a skillet and add the *ancho* mixture. Cook, stirring, for about 5 minutes. Purée the tomatoes in the blender and add to the skillet and simmer for 2 or 3 minutes longer. Add 2 cups of the reserved pork stock, adding chicken stock or water as necessary. If using cooked pork, use chicken stock in place of pork stock. Stir to mix, heat through, and pour over the contents of the casserole. Bake the casserole in a preheated moderate (350° F.) oven until heated through, about 30 minutes. Serve directly from the casserole. Accompany with a green salad.

Mucbi-Pollo   MEXICO
Chicken and Pork Tamal Pie

This is a very old, traditional Mayan dish from Yucatán, a sort of corn pie
wrapped in banana or plantain leaves and baked in a *pib* or earth oven,
though nowadays it is usually cooked in an ordinary gas or electric oven.
As banana or plantain leaves are fairly difficult to come by, kitchen parchment or aluminum foil may be used as substitutes. If the herb *epazote* is
not available, its absence from the dish is no great matter since it is the
achiote (annatto) that gives the *tamal* pie its characteristic flavor and appearance. Traditionally a whole chicken, cut into serving pieces, is used
but there seems to be no logical reason why the chicken should not be
boned for ease in assembling and serving the dish. I have had it both ways
and there is no difference in flavor, which is what matters.

Serves 4 to 6

FOR THE FILLING

1 large onion, chopped
3 medium tomatoes, peeled and
  chopped
2 cloves garlic, chopped
½ teaspoon oregano
¼ teaspoon cumin
2 tablespoons ground achiote
  (annatto)
Salt
A 2½-pound chicken, quartered
1 pound lean, boneless pork, cut
  into 1-inch cubes

1½ cups chicken stock, about
¾ cup masa harina

Put the onion, tomatoes, garlic, oregano, cumin, achiote, and salt to taste in
a blender or food processor and reduce them to a purée. Put the chicken and
pork into a saucepan or casserole and pour the purée over them. Add
enough chicken stock to cover, about 1½ cups. Cover and simmer until
the chicken is tender, about 45 minutes. Lift out the chicken pieces and set
aside. Continue to cook the pork until it is tender, about 30 minutes
longer. Bone the chicken and cut it into large pieces. Set it aside with the
pork. Strain the stock. Put the *masa harina* in a small saucepan and add
enough of the stock to make a very thick sauce, stirring over low heat for a
minute or two. Pour the sauce over the chicken and pork.

FOR THE DOUGH

3 cups masa harina
1 cup (½ pound) annatto oil or
*   lard, page 324*
1 ½ tablespoons achiote (annatto)
*   seeds*
Chicken stock
Salt

Put the *masa harina* in a bowl, stir in the annatto oil or lard and the achiote seeds, and when thoroughly mixed add just enough hot chicken stock and a pinch of salt to make a thick, smooth dough. Cut a 12- by 24-inch strip of kitchen parchment or aluminum foil, or use a banana leaf, if available. Spread half of the *masa harina* dough on the parchment or foil, leaving room at the sides. Arrange the chicken, pork, and sauce on top of the dough. Cover with the rest of the dough. Fold up the parchment into a parcel and put it into a greased baking pan, fold side down. Bake in a preheated hot (400° F.) oven for 30 minutes. Unwrap to serve. The outside will be crisp, the inside, with the chicken and pork filling, moist. Serve with *Ixni-Pec* (Hot Pepper Sauce), page 311.

Queso Relleno
Stuffed Cheese

MEXICO

This dish, though popular for a long time in its birthplace, the Caribbean island of Curaçao (where it is called *Keshy Yena* in the patois of the island), was introduced to Yucatán by Dutch and German coffee men sometime in the last century. Its foreign origins are obvious in that a Dutch Edam cheese is the main ingredient, hollowed out and stuffed with a rich pork mixture. For some reason Yucatecans almost invariably use saffron rather than achiote, which is more characteristic of their kitchen, and they usually steam rather than bake the cheese; the sauce, too, is a further Mayan enhancement. The dish looks quite spectacular when brought to the table as the cheese expands during the cooking and, when cut into wedges and served, the soft cheese shell combines deliciously with the pork filling. All that is needed as an accompaniment is a salad.

Serves 6 to 8

A 4-pound Edam cheese
6 eggs
2 pounds lean pork, ground
Salt
4 tablespoons lard or vegetable oil
1 medium onion, finely chopped
1 red bell pepper, seeded and
    chopped, or use 2 canned
    pimientos
2 cloves garlic, chopped

2 tomatoes, peeled, seeded, and
    chopped
½ teaspoon oregano
¼ teaspoon ground cloves
Freshly ground pepper
¼ cup small, pitted green olives
¼ cup seedless raisins
¼ cup capers
¼ cup dry sherry

FOR THE SAUCE

3 tablespoons butter
3 tablespoons all-purpose flour
The reserved pork stock
⅛ teaspoon powdered saffron, or
    thread saffron ground in a
    mortar with a pestle

1 red bell pepper, seeded and
    chopped, or use 2 canned
    pimientos, chopped
Salt, freshly ground pepper
¼ cup small, pitted green olives,
    halved

Peel the red wax covering off the cheese. Cut an inch-thick slice from the top and hollow it out slightly. Scoop out the cheese, leaving a shell ½ to ¾ inch thick. Reserve the scooped-out cheese for another use. Put the shell and lid in a large bowl of cold water to cover, and soak for 1 hour. Hardboil the eggs and drop them into cold water. When they are cool enough to handle, shell them. Carefully remove the whites, leaving the yolks whole. The best way to do this is with the fingers. Finely chop the whites and set both whites and yolks aside.

Put the pork into a saucepan with enough water to cover and salt to taste. Cover and simmer until the meat is tender, about 30 minutes. Heat the lard or vegetable oil in a skillet and sauté the onion, bell pepper, and garlic until the onion is soft. If using the pimientos, add with the tomatoes. Add the tomatoes and cook until the mixture is quite thick, about 5 minutes. Drain the pork and reserve the stock. Add the onion and tomato mixture to the pork with the oregano, cloves, salt and pepper to taste, the chopped egg whites, olives, raisins, capers, and sherry, mixing well. Remove the cheese shell and lid from the water, drain, and pat dry. Divide the meat mixture into three parts. Put one-third of it into the cheese, patting it down firmly. Halve the egg yolks. Make a layer of 6 halved yolks on top of the meat. Spoon in another third of the meat mixture and pat down lightly. Make a layer of the remaining 6 halved egg yolks, and top with the rest of the meat mixture. Place the lid on the cheese and rub the cheese all over with lard or oil. Wrap it in a double layer of cheesecloth, then place on a rack in a steamer, and steam over boiling water for 40 minutes.

Meanwhile prepare the sauce: Heat the butter in a saucepan. Add the flour and cook, stirring constantly with a wooden spoon, for a minute. Do not let the flour brown. Add the reserved pork stock, making up the quantity with water to 2 cups, if necessary. Add the saffron, the bell pepper or pimientos, salt and pepper to taste, and the olives. Cook, stirring frequently, for 15 minutes. Pour over the cheese just before serving.

Lift the cheese out of the steamer and remove the cheesecloth. Place the cheese on a warmed serving platter and pour the sauce over it. To serve, cut the cheese in wedges.

Arroz com Porco   BRAZIL
Rice with Pork

This dish is typical of São Paulo and the regions the Paulistas developed.

Serves 6

FOR THE MARINADE

½ cup dry white wine
½ cup white vinegar
1 large clove garlic, crushed
1 medium onion, grated
Salt, freshly ground pepper
1 tablespoon chopped fresh
   coriander (cilantro)

1 fresh hot red pepper, chopped, or
   ½ teaspoon hot pepper sauce
   (such as Tabasco or Môlho de
   Pimenta e Limão, page 313)
2 pounds lean boneless pork, loin
   or shoulder, cut into 1-inch
   cubes

FOR THE STEW

2 tablespoons vegetable oil
1 medium onion, chopped
1 green bell pepper, seeded and
   chopped
1 clove garlic, chopped
1 tablespoon chopped fresh
   coriander (cilantro)

2 cups long-grain rice
Salt, freshly ground pepper
¼ pound boiled ham, diced
¼ cup freshly grated Parmesan
   cheese plus 2 tablespoons
1 tablespoon butter

In a large bowl combine the wine, vinegar, garlic, grated onion, salt and pepper to taste, coriander, and hot pepper or hot pepper sauce. Add the pork and mix lightly. Cover the bowl and refrigerate for about 8 hours, stirring once or twice. Lift out the pork pieces and pat them dry with paper towels. Strain and reserve the marinade. Discard the solids.

Now begin the stew: Heat the oil in a casserole and sauté the pork pieces until they are lightly browned. Add the onion, green pepper, garlic, and fresh coriander, and sauté for 3 or 4 minutes longer. Add the strained marinade, cover, and simmer until the pork is tender, about 1 hour.

About 20 minutes before the pork is done, wash the rice, drain, and put it into a heavy saucepan with 4 cups cold water. Bring to a boil over high heat, stir in ½ teaspoon salt, cover, and cook over low heat until the rice is tender and all the liquid absorbed, about 20 minutes.

Taste the pork for seasoning, adding a little more salt and pepper if needed. Add the ham and stir in the ¼ cup of cheese.

Arrange half the rice on an ovenproof serving platter. Spread the pork mixture over the rice, which should be quite dry. Arrange the rest of the rice over the pork. Sprinkle the rice with the 2 tablespoons of Parmesan cheese and the butter, cut into small bits. Put the platter into a preheated moderately hot (375° F.) oven until the top is lightly browned, about 10 minutes. Serve with a freshly made tomato sauce (*Môlho ao Tomate*, see page 318).

Arroz con Chancho   PERU
Pork and Rice

This Peruvian pork and rice dish is much simpler than the Brazilian version, but the annatto used in the cooking liquid for both pork and rice gives the finished dish a pleasantly distinctive flavor and an attractive yellow color.

Serves 6

2 tablespoons lard or vegetable oil
2 pounds boneless pork loin or
   shoulder, cut into 1-inch
   cubes
2 teaspoons finely chopped garlic
½ teaspoon ground annatto
1 tablespoon sweet paprika

1 fresh hot red pepper, seeded and
   chopped, or ½ teaspoon
   cayenne
Salt
2 cups long-grain rice
1½ cups fresh green peas, shelled

Heat the lard or oil in a flameproof casserole and sauté the pork pieces until they are lightly browned all over. Add the garlic, annatto, paprika, fresh hot pepper or cayenne, and salt to the casserole and sauté for a minute or two longer. Add enough water barely to cover and simmer, covered, over low heat until the pork is tender, about 1½ hours. Drain the liquid from the casserole and measure it. Add enough water to make the quantity up to 4 cups. Return the liquid to the casserole, stir in the rice and the peas, cover, and bring to a boil. Reduce the heat as low as possible and cook until the rice and peas are tender and all the liquid absorbed. Serve with a green vegetable or a salad.

Carne Rellena
Stuffed Steak

This is an unusual dish and looks quite spectacular, as the egg and vegetables show attractively in each slice. The flavor matches the looks. The stuffed omelet makes a rich accompaniment to the tender, juicy steak.

Serves 6

A 3-pound flank steak, or two
   1½-pound steaks
4 large cloves garlic, crushed
Salt
¼ cup olive oil
4 eggs

Vegetable oil
A 10-ounce can green asparagus
   tips
2 whole pimientos, cut into strips
2 tablespoons butter
1¼ cups dry red wine

Trim the steak of any fat and place in a baking dish or any shallow dish large enough to hold it comfortably. Mix the garlic with 2 teaspoons salt and the olive oil and rub the mixture into both sides of the steak. Let it stand at room temperature for about 2 hours.

Break the eggs into a bowl and beat them lightly with 1 teaspoon salt and 2 tablespoons water. Heat a 7-inch omelet pan and pour in just enough vegetable oil to film the surface. The pan should be about the same width as the steak. A rectangular Japanese omelet pan is ideal for this; if using a round pan, trim the omelet later to fit the steak. Pour the eggs into the pan and make an omelet in the usual way, stirring vigorously with the flat of a fork over moderate heat until the eggs begin to set, then cook until the eggs have set. Slide the omelet out of the pan and place it on top of the steak. If using 2 smaller steaks, make 2 omelets. Trim the omelet to fit. On top of the omelet lay alternate horizontal rows of asparagus tips and pimiento strips, starting and ending about ½ inch from the edge. Roll up the steak and tie it securely with string. Put the steak into a baking tin and dot it with the butter. Bake in a preheated moderate (350° F.) oven for 45 minutes for rare steak, basting it several times with the wine. Cook for 15 minutes longer if a well-done steak is preferred.

Lift the steak out onto a warmed serving platter and remove the string.

Reduce the wine and pan juices quickly over brisk heat and pour into a sauceboat. Cut the steak into 1-inch slices, and serve with plain white rice, *Caraotas Negras* (Black Beans), and fried plantains or bananas.

Molondrones con Camarones
Okra with Shrimp   DOMINICAN REPUBLIC

This is a lovely dish from the Dominican Republic with okra, bananas, shrimp, and coriander making an unusual combination of flavors.

Serves 3 to 4

½ cup vegetable oil
1 medium onion, finely chopped
4 cups small, fresh okra pods, cut into ¼-inch slices
3 underripe bananas, peeled and cut into ½-inch slices
2 medium tomatoes, peeled and chopped

¼ cup lemon juice
1 small fresh hot red or green pepper, seeded and chopped
1 tablespoon fresh green coriander (cilantro), chopped
Salt, freshly ground pepper
1 pound medium-sized shrimp, shelled and deveined

Heat the oil in a skillet and sauté the onion until it is soft. Add the okra and sauté for 2 to 3 minutes longer. Add the bananas, tomatoes, lemon juice, hot pepper, coriander, and salt and pepper to taste. Simmer the mixture for about 5 minutes, or until the okra is tender. Add the shrimp and cook for about 3 minutes longer, or until the shrimp turn pink. Serve with rice.

Repollo Relleno
Stuffed Whole Cabbage   BOLIVIA

A whole stuffed cabbage with a highly seasoned meat stuffing makes a most delectable luncheon or family supper dish. I've come across it with variations in the filling in the Andean countries of Bolivia, Peru, Venezuela, and Colombia. Its obvious ancestor is *sou-fassum*, the stuffed cabbage of Provence. When I cook it, I borrow a trick from Richard Olney, who wraps his *sou-fassum* in cheesecloth, making it a lot easier to handle than when it is merely tied round with a piece of string. I save the leftover stock for making soup.

Serves 6 to 8

1 large Savoy cabbage, weighing about 3 pounds
1 recipe Picadillo *(Seasoned Chopped Beef), page 131, using pork instead of beef and omitting the apples and almonds*

Beef or chicken stock
1 recipe Salsa de Jitomate *(Tomato Sauce), page 319*

Trim the cabbage, removing any wilted outer leaves. Drop the cabbage into a large saucepan full of briskly boiling water and let it simmer for 10 minutes. Lift out the cabbage into a colander and let it drain thoroughly. When it is cool enough to handle, place it on a large square of double cheesecloth and carefully open the outer leaves, spreading as flat as possible without breaking them off. Cut out the heart of the cabbage, discard the core, chop fine, and add it to the seasoned chopped pork, mixing thoroughly. Cut away as much of the core as possible while leaving the cabbage intact. Form the meat into a ball and pack it into the center of the cabbage. Press the outer leaves back into shape, re-forming the cabbage. Gather up the cheesecloth and tie it up with string. Put the cabbage into a large saucepan into which it fits comfortably and pour in enough stock to cover. Bring to a boil, reduce the heat, and simmer the cabbage for 3 to 3½ hours. Lift out into a round serving dish or soup tureen, untie, and slide out the cheesecloth, lifting the cabbage with a spatula to do so. Spoon a little tomato sauce over the cabbage and serve the rest in a sauceboat. To serve cut the cabbage into wedges. Accompany with rice.

Variation: Reduce the amount of pork to 1 pound and add 1 pound potatoes, peeled and cut into ¼-inch cubes. Serve with crusty bread instead of rice.

Variation: In Venezuela, cooks add 1 teaspoon *Aliño Criollo* (Creole Style Seasoning Powder), page 325, to the meat mixture, which gives it a very interesting flavor.

Variation: In Brazil, where stuffed cabbage is also popular, a mixture of pork and beef, seasoned with ½ teaspoon nutmeg, is used. Two slices of chopped bacon may be added as well as ¼ cup well-washed raw rice.

Flan de Legumbres   ECUADOR
Vegetable Soufflé

Vegetables are handled imaginatively by Ecuadorian cooks. This mixture of eggs and vegetables makes a satisfying meal when served with soup and dessert.

Serves 4 to 6

6 slices bacon, cut into julienne
1 cup fresh breadcrumbs
½ cup milk
3 tablespoons tomato sauce
1 cup chicken stock
2 tablespoons melted butter
1 tablespoon chopped parsley

Salt, freshly ground pepper
2 cups cooked mixed vegetables
    such as corn, peas, carrots,
    cauliflower, green beans, and
    green pepper, all chopped
3 eggs, well beaten
½ tablespoon butter

Cook the bacon in a skillet over moderate heat until crisp, and drain on paper towels. Combine the bacon with the breadcrumbs, milk, tomato sauce, chicken stock, melted butter, parsley, and salt and pepper to taste. Fold in the mixed vegetables. Fold in the eggs and pour the mixture into a buttered 1½-quart soufflé dish. Stand the dish in a baking tin, half-filled with hot water, in a preheated moderate (350° F.) oven, and cook for 1 hour, or until a knife inserted into the soufflé comes out clean.

Torta de Plátano
Savory Green Banana Cake

MEXICO

There is a hint of sweetness in this very original old colonial dish from Oaxaca in Mexico: the bananas go well with the robust flavor of the beans, a combination that is both unusual and good with meat and poultry when served instead of rice or potatoes.

Serves 6 to 8

2 cups cooked kidney beans
1 medium onion, finely chopped
1 bay leaf
4 tablespoons lard or vegetable oil
Salt, freshly ground pepper

6 green (unripe) bananas, or 4
  green plantains
½ cup grated Parmesan cheese
4 tablespoons butter
2 eggs, lightly beaten

If dried beans are used, simmer 1 cup well-washed and picked-over kidney beans in water to cover with ½ medium onion, chopped, and a bay leaf, until the beans are tender, about 2 hours. If the beans dry out during the cooking, add a little hot water. Drain, reserve ½ cup of the cooking liquid, remove and discard the bay leaf, and purée the beans with the reserved liquid in a blender. Black beans may also be used.

Put the beans with about ½ cup of the cooking liquid in a blender or food processor and reduce them to a purée. Heat the lard or oil in a heavy skillet and sauté the onion until it is very soft. Add the beans and cook, stirring with a wooden spoon, until they form a soft paste. They should not be dry. Season to taste with salt and pepper. Set aside.

Cut through the skins of the bananas lengthwise and peel them. Put them into a saucepan with salted water to cover, bring to a boil over moderate heat, reduce the heat, and simmer, uncovered, until they are tender, 10 to 15 minutes. Plantains will take about 30 minutes. Drain and mash with a fork while they are still warm. Mash in the grated cheese and 3 tablespoons of the butter. Stir in the eggs, mixing well. Butter a soufflé dish and make a layer of half the banana mixture, cover with the bean mixture, and top with the remaining banana mixture. Dot with the remaining tablespoon of butter, and bake in a preheated moderate (375° F.) oven for 30 minutes. Serve directly from the dish.

Variation: Some cooks add 4 tablespoons of flour to the banana mixture with the cheese but I find this makes the topping very dense and heavy. However, for another Mexican version of the dish, *Frijoles con Plátanos*

(Beans with Bananas), which is made with ripe bananas, flour is necessary (1 tablespoon flour for each banana), as the ripe fruit has more sugar and less starch. For this the banana mixture is fried in oil, 1 tablespoon at a time as a fritter, until browned on both sides, about 5 minutes. To serve put 1 teaspoon hot mashed black beans in the center and fold the fritter over. These can be eaten with cream cheese as a dessert but are delicious with plainly cooked meats or poultry as a side dish.

Variation: In Oaxaca the *torta* is sometimes made into *Empanadas* (Turnovers). Pat the cooked green banana mixture plus 4 tablespoons flour into flat cakes 2 to 3 inches in diameter, stuff with a little of the bean mixture, fold over, pressing the edges together to seal in the filling, and fry in lard or vegetable oil until golden on both sides.

Variation: I came across a similar dish in Guatemala, *Empanadas de Plátano* (Banana Turnovers), also called, more picturesquely, *Niños Envueltos* (Babies in a Blanket). Green plantains were preferred to green bananas though both were used, and flour was added, but the beans used were black beans, never any other kind. Sometimes the turnovers were stuffed with fresh cream cheese instead of, or as well as, the mashed beans, and the turnovers were deep fried. I once had them sprinkled with sugar and served with cream as a dessert. They were remarkably pleasant.

BEANS

Beans are important in Latin America not only because so many of the world's varieties of this useful vegetable originated there but because they supplied valuable protein in a region where there were none of the sources of high protein that Europe had, such as cattle, sheep, goats, pigs, and so on. Fortunately beans were not pushed out of the kitchen by the Conquest. They are just as popular today as they ever were. They are an essential part of Mexico's main meal, served after the main course and before dessert, in small bowls. They are quite soupy and are eaten with a spoon, accompanied by tortillas, which can also be used to scoop up the beans. I like to serve them, as do many modern Mexicans, with the meal. So essential are beans to the Latin American kitchen that there is a saying when unexpected guests arrive: *"Pónle más agua a los frijoles,"* meaning "Add more water to the beans." They are immensely popular as *frijoles refritos*, refried beans. It took me some time to understand why they are called "refried" when clearly they are fried only once. It is partly a matter of euphony since *frijoles fritos* sounds awful whereas *frijoles refritos* makes a pretty sound.

It is also a nice economy of language as the beans are first boiled then fried, with the "re" standing for twice and pointing out the double cooking.

Venezuelans make a charming joke about their black beans, *Caraotas Negras*. They call them *"caviar criollo,"* creole caviar, and serve them mashed, usually with *Arepas* (Corn Bread) as an hors d'oeuvre. They are also an essential part of the national dish, *Pabellón Caraqueño*. They are the heart of Brazil's national dish, *Feijoada Completa* (Black Beans with Mixed Meats).

Because they were so important, cooks evolved their own special ways of seasoning the slowly simmered beans. I cook my beans according to the rules laid down by my husband's grandmother. I think of her recipe as Seven Precious Beans because seven ingredients are added to the beans, which she, along with lots of other cooks in Mexico, insist must never be presoaked. There are exceptions, notably black beans for *Feijoada*. Soaking instructions are given for the exceptions in the recipes in which they occur. Added are onion, garlic, hot pepper, oil or lard, salt, *epazote* or bay leaf, and tomato. Beans themselves have a good, full flavor and when well seasoned and slowly cooked over the most gentle heat are quite irresistible.

Lentils, which like beans are members of the legume family and also a very ancient food, are very popular all over Latin America though not to the point of rivaling beans.

Frijoles
Beans

MEXICO

Serves 6 to 8

2 cups red kidney, black, pinto, or
    pink beans
2 medium onions, finely chopped
2 cloves garlic, chopped
2 canned serrano chilies, or 1
    jalapeño chili, chopped, or 1
    teaspoon dried hot red
    peppers, crumbled

1 sprig epazote (see page 9), or 1
    bay leaf
2 tablespoons lard or vegetable oil
Salt
1 medium tomato, peeled and
    chopped

Wash and pick over the beans but do not soak. Put the beans into a large saucepan with cold water to cover by about 1 inch. Add half the chopped onions and garlic, the chilies, and the *epazote* or bay leaf. Cover, bring to a boil, and simmer gently, adding hot water as needed. When the beans begin to wrinkle, after about 15 to 20 minutes of cooking, add 1 tablespoon of the lard or vegetable oil. When the beans are tender (cooking may take 1½ to 3 hours), add salt to taste and continue to simmer for 30 minutes longer but without adding any more water. There should not be a great deal of liquid when the beans are done.

In a skillet heat the remaining tablespoon of lard and sauté the remaining onions and garlic until soft. Add the tomato and sauté for 2 or 3 minutes longer. Take about ½ cup of beans and any liquid from the saucepan and add them, by the tablespoon, to the skillet, mashing the beans into the tomato mixture over moderate heat to form a fairly heavy paste. Stir this back into the beans in the saucepan, and simmer over low heat for a few minutes to thicken the remaining liquid.

Variation: For *Frijoles Refritos* (Refried Beans), cook the beans as above but use a large skillet to sauté the onions, garlic, and tomato. Over moderate heat, gradually mash in all the beans, tablespoon by tablespoon, together with any liquid. Add a tablespoon of lard from time to time until the beans form a heavy, creamy paste. The amount of lard or vegetable oil used is a matter of taste.

For *antojitos* the beans are used as a spread. If the beans are served as a side dish, they are formed into a roll, sprinkled with grated cheese, and stuck with *tostaditas*, triangles of crisply fried tortilla.

Frijoles Estilo Mexicano   MEXICO
Beans, Mexican Style

This does not mean beans as cooked all over the republic of Mexico. It means as cooked in the state of Mexico and the federal district, where the capital, Mexico City, is located.

Serves 8

2 cups pinto, pink, or red kidney
    beans
1 onion, chopped
1 sprig epazote (optional; see page
    9), or 1 bay leaf

3 tablespoons lard or vegetable oil
Salt

Wash and pick over the beans and put them into a heavy saucepan with the onion and *epazote*, if available, or the bay leaf. Add enough water to cover the beans by 1 inch. Simmer the beans, covered, until they begin to wrinkle, after about 15 to 20 minutes of cooking. Add 1 tablespoon of the lard or oil and continue to cook the beans, covered, adding hot water as necessary until they are tender (1½ to 3 hours). Add salt to taste. Discard the *epazote* or bay leaf. Remove the beans with a slotted spoon to a bowl. Measure ¼ cup beans and mash them until smooth. Stir the mashed beans into the liquid in the saucepan. In a skillet heat the remaining 2 tablespoons of lard or oil and sauté the remaining beans until they are dry, about 5 minutes. Add them to the liquid in the saucepan and simmer the mixture, stirring frequently, until the liquid is thickened.

Caraotas Negras
Black Beans

VENEZUELA

Serves 6

2 cups black (turtle) beans
3 tablespoons olive oil
1 medium onion, finely chopped
1 red bell pepper, seeded and
    chopped, or 2 pimientos,
    chopped
4 cloves garlic
1 teaspoon ground cumin
1 tablespoon sugar
Salt

Wash and pick over the beans. Put the beans to soak for 2 to 4 hours in a saucepan in enough cold water to cover by 2 inches. Add enough water to cover the beans by 1 inch as they will have absorbed much of the soaking water, bring to a boil, cover, and cook until the beans are tender, about 2 hours. In a skillet heat the oil and sauté the onion and bell pepper until both are soft. Add the garlic, cumin, sugar, and the pimientos, if using instead of bell pepper. Sauté for a minute or two, then stir into the beans. Season with salt to taste, and cook, partially covered, over low heat for ½ hour longer. The beans will be quite dry. Serve as a side dish or with *Pabellón Caraqueño* (Steak with Rice, Black Beans, and Plantains).

Feijão Preto
Black Beans

Serves 6 to 8

2 cups black (turtle) beans
2 tablespoons bacon fat
1 medium onion, grated

1 clove garlic, crushed
Salt, freshly ground pepper

Thoroughly wash the beans and put them into a heavy saucepan. Cover with cold water and soak them for about 4 hours. Add enough water to cover the beans by about 1 inch, bring to a boil, lower the heat, and simmer the beans, covered, until they are tender, about 2 hours. Heat the bacon fat in a skillet and add the onion and garlic. Sauté until the onion is soft, then scoop out a cupful of the beans with their cooking liquid and add to the skillet. Continue cooking, at the same time mashing the beans over low heat until the mixture is smooth and thick. Stir the mixture into the pot with the beans, season to taste with salt and pepper, and cook, uncovered, over very low heat for 30 minutes longer.

Porotos Granados
Cranberry Beans with Corn and Squash

This very popular Chilean dish is also very Indian since its main ingredients are all indigenous foods — beans, tomatoes, corn, and squash. In Chile fresh *porotos* (cranberry beans, sometimes called shell beans) are available almost all year round. If they are not available, dried cranberry or Navy beans can be used. *Calabaza*, the West Indian pumpkin, is best to use if available — otherwise use any winter squash.

Serves 4 to 6

2 cups fresh cranberry beans, or 1
    cup dried cranberry or Navy
    beans
3 tablespoons olive oil
2 tablespoons sweet paprika
1 large onion, finely chopped
4 medium tomatoes, peeled and
    chopped

½ teaspoon oregano
Salt, freshly ground pepper
1 pound (about 2 cups) winter
    squash, peeled and cut into
    1-inch cubes
½ cup corn kernels

Wash the fresh beans and put them into a saucepan with cold water to cover, bring to a boil, lower the heat, and simmer, covered, until the beans are tender, about 45 minutes. If using dried beans, rinse them and put them to soak in cold water for 3 or 4 hours. Simmer the beans in unsalted water to cover until they are barely tender, 1½ to 2 hours. Drain the fresh or dried beans and set aside. Reserve the cooking liquid.

Meanwhile heat the oil in a skillet and stir in the paprika over moderate heat with a wooden spoon, taking care not to let it burn. As soon as the paprika and oil are thoroughly mixed, stir in the onion and sauté until the onion is tender. Add the tomatoes, oregano, salt, and freshly ground pepper, and simmer the mixture, stirring from time to time, until it is thick and well blended. Add this mixture and the squash to the saucepan with the beans, stir to mix, and add enough of the reserved cooking liquid barely to cover. Cover and simmer gently for 15 minutes. The squash will disintegrate and thicken the sauce. Stir in the corn and simmer for 5 minutes longer. Serve in soup plates with a little *Pebre* (Chilean Hot Pepper Sauce), if liked.

Frijoles con Puerco Estilo Yucateco   MEXICO
Beans with Pork, Yucatán Style

Serves 6

2 cups black (turtle) beans
2 pounds lean, boneless pork, cut
    into 1½-inch cubes
2 large onions, finely chopped
1 whole fresh hot pepper, or 1
    canned hot pepper

½ teaspoon chopped epazote, *if
    available*
2 or 3 sprigs fresh coriander
    (cilantro)
Salt, freshly ground pepper

FOR THE GARNISH

1 large onion, finely chopped
½ cup fresh coriander (cilantro),
    chopped

12 small radishes, chopped
6 lemon wedges

FOR THE TOMATO SAUCE

4 medium tomatoes
2 fresh or canned hot green
    peppers
Salt

Thoroughly wash and pick over the beans. Put the beans into a large saucepan or flameproof casserole with water to cover by about 2 inches. Bring the beans to a boil, cover, reduce the heat, and simmer for 1 hour. Strain the beans, measure the liquid, and make it up to 8 cups. Return the beans and liquid to the saucepan. Add the pork, onions, hot pepper, *epazote*, if available, coriander sprigs, and salt and pepper to taste. Simmer, covered, until the meat and beans are both tender, about 1½ hours. Discard the hot pepper and coriander sprigs. Lift out the pork pieces with a slotted spoon and place them in the center of a warmed platter. Strain the beans and arrange them round the pork. Pour the bean liquid into a soup tureen. Serve the soup in bowls and the beans and pork on plates at the same time. Serve the garnishes in bowls at the table to be eaten with both the soup and the beans.

To make the tomato sauce: Peel and chop 4 medium tomatoes and simmer them for 15 minutes with 2 fresh or canned hot green peppers and salt to taste. Pour the mixture into a blender or food processor and reduce to a purée. Pour back into the saucepan and heat through. Pour into a bowl and serve over the meat.

Lentejas
Lentils

COLOMBIA

Serves 6

½ pound lentils
2 tablespoons olive oil
2 medium onions, finely chopped
2 cloves garlic, chopped
2 large tomatoes, peeled, seeded,
    and chopped
Salt, freshly ground pepper

Pinch of sugar
1 teaspoon chopped fresh
    coriander (cilantro)

Put the lentils in a large saucepan with water to cover by about 1 inch and cook until they are almost tender, about 1 hour. The quick-cooking variety (noted on package) will be done in about 25 minutes. Drain and set aside.

In a skillet heat the oil and sauté the onions and garlic until the onions are softened. Add the tomatoes, salt, pepper, sugar, and coriander, and simmer gently until the mixture is thick, about 10 minutes. Stir the sauce into the lentils and cook over very low heat for 10 minutes longer to blend the flavors. Serve instead of potatoes or rice.

Angú de Farinha de Milho   BRAZIL
Molded Cornmeal

Brazilians are fond of this simple corn pudding. Traditionally it is served
with *Picadinho de Porco* (Pork Hash), and *Couve à Mineira* (Kale or Collard Greens, Minas Gerais Style), accompanied by *linguiça* sausages. It may
also accompany any meat or poultry dish, or fish and shellfish.

Serves 6

3 cups water   3 tablespoons butter plus butter
1 teaspoon salt   *for the mold*
1 cup cornmeal

In a heavy saucepan bring the water and salt to a boil and pour in the
cornmeal in a thin, steady stream, stirring constantly with a wooden
spoon. Cook over moderate heat until the mixture is smooth and thick.
Stir in the 3 tablespoons of butter. Butter a 1½-quart mold and turn the
cornmeal mixture into it. Pat it down, then unmold onto a serving dish.
    Bacon fat may be used instead of butter.

RICE

Rice is enormously popular in Latin America and cooks pride themselves
on their ability to cook rice to perfection, as this is often considered the
measure of their skill in the kitchen. There are many ways to cook plain
white rice and all of them produce rice that emerges tender, and with every
grain separate. In Peru, Colombia, and Ecuador, cooked rice is drier than
ours and is called *Arroz Graneado. Graneado* has a dual meaning in Peruvian Spanish — choice or select, and grainy. It is an attractive texture.
There are also more elaborate rice dishes like *Arroz a la Mexicana* (Rice,
Mexican Style), which is served as a separate course, *sopa seca*, or dry soup,
at *comida*, the big midday meal. It comes after soup and before the main
course. I serve it with the main course as our meals are not as elaborate as
they are traditionally in Mexico. In coastal Colombia rice is cooked in
coconut milk and garnished with raisins, giving it a tantalizing hint of
sweetness. In addition to plain white rice and more elaborate rice dishes,
Brazil makes rice into molded puddings that are served with the traditional

dishes of Bahia. It is important always to use a heavy saucepan with a tightly fitting lid. If the rice is not to be used immediately, cover the saucepan with a folded dish towel, then the lid to prevent condensed moisture from making the rice mushy. The rice will stay hot for about 15 minutes.

Arroz Blanco

White Rice

MEXICO

Serves 6

1 ½ cups long-grain rice
¼ cup vegetable oil
1 small onion, finely chopped
2 cloves garlic, finely chopped

3 cups cold water
Salt
1 fresh hot green pepper (optional)

Wash the rice thoroughly in several changes of water, drain, and put into a saucepan with hot water to cover. Let stand 15 minutes. Drain in a sieve, letting it stand for about 10 minutes. Heat the oil in a saucepan, add the rice, onion, and garlic, and sauté over low heat, stirring constantly with a wooden spoon, until the rice begins to take on a pale gold color and the oil is absorbed, 3 or 4 minutes. Add the water and salt to taste. Bring to a boil over high heat, reduce the heat to as low as possible, and cook, covered, until the rice is tender and all the liquid absorbed, about 20 minutes. I sometimes like to add a whole fresh hot green pepper when adding the water. It is discarded when the rice is cooked. This gives just a hint of peppery flavor.

Variation: For *Arroz Graneado* (Peruvian Style Rice), pour 2 tablespoons vegetable oil into a saucepan and add 1 clove crushed garlic. Sauté over low heat for 1 or 2 minutes, being careful not to let the garlic burn. Add 4 cups water, 1 teaspoon lemon juice, and salt to taste, and bring to a boil. Stir in 2 cups long-grain rice, washed and drained, bring back to a boil, cover, and cook on the lowest possible heat until the rice is tender and all the liquid absorbed, about 25 minutes. Serves 4 to 6.

Variation: *Arroz Blanco* (White Rice) from Venezuela is traditionally served with *Pabellón Caraqueño* (Steak with Rice, Black Beans, and Plantains) but may accompany any fish, meat, or poultry dish. Thoroughly wash and drain 1½ cups long-grain rice. Heat 3 tablespoons butter in a saucepan and stir in the rice, 1 medium onion, finely chopped, ½ red or green bell pepper, seeded and chopped, and 1 clove garlic, chopped. Sauté, stirring, over low heat for 3 or 4 minutes, or until the butter is absorbed. Do not let the rice brown. Add 3 cups water and salt to taste, bring to a boil, and cook, covered, over very low heat for about 20 minutes, or until all the liquid is absorbed and the rice tender. Serves 6.

Variation: *Arroz de Amendoim* (Peanut-Colored Rice) is not only the color of roasted peanuts, but has a fine, nutty flavor. Thoroughly wash the rice and let it drain in a sieve for 30 minutes. Pour 2 tablespoons peanut oil into a saucepan, add the rice, and sauté, stirring constantly with a wooden spoon, over low heat until the rice is the color of roasted peanuts, a light brown, about 10 minutes. Be careful not to let the rice get too dark in color as it will have a bitter taste. Add 2 tablespoons lemon juice, 1 teaspoon salt, and 3 cups water. Bring to a boil over high heat, then simmer, covered, over very low heat, 15 to 20 minutes, or until the rice is tender and all the liquid absorbed. Serves 6.

Variation: For *Arroz Brasileiro* (Brazilian Style Rice), thoroughly wash and drain 2 cups long-grain rice. Heat 3 tablespoons vegetable oil or lard in a saucepan and sauté 1 onion, finely chopped, and 1 clove garlic, chopped, until the onion is soft. Add the rice and cook, stirring, until the fat has been absorbed. Add 3½ cups water and salt to taste, bring to a boil, cover, and simmer over very low heat until the rice is tender and all the liquid absorbed, about 20 minutes. An attractive variation is to add 1 peeled, seeded, and chopped tomato to the rice just before adding the water, or add ⅓ cup tomato purée. Serves 6, but should be enough for 8 to 10 when served with a *Feijoada Completa* (Black Beans with Mixed Meats).

Arroz a la Mexicana   MEXICO
Rice, Mexican Style

Serves 6 to 8

2 cups long-grain rice
2 tomatoes, peeled, seeded, and
    chopped
1 medium onion, chopped
1 clove garlic, chopped
3 tablespoons lard or vegetable oil
3 ½ cups chicken stock
2 carrots, scraped and thinly
    sliced
1 cup fresh raw peas or frozen
    peas, thawed

1 fresh, hot green pepper, seeded
    and chopped, or 2 serrano
    (hot, green) chilies, seeded
    and chopped
1 tablespoon chopped fresh
    coriander (cilantro) or
    parsley, preferably flat Italian
    parsley

Thoroughly wash the rice in several changes of water and let it soak for 15 minutes. Drain thoroughly in a sieve. Put the tomatoes, onion, and garlic in a blender or food processor and reduce to a purée. Heat the lard or vegetable oil in a flameproof casserole and sauté the rice, stirring constantly, until it is golden. Be careful not to let it brown. Add the tomato mixture and cook it, stirring occasionally, until all the moisture has evaporated. Stir in the chicken stock, carrots, peas, and green pepper. Bring the mixture to a boil, cover it, and simmer over very low heat until the rice is tender and all the liquid absorbed, about 20 minutes. Serve the rice garnished with the chopped coriander or parsley.

Variation: Slice 2 chorizo sausages, fry in a little oil, drain, and garnish the rice with the sausages, 1 large avocado, sliced, and 2 hardboiled eggs, sliced.

Variation: *Arroz Guatemalteco* (Rice, Guatemalan Style) is traditionally served with *Carne en Jocón* (Beef in Tomato and Pepper Sauce), but it may also be served with any dish that would be accompanied by plain rice, such as a meat or poultry stew. Heat 2 tablespoons peanut oil or butter in a heavy saucepan, add 2 cups long-grain rice, and sauté lightly, stirring with a wooden spoon, until the rice has absorbed all the fat, being careful not to let it color. Add 1 cup mixed vegetables (carrots, celery, sweet red peppers, chopped finely, and green peas), salt and pepper, and 4 cups chicken or beef stock. Bring to a boil, cover, and reduce the heat to low. Cook until the rice is tender and all the liquid absorbed, about 20 minutes. Serves 6 to 8.

Arroz con Coco y Pasas   COLOMBIA
Rice with Coconut and Raisins

There are two versions of this dish, *Arroz con Coco y Pasas* (Rice with Coconut and Raisins) and *Arroz con Coco Frito y Pasas* (Rice with Fried Coconut and Raisins). Either makes an excellent and unusual accompaniment to meat dishes. They are typical of the cooking of coastal Colombia, where coconut is very much used.

Serves 6

½ pound raisins
5 cups coconut milk (see page 7)
2 cups long-grain rice

2 teaspoons sugar
1 tablespoon butter
Salt

Put the raisins into a heavy saucepan with a tightly fitting lid, pour in the coconut milk, and let the raisins soak for 30 minutes. Add the rice, sugar, butter, and salt to taste. Cover, bring to a boil, stir once, reduce the heat to very low, and cook the rice, covered, until it is tender and dry (20 to 25 minutes).

Variation: For *Arroz con Coco Frito y Pasas* (Rice with Fried Coconut and Raisins), heat the thick milk made from 1 coconut, about 1 cup or less, in a saucepan over moderate heat, stirring from time to time until the oil separates from the grainy golden residue. In Colombia this is called *titoté*. Add 1 tablespoon brown sugar and cook, stirring, for a few minutes longer. Add 4 cups thin coconut milk and ½ pound raisins and simmer over low heat for 10 minutes. Add 2 cups long-grain rice and salt to taste and cook, stirring frequently, for 10 minutes longer. Stir in 4 tablespoons (¼ cup) butter, or omit this step if preferred. Cover the rice and cook over very low heat until all the liquid is absorbed and the rice is dry and grainy, 20 to 25 minutes.

Angú de Arroz
Molded Rice

BRAZIL

Brazilians like to make molded puddings of rice or rice flour, which are served at room temperature as an accompaniment to dishes like *Vatapá* or with Bahian fish, shellfish, or meat dishes. They make a pleasant change from plain white rice and look very attractive when unmolded.

Serves 6 to 8

2 cups short-grain rice
1 teaspoon salt
1 cup thin coconut milk (see
    page 7)
Butter

Thoroughly rinse the rice until the water runs clear. Put the rice into a saucepan with 4 cups water and leave it to soak overnight. Stir in the salt, cover, bring to a boil, and cook over low heat for 20 minutes, or until the liquid has been absorbed and the rice is mushy. Stir in the coconut milk and cook, mashing the rice with a wooden spoon, for 2 minutes. Turn the rice into a buttered 1½-quart mold and allow to cool. Unmold the rice by covering with a platter and turning over quickly. If it doesn't unmold readily, hit the bottom of the mold with the flat of your hand. Serve at room temperature.

Variation: For *Pirão de Arroz* (Rice Flour Pudding), which goes with the same dishes as does *Angú de Arroz*, combine 1 cup rice flour, 1 teaspoon salt, and 2½ cups coconut milk made by combining both thick and thin coconut milk (see page 7) in a saucepan. Cook over low heat, stirring constantly with a wooden spoon, until the mixture is smooth and thick, about 5 minutes. Pour the mixture into a buttered bowl and let it stand for a few minutes. Turn out onto a serving dish and serve at room temperature. Serves 6 to 8.

Arroz de Haussá
Haussá Rice
BRAZIL

This is an Afro-Brazilian specialty named for the Haussa tribe of Nigeria, who are great rice eaters. The jerked beef used is Brazilian sun-dried salt beef, *carne sêca*, often available in specialty stores. It makes a fine main course for rice lovers.

Serves 4

1 *pound* carne sêca *(jerked beef)*,
   see page 6
4 *tablespoons butter*
2 *medium onions, thinly sliced*
1 *recipe* Arroz Brasileiro *(Brazilian*
   Style Rice), page 249
1 *recipe* Môlho de Acarajé
   (Black-Eyed Pea Fritter
   Sauce), page 23

Soak the beef overnight in cold water to cover. Drain, put into a saucepan with fresh cold water to cover, bring to a boil over moderate heat, and drain. When the beef is cool enough to handle, chop it coarsely, or shred it with the fingers. Heat the butter in a skillet and sauté the onions until they are lightly browned. Add the beef and cook, stirring, until it is lightly browned and heated through. Arrange the rice in the center of a serving dish and surround it with the beef and onion mixture. Serve with *Môlho de Acarajé* (Black-Eyed Pea Fritter Sauce), a hot sauce.

Vegetables and Salads

Verduras y Ensaladas

One of the great excitements of Latin American markets is the vegetable stalls with great heaps of orange carrots, little tender green zucchini, bright red tomatoes, bursting with ripeness, green beans, crisply tender, corn, young onions looking like giant scallions, great, green pumpkins cut to show the vivid yellow flesh inside, bright green okra pods, new potatoes so clean and unblemished they look as though they had sprung from some celestial soil, avocados, black- and green-skinned, green globes of cabbage, peas ready shelled for the buyer, deep red beets, and peppers — vivid green, red, yellow, and orange, in more shapes and sizes than seems possible — spinach, Swiss chard, and a bewildering array of root vegetables — the sweet potatoes, the yams, the taros and malangas, dark brown and light brown, enormous or tiny, smooth-skinned and rough-skinned, knobbly or nicely symmetrical in shape — and the dried beans, black, red, creamy yellow, pink, and speckled, in lavish heaps.

It is no wonder that vegetables play such an important role in the Latin American kitchen — so much so that they are often served as a separate course. What I have learned from South America has changed my own cooking habits considerably. Now I love to serve whole platters of cooked vegetables, lightly dressed with oil and vinegar, at room temperature, either as an accompaniment or as a first course, and I have picked up so many new uses for our more familiar produce that vegetables are never uninspired.

AVOCADOS

Aguacates Rellenos   ECUADOR
Stuffed Avocados

Avocados are much more widely used in soups and sauces than in the States but they're most popular as a first course, stuffed. For a grand occasion, especially a meal in the Latin American tradition, this is fine. I also find that, accompanied by a glass or two of dry white wine and a dessert or cheese, stuffed avocados make a delicious lunch or light supper.

Serves 6

3 large avocados
1 cup chopped, cooked ham
3 hardboiled eggs, chopped
Salt, freshly ground pepper

1 cup mayonnaise, about
Romaine or iceberg lettuce,
   shredded

Carefully peel the avocados, cut into halves lengthwise, and remove and discard the pits. In a bowl combine the ham and hardboiled eggs, season to taste with salt and pepper, and fold in enough mayonnaise to bind the mixture, about 1 cup. Fill the hollows of the avocados with the mixture. Make a bed of lettuce on six salad plates and put half an avocado on each. Serve as a first course or light luncheon dish. A vinaigrette sauce may be used instead of mayonnaise.

Avocados discolor quickly, so if it is necessary to prepare this ahead of time, dip the avocados in lemon juice, or leave them unpeeled, though they will look less elegant. Chopped cold roast pork or chicken may be used instead of the ham mixed with 1 cup cooked mixed vegetables instead of the hardboiled eggs. This is a dish that welcomes the improviser. Ecuadorian cooks sometimes substitute tomato sauce or béchamel for mayonnaise, though I find this less attractive.

Variation: For *Paltas Rellenas con Mariscos* (Avocados Stuffed with Shrimp) from Chile, peel and halve 3 avocados and arrange them on a bed of lettuce on six salad plates. Make 1 recipe *Salsa Golf* (Tomato- and

Cognac-Flavored Mayonnaise), page 327, and mix half of it with 1 pound cooked shrimp, quartered if large, left whole if small. Pile the shrimp mixture into the avocados and serve the rest of the mayonnaise in a sauceboat.

Variation: Venezuela varies the Chilean shrimp-stuffed avocado slightly and calls it *Aguacates Rellenos con Camarones.* The avocados are not peeled, just halved, with the pits removed. The flesh is mashed lightly with a fork and a little vinaigrette dressing is mixed in. They are then stuffed with shrimp in vinaigrette. If small avocados are used, this does make a very nice first course.

Variation: For *Paltas Rellenas* (Stuffed Avocados) from Peru, halve and remove the pits from 3 avocados. Mash a fourth avocado with 1 fresh hot pepper, seeded and chopped, and about ¾ cup vinaigrette dressing made with mustard. Toss the dressing with ½ cup each cooked diced green beans and carrots, ½ cup cooked green peas, ½ cup finely chopped celery, 6 small pimiento-stuffed olives, chopped, and 2 hardboiled eggs, finely chopped. Fill the avocados with the mixture and mask them with mayonnaise. Garnish with slices of hardboiled egg and a little finely chopped parsley. If liked, garnish also with a fresh hot red pepper, cut into a flower shape by slicing it into thin strips almost its full length, stopping short of the stem end. Put the peppers into ice water for several hours, or until the cut ends curl back.

Variation: A simpler version of the Peruvian dish, which is very rich, comes from Cuba. For *Aguacates Rellenos* (Stuffed Avocados), peel the avocados and dip them in lemon juice to prevent discoloring. Cut them in half lengthwise and discard the pits. Arrange each half on a bed of lettuce and fill with a mixture of diced cooked vegetables, using any of the following: potatoes, carrots, beets, green peas, green beans, asparagus tips, finely chopped green or red bell peppers, or chopped cucumbers. Toss the vegetables in a vinaigrette dressing before putting into the avocados, and mask with mayonnaise.

Variation: For *Paltas Rellenas con Salsa Cruda* (Avocados with Uncooked Tomato Sauce) from Bolivia, peel and halve the avocados lengthwise, or simply halve them and remove and discard the pits. Fill them with a sauce made by combining 2 medium tomatoes, peeled and chopped, 1 medium onion, finely chopped, ½ green bell pepper, seeded and chopped, salt and freshly ground pepper to taste, 1 teaspoon vinegar, and 1 tablespoon vegetable oil. This should be made at the last minute if possible, as the sauce loses its fresh flavor if it stands for long.

Variation: For *Paltas Rellenas con Pollo* (Avocados Stuffed with Chicken) from Chile, peel 3 large avocados, dip them in lemon juice, halve them lengthwise, and remove and discard the pits, or simply halve them without peeling. Peel and mash a fourth large avocado and mix it with 1 whole cooked chicken breast, finely chopped. Season to taste with salt, pepper, and lemon juice and fill the avocados with the mixture.

Variation: In Chile leftover cooked rice is also used as a filling. The avocados are prepared as above. Season the mashed avocado with salt, pepper, and ½ cup vinaigrette dressing made with lemon juice. Mix with the rice, about 1 cup, and 12 pimiento-stuffed green olives, sliced. Fill the avocados with the mixture.

ZUCCHINI

Calabacitas Picadas   MEXICO
Chopped Zucchini

Zucchini are surely Mexico's favorite green vegetable, perhaps because they have so long a history in the country, going back to 7000 B.C. They are available all year round and are picked when they are only 3 to 4 inches long, young and tender. Though vegetables in Mexico are traditionally served as a separate course before the main dish, I find they go admirably with meat, poultry, or fish, and in today's Mexico more and more people are serving them in this way.

Serves 4 to 6

3 tablespoons vegetable oil
1 medium onion, finely chopped
1 clove garlic, chopped
3 medium tomatoes, peeled, seeded, and chopped
1 sprig coriander (cilantro) or epazote
2 small fresh hot green peppers, seeded and chopped, or canned serrano or jalapeño chilies

Salt, freshly ground pepper
1 pound small, young zucchini, cut into ½-inch cubes
1 cup corn kernels (optional)

Heat the oil in a saucepan and sauté the onion and garlic until the onion is soft. Add the tomatoes, coriander or *epazote*, the hot peppers, salt and pepper to taste, the zucchini, and the corn, if using. Cover and simmer over very low heat until the zucchini is tender, 30 to 40 minutes, which may seem excessively long. It is because the acid in the tomatoes slows up the cooking of the zucchini.

The corn makes the dish more robust. I add it when the main dish is a light one and leave it out when I want a more purely green vegetable dish to go with a hearty meat.

Calabacitas Poblanas MEXICO
Zucchini, Puebla Style

The state of Puebla in Mexico, home of the country's most famous dish, the *mole poblano*, is noted for its cooking and for the wonderfully rich flavor of the *poblano* chili, a large, deep green pepper that can be mild or quite hot. Since I cannot get *poblanos*, I use green bell peppers, with very good results, for this unusual vegetable dish.

Serves 4 to 6

3 green bell peppers, toasted,
    peeled (see page 15), and
    seeded
1 medium onion, chopped
1 clove garlic, chopped

3 tablespoons vegetable oil
1 pound small, young zucchini,
    cut into ½-inch cubes
Salt, freshly ground pepper
⅓ cup heavy cream

Chop the peppers coarsely and purée them in a blender or food processor with the onion and garlic. Heat the oil in a saucepan and sauté the purée, stirring constantly with a wooden spoon, for 3 or 4 minutes. Add the zucchini, and season to taste with salt and pepper. Add a little water, about ½ cup is all that should be needed, cover, and simmer until the zucchini is tender, about 30 minutes. Check to see if more water is needed — there should be only just enough liquid to cook the zucchini. Stir in the heavy cream and simmer, uncovered, just long enough to heat it through. Serve as a green vegetable with any plainly cooked meat, poultry, or fish.

Variation: Topped with slices of fresh cheese (Spanish *queso blanco* or *queso fresco*, or if not available Münster), about 2 ounces per person, this makes an attractive vegetarian luncheon dish. Serves 2 as a main course.

SPINACH

Espinacas con Anchoas   VENEZUELA
Spinach with Anchovies

Here anchovies add a flavorful salty accent to the blandness of the spinach.
I borrow a Japanese trick of squeezing the excess moisture out of the
spinach by rolling the drained spinach in a *sudare* (a matchstick bamboo
mat like a place mat), and squeezing gently. Swiss chard can be used in any
of the spinach recipes.

Serves 6

2 pounds spinach or Swiss chard
3 tablespoons olive or vegetable
    oil

Freshly ground pepper
A small can anchovy fillets,
    drained and mashed

Wash and drain the spinach or Swiss chard and trim any coarse stems.
Drop the spinach into a large saucepan of briskly boiling water. Bring back
to a boil over high heat and boil for 5 minutes. Drain the spinach, rinse
quickly under cold water, and drain again. Squeeze out the excess moisture
by hand or by rolling the spinach in a bamboo mat and squeezing gently.
Chop the spinach coarsely. Heat the oil in a large skillet, add the spinach,
and sauté, stirring frequently, for about 3 minutes. Season generously with
freshly ground pepper. Add the mashed anchovies, tossing to mix well.
Serve as a vegetable with any plainly cooked meat or poultry, or topped
with fried or poached eggs as a dish by itself.

Espinacas Saltadas   PERU
Spinach with Tomatoes

Serves 6

2 pounds spinach or Swiss chard
3 tablespoons vegetable oil
1 medium onion, finely chopped
2 cloves garlic, chopped
4 medium tomatoes, peeled and
    chopped

1 fresh hot red or green pepper,
    seeded and chopped
Salt, freshly ground pepper
Grated rind of ½ lemon

Cook the spinach or Swiss chard as for *Espinacas con Anchoas* (Spinach with Anchovies) and set aside. Heat the oil in a skillet and sauté the onion and garlic until the onion is soft. Add the tomatoes and hot pepper, season with salt and pepper, and cook until the mixture is well blended, about 5 minutes. Add the grated lemon rind. Stir the spinach into the tomato mixture and cook just long enough to heat through. Serve as a vegetable with any plainly cooked meat, poultry, or fish. For a more robust dish add 6 medium potatoes, boiled and tossed in butter.

Variation: For this version from the Dominican Republic, cook the spinach as above and set aside. Heat 2 tablespoons butter in a skillet and sauté 1 medium onion, finely chopped, until it is soft. Add 2 cups tomatoes, peeled and chopped, salt, pepper, a pinch of sugar, a pinch of ground cloves, and a bay leaf, and simmer until the mixture is thick and well blended. Add the spinach and cook until heated through.

Variation: For *Espinacas con Crema* (Spinach with Cream) from Mexico, cook the spinach as above and set aside. Peel, seed, and chop 2 green bell peppers (page 15) and purée in a blender or food processor with 1 medium onion, chopped. Heat 3 tablespoons oil in a skillet, add the purée, and sauté for 3 or 4 minutes, stirring with a wooden spoon. Add the spinach and season with salt and pepper. Stir in ⅔ cup heavy cream and simmer just long enough to heat through. Serve as a vegetable dish or as a dish by itself garnished with 6 halved hardboiled eggs.

Acelgas en Crema   ARGENTINA
Swiss Chard in Cream Sauce

Both the white and green parts of the chard are used here. When only the green part is called for, I use the white part the next day, cut into 1-inch pieces, boiled in salted water until tender (about 10 minutes), and served either with a plain béchamel sauce or with a cup of grated cheddar stirred into the sauce. Not Latin American, but it avoids wasting this attractive vegetable.

Serves 6

3 tablespoons butter
1 medium onion, finely chopped
1 medium carrot, cut into julienne
    strips
1 medium-sized potato, cut into
    ½-inch cubes

1½ pounds Swiss chard
Salt, freshly ground pepper
3 tablespoons heavy cream

Heat the butter in a saucepan and sauté the onion, carrot, and potato until the vegetables are tender. Wash and drain the Swiss chard and cut both white and green parts into thin strips crosswise. Add to the saucepan, stir to mix, and season to taste with salt and pepper. Cover and simmer over very low heat until the chard is tender, about 10 minutes. Stir in the heavy cream and simmer, uncovered, for a few minutes longer.

KALE OR COLLARD GREENS

Couve a Mineira
Kale or Collard Greens, Minas Gerais Style

BRAZIL

Collard greens, or simply collards, are a variant of kale. Both vegetables are members of the enormous crucifer family and can best be described as a sort of nonheaded cabbage. They can be used interchangeably in this recipe.

Serves 6

2 pounds kale or collard greens
Salt

¼ cup bacon fat
1 clove garlic (optional)

Wash the kale or collard greens under cold running water. Trim the leaves from the stems and shred the leaves finely. Put the leaves in a large bowl and pour boiling salted water over them. Allow to stand for 5 minutes, then drain thoroughly. Heat the bacon fat in a large skillet with the clove of garlic, if liked. Add the kale and sauté for a minute or two. Season to taste with salt, cover the skillet, and cook until the kale is tender, about 15 minutes. Discard the garlic and serve.

Variation: For a slightly different, but equally traditional, dish cut enough salt pork into ¼-inch cubes to make 1 cup and sauté them in a skillet until they have given up all their fat and are crispy and brown. Lift them out and reserve. Cook the kale as above in the fat and just before serving fold in the pork fat cubes.

CABBAGE
Guiso de Repollo   BOLIVIA
Cabbage in Sauce

Cabbage, that universal vegetable, is found all over Latin America often cooked in borrowed ways. Green, white, and red varieties are all available. Cole slaw turns up everywhere, usually as *ensalada de repollo crudo* (raw cabbage salad) and I have found *choucroute* (sauerkraut), another popular borrowed dish, as *chuckrut*. But there are also attractive and original recipes for cabbage that are worth our borrowing. The Bolivian *Guiso de Repollo* (Cabbage in Sauce) is a hearty dish that needs only a broiled lamb chop, a small steak, or a piece of fried chicken to make a complete main course since it combines cabbage with potatoes in a pleasantly spicy tomato sauce.

Serves 4

1 small white or green cabbage,
    weighing about 1 pound
Salt
3 tablespoons vegetable oil
1 medium onion, finely chopped
3 medium tomatoes, peeled and
    chopped
1 fresh hot red or green pepper,
    seeded and chopped

Salt, freshly ground pepper
1 tablespoon tomato purée
2 tablespoons fresh coriander
    (cilantro) or parsley, chopped
4 medium potatoes, freshly cooked
    and halved

Wash the cabbage and shred it finely. Drop it into a large saucepan of boiling salted water, bring back to a boil, and simmer for 5 minutes. Drain thoroughly and set aside. In a skillet heat the oil and sauté the onion until it is soft. Add the tomatoes and hot pepper and cook until the mixture is well blended, about 5 minutes. Season with salt and pepper. Stir in the tomato purée and the coriander or parsley. Fold in the cabbage, add the potatoes, and cook until the mixture is heated through.

Variation: For the Brazilian version of the dish, *Repôlho com Vinho* (Cabbage with Wine), omit the potatoes. Sauté 1 green bell pepper, seeded and chopped, with the onion in olive oil. When adding the tomato purée, stir in ½ cup chopped parsley, and when adding the cabbage, stir in ½ cup dry white wine.

CAULIFLOWER

Cauliflower is a popular vegetable in all of Latin America and most ways of cooking it are common to a number of countries, but here are some new twists.

Coliflor en Salsa de Almendra   CHILE
Cauliflower in Almond Sauce

This is an exquisitely delicate dish that makes cauliflower into something special.

Serves 6

1 medium-sized cauliflower, about 8 inches across
Salt

1 recipe Béchamel (White Sauce), page 325
½ cup finely ground almonds

Trim the cauliflower and cut a cross in the bottom of the stem end. This speeds up the cooking of the stalk so that it is tender at the same time as the flowerets. Drop, stem end down, into a large saucepan of boiling salted water, cover, and simmer for 15 to 20 minutes, or until just tender. Lift out and place in a serving dish, preferably round, to show off the cauliflower.

Meantime make the Béchamel. Stir in the ground almonds, and cook, stirring, over low heat for about 2 minutes to blend the flavors. Mask the cauliflower with the sauce and serve as an accompaniment to any plainly cooked meat, poultry, fish, or shellfish.

Variation: Use ground walnuts instead of the almonds — less delicate but very rich tasting.

Variation: Mask the cauliflower with 1 recipe *Salsa de Choclos* (Sweetcorn Sauce), page 323, for a marvelous combination of flavors, the delicate taste of the cauliflower enhanced by the rich taste of the corn.

Variation: Heat 4 tablespoons olive or vegetable oil in a skillet and add 2 large cloves garlic, crushed in a garlic press, and ¼ cup finely chopped parsley. Sauté for a minute or two, then stir in 1 tablespoon red wine vinegar, salt, and freshly ground pepper, and pour, hot, over the cooked cauliflower. This pleasant, simple dish is from Bolivia.

Variation: Put the freshly cooked cauliflower into a flameproof serving dish and mask with 1 recipe *Môlho ao Tomate* (Tomato Sauce), page 318. Sprinkle with ¼ cup freshly grated Parmesan cheese and run under a broiler just long enough to brown the cheese. I have found it makes a pleasant change to leave out the cheese and instead sprinkle the cauliflower with 2 tablespoons finely chopped fresh coriander or parsley.

Variation: This dish from the Dominican Republic is robust enough to serve 4 as a main course at lunch. Heat 4 tablespoons butter in a large skillet and sauté 1 finely chopped onion until it is soft. Stir in 1 clove garlic, crushed in a garlic press. Add 4 medium tomatoes, peeled and chopped, 1 tablespoon tomato purée, 1 tablespoon lemon juice, a pinch of sugar, salt and pepper to taste, and 1 bay leaf. Simmer for about 10 minutes to blend the flavors. Remove and discard the bay leaf and fold in 1 large freshly cooked potato, cubed, 1 medium-sized cauliflower, cooked and separated into flowerets, and 1 cup cooked cut green beans. Cook the mixture just long enough to heat through. Serve with freshly grated Parmesan cheese separately.

CHAYOTE

Chayotes Rellenos   COSTA RICA
Stuffed Chayotes

Chayotes, with their crisp texture and delicate flavor, are a favorite vegetable from the Caribbean to Brazil. Often they are just peeled, sliced, and simmered until tender in salted water, drained, and served with butter and perhaps a few grinds of black pepper. This is a more elaborate recipe and is served as a separate course before the main dish. It makes a good lunch or light supper dish if the servings are doubled. In Brazil almost identical ingredients are made into a pudding, *Pudim de Chuchu*.

Serves 3 to 6

3 chayotes, peeled and halved
Salt
3½ cups freshly made
*   breadcrumbs*
2 cups grated Münster or mild
*   cheddar cheese*
Freshly ground pepper
2 eggs, lightly beaten

3 tablespoons grated Parmesan
*   cheese*
Butter

Parboil the chayotes in salted water for 10 minutes. Drain thoroughly, then scoop out the flesh, leaving a ½-inch shell and taking care not to break the vegetables. Chop the flesh coarsely and mix with 3 cups of the breadcrumbs, the grated Münster or cheddar cheese, salt and pepper, and the eggs. Pile the mixture back into the shells. Mix the remaining ½ cup breadcrumbs with the Parmesan cheese and sprinkle over the chayotes. Dot with butter and bake in a preheated hot (450° F.) oven for 15 to 20 minutes, or until the dish is heated through and the top nicely browned.

Variation: *Pudim de Chuchu* is an interesting example of how very similar ingredients can result in a very different dish. This is closer to a soufflé than anything else. Peel and halve 2 large chayotes, each weighing about ¾ pound. Simmer in salted water to cover until tender, about 15 minutes. Drain and allow to cool. Remove the edible seed. Chop the vegetable coarsely and set aside. In a bowl mix together 1 cup freshly made breadcrumbs, 1 cup grated cheese such as Münster, Gruyère, or cheddar, salt and freshly ground pepper, 2 tablespoons melted and cooled butter, and 3 lightly beaten egg yolks. Beat 3 egg whites until they stand in stiff peaks. Fold into the chayote mixture. Pour into a buttered 1-quart mold and bake in a preheated moderate (375° F.) oven for about 30 minutes, or until a knife inserted in the pudding comes out clean. Serve with *Môlho ao Tomate* (Tomato Sauce), page 318, as a light lunch or supper dish, or as a separate course, or to accompany any plainly cooked meat, poultry, or fish. Serves 3 to 4.

Tayotes Revueltos con Huevos
Chayotes Scrambled with Eggs

DOMINICAN REPUBLIC

Chayotes are called tayotes in the Dominican Republic, where the cuisine is remarkably rich and varied. This dish is most versatile since it could serve for a late breakfast, light lunch, or supper, or accompany plainly cooked meat, poultry, or fish. The cooked seed of the chayote is delicious. I always claim it as cook's perks.

Serves 2

1 large chayote, weighing about ¾ pound	1 small fresh hot red or green pepper, seeded and chopped
Salt	Freshly ground pepper
3 tablespoons vegetable oil	1 tablespoon tomato purée
1 medium onion, finely chopped	4 eggs, lightly beaten
1 clove garlic, finely chopped	
2 medium tomatoes, peeled and chopped	

Peel and halve the chayote and cook in salted water to cover until tender, about 15 minutes. Remove the seed and eat it. Drain thoroughly and cut into ½-inch cubes. Set aside. Heat the oil in an 8-inch skillet and sauté the onion over medium heat until it is soft. Add the garlic, tomatoes, and the hot pepper and simmer until the mixture is well blended and most of the liquid evaporated. Season with salt and pepper and stir in the tomato purée. Add the chayote and cook until heated through. Add the eggs and cook, stirring with the flat of a fork to reach all the surfaces of the pan until the eggs are set. Serve immediately.

Variation: For a more robust dish, add 4 ounces chopped ham to the skillet with the cubed chayotes.

EGGPLANT

Eggplant is a much-loved vegetable throughout Latin America. It may be simply sliced and fried in oil, or dipped in beaten egg and breadcrumbs, or in batter, before frying. It is served stuffed with a cheese and ham mixture, or with a *picadillo* (hash) made of pork or beef, or cooked with shrimp. Recipes do not differ a great deal from country to country. Stuffed eggplant may be served as a separate course or as a main dish for lunch or supper. A perennial favorite is *Caviar de Berengena* (Eggplant Caviar), sometimes called *berengena Rusa* (Russian eggplant), served as a cold hors d'oeuvre or salad. It is amusing to note that this dish, an international favorite, is known in both the Caucasus and the Middle East as poor man's caviar. The type of eggplant found in Latin America is the beautiful shiny deep purple kind.

Berenjena Rellena con Picadillo
Eggplant Stuffed with Hash

Serves 2

1 medium eggplant, weighing
    about 1 pound
Salt
4 tablespoons vegetable oil
½ pound chopped pork or beef
1 medium onion, finely chopped
1 clove garlic, chopped
3 medium tomatoes, peeled,
    seeded, and chopped

1 tablespoon tomato purée
1 tablespoon red wine vinegar
2 tablespoons parsley or fresh
    coriander, chopped
Salt, freshly ground pepper
2 tablespoons grated Parmesan
    cheese

Cut the eggplant in half lengthwise and score with a small sharp knife in both directions at ½-inch intervals. Sprinkle with salt and leave for 30 minutes. Squeeze the eggplant gently to remove the bitter juice, rinse quickly in cold water, squeeze again, and pat dry. With a grapefruit knife cut round the eggplant, leaving a ½-inch shell. Pull out the flesh and cut away any bits left in the shells. Chop the eggplant coarsely and set aside. Heat the oil in a skillet and sauté the pork or beef with the onion and garlic until the onion is soft and the meat lightly browned. Add the eggplant and sauté, stirring, for 2 or 3 minutes longer. Add the tomatoes, the tomato purée, vinegar, parsley or coriander, and salt and pepper. Stir to mix and simmer for 5 minutes longer. Spoon the mixture into the eggplant shells, sprinkle with the cheese, and arrange on a baking sheet or in a baking pan. Bake in a preheated moderate (350° F.) oven for 30 minutes.

Variation: For *Berenjena Rellena con Queso* (Eggplant Stuffed with Cheese), sauté 1 medium onion, finely chopped, in 3 tablespoons butter. Add the chopped eggplant and sauté for a few minutes longer. Stir in 1 cup freshly made breadcrumbs, 1 cup grated Münster or cheddar cheese, 2 ounces ham, coarsely chopped, salt, pepper, ⅛ teaspoon cayenne, and 1 egg, lightly beaten. Pile the mixture into the eggplant shells, sprinkle with 2 tablespoons Parmesan cheese, dot with butter, and bake in a preheated moderate (375° F.) oven for 30 minutes. Serve with *Môlho ao Tomate* (Tomato Sauce), page 318.

Variation: For *Berinjela com Camarão* (Eggplant with Shrimp) from Brazil, sauté 1 medium onion, finely chopped, 1 clove garlic, chopped, 1 small fresh red or green pepper, seeded and finely chopped, and the eggplant in 3 tablespoons olive or vegetable oil until the onion is soft. Stir in ½ pound raw, coarsely chopped shrimp and sauté for 1 minute longer. Add 1 cup freshly made breadcrumbs, ½ cup chopped parsley or fresh coriander, 1 cup tomatoes, peeled, seeded, and chopped, 1 tablespoon tomato purée, and salt and pepper. Mix thoroughly, then pile into the eggplant shells. Sprinkle with 2 tablespoons grated Parmesan cheese, dot with butter, and bake in a preheated moderate (350° F.) oven for 30 minutes.

Berenjenas con Vainitas   VENEZUELA
Eggplant with Green Beans

A very pretty dish, it is also the sort of combination of vegetables that is popular in Latin America. Excellent with broiled meats, poultry, or fish, it also makes a fine salad, tossed with vinaigrette instead of butter, and served slightly chilled or at room temperature.

Serves 6

2 pounds eggplant	*1 pound green beans, cut into*
Salt	*1-inch pieces*
6 tablespoons vegetable oil	*2 tablespoons butter, or 4*
1 medium onion, finely chopped	*tablespoons Vinaigrette*
4 medium tomatoes, peeled and	*(page 326)*
chopped	*2 tablespoons finely chopped*
Pinch of sugar	*parsley*
Freshly ground pepper	
20 small pimiento-stuffed olives,	
about 2 ounces	

Cut the eggplant into ½-inch slices, then cut each slice into fingers crosswise. Put into a colander, sprinkle with salt, and leave for about ½ hour to drain the bitter juice. Rinse in cold water, squeeze lightly, and pat dry with paper towels. Heat the oil in a skillet, add the onion and eggplant. Sauté, turning the eggplant pieces once or twice, until the onion and eggplant are both soft. Add the tomatoes, salt to taste, sugar, and pepper. Stir in the olives and cook for about 5 minutes longer, or until the mixture is fairly dry. Cook the beans in boiling salted water until they are tender, 10 to 15 minutes. Drain thoroughly, return to the saucepan with the butter, and toss over moderate heat until the butter is melted. Arrange the eggplant mixture in the center of a serving dish, surround it with the beans, and sprinkle with the parsley.

Caviar de Berenjena
Eggplant Caviar

DOMINICAN REPUBLIC

1 large eggplant, weighing about 2
    pounds, or two 1-pound
    eggplants
1 medium onion, finely chopped
1 sweet red pepper, peeled (page
    15), seeded, and chopped
2 medium tomatoes, chopped
2 tablespoons fresh coriander,
    chopped

Salt, freshly ground pepper
4 tablespoons olive oil
1 tablespoon red wine vinegar or
    lime or lemon juice
Lettuce leaves and black olives

Bake the eggplant on the middle rack of a preheated moderate (375° F.)
oven for about 45 minutes, or until tender. Cool, peel, and chop coarsely.
Add the onion, sweet pepper, tomatoes, coriander, salt and pepper, and mix
well. Beat the oil and vinegar together and stir into the eggplant mixture.
Serve garnished with lettuce leaves and black olives as an hors d'oeuvre
with crackers, or as a salad.

STUFFED PEPPERS
Chiles Rellenos

Stuffed peppers are eaten all over Latin America but it is in Mexico, where
they use the lovely dark green *poblano* pepper, that they are most famous (I
substitute bell peppers instead with fine results). The best known of all the
stuffed peppers is *Chiles en Nogada* (Peppers in Walnut Sauce) from Puebla. They are traditionally served on St. Augustine's Day, August 28, and
also on September 15, Mexican Independence Day, the colors of the
dish — red, white, and green — being the colors of the Mexican flag. Fresh
walnuts, which are in season in late August and early September, are used
in the sauce, but packaged walnut meats will do.

Chiles en Nogada

MEXICO

Peppers in Walnut Sauce

Serves 6

6 poblano or *large green bell
    peppers, peeled (page 15)*
1 recipe Picadillo *(Seasoned
    Chopped Beef), made with
    pork and 1 of the apples
    replaced by a peach (page 131)*
2 eggs, *separated*
½ teaspoon salt
Flour
Vegetable oil for frying

FOR THE SAUCE

1 cup walnuts, *finely ground*
An 8-ounce package cream cheese
1 cup light cream, *about*
1 tablespoon sugar *(optional)*
Pinch of ground cinnamon
    (optional)
Salt

FOR THE GARNISH

Seeds from 1 pomegranate

Slit the peppers down one side and remove the seeds, taking care not to break the peppers. Stuff with the *Picadillo*. Beat the egg whites until they stand in firm peaks. Beat the egg yolks lightly with the salt and fold into the whites. Pat the peppers dry with paper towels and dip them in the flour, then in the egg. Heat enough oil in a heavy skillet to come to a depth of at least ½ inch. Fry the peppers, in more than one batch so as not to crowd the pan, until they are lightly golden all over. The egg will seal in the filling. Drain on paper towels. Arrange them on a shallow platter.

In a blender or food processor fitted with a steel blade, combine the walnuts, cream cheese, cut into bits, and half the cream. Traditionally sugar and cinnamon are added but this is not to everyone's taste so it may be left out. (I personally prefer the sauce without.) Add a little salt and blend the mixture until it is smooth with the consistency of heavy mayonnaise, adding as much of the cream as necessary. Mask the peppers with the sauce, and garnish with the pomegranate seeds.

Variation: Of all the stuffed peppers, the one simply known as *Chiles Rellenos* (Stuffed Peppers) is most often served. Taste and texture combine to make this a splendid dish. Prepare the peppers and stuff them with *Picadillo* (Seasoned Chopped Beef), page 131, or *Picadillo de la Costa* (Seasoned Meat, Coastal Style), page 132. Coat with the egg mixture and fry in oil until golden brown. Drain on paper towels. Make 1 recipe *Salsa de Jitomate* (Tomato Sauce), page 319, and thin it to the consistency of a heavy broth with chicken stock, about 1 cup, and pour it into a large saucepan. Add the stuffed peppers. The broth will come about halfway up them. Simmer just long enough to heat through and serve with the broth. The peppers can be prepared ahead of time and added to the tomato broth to heat through just before serving.

Variation: For *Chiles Rellenos con Frijoles* (Peppers Stuffed with Beans), prepare the peppers and stuff them with about 3 cups of *Frijoles Refritos* (Refried Beans), page 242. Coat in the egg mixture in the usual way and fry in oil. Drain on paper towels. Arrange in an ovenproof dish, pour ½ cup heavy cream over them, and sprinkle with 4 ounces shredded Münster, Monterey Jack, or mild cheddar cheese. Heat the dish in a preheated moderate (350° F.) oven for 30 minutes, or until it is heated through and the top lightly browned.

Variation: Make the peppers in the usual way but stuff with slices of Münster or mild cheddar cheese, and serve with *Salsa de Jitomate* (Tomato Sauce), page 319.

Variation: The Chileans have a good way of using up leftover cooked beef or pork. Prepare the peppers for stuffing in the usual way. To make the filling sauté 1 finely chopped medium onion in 2 tablespoons butter, add 2 cups cooked meat, chopped or shredded, 2 cups cooked corn kernels, 1 cup freshly made breadcrumbs, ½ cup chopped parsley, 1 fresh hot red or green pepper, seeded and finely chopped, ½ teaspoon oregano, and salt and pepper to taste. Stir to mix and sauté for a minute or two. Stuff the peppers and fry in the egg batter in the usual way. Serve with *Pebre* (Chilean Hot Pepper Sauce), or with *Salsa Chilena* (Chilean Sauce), or with *Salsa de Jitomate* (Tomato Sauce).

POTATOES

Papas Chorreadas   COLOMBIA
Potatoes with Cheese, Tomato, and Onion Sauce

This is a marvelously rich, beautifully flavored potato dish.

Serves 6

6 large potatoes, scrubbed
1 tablespoon lard and 1
    tablespoon butter, or 2
    tablespoons butter
1 medium onion, finely chopped

2 large tomatoes, peeled and
    chopped
Salt, freshly ground pepper
½ cup heavy cream
1 cup grated Münster cheese

In a large saucepan boil the potatoes until they are tender. Drain the potatoes, peel, and keep them warm. In a skillet heat the lard and butter, or the butter, and sauté the onion until it is softened. Add the tomatoes and salt and pepper to taste, and cook, stirring, for about 5 minutes. Stir in the cream and cheese and cook, stirring, until the cheese is partially melted. Pour the sauce over the potatoes.

Llapingachos   ECUADOR
Potato Cakes

This is a typical *sierra* (mountain) dish with a number of variations. It may be served as a first course, 2 cakes to a serving, accompanied by lettuce, avocado slices, and tomato. The potato cakes may be topped with fried eggs, and on the coast it is usual to add slices of fried, ripe plantains and *Salsa de Maní* (Peanut Sauce). Often served with slices of fried bass as a main course, the *Llapingachos* are then accompanied by hot white rice and tomato, lettuce, avocado, cauliflower, green beans, and green peas, all at room temperature, as a salad.

Serves 6

2 pounds potatoes, peeled and
    sliced
Salt
4 tablespoons (¼ cup) butter

2 medium onions, finely chopped
2 cups Münster cheese, shredded
Lard, butter, or oil, or annatto lard
    or oil (page 324) for frying

Boil the potatoes in salted water until soft. Drain and mash. Heat the butter in a skillet and sauté the onions until they are very soft. Add the onions to the mashed potatoes, mixing well. Shape the potatoes into 12 balls. Divide the cheese into 12 parts and stuff each of the potato balls with the cheese, flattening them as you do so into cakes or patties about 1 inch thick. Chill in the refrigerator for about 15 minutes. In enough lard, butter, or oil (with or without annatto as you please) to cover the bottom of a skillet, sauté the potato cakes until they are golden brown on both sides. The onions may be omitted, or the potato may be mixed with the cheese instead of the cheese being used as a stuffing.

TROPICAL ROOT VEGETABLES

Tropical root vegetables like the taros, malangas, cassava (yucca), yams, sweet potatoes (including the white sweet potato better known as *boniato*), *arracacha*, *apio*, and Jerusalem artichokes add a new dimension to any meal whether it is a Latin American one or not. Generally speaking they can be cooked as potatoes are, peeled and boiled, then dressed with butter, salt, and freshly ground pepper, or mashed to a purée with butter and a little milk or cream, or baked in the oven, unpeeled like potatoes in their jackets. It is not possible to give exact cooking times for all the root vegetables as they vary so much in size, shape, and texture. However, as a guide, a *boniato* weighing 1 pound takes about 1½ hours in a preheated moderate (350° F.) oven. There is one yam called a *mapuey* that has a marvelously dry texture and positively thirsts for butter. I like to bake or boil it and serve the butter with a lavish hand. Other root vegetables have a moist texture and are nice just with sauce or gravy from the main course. West Indian pumpkin, also called *calabaza*, and other winter squash, though they're not root vegetables, are also marvelous baked or boiled and mashed with butter, or with sauce or gravy. Many of the tropical root vegetables discolor quickly when exposed to the air, so it is wise to peel them under running water and drop them into cold water as soon as they are peeled.

The best way to get to know these enchanting vegetables is to buy and cook them. Markets specializing in tropical foods carry them and the men and women in the markets are usually a mine of information. The various types are discussed in the ingredients section.

✳ Jerusalem Artichokes

Jerusalem artichokes, despite their name, are a root vegetable native to North America. There are not many recipes for them in Latin America.

Topinambur al Horno   CHILE
Baked Jerusalem Artichokes

I found these in Chile. They make a nice change as an accompaniment to steaks or chops.

Serves 6

2 pounds Jerusalem artichokes
Salt
Butter

1 recipe Béchamel (White Sauce), page 325
½ cup grated Parmesan cheese

Wash and scrape the artichokes and cook in salted water until tender, about 10 to 15 minutes. Drain and slice. Butter a shallow Pyrex or similar dish and arrange the sliced vegetables in it. Pour the Béchamel over the artichokes, sprinkle with the cheese, dot with butter, and bake in a preheated moderate (375° F.) oven for 20 minutes, or until the dish is heated through and lightly browned on top. Serve with steak, chops, or any plainly cooked meat or poultry.

Variation: There is an interesting interplay of textures in this recipe, which is also from Chile. Instead of all Jerusalem artichokes, use 1 pound Jerusalem artichokes and 1 pound potatoes, arrange roughly in layers in the baking dish, and cook as above.

✳ Cassava

Cassava root, whether eaten as a root vegetable or made into cassava meal as the Brazilians do, is much appreciated throughout Latin America.

Farofa de Azeite de Dendê
Cassava Meal with Palm Oil

BRAZIL

A Brazilian meal would not be complete without some form of *farinha de mandioca* (cassava, or manioc, meal). It may be toasted in a skillet on top of the stove or in a shallow pan in the oven until it is a very light brown. It is then put into a *farinheira*, a sort of shaker, and sprinkled on meat, poultry, and vegetables at the table. As I don't have the traditional shaker, I serve it from a small bowl, and spoon it over foods. It has a light, nutty flavor, quite subtle. The *farofas* are more elaborate and are served with any main course.

Serves 6 to 8

2 cups cassava (manioc) meal
4 tablespoons dendê (palm) oil

In a skillet, over low heat, toast the cassava meal until it begins to turn a very pale brown. Stir frequently so that it does not burn. Stir in the *dendê* (palm) oil and cook until it is well blended and the mixture is bright yellow. Transfer to a serving bowl. Serve with *Xinxim de Galinha* (Chicken with Shrimp and Peanut Sauce), or with any meat or poultry.

Variation: For *Farofa de Manteiga* (Cassava Meal with Butter), use butter instead of *dendê* (palm) oil. If liked 1 small onion, finely chopped, may be sautéed in the butter, then scrambled with 1 egg, lightly beaten. The cassava meal is then added, seasoned with salt, and garnished, when ready to serve, with a little finely chopped parsley.

Farofa de Ouro   BRAZIL
Cassava Meal with Hardboiled Eggs

2 cups cassava (manioc) meal
¼ pound (½ cup) butter
Salt
3 hardboiled eggs, peeled and
    chopped

In a heavy skillet, preferably iron, toast the cassava meal until it turns a
pale beige, stirring constantly with a wooden spoon so that it colors evenly.
Put the butter into a small saucepan and melt it over low heat. Pour the
butter over the cassava meal, stirring to mix evenly. Season to taste with
salt and stir in the eggs. Serve in a bowl as an accompaniment to meats or
poultry, or with *Feijoada Completa* (Black Beans with Mixed Meats).

Variation: Garnish the *Farofa* with 1 cup small pitted black or green olives.
If liked, chop 6 slices bacon and fry until crisp. Drain and discard the fat.
Fold the bacon bits into the cassava meal after the butter has been added.

Picante de Yuca   PERU
Cassava Root with Cheese Sauce

One of the most original cassava dishes is this Peruvian one where the
vegetable is masked by a lively cheese sauce made hot with fresh peppers.
The peppers used should be quite large ones, 3 or 4 inches in length, not the
tiny very hot ones, as they lend flavor as well as heat. The number of
peppers can, of course, be reduced according to individual taste but Peruvians like their food hot and this is how they would have it. They would
also use an herb called *huacatay*, of the marigold family, in the sauce, but
it is not available here and there is no substitute. The flavor is unusual, a
little rank, and it is certainly an acquired taste. I find the sauce good
without it. The dish makes an attractive accompaniment to plainly cooked
meats or poultry and is also good by itself. The recipe makes about 2½
cups of sauce, which is lovely with corn on the cob or over green vegetables
such as green beans or cauliflower to make a vegetarian luncheon dish.

Serves 6

½ *pound Spanish fresh cheese*
  *(*queso fresco *or* queso blanco*),*
  crumbled, or use grated
  Münster cheese
10 *fresh hot red or green peppers,*
  seeded and chopped
1 *cup olive or vegetable oil*

Salt, freshly ground pepper
2 *pounds cassava (yucca) root,*
  peeled and sliced
2 *hardboiled eggs, sliced*
Black olives
Lettuce leaves

Put the cheese into a blender or food processor with the peppers and the oil and reduce it to a heavy cream. Season to taste with salt and pepper and set aside. Boil the cassava (yucca) root in salted water until it is tender, about 30 minutes. Drain and arrange the slices on a serving platter and pour the sauce over them while they are still hot. Garnish the platter with the eggs, olives, and lettuce leaves.

Budín de Yuca   GUATEMALA
Cassava Root Soufflé

Guatemala has an interesting way of making cassava root into a soufflé, which can be served instead of rice or other starchy vegetables with meat and poultry dishes, or with *Môlho ao Tomate* (Tomato Sauce), page 318, or *Salsa de Jitomate* (Tomato Sauce), page 319, and grated Parmesan cheese as a first course or light luncheon dish.

Serves 4

1 *pound cassava (yucca) root*
Salt, freshly ground pepper
6 *tablespoons butter*

1 *cup milk, about*
4 *egg yolks*
5 *egg whites*

Peel the cassava (yucca) root under cold running water, as it discolors quickly. Slice it and drop it into a saucepan of salted water. Bring to a boil, lower the heat, cover, and simmer until tender, about 30 minutes. Drain the cassava, mash, season to taste with salt and pepper, and beat in the butter. Heat the milk and stir it gradually into the mashed vegetable until it has the consistency of mashed potatoes. Use a little more hot milk if necessary. Beat in the egg yolks one by one. Beat the egg whites with a pinch of salt until they stand in firm peaks. Fold them into the vegetable mixture lightly but thoroughly and pour into a 2-quart soufflé dish. Bake in a preheated moderate (350° F.) oven for 35 minutes or until well puffed and lightly browned.

SALADS

Ensalada Mixta   ECUADOR
Mixed Salad

Of all the countries in Latin America, Ecuador has the most imaginative
and original approach to vegetables. Cooks there never cease to astonish
me with the variety of their salads, many of which I find pleasant for a
simple lunch if served in double portions. Because it is only 15 miles from
the equator, Quito, Ecuador's capital, has equal day and night so that all
year round 12 hours of sunshine encourage fruits and vegetables to grow.
This part of the country also has a fantastically deep subsoil and good
rainfall so that the raw materials for making salads are of superb quality.
At 9,500 feet above sea level, water boils at a lower temperature and vegetables do not get overcooked, and since at this altitude it is always cool in
the shade, salads are served at room temperature rather than chilled. I find
this enhances flavor, though at sea level in hot summer an unchilled salad
will be a wilted and drooping one.

Serves 4

2 cups chopped lettuce
2 hardboiled eggs, chopped
2 cups cooked, cubed potatoes
2 cups cooked green beans, cut
    into ½-inch pieces

½ cup Vinaigrette dressing (page
    326)

Combine all the ingredients in a salad bowl and toss lightly to mix.

Variation: For *Ensalada de Hongos* (Mushroom Salad), combine equal
amounts of cooked corn kernels, cooked chopped carrots, cooked green
beans, cut into ½-inch pieces, cooked green peas, and sliced mushrooms,
and toss in vinaigrette dressing.

Variation: For *Ensalada de Garbanzos* (Chickpea Salad), combine cooked
chickpeas with half the amount of cooked, coarsely chopped Brussels
sprouts and toss in Vinaigrette dressing made with mustard (page 326).
Chopped lettuce and cubed boiled potatoes may be added and the Brussels
sprouts omitted.

Variation: For *Ensalada de Alcachofas* (Artichoke Heart Salad), mix together equal amounts of cooked, sliced artichoke hearts and sliced apples
with Mayonnaise (page 326) to taste.

Variation: For *Ensalada de Papas* (Potato Salad), omit the lettuce, add 2 cups chopped celery and 1 medium tomato, peeled and chopped.

Variation: For *Ensalada de Tomate* (Tomato Salad), combine 4 medium tomatoes, peeled and chopped, with 4 hardboiled eggs, chopped, and 1 cup chopped lettuce. Toss with vinaigrette dressing made with lemon juice.

Variation: For *Ensalada de Pepinos* (Cucumber Salad), peel 2 cucumbers if they are waxed, if not leave them unpeeled and slice very thinly. Put them in a bowl with 1 teaspoon salt, mixing well, and let stand for 30 minutes. Rinse and drain thoroughly. Peel and chop 2 medium tomatoes and combine with the cucumbers. Toss with a vinaigrette dressing.

Variation: For *Ensalada de Papas y Pimientos* (Potato and Sweet Red Pepper Salad), combine 2 cups cooked sliced potatoes, 2 sweet red bell peppers, peeled and sliced, 2 medium-sized mild onions, sliced, or 1 large, halved and sliced, and 2 cucumbers, peeled, seeded, and sliced with ¾ cup Vinaigrette dressing (page 326), made with lemon juice and seasoned with 2 pinches nutmeg. Let the salad stand for 1 hour before serving. Mix lightly just before serving.

Ensalada de Habas
Fresh Broad Bean Salad

ECUADOR

Fresh young broad beans are often hard to get. If the beans are older, shell them, drop them into boiling water, let them stand a few minutes, then peel off the tough outer skin. I find English canned broad beans or Italian canned broad beans labeled fava beans a good substitute. These need no cooking and should just be rinsed and drained. I sometimes use baby lima beans. The 12-ounce package of frozen baby limas serves 4.

Serves 4

2 cups young broad beans, shelled
2 tablespoons butter
Salt, freshly ground pepper

1 tablespoon white vinegar or
lemon juice

Cook the beans in water to cover until they are tender, about 15 minutes. Drain and cool. Melt the butter in a saucepan, add the beans, season to taste with salt and pepper, and cook for about 1 minute, turning the beans with a rubber spatula so that all are coated with the butter. Remove from the heat and pour the vinegar or lemon juice over them, stirring to mix. Serve at room temperature as an accompaniment to meats or poultry.

Salada de Palmito
Hearts of Palm Salad

Serves 6 to 8

Two 1-pound cans hearts of palm

FOR THE *MÔLHO PARA PALMITO* (Hearts of Palm Dressing)

1 tablespoon lime or lemon juice   *Salt, freshly ground pepper*
1 tablespoon Dijon mustard   *4 tablespoons vegetable oil*

Thoroughly drain the hearts of palm and cut them into ½-inch slices. Set aside.

In a bowl beat together the lime or lemon juice with the mustard and salt and pepper to taste. Gradually beat in the oil. Pour the dressing over the palm heart slices and toss lightly.

Ensalada de Aguacate
Avocado Salad

This salad is simplicity itself as well as being surprisingly good. The true flavor of the avocado comes through in all its buttery richness.

Serves 6 to 8

6 tablespoons olive oil   *Salt, freshly ground pepper*
2 tablespoons white wine vinegar   *2 large, ripe avocados*

In a salad bowl beat together the oil and vinegar. Season to taste with salt and pepper. Peel the avocados and remove the pits. Cut the flesh into cubes and toss lightly with the dressing. If liked, serve in a bowl lined with lettuce leaves.

Chojín
Radish and Fried Pork Rind Salad

Serves 6 to 8

24 small red radishes, ½ pound about, finely chopped
12 fresh mint leaves, finely chopped
3 cups chicharrones *(fried pork rinds), finely chopped*

Salt to taste
¼ cup Seville (bitter) orange juice, or use two-thirds orange juice to one-third lemon juice

Combine all the ingredients in a bowl and serve as a salad first course. If possible, use a Latin American type of *chicharrón*, as it is more flavorful.

Variation: For *Picado de Rábano* (Radish Salad), omit the *chicharrones* (fried pork rinds) and serve as a salad.

Ensalada de Coliflor
Cauliflower Salad

This cauliflower salad looks quite grand on a buffet, the white of the vegetable just visible beneath the pale green of the masking avocado sauce, very summery and pretty especially when garnished with radish roses.

Serves 4 to 6

1 medium-sized cauliflower, cooked and placed in a serving dish (page 263)

½ recipe for Guacamole *(Avocado Sauce), page 316, or* Guacamole del Norte *(Avocado Sauce, Northern Style), page 317*

Allow the cooked cauliflower to cool, then mask it with the avocado sauce. Serve immediately as avocado tends to darken. Garnish with radish roses.

Variation: Dominican Republic cooks have their own way of doing this. Mash 1 large avocado with salt, pepper, 1 tablespoon white wine vinegar, 3 tablespoons vegetable oil, and ¼ cup finely ground almonds. Mask the cauliflower with the mixture. The oil and vinegar used in this recipe help to keep the avocado sauce from darkening. Garnish with radish roses.

Ensalada de Topinambur
Jerusalem Artichoke Salad

A good change from potato salad. Choose the largest artichokes available to give the finished salad a more attractive look, and be careful not to overcook them as they should be crisp not mushy.

Serves 6

2 pounds Jerusalem artichokes
Salt

1 recipe Vinaigrette (Oil and Vinegar Dressing), page 326

Wash and scrape the artichokes and cook in salted water until tender, about 10 to 15 minutes. Drain and slice. Allow to cool, then toss with the Vinaigrette.

For a richer salad, mix the artichokes with 1 cup Mayonnaise (page 326), or *Salsa Golf* (Tomato- and Cognac-Flavored Mayonnaise), page 327.

Ensalada de Verduras   ECUADOR
Vegetable Salad

This is a favorite way of serving vegetables in Ecuador and is often presented as a separate course, before the main course. The vegetables are arranged in rows on a large platter and are served freshly cooked at room temperature. I have had them without any dressing, simply seasoned with salt during the cooking, with a dressing only of oil, salt, and pepper, and with a vinaigrette made with 3 parts oil to 1 part vinegar or lemon juice, and seasoned with salt and pepper. The platter may be decorated with shredded lettuce or garnished with slices of hardboiled egg, or with olives, green or black. The vegetables should be cooked and tossed with the dressing separately. The dressing should not be abundant. The vegetables may be arranged as the cook sees fit: in rows, in heaps, or in circles. The vegetables listed below are the ones most frequently used. I like to serve the platter of mixed vegetables to accompany a main course, especially an Ecuadorian one.

Green peas	*Diced celery*
Diced beets	*Asparagus, cut into 1-inch pieces*
Cauliflower, separated in flowerets	*Artichoke hearts, halved or quartered*
Green beans, cut into ½-inch slices	*Tiny sliced raw zucchini, or larger zucchini, cooked and diced*
Corn kernels	*Sliced raw tomatoes*
Diced carrots	*Sliced avocados*
Diced potatoes	

Ensalada de Nopalitos
Cactus Salad

MEXICO

This is Mexico's most traditional salad. It is lovely for summer as the juicy yet crisp young cactus pieces are very refreshing.

Serves 6

Two 10-ounce cans nopalitos *(cactus pieces)*	*2 tablespoons fresh coriander, chopped*
3 medium tomatoes, peeled, seeded, and chopped	*½ cup Vinaigrette dressing (page 326)*
½ medium white onion, finely chopped	

Rinse the cactus pieces gently in cold water and drain them thoroughly. Combine all the ingredients in a salad bowl and mix lightly. Chill before serving.

Variation: For a more elaborate salad, line the bowl with lettuce leaves, add the salad, and garnish it with canned *jalapeño* chili rinsed, patted dry, and cut into strips, about ¼ pound crumbled fresh cheese (*queso fresco* or *queso blanco* or cottage cheese), or 3 tablespoons grated Parmesan cheese, with ¼ teaspoon oregano sprinkled on top of the salad.

Pico de Gallo
Rooster's Beak

MEXICO

The root vegetable used in this salad, *jícama*, comes originally from Mexico but is now grown in the States and can be found in tropical markets. This is the traditional recipe from Jalisco, where the salad is most often served as an hors d'oeuvre with drinks. I like it served as a salad in lieu of dessert.

Serves 6

2 small jícamas, *weighing about 1 pound, peeled and coarsely chopped*

4 navel oranges, *peeled, sectioned, and coarsely chopped*

Salt
Cayenne pepper

Combine the *jícama*, oranges, and salt to taste in a bowl. Sprinkle with cayenne and chill thoroughly before serving.

Breads and Desserts

Panes y Postres

The people of pre-Columbian America had no breads as we know them but they had their own special flat breads made from corn, *Arepas* and *Tortillas* (already discussed as appetizers). In the colonial period other breads like *Sopa Paraguaya* were invented. Modern Latin American bakeries produce commercial breads like our own as well as *pan dulce*, the sweet breakfast breads of Spain. They are truly international. I have chosen breads that are either indigenous or colonial, like a delicious banana bread from Guatemala, *Pan de Banano*; Mexico's bread rolls, *Bolillos*; Venezuela's corn pancakes, *Cachapas de Jojoto*; and Paraguay's rich and splendid corn bread, *Sopa Paraguaya*. They are not hard to make and add an authentic and different touch to a Latin American meal.

There were few indigenous desserts; people mostly finished a meal with fresh fruits. Some, like pineapple, papaya, the *zapotes* and *anonas*, and *tuna* (fruit of the *nopal* cactus), were unknown to Europe at the time. The Aztecs stuffed tamales with strawberries, that universal fruit; honey was used as a sweetening by both Mayas and Aztecs; and the Incas made desserts from squash and sweet potatoes, but they lacked wheat flour, butter, cream, and sugar to make the pies, puddings, and rich desserts of

Europe. It was not until the colonial period and the introduction of sugar cane that desserts began to flourish. Spanish nuns in Peru and Mexico, especially in Puebla, made colonial desserts famous. In Brazil, primarily in Bahia, cooks in the great houses of the sugar plantations created a whole new world of cakes and sweet things for desserts. They drew on the Portuguese tradition of using lots of egg yolks and sugar. Out of this huge array I have chosen a small selection of favorites which I think are suited to the modern palate.

BREADS

Sopa Paraguaya   PARAGUAY
Paraguayan Corn Bread

This is a wonderfully hearty well-flavored corn bread with two kinds of cheese to enrich it and onions sautéed in butter to add to the flavor. It is traditionally served with *So'O-Yosopy* (Beef Soup) and with grilled steaks, but is fine with any meat or poultry dish, or by itself.

8 tablespoons (½ cup) butter
2 medium onions, finely chopped
½ pound farmer or cottage cheese
½ pound Münster cheese, grated
2 cups cornmeal
2 cups grated corn kernels, or a
*   1-pound can cream-style*
*   sweet corn*

1 teaspoon salt, preferably coarse
1 cup milk
6 eggs, separated

Grease a baking tin, about 10 by 13 inches, and sprinkle with 1 tablespoon flour. Shake to remove the excess.

In a skillet heat 4 tablespoons of the butter and sauté the onions until they are softened. Set aside. Cream the remaining 4 tablespoons of butter and add to the farmer or cottage cheese, blending thoroughly. Add the Münster cheese and the onions. In another bowl combine the cornmeal, corn, salt, and milk, and mix thoroughly. Combine the corn mixture with the cheese mixture, blending thoroughly.

Beat the egg whites until they form soft peaks and beat the yolks separately. Combine the two and stir them into the cornmeal and cheese mixture. Pour the batter into the baking tin. Bake in a preheated hot (400° F.) oven for 45 minutes, or until a cake tester comes out clean.

A pinch of ground aniseed may be added to the mixture, if liked. Another pleasant variation is to cut enough of the Münster into tiny cubes to measure ½ cup and stir this into the batter at the last moment, if liked. This gives a slightly different texture to the finished bread.

Pan de Banano
GUATEMALA
Banana Bread

This easy-to-make banana bread is lovely for a snack. Spread with honey or topped with fresh fruit, it can be dressed up with cream or ice cream to make an attractive dessert.

Makes one 9-inch loaf

¼ pound (½ cup) butter
½ cup sugar
1 pound ripe bananas (2 or 3 large)
½ teaspoon salt
1 teaspoon ground cinnamon

1 tablespoon lemon juice
1 egg, well beaten
1½ cups all-purpose flour
2 teaspoons baking powder

Soften the butter at room temperature and cream it with the sugar in a mixing bowl until light and fluffy. Mash the bananas and add to the butter and sugar mixture. Add the salt, cinnamon, lemon juice, and egg. Sift the flour with the baking powder and fold it into the liquid mixture. Pour the batter into a greased (9- by 5-inch) loaf pan. Bake in a preheated moderate (350° F.) oven for 1 hour, or until a cake tester comes out clean. Serve with honey as a cake bread, or as a pudding with cream or ice cream.

Tortillas
MEXICO
Makes about eighteen 4-inch tortillas

To make tortillas, see page 44.

Tortillas that are served instead of bread with Mexican meals may be made slightly larger, 5 or 6 inches across, though the 4-inch ones are perfectly acceptable. When they are eaten in this way, or made into soft tacos (stuffed, rolled tortillas), they should be brought to the table wrapped in a napkin, then placed in a small woven reed or straw basket. The napkin is always folded back over the tortillas when one is taken so as to keep them warm and soft. In Mexico no one ever takes the top tortilla of the stack, always the second or third to be sure of getting a good hot one. Leftover tortillas are never wasted, as they are the prime ingredient of *chilaquiles*, fried strips of day-old tortilla baked in a chili sauce. They are also used as a garnish in certain soups.

Arepas
Corn Bread

VENEZUELA AND COLOMBIA

The *Arepas* of Venezuela and Colombia are made from corn processed into flour in the same way as the flour for Mexican corn tortillas, but the *arepa* is not a flexible pancake like the tortilla. It looks rather like a pure white round bread roll. The outside is crisp, the inside doughy. In Caracas I have had *Arepas* served with cream cheese as an unusual first course. The doughy inside is pulled out of the *arepa* and it is then filled with the delicious local runny cream cheese. French *crème fraîche* (page 9) is a good substitute, as it is very like the Caracas cream cheese. I've found that cream cheese softened at room temperature and mashed with a little heavy cream also serves nicely as a substitute for the Venezuelan original. Easy to make and taking little time, *Arepas* make a pleasant change from everyday bread and are especially good with Venezuelan dishes. When eaten as bread, the doughy inside is split open, pulled out with the fingers, and the remaining shell is buttered, or the *Arepas* are simply split and buttered. I often top the butter with a little cream cheese as I find the combination irresistible.

Makes 8 to 10

2 cups corn flour for **Arepas** (see page 4)	1 teaspoon salt 2 cups water, about

In a bowl mix the *arepa* flour with the salt. Stir in the water to make a stiffish dough. Add a little more if necessary. Let the dough stand for 5 minutes, then form into balls flattened slightly to 3 inches across and about ½ inch thick. Cook on a heavy, lightly greased griddle over moderate heat for 5 minutes a side, then bake in a preheated moderate (350° F.) oven for 20 to 30 minutes, turning them two or three times during cooking.

They are done when they sound hollow when tapped. Serve hot. Traditionally they are wrapped in a napkin and served in a straw basket.

Variation: For *Arepas de Queso* (Corn Bread with Cheese), add 1 cup finely chopped or crumbled *queso fresco* or *queso blanco* (Spanish fresh cheese), or grated Münster cheese.

Variation: For *Arepas de Chicharrones* (Corn Bread with Pork Rinds), add 1 cup *chicharrones* (fried pork rinds), crumbled.

Variation: For *Arepas Santanderinas* (Corn Bread, Santander Style), mix 2 tablespoons lard into the flour before adding the water, working it in thoroughly with your fingers, then make as usual.

Variation: For *Arepas Fritas* (Fried Corn Bread), mix 1 cup grated cheese with the flour. Beat an egg yolk with the water and salt, and mix it with the flour and cheese, kneading the dough thoroughly (about 5 minutes). Roll out into thin circles about 4 inches in diameter and fry in lard or oil until lightly browned on both sides. These may be made smaller, about 1½ inches in diameter, and served as an accompaniment to drinks.

Variation: For *Arepas Fritas Infladas* (Puffed Fried Corn Bread), add to the dough 1 cup grated cheese, ½ cup all-purpose flour, ¼ teaspoon ground anise, and 1 tablespoon sugar, preferably brown. Knead the dough until it is very smooth, about 5 minutes. Form it into small balls and roll them out on a lightly floured board to make thin 3-inch pancakes. Deep fry in hot oil. They should puff up. Serve immediately. I find it easier to lift them with a slotted spoon as they are very soft.

Cachapas de Jojoto   VENEZUELA
Corn Pancakes

These are pleasant eaten instead of bread with a meal. Miniaturized (about 1½ inches across) and wrapped round a piece of Spanish fresh cheese, (*queso fresco* or *queso blanco*), or Münster, they make an attractive cocktail nibble.

Makes about 12

*1½ cups corn kernels, if frozen
    thoroughly defrosted*
½ cup heavy cream
1 egg
3 tablespoons all-purpose flour

¼ teaspoon sugar
½ teaspoon salt
2 teaspoons butter, melted
Butter for frying

Put all the ingredients into a blender or food processor and mix until smooth. Grease a skillet or omelet pan by rubbing a piece of crumbled wax paper over a stick of butter, then rubbing the pan with the paper. Repeat this process for each pancake. Drop the mixture, 2 tablespoons at a time, into the skillet and fry until lightly browned on both sides, turning once. Serve hot.

Variation: For *Cachapas de Hojas* (Corn Mixture Steamed in Leaves), put 2 tablespoons of the corn mixture into the center of a dry corn husk and fold it up into a package. Arrange the corn husks in a steamer, and steam, covered, over boiling water until firm, about 30 minutes. *Cachapas de Budare* (Corn Mixture in Banana Leaves) are made by stuffing a piece of banana leaf with the corn mixture, folding the leaf into a package, and cooking it over moderate heat on a griddle, turning it twice, then standing it at the side of the griddle to finish cooking. Ideally the *Cachapas* should be baked on a *budare*, a special Venezuelan griddle, and finished at the back of a wood-burning stove. It is possible to improvise using aluminum foil and a heavy griddle, setting both over very low heat on top of two asbestos mats. Faced with the difficulty of getting fresh banana leaves, I have contented myself with *Cachapas de Jojoto*, which are extremely good and present no difficulties at all.

Bolillos   MEXICO
Mexican Bread Rolls

These are the marvelous *petits pains* of Mexico, acquired during the short, unhappy reign of Maximilian and Carlota, wished on the Mexicans by Napoleon III and vigorously resisted by the infant republic. Mexico preferred to remain independent but was in no way reluctant to accept the world's best bread — French bread. To this day I find that *Bolillos*, the spindle-shaped rolls that are sold fresh twice a day in the bakeries of Mexico, are equaled only by bread in France. I find I can make a good approximation of them with little trouble if I get a good, hard wheat flour.

Makes 18

1 package (¼ ounce) active dry yeast, or ½ ounce fresh yeast	5 cups sifted bread flour*
	Butter for the bowl
1 ½ teaspoons salt	

*Bread flour is one with a higher mixture of hard wheat. All-purpose flour may be substituted.

Put the yeast into a large bowl and soften it in ¼ cup lukewarm water. When it has liquefied completely, stir in 1¾ cups lukewarm water and the salt, and stir to mix. Gradually mix in the flour to make a dough that comes away from the sides of the bowl with a little stickiness. Knead the dough on a lightly floured board for 10 minutes, or until it is smooth and elastic and has lost all its stickiness. Put the dough in a buttered bowl, cover it with a clean cloth, and leave it to rise in a warm place until it has doubled in bulk, about 2 hours.

The oven with just the pilot light lit is a good place to put the dough to rise in cold weather. This is a slow-rising dough and it is important to allow it enough time.

At the end of this time punch the dough down, cover it, and let it rise a second time until again doubled in bulk, about 1 hour. Turn it out onto a lightly floured board and knead it for about 5 minutes. Divide the dough in half. Roll each piece out into an oblong, about 18 inches by 6 inches. Roll each piece up like a jelly roll. Cut each roll into 9 slices, making 18 in all. Pinch the ends of each slice to form a spindle shape and arrange on a buttered baking sheet. Cover and let the rolls rise until they have doubled in bulk, about 1 hour. Brush them lightly with water and bake in a pre-heated hot (400° F.) oven for about 30 minutes, or until they are golden brown.

DESSERTS

Creme de Abacate   BRAZIL
Avocado Cream

Apart from avocado ice cream, which I confess I do not care for, this is the only dessert using avocados that I have come across. It was part of our kitchen repertoire during the years we lived in Jamaica, and later on I was puzzled by this as it was so clearly not a Jamaican dish. The mystery was solved by my mother, who told me it had been given her by the Brazilian lady who was the previous tenant of the house we rented — a sort of parting gift.

Serves 6

3 large, ripe avocados, chilled
4 tablespoons fresh lime juice
6 tablespoons superfine sugar

Halve the avocados, remove the pits, and mash them in their shells with a fork. Turn them out into a bowl and mash until smooth with the lime juice and sugar. Pile the mixture into glass serving dishes and garnish, if liked, with a little grated lime peel or a slice of lime.

Mazamorra Morada   PERU
Peruvian Fruit Compote

Mazamorra is a dish made with cornstarch and sugar or honey. This *Mazamorra* is made with *maíz morado*, the purple corn of Peru that gives off a most beautiful deep purple color when it is simmered in water. It has a delicate, flowery, lemony taste. Purple corn is not readily available outside Peru but fortunately the Hopi Indians grow it in Arizona and it can be ordered by mail. However, I have found I can get the same lovely color by using blackberries, and, by orchestrating the flavors a little differently, the same flavor may be obtained as well. This is a luscious and refreshing dessert, lovely for a summer buffet.

Serves 8 to 10

½ pound purple corn kernels
6 cups water
2 cups sugar
6 cloves
A 3-inch piece of stick cinnamon
½ small pineapple, peeled, cored, and cubed
2 quinces, peeled and sliced
2 pears, peeled and sliced

2 peaches, pitted, peeled, and sliced
1 pound cherries, pitted
½ pound dried apricots, halved
½ pound dried peaches, quartered
4 tablespoons cornstarch
Juice of 2 lemons, about 6 tablespoons
Ground cinnamon (optional)

Put the purple corn kernels into a saucepan with the water, bring to a boil, and simmer until the corn is cooked, about 30 minutes, and the water is a deep purple. Strain and discard the corn. Measure the liquid and add more water to make 6 cups, if necessary. Return the purple water to the saucepan and add the sugar, cloves, cinnamon stick, pineapple, quinces, pears, peaches, cherries, dried apricots, and dried peaches. Bring the liquid to a simmer, cover the saucepan, and cook gently over low heat until the fruit is tender, about 15 minutes. Remove and discard the cloves and cinnamon. Dissolve the cornstarch in ¼ cup water and stir it into the fruit mixture. Cook until the liquid is thickened, then stir in the lemon juice. Chill the compote and serve it sprinkled with a little cinnamon, if liked.

Variation: Cook the fruit in plain water. Add 2 apples, peeled and sliced, and ½ pound blackberries to the other fruit, otherwise make the dish in the same way.

Flan de Piña   COLOMBIA
Pineapple Custard

This is a very old family recipe given to me by my friend Cecilia Blanco de Mendoza, an authority on traditional Colombian cooking.

Serves 6

¼ cup sugar
1 cup unsweetened pineapple
    juice

1 cup sugar
4 eggs

In the top of a double boiler (6½-cup size) over boiling water melt the ¼ cup sugar over moderate heat, stirring constantly, until it has melted and is a rich caramel color. Dip the bottom of the container into cold water for a second or two, then turn the mold so that the caramel coats sides as well as bottom. Set aside.

In a saucepan combine the pineapple juice and 1 cup sugar and cook, stirring, until the liquid is reduced to half and is quite thick. Cool the syrup. Beat the eggs until they are thick and lemon-colored. Pour the syrup into the eggs in a thin, slow stream, beating all the time. Pour the mixture into the prepared caramelized container. On the top of the stove cook the custard, covered, over barely simmering water for about 2 hours, or until it is set. Cool and refrigerate until ready to serve. Before serving unmold by running a knife between the custard and the container, then place a serving dish over the mold and invert quickly.

Dulce de Piña con Arracacha   COLOMBIA
Arracacha and Pineapple Dessert

This is an unusual use of a root vegetable. The leggy vegetable (page 4) can be found in tropical markets and is well worth looking for. It has a taste reminiscent of celery, which marries well with the pineapple juice it is simmered with. The sweet has a fresh, invigorating flavor.

Serves 4 to 6

1 ½ pounds apio   1 cup sugar, or more to taste
4 cups unsweetened pineapple
    juice

Peel and slice the *apio* and put it on to cook in a saucepan with cold water
to cover. Simmer, covered, until it is tender, about 30 minutes. Drain and
mash. Add the pineapple juice and the sugar and cook the mixture, uncovered, over low heat, stirring frequently, until it forms a thick paste and the
bottom of the saucepan can be seen when the spoon is drawn across it.
Transfer to a dessert dish and chill. Serve by itself, or with whipped cream
or ice cream.

Mousse de Castanhas de Caju e Chocolate

BRAZIL

Cashew Nut and Chocolate Mousse

Serves 6 to 8

2 ounces (2 squares) unsweetened
    chocolate
½ cup sugar
5 egg yolks
1 cup roasted cashew nuts, finely
    ground
1 cup heavy cream
5 egg whites

Break the chocolate into small pieces and put with 2 to 3 tablespoons of
water into the top of a double boiler over boiling water. Add the sugar and
stir until the chocolate is melted and the sugar dissolved. Remove the pan
from the heat and beat in the egg yolks, one at a time, beating well after
each addition. Stir in the ground cashew nuts. Beat the cream until it
stands in firm peaks and fold it into the chocolate mixture. Beat the egg
whites until they stand in firm peaks and fold into the chocolate mixture,
lightly but thoroughly. Pour into a 1-quart soufflé dish and refrigerate
overnight or for several hours. Serve, if liked, with sweetened whipped
cream.

Capirotada

Bread Pudding

This is a very special bread pudding, a great favorite in Mexico during Lent and a marvelous dessert at any time, especially for a holiday buffet. I make my *Capirotada* from a recipe given me by my husband's grandmother, and I use brown sugar flavored with cinnamon and cloves for the syrup in which it is drenched before baking. A good friend, the writer Elizabeth Borton de Treviño, sent me a grandly extravagant recipe for the syrup, which she was given by a friend, Señora Estela Santos Coy de Cobo, who had it from her grandmother. It is a blend of disparate flavors — orange rind, tomato, onion, cloves, green or red pepper — which one would never expect to work, yet work it does, lusciously.

Serves 6 to 8

FOR THE SYRUP

*2 cups piloncillo or brown sugar,
    firmly packed*
A 2-inch piece of stick cinnamon
1 small onion, stuck with 3 cloves
*1 medium red or green bell pepper,
    seeded and halved*
*Peel from 1 medium orange,
    shredded*

*½ cup fresh coriander (cilantro),
    chopped*
*1 small tomato, peeled, seeded,
    and chopped*
4 cups water

Combine all the ingredients in a saucepan, bring to a boil, reduce the heat, and simmer, partially covered, for 30 minutes. Allow to cool a little. Strain, discard the solids, and set the syrup aside.

FOR THE PUDDING

Butter
*6 cups of ½-inch cubes toasted
    French or firm white bread*
*3 apples, peeled, cored, and thinly
    sliced*

1 cup raisins
1 cup chopped blanched almonds
*½ pound Münster, Monterey Jack,
    cheddar, or similar cheese,
    coarsely chopped*

Butter a 2-quart ovenproof casserole or soufflé dish and make a layer of cubes of toast. Add a layer of apple slices, raisins, almonds, and cheese. Repeat until all the ingredients are used up. Pour the syrup over the dish. Bake in a preheated moderate (350° F.) oven for 45 minutes, or until heated through. Serve hot.

Variation: For a slightly richer dish sauté the bread cubes in ½ cup vegetable oil or butter.

Variation: For a simpler syrup simmer 2 cups brown sugar with a 2-inch piece of stick cinnamon, 2 cloves, and 4 cups water to make a light syrup. Remove the cinnamon and cloves before using.

Dulce de Queso   COLOMBIA
Cheese Sweet

Serves 4 to 6

1 pound mozzarella cheese, about   *1 cup water*
2 cups dark brown sugar   *A 2-inch piece of stick cinnamon*

Let the cheese come to room temperature. Using a very sharp knife, cut the cheese horizontally into ¼-inch slices and arrange them in a shallow Pyrex dish. In a small saucepan combine the sugar, water, and cinnamon, and bring to a boil, stirring to dissolve the sugar. Boil for 5 minutes without stirring. Pour the syrup over the cheese and serve immediately. For a softer cheese, put the prepared dish in a preheated 350° F. oven for 5 minutes.

✳ Coconut Desserts

Coconut is used a great deal in Latin American desserts. Since fresh coconuts are available in tropical markets and supermarkets all year, I prefer to use them rather than packaged coconut. Brazilian cooks have worked out an excellent method of getting the coconut out of the shell, and a food processor makes the rest of the work easy (see page 7).

Cocada   MEXICO
Coconut Custard

Serves 6

1½ cups sugar   *3 cups milk*
A 2-inch piece of stick cinnamon   *4 whole eggs, lightly beaten*
Liquid from a medium-sized   *2 tablespoons butter, or ½ cup*
*   coconut, ½ cup, about*   *   toasted slivered almonds*
2 cups grated coconut (page 7)

In a saucepan combine the sugar, cinnamon stick, and coconut water. Stir the mixture over low heat until the sugar is dissolved. Add the coconut and continue to cook the mixture, stirring, until the coconut is transparent, about 5 minutes. Remove and discard the cinnamon stick. Stir in the milk, mixing thoroughly. Simmer, over moderate heat, stirring from time to time, until the mixture has thickened and a spoon drawn across the bottom leaves a clean path. Pour ½ cup of the mixture into the eggs, beating constantly with a whisk. Pour the egg mixture back into the saucepan and cook, stirring constantly, over low heat until it has thickened. Do not let it boil. Remove from the heat and pour into a flameproof serving dish (a 1-quart soufflé dish is fine), cool, then refrigerate for several hours. Just before serving, dot the pudding with the butter, and put it under the broiler until the top is lightly browned; or garnish with the slivered almonds.

Variation: For *Dulce de Coco* (Coconut Sweet) from Colombia, soak ¾ cup raisins in hot water for 15 minutes, drain, and put into a heavy saucepan with 4 cups grated coconut, the coconut water made up to 1 cup with water, 4 tablespoons lemon juice, 1½ cups sugar, and a 3-inch piece of stick cinnamon. Bring to a boil, reduce the heat, and simmer until the syrup forms a thread when tested in cold water. Remove and discard the cinnamon stick. Beat 3 egg yolks in a bowl until they are thick and lemon-colored. Beat in 3 tablespoons of the coconut syrup, a tablespoon at a time. Gradually pour the yolk mixture into the coconut mixture and cook over low heat, stirring constantly, for 5 minutes without letting it boil. Cool and refrigerate several hours before serving. Serves 6.

Variation: *Doce de Leite Baiana* (Bahian Style Coconut and Milk Pudding) is a simpler, but still delicious, version of coconut custard. Combine 4 cups finely grated fresh coconut with 4 cups milk and 2¼ cups firmly packed light brown sugar in a heavy saucepan and cook over moderate heat until the mixture is thick and has the consistency of custard. Stir the mixture from time to time with a wooden spoon until it begins to thicken, then stir constantly. Transfer the pudding to a serving dish and serve at room temperature. Serves 6 to 8.

Variation: Writer and friend Elizabeth Borton de Treviño gave me this recipe, given her by the Acapulco cook of the Limantour family at their *quinta* Los Bichitos. It needs less watching than top-of-the-stove versions and has a rather denser texture. For this *Cocada*, simmer 3 cups milk with 1½ cups sugar in an uncovered saucepan for 20 minutes, or until the mixture is slightly thickened. Let it cool. Lightly beat 6 eggs, then beat them into the milk mixture. Stir in ½ teaspoon almond extract and 3 cups freshly grated coconut. Pour into a buttered Pyrex dish. Set in a pan of water so that the water comes 2 inches up the side and bake in a preheated moderate (350° F.) oven for 1½ hours, or until a cake tester comes out clean. Cool and chill before serving. Serves 6 to 8.

Variation: *Pudim de Côco* (Coconut Pudding) from Brazil is a rather richer version of coconut custard. Combine 1 cup sugar with ⅓ cup water in a small saucepan and simmer until it spins a thread (234° F. on a candy thermometer). Remove from the heat and stir in 4 tablespoons (¼ cup) butter. Cool. Stir in 2 cups grated coconut. Thoroughly beat 5 egg yolks until they are very light, and fold into the coconut mixture. Pour into a buttered 3-cup baking dish or soufflé dish, set in a pan of water so that the water extends 2 inches up the side, and bake in a preheated moderate (350° F.) oven for 1 to 1½ hours, or until a cake tester comes out clean. Serve at room temperature. Traditionally the pudding is served with cheese. Use Spanish fresh cheese (*queso fresco* or *queso blanco*), Münster, or similar cheese. Serves 6.

Manjar de Coco com Môlho de Ameixas

BRAZIL

Coconut Blancmange with Prune Sauce

Serves 6

FOR THE BLANCMANGE

4 cups finely grated fresh coconut	*Sugar to taste*
4 cups milk	*4 tablespoons cornstarch*

In a saucepan combine the coconut and milk and bring to a simmer. Remove from the heat and steep for 30 minutes. Strain the liquid through a cheesecloth-lined sieve into a bowl, squeezing the cloth to extract all the liquid. There should be 4 cups. If necessary add a little milk to make up the quantity. Season with sugar to taste. Rinse out and dry the saucepan. Mix a little of the coconut milk with the cornstarch and stir it into the rest of the milk. Pour the mixture into the saucepan and cook, stirring constantly with a wooden spoon, over moderate heat until it is smooth and thick, about 5 minutes. Pour it into a 1-quart mold rinsed out with cold water and refrigerate until set. Unmold onto a serving plate and surround with the prune sauce.

FOR THE SAUCE

½ *pound, about 24, pitted prunes*   1 ½ *cups sugar*
¾ *cup tawny port*   ½ *cup water*

Put the prunes into a bowl with the port and let them macerate for 30 minutes. In a medium saucepan combine the sugar and water. Simmer for 5 minutes to make a fairly heavy syrup. Add the prunes and port and simmer for 5 minutes longer. Cool, chill, and use to garnish the *Manjar de Coco.*

Quindins de Yáyá   BRAZIL
Coconut Cupcake Dessert

Makes 24

2 *cups freshly grated coconut*
2 *tablespoons softened butter*
1 ½ *cups light brown sugar*
8 *large egg yolks*
1 *egg white, well beaten*
Butter
1 *cup sifted all-purpose flour*
  (optional)

In a large bowl mix together the coconut, butter, and sugar, beating to mix thoroughly. One by one beat in the egg yolks, beating thoroughly after each addition. Fold in the egg white beaten until stiff peaks form. Some cooks add a little flour, in which case beat in the flour after all the other ingredients have been combined. The addition of flour gives a lighter, more cakelike texture. Butter 24 muffin tins. Pour the mixture into the tins and stand them in a baking pan with hot water to reach about halfway up the sides of the tins. Bake in a preheated moderate (350° F.) oven for about 45 minutes, or until a toothpick inserted into the cakes comes out clean.

   Some modern cooks use a 9- or 10-inch pie plate instead of individual muffin tins. The cooking time should be increased to 1½ or 2 hours, or until a toothpick inserted into the cake comes out clean.

✳ Pumpkin and Squash Desserts

Torta de Zapallo   ECUADOR
Pumpkin Cake

Calabaza (West Indian pumpkin), which is used so much all over Latin
America as a vegetable and in soups and stews, is also used in some delectable puddings, cakes, and fritters.

Serves 8

1 ½ pounds peeled and cubed
    West Indian pumpkin
    (calabaza) or any winter
    squash, or use two 12-ounce
    packages cooked, frozen
    squash
½ teaspoon cinnamon

1 cup sugar
½ cup heavy cream
2 tablespoons butter
2 ounces dark rum
1 cup seedless raisins
1 cup grated Münster cheese
3 large eggs, well beaten

Cook the squash in water to cover until tender, about 15 minutes. Drain
thoroughly. If using frozen squash, simply thaw it. Put the squash in a
saucepan and stir in the cinnamon, sugar, heavy cream, and 1 tablespoon of
the butter. Mash the squash and cook it over low heat until the sugar has
dissolved and the mixture is fairly firm, not watery. Remove from the heat
and allow to cool. Add all the remaining ingredients, except the reserved
butter. Using the butter, grease a 2-quart soufflé dish and pour in the
squash mixture. Bake in a preheated moderate (350° F.) oven until the cake
is firm to the touch, about 1 hour. An ounce of rum may be poured over the
cake while it is still hot, if liked. Serve as a pudding from the soufflé dish
plain, or with whipped or sour cream.

Pudim de Abóbora   BRAZIL
Pumpkin Pudding

Serves 6

4 large eggs
½ teaspoon salt
½ cup light brown sugar
½ teaspoon ground ginger

¼ teaspoon ground cinnamon
¼ teaspoon ground cloves
¼ teaspoon ground nutmeg

1 ½ cups cooked mashed winter
squash or, preferably, West
Indian pumpkin (calabaza)

1 cup evaporated milk or light
cream
Butter for the mold

Break the eggs into a large bowl and beat them lightly. Beat in the salt, brown sugar, ginger, cinnamon, cloves, nutmeg, squash, and evaporated milk or cream. Butter a 1-quart mold or pudding basin and pour in the custard. Set it in a pan of hot water so that the water extends 2 inches up the side and bake in a preheated moderate (350° F.) oven until a toothpick inserted into the custard comes out clean, about 1½ hours.

Picarones

Sweet Fritters

PERU

Serves 8 to 12

½ pound West Indian pumpkin
(calabaza) or any winter
squash, peeled and sliced
½ pound sweet potato, preferably
white sweet potato (boniato),
peeled and sliced
1 teaspoon salt

¼ teaspoon ground aniseed
4 cups all-purpose flour, sifted
1 envelope (¼ ounce) yeast
Vegetable oil for deep frying

Cook the pumpkin or squash and sweet potato in water to cover until they are tender. Drain the vegetables, mash them, and force them through a sieve. Mix in the salt, aniseed, and flour. Soften the yeast in ¼ cup of lukewarm water and mix it into the flour to make a fairly firm dough, adding a little more water if necessary, though the pumpkin and sweet potato will probably supply enough moisture. Knead the dough until it is smooth and satiny, about 5 minutes. Place it in a bowl, cover with a cloth, and allow to stand in a warm, draft-free place for 2 or 3 hours, or until it has doubled in bulk. Pull off pieces of dough by tablespoons and shape them into rings. Deep fry them in hot oil (370° F.) until they are browned on both sides. Drain on paper towels and serve with *Miel de Chancaca* (Sugar Syrup).

MIEL DE CHANCACA (Sugar Syrup)

2 cups dark brown sugar
1 cup sugar
2 cups water

1 piece lemon peel
1 piece orange peel

Combine all the ingredients in a saucepan and simmer until the syrup is quite thick. Remove and discard the orange and lemon peel. Serve as a dipping sauce with the *Picarones*.

Pristiños
Pumpkin Fritters

ECUADOR

Serves 6

2 cups all-purpose flour	¼ pound (½ cup) butter, softened
1 teaspoon baking powder	at room temperature
1 teaspoon salt	1 cup cooked, mashed West
2 tablespoons grated Parmesan	Indian pumpkin (calabaza)
cheese	Oil or lard for deep frying

Sift the flour, baking powder, and salt into a bowl. Add the cheese. Work the butter into the mixture with your fingers, then the pumpkin with a fork. The pumpkin should supply enough moisture to make a soft but not sticky dough. Turn the dough onto a floured board and roll out to a ½-inch thickness. Cut it into strips 1 inch wide and 6 inches long. Form each strip into a ring, pinching the ends lightly together. Deep fry in hot oil or lard (350° F. to 365° F.) until golden brown on all sides. Drain on paper towels and serve with cinnamon syrup.

CINNAMON SYRUP

2 cups dark brown sugar, firmly	A 1-inch piece of stick cinnamon
packed	

In a saucepan combine the sugar with 1 cup water and the cinnamon stick. Stir the mixture to dissolve the sugar and simmer over moderate heat for 5 minutes. Discard the cinnamon stick.

✳ Milk Pudding

There is a dessert made from milk simmered with sugar until it is thick that is popular throughout Latin America. It has a variety of names — *Manjar Blanco, Natillas Piuranas, Arequipe, Dulce de Leche, Cajeta de Celaya* — and the cooking technique varies slightly from country to country. I think milk pudding is about the most practical translation. Making this can be time-consuming, about 1½ hours, if one stands at the stove and conscientiously stirs the mixture with a wooden spoon, but I have found that if the heat is kept low one can make the pudding, stirring from time to time, while doing other things in the kitchen. Once the mixture begins to thicken, however, it does need constant stirring or the texture suffers and is grainy instead of smooth. But this is only in the last 5 minutes or so. Everyone in Latin America knows the *truco*, or trick, of boiling an unopened can of sweetened condensed milk until it caramelizes, but most cooks prefer the results of the longer method. However, there is a very quick Colombian version using sweetened condensed milk and evaporated milk that is delicious, and a nice compromise. It is amazing how great a difference in taste and texture is produced by small differences in proportions and cooking methods for this most delicate of desserts.

Natillas Piuranas
Brown Sugar Pudding

PERU

Ideally this should be made with goat's milk but I have found that using a mixture of milk and cream or evaporated milk gives a very good result.

Serves 4 to 6

2 cups dark brown sugar
¼ cup water
3 cups milk
1 cup light cream or evaporated
    milk

½ teaspoon baking soda
½ cup finely ground walnuts

In a large, heavy saucepan combine the brown sugar and the water and cook over low heat, stirring constantly with a wooden spoon, until the sugar is dissolved. In another saucepan combine the milk, light cream or evaporated milk, and the baking soda. Stir to mix and bring almost to a boil over fairly high heat. Pour into the dissolved sugar, stirring to mix thoroughly, and cook, stirring frequently, until the mixture is thick and caramel-colored and the bottom of the pan can be seen when the spoon is drawn across it. Stir in the walnuts, mixing well. It will take about 1 hour. Serve either chilled or at room temperature.

Manjar Blanco
Milk Pudding

CHILE

Serves 6

8 cups milk
2½ cups sugar

A 2-inch piece of vanilla bean

In a heavy saucepan combine all the ingredients and bring to a simmer. Cook, stirring from time to time, over low heat until the mixture begins to thicken. Remove the piece of vanilla bean. Simmer, stirring constantly with a wooden spoon, until the mixture is thick enough so the bottom of the pan can be seen when the spoon is drawn across it. It will take about an hour. Do not overcook or the pudding will turn into candy. Turn into a serving bowl and serve either slightly chilled or at room temperature.

Variation: For *Dulce de Leche* (Milk Sweet or Dessert) from Paraguay, combine 10 cups milk, 1 teaspoon vanilla essence, ½ teaspoon baking soda, and 2 cups sugar in a saucepan and stir from time to time, off the heat, until the sugar is dissolved. Bring to a simmer and cook over very low heat, to prevent the milk from boiling over, stirring occasionally with a wooden spoon until the mixture is thick and caramel-colored. When the mixture begins to thicken, stir constantly. The pudding is ready when the bottom of the saucepan can be seen when the spoon is drawn across it, or when a spoonful on a plate no longer runs but retains its shape. The pudding may be varied by increasing the amount of sugar to 3 cups or by increasing the amount of milk to 12 cups. Serves 6 to 8.

Variation: For *Arequipe* (Milk Pudding) from Colombia, there is a recipe almost identical to the one above from Paraguay but using 12 cups milk to 4 cups sugar.

Variation: There is another *Arequipe* that is very successful and a splendid shortcut. Put 2 cups evaporated milk and 2 cups sweetened condensed milk into a heavy saucepan, stir to mix thoroughly, bring to a simmer, and cook, stirring constantly, until the mixture is thick and golden and the bottom of the pan can be seen when the spoon is drawn across it. Serve with wedges of cheese, preferably Spanish fresh cheese (*queso fresco* or *queso blanco*), or with Münster, Edam, or Gouda.

Variation: For *Dulce de Leche Con Huevos* (Milk Sweet with Eggs), simmer 8 cups of milk with 2 cups sugar, a vanilla bean, and a 2-inch piece of stick cinnamon until the mixture begins to thicken. Remove the vanilla bean and cinnamon stick. When the pudding is thick, remove from the heat and stir in 4 well-beaten egg yolks. Return the pudding to the heat and cook, stirring, for 2 minutes. Remove from the heat. Beat 4 egg whites until they stand in peaks and add to the pudding, off the heat. Return the pudding to the heat and cook, stirring constantly, until it is again thick. Off the heat beat the pudding until it is cool. Turn into a dessert dish and chill until ready to serve. Serves 6 to 8.

Variation: The best milk puddings of Mexico come from the rich mining and farming state of Guanajuato. The most famous of them is *Cajeta de Celaya*, which means literally box from the town of Celaya and refers to the small wooden boxes in which the sweet is packaged. Put 3 cups each cow's and goat's milk, mixed with ½ teaspoon baking soda and 2 teaspoons cornstarch, in a heavy saucepan with 2 cups sugar and a fig leaf, if available, and simmer the mixture in the usual way until thick. Discard the fig leaf and pour the pudding into a serving bowl. Serve chilled or at room temperature. Goat's milk is sometimes available in health or specialty stores.

For *Cajeta Envinada* (Milk Pudding with Wine), stir ½ cup sherry, muscatel, or Madeira into the finished sweet. For *Cajeta de Leche Quemada* (Pudding of Burned Milk), the sugar is caramelized before the milk is added. To do this the sugar is put into a heavy saucepan over low heat and stirred constantly with a wooden spoon until it melts and turns coffee color. The milk should be added little by little, off the heat, and stirred well to mix. The pudding is then cooked in the usual way. It is a deep, rich amber color. There is a little *truco* here that some cooks use — they substitute light brown sugar for white sugar. For *Cajeta de Almendra Envinada* (Milk Pudding with Almonds and Wine), add ¼ cup ground almonds and ½ cup sherry, muscatel, or Madeira. Serve the pudding by itself, or with ice cream or slices of pound cake or cookies. Serves 6.

Chongos Zamoranos   MEXICO
Custard Squares in Syrup

This is a different kind of milk pudding, and as great a favorite in Mexican households today as it was in colonial times. There are many versions. This one from Zamora in Michoacán is the one I like best. *Chongo* means a tuft of hair tied on top of the head — a very fanciful way to describe this dessert.

Serves 8

2 quarts (8 cups) milk
4 egg yolks, lightly beaten
4 rennet tablets

1½ cups sugar
A 2-inch piece of stick cinnamon

Heat the milk to lukewarm. Off the heat, beat in the egg yolks. Pour the mixture into a deep, straight-sided flameproof dish about 8 inches by 10 inches. Dissolve the rennet tablets in ¼ cup cold water and add to the milk mixture. Let the mixture stand in a warm place until it is set, about 1 hour. Using a sharp knife cut it into 2-inch squares disturbing it as little as possible. Sprinkle with the sugar. Break up the cinnamon stick and sprinkle the bits over the junket. Place over the lowest possible heat, using an asbestos mat if necessary to keep the liquid below simmering point, for about 2 hours. The sugar and the whey from the junket will form a thick syrup. Chills before serving.

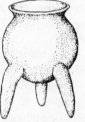

Quimbolitos
Steamed Puddings

ECUADOR

Serves 6

4 tablespoons (¼ cup) butter
6 tablespoons sugar
2 eggs, well beaten
¼ cup milk
½ cup all-purpose flour

½ cup cornstarch
2 teaspoons baking powder
½ cup grated Parmesan cheese
⅓ cup seedless raisins
2 tablespoons cognac or light rum

Soften the butter at room temperature. In a bowl cream together the butter and sugar until the mixture is light and fluffy. Add the eggs mixed with the milk. Sift together the flour, cornstarch, and baking powder, and stir into the batter mixture. Stir in the cheese, raisins, and cognac or rum.

Cut either kitchen parchment or aluminum foil into six 8- by 12-inch rectangles. Drop a scant 3 tablespoons of the mixture into the center of each, and fold up into an envelope. Arrange in a steamer and cook over boiling water for 45 minutes. Serve hot, with or without cream.

In Ecuador the *Quimbolitos* are cooked in *achira* leaves, the leaf of the taro plant, perhaps better known as *dasheen* or *yautía*. Nothing seems to be lost by cooking them in parchment or foil, however.

✳ Cakes

Torta del Cielo   MEXICO
Heavenly Cake

This cake is served on all kinds of special occasions in Yucatán: engagement parties, weddings, baptisms, first communions, birthdays, and so on. There are many versions, some using no flour at all, just ground almonds. This is the version I prefer and I find it aptly named.

Serves 12

8 ounces blanched almonds
½ cup cake flour
1 teaspoon baking powder
10 eggs, separated
1 ¼ cups sugar

1 teaspoon vanilla extract
Pinch of salt

Cut a piece of wax paper to fit a 10-inch springform pan and oil it lightly. Fit it into the bottom of the pan. Do not oil the sides.

Grind the nuts, ½ cup at a time, in a blender, food processor, or nut grinder, and shake them through a sieve. Sift the flour with the baking powder into a bowl and mix thoroughly with the nuts. In another bowl beat the egg yolks, adding the sugar gradually until they are light, thick, and lemon-colored and form a ribbon when lifted from the bowl. Stir in the vanilla. Beat the egg whites with the pinch of salt until they stand in firm peaks. Sprinkle the flour and nut mixture onto the egg yolks, add the whites, and, using a rubber spatula, lightly fold them all together. Do not overmix, fold only until the last patches of white disappear. Pour the mixture into the prepared pan and bake in a preheated moderate (375° F.) oven for 50 minutes, or until a cake tester comes out clean. Invert on a wire rack and allow to cool thoroughly for 1 to 2 hours. Remove from the pan and peel off the wax paper. Turn right side up and dust with confectioners' sugar. The cake may be served with whipped cream, ice cream, fruit salad, or by itself. It may be frosted with a butter cream frosting, if liked.

Variation: Use 1 pound ground almonds and omit the flour and baking powder. Beat the egg whites until they stand in firm peaks, then beat in the yolks, two at a time, adding 2 extra yolks. Then beat in the almonds, ¼ cup at a time, and 1 pound confectioners' sugar, ¼ cup at a time. Stir in the vanilla.

Torta de Castanhas-Do-Pará   BRAZIL
Brazil Nut Cake

This rich yet light cake from Brazil makes a splendid dessert. I like it as a change from *Quindins de Yáyá* (Coconut Cupcake Dessert) to follow *Feijoada Completa* (Black Beans with Mixed Meats). Brazil nuts take the place of flour in the cake itself, an airy thing of egg whites. The egg yolks make a luscious filling, while the chocolate frosting adds the final luxurious touch.

Serves 12 to 14

FOR THE CAKE

12 *egg whites*   8 *ounces Brazil nuts, finely ground*
1 *cup sugar*   *Butter*

Beat the egg whites until they stand in firm, unwavering peaks. Gradually beat in the sugar. Fold in the nuts, gently but thoroughly. Have ready two 8-inch cake tins lined with buttered wax paper or kitchen parchment. Pour in the cake batter and bake in a preheated moderate (350° F.) oven for 40 minutes. The cakes will puff up but will fall as they cool. When they are cool, spread generously with the filling and sandwich the cakes together. Cover with chocolate frosting.

FOR THE FILLING

1 *cup sugar*   6 *egg yolks*
½ *cup water*

Combine the sugar and water in a small saucepan and cook over moderate heat until the syrup reaches the soft ball stage, when a little of the syrup dropped on a saucer holds its shape but flattens out, 234° F. on a candy thermometer. Beat the egg yolks until they are thick and lemon-colored, then beat in the cooled syrup. Pour into the top of a double boiler and cook, stirring constantly with a wooden spoon, over low heat until the mixture is thick. Cool before using to fill the cake.

FOR THE FROSTING

2 *ounces semisweet chocolate,*   ¼ *cup coffee or water*
   broken into bits   ½ *egg white, beaten until stiff*
¼ *cup sugar*

In the top of a double boiler over moderate heat, combine the chocolate, sugar, and coffee or water, and cook, stirring, until the sugar is dissolved and the mixture smooth. Cool. Beat in the egg white. Spread over the cake. Refrigerate the cake until the frosting is firm.

For a simpler frosting melt 2 ounces semisweet chocolate in 2 tablespoons coffee or water in the top of a double boiler over moderate heat. Off the heat, beat 4 tablespoons unsalted butter, cut into bits, into the chocolate mixture. Continue to beat the mixture until it is cool. Spread over the cake.

Sauces
Salsas

Because the sauce is incorporated into so many Latin American dishes, there is not a large body of separate sauces. At the same time it could be said with justification that Mexican cuisine is one of sauces with infinite variations played on a theme. The same is true of Peruvian cooking. No one has ever codified these sauces and it might, if it could be done, complicate rather than simplify matters. Every country has some form of hot pepper sauce, always present on family tables, so that the amount of fire in one's food is discretionary, though Peruvian dishes tend to be pretty hot in their own right. French sauces, sometimes with names that startle a little, have migrated to Latin America, and so has the technique of the *sofrito*, that useful mixture of sautéed onion and garlic, which began in Spain and Portugal and was expanded during the colonial period from its simple original form to include peppers and tomatoes, gifts of the New World. The avocado-based sauces are well represented, as are sauces with tomato.

Pebre

CHILE

Chilean Hot Pepper Sauce

The number of hot peppers used in this sauce is purely discretionary. Some people like it very hot, and it is then just called *Salsa Picante* (Hot Sauce). As many as 8 hot peppers might be used. Others prefer it mild. Hot red peppers may be used instead of green.

Makes about 1 cup

1 medium onion, finely chopped
1 clove garlic, minced
2 tablespoons finely chopped fresh
   coriander (cilantro)
1 tablespoon finely chopped
   parsley

1 or more fresh hot green peppers,
   seeded and finely chopped
3 tablespoons olive oil
1 tablespoon lemon juice
Salt to taste

Combine all the ingredients in a bowl and let stand for about 1 hour before serving for the flavor to develop. Serve with any meat and with *Porotos Granados* (Cranberry Beans with Corn and Squash).

Salsa de Ají

COLOMBIA

Hot Pepper Sauce

Makes about 1 cup

½ pound fresh hot red or green
   peppers

1 teaspoon salt, or to taste
1 medium onion, finely chopped

Remove the seeds from the peppers and chop them coarsely. In a blender or food processor grind them to a pulp with the salt. Add the chopped onion and mix well.

Salsa de Ají Picante

ECUADOR

Hot Pepper Sauce

There are many versions of hot pepper sauce. This one is from the coast.

Fresh hot red or green peppers   *Lemon juice*
Red onion   *Salt*

Seed the peppers and cut them into small strips. Combine the peppers with an equal amount of finely chopped red onion in a wide-mouthed glass jar. Cover the vegetables with lemon juice, add salt to taste, and let the sauce stand for 3 to 4 hours before using. The lemon juice may be diluted by adding a little hot water.

Ixni-Pec   MEXICO
Hot Pepper Sauce

Pronounced roughly schnee-peck, this is the fresh, hot pepper sauce that always appears on Yucatecan dining tables in a small bowl or sauceboat. It should be taken with discretion for, though it has a lovely flavor, it is very hot. The pepper used is the yellow *habanero*. I have found that pickled hot peppers from the Caribbean, usually from Trinidad or Jamaica, have an almost identical flavor and make a splendid substitute.

Makes about 1 cup

¼ cup each finely chopped onion,   *Seville (bitter) orange juice, or use*
tomato, and hot chili pepper,   *two-thirds orange juice to*
rinsed if pickled   *one-third lime juice*
                                      Salt

In a bowl combine the onion, tomato, and hot pepper and add enough orange juice to make it soupy, about ¼ cup. Season to taste with salt. Serve with Yucatecan dishes or whenever a hot pepper sauce is called for. The sauce should be eaten the same day or the next.

Variation: Though *Ixni-Pec* is very hot indeed, I have encountered an even hotter sauce called simply *Salsa Picante* (Hot Sauce). It consisted of green *habaneros* peeled by toasting over a flame, seeded and chopped and diluted with a little Seville (bitter) orange juice.

Môlho de Pimenta e Limão   BRAZIL
Hot Pepper and Lime Sauce

The peppers used in Brazil are the small, very, very hot *malagueta* peppers not usually available here. Any very hot pepper can be substituted but I have found pickled Caribbean peppers, usually from Jamaica or Trinidad, a good substitute.

Makes about ¾ cup

3 or 4 hot red or green peppers,
    seeded
1 onion, chopped

1 clove garlic, chopped
Salt
½ cup lime or lemon juice

Crush the peppers, onion, and garlic with salt to taste in a mortar with a pestle, adding the lime or lemon juice little by little, or purée in a blender or food processor. Serve in a bowl to accompany meat, poultry, or fish dishes and with *Feijoada Completa* (Black Beans with Mixed Meats).

Môlho de Pimenta
e Azeite de Dendê   BRAZIL
Hot Peppers in Dendê (Palm) Oil

This is a common sauce on Bahian tables. The pepper used is the tiny, ferociously hot *malagueta* pepper.

Makes about ½ cup

6 or more small fresh hot red or
    green peppers

Dendê *(palm) oil, to cover*

Put the peppers in a small bowl and pour in enough oil to cover them. Let them stand for several hours before using. The oil will be quite hot and flavored by the peppers, while the heat of the peppers themselves will be slightly reduced.

Variation: For *Môlho de Pimenta e Azeite de Oliva* (Hot Peppers in Olive Oil), use olive oil instead of palm oil. This is a more usual hot sauce in other parts of Brazil, where palm oil is not used.

Salsa de Ají Colorado
CHILE
Red Pepper Sauce

Makes about 2½ cups

24 fresh hot red peppers, seeded
    and cut into strips
1 cup wine vinegar

1 clove garlic, chopped
1 teaspoon salt
¾ cup vegetable oil

Put the pepper strips into a bowl and add the vinegar. Leave overnight, stirring with a wooden spoon once or twice. Drain, reserving the vinegar. Put the peppers into a blender or food processor with the garlic, the salt, and enough of the vinegar to reduce them to a purée. Beat in the oil, adding about ¼ cup of the vinegar to give the sauce the consistency of mayonnaise. For a milder sauce discard the vinegar in which the peppers were soaked and use fresh vinegar. A lot of the heat of the peppers will have soaked out into the vinegar.

Serve with *Chancho a la Chilena* (Pork Loin, Chilean Style) or with any plainly cooked meat, poultry, or fish, or with cold meats.

Ajíes en Leche
VENEZUELA
Hot Peppers in Milk

The hot peppers used in Venezuela are medium-sized round or lantern-shaped ones, extremely hot and very well flavored. Any hot peppers may, of course, be used.

Makes about 1¼ cups

1 cup milk
½ teaspoon salt
6 fresh hot red or green peppers,
    stemmed and halved
    lengthwise

1 slice onion
1 clove garlic
3 or 4 fresh mint leaves (optional)

Pour the milk into a saucepan, add the salt, bring to a boil and immediately remove from the heat. Allow to cool. Put the hot peppers, onion, garlic, and mint leaves in a glass jar and pour the milk over them. Let stand overnight. To serve, pour into a bowl and eat the peppers as a sauce with any meat, poultry, or fish dish.

Salsa de Chile Ancho y Almendra   MEXICO
Mild Red Chili and Almond Sauce

The Mexican kitchen is extraordinarily rich in sauces, *mollis* in Nahuatl, the language of the Aztec empire, modified to *moles* in Spanish. This mild and gentle sauce was probably made originally with peanuts, which were indigenous, having found their way north from Brazil, instead of almonds. Certainly almonds make a subtler sauce than do peanuts, though both are good.

The sauce is used with salt cod, another import, in *Bacalao en Salsa de Chile Ancho y Almendra* (Salt Cod in Mild Red Chili and Almond Sauce). It is also excellent with poultry, pork, or veal (chicken stock is fine for all three). The meat is poached in stock or water until it is almost tender. The sauce is then thinned with a little of the stock and the meat is simmered in the sauce until it is tender and the flavors are blended, about 5 minutes.

Makes about 5 cups

6 ancho *chilies*
1 medium onion, *chopped*
¼ pound (¾ cup, about) toasted almonds, *ground*
⅛ teaspoon ground cinnamon
⅛ teaspoon ground cloves
¼ teaspoon oregano
¼ teaspoon sugar
Salt
4 tablespoons vegetable oil
2 cups chicken, beef, or fish stock

Pull the stems off the chilies, shake out and discard the seeds, rinse in cold water, tear into pieces, and put into a bowl with 1 cup hot water. Let soak for about 1 hour, longer if the chilies are very dry, turning them from time to time. Put the chilies, any soaking water, and the onion into a blender or food processor and reduce to a purée. Add the almonds to the chili mixture with the cinnamon, cloves, oregano, sugar, and salt to taste. The mixture will be quite heavy, almost a paste. Heat the oil in a heavy skillet and sauté the chili mixture, stirring constantly with a wooden spoon, for 5 minutes over moderate heat. Add 2 cups of the appropriate stock, stir to mix, and simmer for a few minutes longer. Clam juice may be used instead of fish stock.

The sauce, which should be of medium consistency, is now ready to use with salt cod, poultry, pork, or veal. It may also be used with fresh fish, preferably fillets, in which case the uncooked fish may be simmered in the sauce until done, or put into a greased, shallow flameproof casserole with the sauce poured over it and baked in a preheated moderate (350° F.) oven until tender, about 20 minutes.

Guacamole

MEXICO

Avocado Sauce

In Mexico *Guacamole* is eaten with everything — meat, poultry, fish, shell-fish, beans, cheese, and by itself with *tostaditas*, triangles of fried tortilla. *Antojitos* are unthinkable without it. Very old recipes give *guacamole* simply as avocado with chili and I have had it simply mashed with a little salt, very elegant. However, recipes from the seventeenth century on give it as a mixture of tomatoes, fresh green coriander (cilantro), onion, and chopped *serrano* chilies, the small hot green mountain peppers very much used in the Mexican kitchen. I find the canned *serranos* are a better choice than fresh hot peppers of another variety, since it is their flavor as well as their heat that is needed. Fresh *serranos* are sometimes available in Latin American markets.

There is a lot of superstition about preventing *Guacamole* from dark-ening when exposed to air. One is that putting the avocado pit in the center of the finished sauce will do this. Long and careful research has convinced me of the falseness of this claim but I must confess I like the look of the brown pit sitting in the bowl of creamy green sauce. Next to making the sauce at the last minute the best solution is to cover the bowl tightly with plastic wrap and refrigerate it.

There are two basic versions of *Guacamole*, one with tomatoes, the other *Guacamole del Norte* (Avocado Sauce, Northern Style) made with Mexican green husk tomatoes, which does not discolor quite so quickly, perhaps because the green tomato is more acid than ordinary tomatoes. Certainly sprinkling lime or lemon juice on a cut avocado does help pre-vent darkening. Also a very ripe avocado will darken more quickly than one that is just at its moment of ripe perfection but not a minute over it.

I find that the best way to mash an avocado is to cut it in half, un-peeled, remove the pit, and holding the pear in the left hand mash the flesh with a fork, scoop it out with a spoon and mash any solid bits that have escaped. This gives the finished purée a good texture.

Makes about 4 cups

2 large ripe avocados, pitted and
    mashed
2 medium tomatoes, peeled,
    seeded, and chopped
1 tablespoon onion, finely
    chopped

3 canned serrano chilies, or 1
    teaspoon seeded and finely
    chopped fresh hot green
    pepper
1 tablespoon fresh green coriander
    (cilantro), chopped

Salt to taste

Mix all the ingredients thoroughly and place in a serving dish with the pit of one of the avocados in the center, if liked. Serve as a dip with triangles of fried tortilla, or as a sauce.

Variation: For *Guacamole del Norte* (Avocado Sauce, Northern Style), substitute half of a 10-ounce can of Mexican green tomatoes (about 6), drained and mashed, for the tomatoes. If fresh green husk tomatoes are available, peel off the papery husk and drop them into boiling salt. Cook for 2 minutes, drain, and allow to cool. Chop finely. Then proceed as for *Guacamole.*

Guasacaca
Avocado Sauce

VENEZUELA

There was a great deal of trade between Mexico and South America in pre-Conquest times and it is entirely possible that this is a migrant version of an original *guacamole* somewhat modified in later colonial days.

Serves 4

4 tablespoons olive oil
1 tablespoon red wine vinegar
Salt to taste
½ teaspoon finely chopped,
    seeded, fresh hot red pepper, or
    ½ teaspoon ground hot red
    pepper

1 large avocado, peeled and diced
1 medium tomato, peeled and
    chopped
1 medium ripe red bell pepper, or
    use a green pepper, finely
    chopped
1 small onion, finely chopped

In a bowl combine the oil, vinegar, salt, and hot pepper, and beat with a fork to mix thoroughly. Add the rest of the ingredients, tossing to mix. Serve with grilled meats.

Variation: Add 1 tablespoon of finely chopped fresh green coriander (cilantro) or parsley.

Variation: Add 1 hardboiled egg, finely chopped.

Ají de Huevo   COLOMBIA
Avocado Sauce

This is another migrant recipe that evolved when the Chibcha of Colombia used to export their exquisite gold work to Mexico. I suspect the reverse trade included more than recipes. It is interesting to see how this one differs from the original Mexican recipe and from the next-door Venezuelan one. The name of the sauce really defies translation. *Ají* is the South American word for hot pepper. *Huevo* is egg. Literally one gets "hot pepper of egg." Avocado sauce is a better way of describing it.

Makes about 1 ½ cups

1 large avocado, pitted and
   mashed
1 hardboiled egg yolk, mashed
1 tablespoon finely chopped fresh
   green coriander (cilantro)
1 fresh hot green pepper, seeded
   and chopped

1 finely chopped scallion, using
   white and green parts
1 hardboiled egg white, finely
   chopped
1 tablespoon white wine vinegar
Salt, freshly ground pepper

Mix the avocado and egg yolk thoroughly. Add all the rest of the ingredients and mix well. Serve as a sauce with *Sobrebarriga Bogotana* (Flank Steak, Bogotá Style) or *Ajiaco de Pollo Bogotano* (Bogotá Chicken Stew).

Môlho ao Tomate   BRAZIL
Tomato Sauce

Makes about 2 cups

3 tablespoons olive oil
6 large, ripe tomatoes, coarsely
   chopped
1 clove garlic, minced

3 or 4 fresh basil leaves, chopped,
   or 1 teaspoon dried basil
Salt, freshly ground pepper

Heat the oil in a saucepan and add the tomatoes, garlic, and basil. Simmer over low heat for 3 or 4 minutes, stirring occasionally. Season to taste with salt and pepper and stir in ½ cup warm water. Simmer over low heat, stirring from time to time, until the mixture is quite thick. Work the mixture through a sieve.

Salsa de Jitomate
Tomato Sauce

Makes about 2½ cups

1 medium onion, chopped
1 clove garlic, chopped
3 large tomatoes, peeled and
    chopped
2 canned serrano chilies, chopped

⅛ teaspoon sugar
Salt to taste
2 tablespoons vegetable oil
1 tablespoon chopped fresh green
    coriander (cilantro)

Combine the onion, garlic, tomatoes, and chilies in a blender or food processor and purée briefly. The purée should retain some texture and not be too smooth. Season with the sugar and salt. Heat the oil in a skillet, pour in the tomato mixture, and cook, stirring, over moderate heat until it is thick and well blended, about 5 minutes. Stir in the coriander.

Salsa Chilena
Chilean Sauce

Serve this with plainly cooked meat or any cold dish.

Makes about 2½ cups

2 cups beef stock
1 medium onion, finely chopped
2 medium tomatoes, peeled and
    chopped

2 tablespoons lemon juice
Salt, freshly ground pepper
¼ cup olive or vegetable oil

Put the stock and onion into a saucepan and simmer, uncovered, over moderate heat until the onion is tender. Pour into a blender or food processor and reduce to a purée. Set aside.

Put the tomatoes into the blender or food processor and reduce them to a purée. Pour the purée into a small saucepan and cook, stirring, until it is thick. Stir the tomato into the stock and onion mixture. Add the lemon juice and salt and pepper to taste. Allow to cool, then gradually beat in the oil. The sauce should be thick. If necessary, beat in more oil.

Salsa Cruda
MEXICO

Uncooked Tomato Sauce

This sauce appears on Mexican tables as often as salt and pepper. It is served with cooked meats, poultry, fish, eggs, and beans and is added to tacos (stuffed tortillas) and other *antojitos* (appetizers). The beautifully ripe, red tomatoes of Mexico have very thin skins and though these can simply be peeled off by hand, they are usually left on for *Salsa Cruda*. I peel the tomatoes for this sauce only if they have thick skins.

Makes about 2½ cups

2 large ripe tomatoes, finely
    chopped
1 small onion, finely chopped
2 or more fresh hot green peppers,
    seeded and chopped, or use
    canned serrano chilies, seeded
    and chopped

1 tablespoon chopped fresh green
    coriander (cilantro)
Pinch of sugar
Salt to taste

Mix all the ingredients together. Serve in a bowl or gravy boat. It is best made at the last minute and served at room temperature.

Salsa Criolla
ARGENTINA

Creole Sauce

Serve this with roasted or grilled meats.

Makes about 3 cups

2 medium onions, finely chopped
3 medium tomatoes, finely
    chopped
1 fresh hot green pepper, seeded
    and finely chopped
1 clove garlic, chopped

2 tablespoons finely chopped
    parsley
Salt, freshly ground pepper
½ cup olive oil
3 tablespoons red wine vinegar

In a bowl combine the onions, tomatoes, pepper, garlic, and parsley, mixing lightly. Season with salt and pepper. In a small bowl beat together the oil and vinegar with a fork, then pour the mixture over the vegetables. Stir to mix.

Salsa de Tomatillo
Mexican Green Tomato Sauce

This is, I think, the most distinctive of all the Mexican sauces and the most delicious. It is made with the green husk tomato available fresh in markets in the Southwest and canned from stores specializing in Mexican foods. Green husk tomatoes must not be confused with green (unripe) ordinary tomatoes. They are in the same family but a different species altogether (see page 17).

Makes about 1 cup

A 10-ounce can Mexican green
    tomatoes, drained
1 tablespoon finely chopped white
    onion
½ clove garlic, chopped
2 or more canned serrano chilies,
    chopped

1 tablespoon fresh green coriander
    (cilantro), chopped
Salt to taste

Thoroughly mix all the ingredients, mashing the green tomatoes, or whirl very briefly in a blender or food processor. Serve in a bowl or gravy boat.

Variation: Some cooks omit the onion and garlic and increase the amount of coriander to taste. Whirl very briefly in a blender or food processor.

Salsa de Tomate Verde
Another Green Tomato Sauce

This sauce, which can be used with any plainly cooked meat, poultry, fish, or shellfish, will keep for some time.

Makes about 2½ cups

Two 10-ounce cans Mexican green
    tomatoes, drained, about 2
    cups
3 cloves garlic, crushed
3 fresh hot red or green peppers,
    seeded and finely chopped

½ cup white vinegar
¼ teaspoon ground allspice
¼ teaspoon oregano
Salt, freshly ground pepper

Put the tomatoes, garlic, and hot peppers into a small saucepan and cook together for a few minutes until the tomatoes have disintegrated, stirring two or three times. Add the rest of the ingredients and cook for a few minutes longer, or until the mixture is well blended. Bottle and refrigerate.

Salsa de Perejil   CHILE
Parsley Sauce

Makes about 1 ¾ cups

1 cup olive or vegetable oil
4 tablespoons red or white wine
    vinegar or lemon juice

1 teaspoon prepared mustard
½ cup finely chopped parsley
Salt, freshly ground pepper

Mix all the ingredients together. Serve with fish or shellfish or as a dressing with tomatoes.

    For *erizos* (sea urchins), make the dressing with lemon juice, omit the mustard, and add ½ cup finely chopped onion.

Ají de Queso   ECUADOR
Cheese Sauce

Makes about 2 cups

1 large tomato, peeled, seeded,
    and coarsely chopped
1 fresh hot red or green pepper
½ pound Spanish fresh cheese
    (queso blanco or queso fresco)
    or ricotta

Salt, freshly ground pepper
1 medium onion, finely chopped
1 hardboiled egg, chopped

In a blender or food processor combine the tomato, pepper, and cheese and reduce to a purée. Be careful not to overblend. Season to taste with salt and pepper and put into a bowl. Sprinkle with the onion and egg. Serve as a sauce with potatoes and cooked green vegetables.

Salsa de Maní
ECUADOR

Peanut Sauce

Serve this with *Llapingachos* (Potato Cakes).

Makes about 1½ cups

2 tablespoons annatto (achiote) oil or lard (see page 324)
1 onion, finely chopped
1 clove garlic, chopped
1 medium tomato, peeled, seeded, and chopped

½ cup finely ground peanuts, or 2 tablespoons peanut butter
Salt, freshly ground pepper

Heat the annatto oil or lard in a skillet and stir in the onion, garlic, and tomato. Cook over moderate heat until the onion is tender and the mixture well blended. Stir in the peanuts, season to taste with salt and pepper, and cook for a few minutes longer. The sauce should be thin enough to pour. If necessary, add a little tomato juice or water and cook just long enough to blend.

Salsa de Choclos
CHILE

Sweetcorn Sauce

This is a colonial sauce developed at a time when corn was a make-do vegetable, not yet esteemed in its own right, as it was later on. The sauce is light and delicious, the flavor of the fresh sweetcorn coming through beautifully. It can be used as a sauce with meats or poultry, but I prefer it over green vegetables and especially with cauliflower.

Makes about 3 cups

2 cups sweetcorn kernels; if using frozen corn, thaw thoroughly
1 cup milk
1 teaspoon sweet paprika

Salt, freshly ground white pepper
1 or 2 eggs, lightly beaten (optional)

In a blender or food processor combine the corn, milk, sweet paprika, salt, and pepper and reduce to a smooth purée. Pour into a saucepan and cook, stirring constantly, over low heat for 5 minutes, or until the mixture is well blended. If necessary, thicken the sauce by stirring in 1 or 2 eggs, lightly beaten, and cooking over low heat, stirring, until the sauce is thickened. I find corn varies considerably, so I use my judgment about thickening the sauce, using no eggs, or 1 or 2 as required.

Color Chilena   CHILE
Paprika Oil

This oil is used a great deal in Chilean cooking, and since it keeps indefinitely can be made in quantity. However, if you want to make less, paprika can simply be added to oil in the ratio of 1 teaspoon paprika to every 2 tablespoons oil, with garlic used proportionately.

Makes 2 cups

2 cups vegetable oil or lard   5 tablespoons sweet paprika
3 cloves garlic

Heat the oil or lard in a saucepan and add the garlic cloves. Sauté the garlic until it is brown, then lift out and discard. Off the heat, stir in the paprika until it is well mixed with the oil. Cool and bottle.

Aceite o Manteca de Achiote   COLOMBIA
Annatto Oil or Lard

This is used a good deal as both a coloring and a flavoring in the Caribbean, Colombia, Ecuador, and Venezuela (see page 4).

Makes ½ cup

4 tablespoons annatto seeds   4 tablespoons vegetable oil or lard
  (achiote)

Combine the annatto seeds and oil in a small, heavy saucepan and place over moderate heat until the seeds begin to give up their color, a deep orangey-red. If the seeds are fresh, the color will be abundant and deep and will be given off very quickly, within about 1 minute. Watch for the moment when the color starts to change to golden and remove immediately from the heat. Strain and bottle. The oil or lard will keep indefinitely.

Aliño Criollo VENEZUELA
Seasoning Powder, Creole Style

This mixture of ground herbs and spices, which varies slightly from cook to cook, is used as a seasoning in many Venezuelan dishes, and I have found it a pleasant addition to stews and casseroles even outside the Venezuelan or Latin American kitchen. It can be bought ready-made from spice shelves in Venezuelan supermarkets as *Aliño Preparado* (Prepared Seasoning). I make it without garlic so that it keeps, but I add a large clove of crushed garlic to 2 tablespoons of the powder when I use it in cooking.

Makes about ½ cup

1 tablespoon garlic salt
1 ½ teaspoons ground cumin
1 tablespoon ground annatto
   (achiote) seeds

¼ teaspoon ground black pepper
1 tablespoon oregano
3 tablespoons sweet paprika

Thoroughly mix all the ingredients and put into a small glass jar. Store in a cool, dark place. Keeps indefinitely.

BASIC SAUCES

Béchamel
White Sauce

Makes about 2 cups

2 tablespoons butter
2 tablespoons flour
2 cups milk

Salt, white pepper
Pinch of nutmeg

In a small, heavy saucepan melt the butter. Stir in the flour with a wooden spoon and cook, stirring, over low heat for 2 minutes. Gradually pour in the milk, stirring constantly to mix, and bring to a boil. Simmer, stirring frequently, for 5 minutes. Season to taste with salt, white pepper, and nutmeg.

For a thick béchamel, use only 1 cup of milk. For a medium sauce, use 1½ cups, and for the more usual, creamy sauce, use 2 cups.

If the sauce should be lumpy, which is unlikely if it is properly made, simply whirl it in a blender or food processor.

Vinaigrette
Oil and Vinegar, or French, Dressing

Makes about ½ cup

2 tablespoons wine vinegar or
    other mild vinegar
Salt, freshly ground pepper

1 teaspoon Dijon mustard
8 tablespoons peanut, corn, or
    olive oil

Put the vinegar in a bowl with the salt and pepper to taste and the mustard and beat with a fork to mix well. Then beat in the oil, little by little, until the sauce is well blended. Taste for seasoning, adding more vinegar, or salt and pepper.

Lemon juice may be used instead of vinegar. For a mustard-flavored vinaigrette, increase the amount of Dijon mustard to 2 tablespoons.

Mayonnaise

This is my preferred recipe for mayonnaise. Any standard recipe may be used, and blender mayonnaise is perfectly acceptable. However, I find this is richer with a better texture, and since it takes only minutes to make I will give it in detail.

Makes about 1½ cups

2 large egg yolks
½ teaspoon Dijon mustard
Salt, freshly ground pepper
1 cup corn, peanut, or olive oil,
    about

4 teaspoons vinegar or lemon
    juice, or 2 teaspoons each
    vinegar and lemon juice

Put the egg yolks into a rimmed soup plate. I find this makes beating easier than using a bowl, though a bowl, of course, will do. Beat the egg yolks lightly with a fork, and beat in the mustard, and salt and pepper to taste. Drop by drop beat in the oil until the yolks thicken. When about half the oil is beaten in and the mixture is very thick, beat in the vinegar or lemon juice, or a mixture of the two. Beat in the remaining oil, pouring it in a thin, steady stream. Taste the mayonnaise and add more vinegar or lemon, or salt and pepper, if liked. If the mayonnaise is too thick for personal taste, thin with a teaspoon or so of hot water.

If the mayonnaise fails to thicken, or separates, place an egg yolk in a bowl and beat in the failed mayonnaise, tablespoon by tablespoon, to restore the sauce.

The type of vinegar used is a matter of choice, but it should never be a coarse vinegar. Wine vinegar is the most commonly used, but I do find that a Japanese rice vinegar gives a delicious result, as of course do the herb-flavored tarragon or basil vinegars.

Salsa Golf   CHILE
Tomato- and Cognac-Flavored Mayonnaise

This is a delicious mayonnaise. I have come across it served in Colombia as a dressing for avocado and described as an international recipe; it may also be used with any cold fish or shellfish. It is generally credited to Chile, where perversely it is sometimes called *Salsa Americana.* I can find no explanation whatever for its being called *Salsa Golf* and my imagination fails me.

Makes about 1 ½ cups

2 egg yolks
1 teaspoon Dijon mustard
Pinch of cayenne pepper, or dash
    of Tabasco
Salt to taste
2 teaspoons lemon juice
1 tablespoon white wine vinegar
1 cup vegetable oil
¼ cup olive oil
2 tablespoons tomato ketchup or
    thick tomato purée
1 tablespoon cognac

Put the egg yolks, mustard, cayenne or Tabasco, salt, lemon juice, and vinegar in a bowl, and beat until thick and well blended. Beat in the vegetable and olive oil, drop by drop, until the mayonnaise begins to thicken, then beat in the remaining oil in a thin, steady stream. Add the tomato ketchup or purée and the cognac. The finished mayonnaise will be a delicate pink.

For *Palta Rellena* (Stuffed Avocado), peel and halve an avocado and remove the pit. Fill the center of each half with *Salsa Golf.* Serves 2 as an appetizer, 1 as a luncheon.

BASIC PROCEDURES

Beurre Manié to Thicken a Sauce

Thoroughly mix 1 tablespoon butter, softened at room temperature, with 1 tablespoon flour. The most convenient way to do this is to put the flour and butter in a cup and mix with a fork. Stir bit by bit into the liquid to be thickened, over moderate heat. This is enough to lightly thicken the average stew. Quantities can be adjusted as required.

To Clarify Butter

Cut the butter into chunks and put into a heavy saucepan over moderate heat. Skim the foam off the surface as it rises. When the butter has melted and looks quite clear let it stand for a few minutes for all the solids to sink to the bottom. Strain the butter through a sieve lined with damp cheese-cloth. The residue need not be thrown away but can be poured over green vegetables or stirred into a stew.

To Peel and Seed Tomatoes

Ripe tomatoes picked off the vine in one's own garden can often be peeled simply by pulling off the skin with the fingers. I've often peeled market-bought tomatoes in Latin America this way and hothouse tomatoes are sometimes peelable in this manner. Otherwise, choose ripe, red tomatoes and drop them into boiling water, one at a time, for 10 seconds. Lift out, rinse quickly under cold water, and peel with a paring knife from the stem end. To remove the seeds, cut the tomato in half crosswise and squeeze out the seeds gently.

Drinks
Bebidas

Latin America does very well with drinks from tea, coffee, wine, and beer, which were introduced there, to native chocolate, *mate*, tequila, *pisco*, rum, and the beerlike drinks, *pulque*, *chicha*, and *tepache*. There is lots of Scotch whisky, gin, and vodka as well as the soft drinks of both the antique and colonial past, and modern soft drinks.

Thanks to Germans, who missed the beer of their homeland, all of Latin America has very good beer indeed. And thanks to French, Spanish, Portuguese, Italians, Germans, and Swiss, who missed their native wines, Chile and Argentina, and to a lesser extent Brazil, Uruguay, Paraguay, and Mexico, have either good or acceptable wines.

Brazil's coffee is notable and one drinks it as *cafezinho*, very strong demitasse with a lot of sugar, often as not with *bôlos* (cakes), while in Colombia, whose coffee is also notable, what one takes in a demitasse is called a *tinto*. Other fine coffees are produced in smaller quantities in Guatemala, El Salvador, Costa Rica, and Mexico. For breakfast Brazil takes its coffee as *café com leite*, the same strong coffee of the demitasse diluted with hot milk, the *café con leche* of the rest of the continent. Mexico adds brown sugar, cinnamon stick, and cloves to make its *Café de Olla* (Pot Coffee).

Tea is not as popular as coffee, though it is esteemed for afternoon tea. Also popular are the herbal teas, the *tisanas* like mint and chamomile, and, of course, *mate*. Chocolate is a popular drink especially in Mexico, where it is packaged already sweetened, flavored with cinnamon and cloves, and mixed with ground almonds. It can be bought in specialty food shops here.

Many of the local soft drinks or beerlike drinks are either not available here, or are impractical to make at home, but I have sometimes come across a concentrated bottled form of *guaraná* in shops selling Brazilian foods. This is made from a Brazilian shrub and is delicious as a soft drink as well as being a good mix for gin, vodka, or rum.

Many of the mixed drinks of Latin America are as international as Scotch and soda, or gin and tonic. I have chosen local drinks I have enjoyed in their home countries and which I have been able to make in the States.

Pisco Sour
Peruvian Brandy Sour

PERU

Pisco, Peruvian brandy, is used in this sour, which is also popular in Chile, where they use the very similar Chilean *pisco*. *Pisco* is also popular in Bolivia. The small tropical lemon-limes used in the drink have a very subtle flavor. They are sometimes available in California. Our limes and lemons are rather more strongly flavored, and a little more sugar may be needed.

Serves 1

1 teaspoon egg white
1 teaspoon superfine sugar
2 teaspoons lime or lemon juice

2 ounces pisco (Peruvian brandy)
2 or 3 ice cubes
Angostura bitters

Combine all the ingredients except the Angostura bitters in a cocktail shaker and shake vigorously. Strain into a sour glass and shake a few drops of Angostura bitters on top.

Biblia con Pisco
Peruvian Brandy Eggnog

Serves 1

1 whole egg
1 tablespoon superfine sugar
1 ½ ounces pisco (Peruvian
    brandy)

⅛ teaspoon ground cinnamon or
    nutmeg

Beat the egg with the sugar, either by hand or with an electric beater, until the sugar is dissolved. Beat in the *pisco.* Pour into a 6-ounce goblet or punch cup, chill thoroughly, sprinkle with cinnamon or nutmeg, and serve. If preferred, 1 or 2 ice cubes may be added to the drink instead of chilling it.

Yungueño
Peruvian Brandy with Orange Juice

Serves 1

1 ½ ounces pisco (Peruvian
    brandy)
1 ½ ounces orange juice

¼ teaspoon superfine sugar
½ cup cracked ice

Combine all the ingredients in a cocktail shaker and shake vigorously. Pour, unstrained, into an 8-ounce wine glass or a tumbler.

Gin Fizz

It was said to me once that the greatest glory of Uruguay was the gin fizz (pronounced jeen feez) made in the capital city of Montevideo. This may well be true, and I think the secret lies in the delicate flavor of the tropical lemon-limes of the region. I find using a little more sugar with our lemons balances the flavor and gives almost the same result.

Serves 1

2 teaspoons superfine sugar   2 ounces gin
2 tablespoons lemon juice   ½ cup crushed ice

Combine the sugar and lemon juice in a cocktail shaker and stir until the sugar is dissolved. Add the gin and crushed ice and shake very thoroughly. Strain into a narrow straight-sided glass about 4 inches high, or into a small tumbler.

Coco Fizz

MEXICO

Serves 4

2 cups coconut water   1 cup crushed ice
3 tablespoons superfine sugar   ⅓ cup lime juice
1 cup gin   Club soda

In a cocktail shaker combine the coconut water and the sugar and stir until the sugar is dissolved. Add all the remaining ingredients, except the club soda, and shake vigorously. Pour into four 9-ounce glasses and add a splash of soda to each.

Coconut water is the liquid in the green coconut, sometimes available in tropical markets. There is some coconut water in mature coconuts, about 1 cup usually, enough for 2 drinks.

Cola de Lagarto
Lizard's Tail

MEXICO

Serves 1

¾ cup dry white wine   1 teaspoon superfine sugar
⅓ cup vodka or gin   1 teaspoon crème de menthe
1 tablespoon lime juice   3 or 4 ice cubes

Combine all the ingredients in a cocktail shaker and shake vigorously. Strain into a chilled tumbler.

Caipirinha
Rum Sour

The name of this drink means literally "country bumpkin," perhaps because the lime is coarsely chopped and the drink served unstrained, unlike the *Batida de Limão* (Lime Batida), where only juice is used and the drink is strained, refined. Or perhaps because it is a splendid drink for that country feast, *Churrasco à Gaucha*, the Brazilian barbecue.

Serves 1

½ *lime*
1 *teaspoon superfine sugar*

2 *ounces* Cachaça *(Brazilian rum) or white rum*

½ *cup crushed ice*

Coarsely chop the lime and transfer it to the mixing glass of a cocktail shaker with the sugar, adding more if liked. Muddle thoroughly to extract all the juice and oil from the lime peel. Add the rum and ice. Shake vigorously and pour, unstrained, into a cocktail glass.

Batida de Limão
Lime Batida

Serves 1

2 *tablespoons lime or lemon juice*
1 *teaspoon sugar*

2 *ounces* Cachaça *(Brazilian rum) or white rum*

½ *cup crushed ice*

Combine all the ingredients in a cocktail shaker and shake vigorously. Strain into a cocktail glass.

Variation: For *Batida de Coco* (Coconut Milk Batida), substitute 2 tablespoons thick coconut milk (see page 7) for the lime juice.

Variation: For *Batida de Maracujá* (*Granadilla* or Passion Fruit Batida), substitute 2 tablespoons of *granadilla* or passion fruit juice for the lime juice and increase the sugar to 1½ teaspoons. *Granadilla* or passion fruit juice is often available in specialty food shops.

Variation: For *Batida de Abacaxi* (Pineapple Batida), substitute 2 ounces pineapple juice for the lime juice.

Margarita

Serves 1

½ *shell of lime or lemon*
Salt
1 ½ *ounces white tequila*

½ *ounce Triple Sec or Curaçao*
1 *ounce lime or lemon juice*
2 *or 3 ice cubes*

Rub the rim of a cocktail glass with the rind of the lime or lemon. Pour salt into a saucer and spin the rim of the glass in it. Combine the remaining ingredients in a bar glass and stir until thoroughly chilled. Strain into the prepared cocktail glass.

Tequila Sunrise

This and its variation, Tequila Cocktail, are very popular tequila drinks.

Serves 1

½ *lime*
2 *ounces white tequila*
½ *teaspoon crème de cassis*
1 *teaspoon grenadine syrup*
Club soda
Ice cubes

Squeeze the lime, pour the juice into an 8-ounce highball glass together with the shell of the lime. Add the tequila, *crème de cassis*, and grenadine syrup. Add enough club soda to fill the glass three-quarters full, stir to mix, then drop in 2 or 3 ice cubes.

Variation: For Tequila Cocktail, combine 1½ ounces tequila with the juice of 1 lime, about 3 tablespoons, and ½ ounce grenadine syrup or to taste. Stir to mix and pour over crushed ice in a cocktail or saucer champagne glass. Serve with two short straws. Serves 1.

Vampiros
Tequila Bloody Marys

MEXICO

Serves 4

1 ¼ cups tomato juice
½ cup orange juice
2 tablespoons lime juice
2 tablespoons chopped onion

½ teaspoon Worcestershire sauce
Salt, cayenne pepper to taste
6 ounces white tequila

Combine all the ingredients, except the tequila, in a blender and blend until smooth. Pour into a jug and chill for at least 4 hours. To serve pour 1½ ounces white tequila into each of four Old-Fashioned glasses and pour in ½ cup of the tomato mixture. Stir to mix. If liked, the drink may be served over ice cubes.

Aperitivo Chapala

MEXICO

There is a lot of controversy over this drink, a chaser for tequila, created by the widow Sanchez at her restaurant at Lake Chapala. Her original was made without tomato juice and had Seville (bitter) orange juice and grenadine syrup. I find ordinary orange juice just as good. The hot pepper gives it a nice lift. I was served it as *Aperitivo Chapala* when I stayed at the lake so I have kept that name here.

Makes about 6 servings

1 cup orange juice
3 tablespoons grenadine syrup
½ teaspoon salt

½ teaspoon cayenne pepper or any ground hot red pepper

Mix all the ingredients thoroughly and chill. Serve in small, straight-sided 1½- to 2-ounce tequila glasses with another glass of tequila served separately. Drink alternately sip by sip. Traditionally the drink is accompanied by small, dried, fried fish, available packaged in many specialty food shops.

Sangrita

Sangrita made with tomato juice is also a splendid accompaniment to tequila. I like the modern way of serving it, combining the Sangrita and the tequila over ice cubes in an Old-Fashioned glass.

Makes 18 to 24 servings

3 cups tomato juice
1 cup orange juice
½ cup lime juice
½ small white onion, chopped
1 teaspoon sugar
1 teaspoon salt, or to taste

2 teaspoons seeded and chopped
    fresh hot green or red pepper,
    or 1 teaspoon cayenne pepper
White tequila
Halved limes
Salt

Combine the tomato juice, orange juice, lime juice, onion, sugar, salt, and hot pepper or cayenne in a blender or food processor and blend until smooth. Strain into a jug and chill thoroughly. Serve in small, straight-sided 1½- to 2-ounce tequila glasses with another glass of tequila served separately. Squeeze a little lime juice into either the Sangrita or the tequila and drink sip by sip, or put a little salt on the lime and take a little suck of it as liked.

Sangría

This is the Spanish wine drink that Mexico has both adopted and adapted to its own use. It is light and pleasant, especially in hot weather.

Makes about 10 servings

1 cup orange juice
½ cup lime or lemon juice
¼ cup superfine sugar, or to taste

1 bottle dry red wine, preferably
    Spanish
Ice cubes

In a jug combine the orange juice, lime or lemon juice, and the sugar and stir until the sugar is dissolved. Taste and add a little more sugar if liked. Pour in the wine, stir to mix, and chill thoroughly in the refrigerator. To serve, put 2 or 3 ice cubes in a 6-ounce goblet or tumbler and fill with Sangría.

Agua de Jamaica   MEXICO
Sorrel or Rosella Drink

This is a popular soft drink and is made from the sepals of a tropical flower known in Mexico as *flor de Jamaica* and in Jamaica as sorrel, elsewhere as rosella or roselle. It can be bought dried in tropical markets usually as rosella or sorrel.

Makes about 10 servings

2 cups rosella sepals   *Sugar to taste*
2 quarts water

Rinse the rosella sepals and put them into a large saucepan with the water. Bring to a boil over moderate heat, remove from the heat, and allow to cool. Strain into a jug. Sweeten to taste and chill thoroughly. Serve in tumblers with ice cubes.

Mate   PARAGUAY

Mate, from the Quechua word, is a mildly stimulating, nonalcoholic drink made from the powdered dried leaves of the South American evergreen *Ilex paraguayensis*. It can be bought in many health or specialty food shops and made according to package directions. It is not necessary to have the special silver-trimmed gourd and the *bombilla*, a special silver straw, to sip it through. A teapot and a cup do just as well, and it may be drunk either hot or cold. The *mate*, the name for the gourd in which the tea is made, is called a *chimarrao* in southern Brazil, where the drink is as popular as it is in Paraguay, Uruguay, and Argentina. In South America, especially in Argentina, the rules for making *mate* can be quite complicated, and many lovers of the tea insist that the water must be just under a boil.

To make the tea, heat a teapot by rinsing it out in boiling water, add 1 tablespoon *mate* per cup, pour in boiling water, let the tea steep for 5 minutes, strain, and serve either plain, or with sugar and/or milk, if liked. To drink cold, make the *mate* double strength and pour it over ice cubes. Serve plain or with sugar and lemon.

Café de Olla
Pot Coffee

In Mexico, which is coffee country, this is served in small pottery mugs each holding 4 ounces (½ cup) as an after-dinner coffee. In Mexico *piloncillo*, the local brown sugar, would be used. Our dark brown sugar is about the same. Coffee for breakfast, *Café con Leche* (Coffee with Milk), is very strong, served in large cups, and diluted half and half with hot milk.

Serves 6

3 cups water
⅓ cup dark brown sugar
2-inch piece of stick cinnamon

3 whole cloves
3 tablespoons regular-grind
    dark roasted coffee

Combine the water, sugar, cinnamon, and cloves in an earthenware or any heatproof coffee pot and bring the water to a boil over moderate heat. Add the coffee, bring again to a boil, simmer for 1 minute, stir, cover, and leave in a warm place for a few minutes for the grounds to settle. Pour through a strainer into earthenware mugs, or use any demitasse cups.

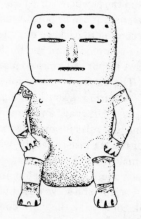

Sources of Latin American Foods

New York

Casa Moneo
210 West 14th Street
New York, N.Y. 10011
Casa Moneo carries a very wide range of Mexican and South American specialties. Mail order.

La Marqueta is an enclosed market that extends from 112th to 116th streets on Park Avenue.

Mara's West Indies Market
718 Nostrand Avenue
Brooklyn, New York 11216

H. Roth & Son
1577 First Avenue
New York, New York 10028
Roth's has a lot of Brazilian foods including *carne séca* and cassava (manioc) meal.

Trinacria Importing Company
415 Third Avenue
New York, New York 10016

Perello, Inc.
2585 Broadway
New York, New York 10025
I've been able to get Seville (bitter) oranges here.

Ninth Avenue from about 38th Street to the fifties is a marvelous source for root vegetables, seafood, special cuts of pork, and so on.

Washington, D.C.

La Sevillana, Inc.
2469 18th Street, N.W.
Washington, D.C.

Safeway International
1110 F Street, N.W.
Washington, D.C. 20004

Casa Peña
1638 17th Street
Washington, D.C. 20009

Chicago
La Preferida, Inc.
117-181 W. South Water Market
Chicago, Illinois 60608

La Casa del Pueblo
1810 Blue Island
Chicago, Illinois 60608

Casa Esteiro
2719 West Division
Chicago, Illinois 60622

Los Angeles
El Mercado
First Avenue and Lorena
East Los Angeles, California 90063

San Francisco
Mi Rancho Market
3365 20th Street
San Francisco, California 94110

Casa Lucas Market
2934 24th Street
San Francisco, California 94110

La Palma
2884 24th Street
San Francisco, California 94110

San Antonio, Texas
Frank Pizzini
202 Produce Row
San Antonio, Texas 78207

Dallas
J. A. Mako Horticultural Enterprises
P.O. Box 34082
Dallas, Texas 75234
J. A. Mako has authentic Mexican
chili pepper seeds, for those who
want to grow their own. Mail order.

Boston
Garcia Superette
367 Center Avenue
Jamaica Plain
Boston, Massachusetts 02130

Cambridge
Star Market
625 Mt. Auburn Street
Cambridge, Massachusetts 02238

Cardullo's Gourmet Shop
6 Brattle Street
Cambridge, Massachusetts 02138

Miami
The Delicatessen Burdine's
Dadeland Shopping Center
Miami, Florida 33156

Albuquerque
Hopi Indians
Bucks General Store
P.O. Box 13561
Albuquerque, New Mexico 87112

Blue corn can be ordered from the
Hopi.

Index

custard(s) *(continued)*
  pineapple, 293
  squares in syrup, 305–6

dendê (palm) oil, 9
doce de leite Baiana, 297
Dominican Republic, food of, xvi
Dominican Republic, recipes of
  cauliflower salad, 281
  chayotes scrambled with eggs, 265–6
  chicken with rice, 192
  eggplant caviar, 269
  okra with shrimp, 236
  pork chops with dried fruit, 115
  sausage and bacon stew, 167
  Spanish stew, Dominican style, 166
  turkey stew, Dominican style, 197
drunken chicken, 179–80
drunken duckling, 208
duck or duckling, 206–9
  drunken, 208
  in orange juice, 208–9
  with prunes, 208
  with rice, 206–7
  in wine, 207
dulce: de coco, 297
  de leche, 304
  de leche con huevos, 304–5
  de piña con arracacha, 293–4
  de queso, 296

Ecuadorian food, xviii–xix
Ecuadorian recipes
  artichoke heart salad, 278
  avocados, stuffed, 255
  bass marinated in lime juice, 30
  beef in fruit sauce, 114
  beef tongue, 143
  broad bean salad, fresh, 279
  cheese sauce, 322
  chicken, Creole style, 189
  chicken in almond sauce, 189
  chicken with cheese, 190
  chicken in egg sauce, 188–9
  chicken with lemon, 189
  chicken in nut sauce, 189
  chicken with olives, 189
  chicken in orange juice, 190
  chicken with sherry, 190
  chicken with sweet red peppers, 189
  chickpea salad, 278
  chickpeas, toasted, 24
  corn, toasted, 24
  corn soufflé, 227
  cucumber salad, 278
  hot pepper sauce, 311–12

Ecuadorian recipes *(continued)*
  mixed salad, 278
  mushroom salad, 278
  peanut sauce, 323
  peanut soup, 61–2
  pork loin in orange juice, 126
  pork loin with shrimp, 124
  pork stew, 106
  potato cakes, 272–3
  potato salad, 278
  potato soup, 60
  potato soup with shrimp fritters, 60–1
  potato and sweet red pepper salad, 279
  pudding, steamed, 306
  pumpkin cake, 300
  pumpkin fritters, 302
  shrimp, marinated, 30
  spring soup, 72
  striped bass and shrimp stew, 70–1
  striped bass stew, 71
  tripe with peanut sauce, 141
  vegetable salad, 282
  vegetable soufflé, 238
  winter squash soup, 60
egg(s): chayotes scrambled with, 265–6
  hardboiled, cassava meal and, 276
  milk pudding with, 305
  milk sweet with, 304–5
  salt cod with, 96–7
eggplant: caviar, 269
  with green beans, 268
  with shrimp, 267–8
  stuffed with cheese, 267
  stuffed with hash, 267
empanadas, 32–41, 240
  de locos, 33
  de plátano, 240
  See also turnover(s)
empanaditas, 40–1
ensalada: de aguacate, 280
  de alcachofas, 278
  de coliflor, 281
  de garbanzos, 278
  de habas, 279
  de hongos, 278
  mixta, 278
  de nopalitos, 283
  de papas, 279
  de papas y pimientos, 279
  de pepinos, 279
  de tomate, 279
  de topinambur, 282
  de verduras, 282
epazote, 10
escabeche de atun, 86

A Note About the Author

Elisabeth Lambert Ortiz has written three cookbooks on Mexican, Caribbean, and Japanese cuisines, and has edited and contributed to several others. A principal consultant to the Time-Life Foods of the World book on Latin America and the Caribbean, she is also a regular writer for *Gourmet* magazine. She and her husband — a Mexican diplomat — have lived all over the world, including many of those countries represented in this book. For a long time they made their home in New York City; they now live in London.